Reducing Cyberbullying in Schools

Reducing Cyberbullying in Schools

International Evidence-Based Best Practices

Edited by

Marilyn Campbell
Queensland University of Technology (QUT), Brisbane, QLD, Australia

Sheri Bauman
University of Arizona, Tucson, AZ, USA

ELSEVIER

ACADEMIC PRESS
An imprint of Elsevier

Academic Press is an imprint of Elsevier
125 London Wall, London EC2Y 5AS, United Kingdom
525 B Street, Suite 1800, San Diego, CA 92101-4495, United States
50 Hampshire Street, 5th Floor, Cambridge, MA 02139, United States
The Boulevard, Langford Lane, Kidlington, Oxford OX5 1GB, United Kingdom

Library of Congress Cataloging-in-Publication Data
A catalog record for this book is available from the Library of Congress

British Library Cataloguing-in-Publication Data
A catalogue record for this book is available from the British Library

ISBN: 978-0-12-811423-0

For information on all Academic Press publications
visit our website at https://www.elsevier.com/books-and-journals

Publisher: Nikki Levy
Acquisition Editor: Dennis McGonagle
Editorial Project Manager: Karen R. Miller
Production Project Manager: Punithavathy Govindaradjane
Cover Designer: Matthew Limbert

Typeset by SPi Global, India

To Brian for his love, support, humour, and his endless insertions of commas in my writing. – Marilyn Campbell

To Bob, my patient and loving cheerleader, for his unwavering confidence in me. – Sheri Bauman

Contents

About the Editors

Marilyn Campbell, PhD is a Professor in the School of Early Childhood and Inclusive Education, Faculty of Education at Queensland University of Technology. She currently lectures in the Masters of Education program preparing teachers for school counseling and in the Masters of Educational and Developmental Psychology preparing psychologists to work in a range of educational and developmental positions. Marilyn has worked as a teacher and psychologist in early childhood, primary, and secondary schools. She has also been a teacher-librarian, school counselor, and supervisor of school counselors. Her research interests are on behavioral and emotional problems in children and adolescents. Her recent work has included research on anxiety prevention and intervention as well as the effects of bullying and especially cyberbullying in schools. She is the author of the Worrybusters' series of books for anxious children.

Sheri Bauman, PhD is a Professor and Coordinator of the School Counseling Master's Degree Program at the University of Arizona in Tucson, Arizona, United States. Prior to earning her doctorate in 1999, she worked for 30 years as a teacher and school counselor in public schools. She is a licensed psychologist (currently inactive). Dr. Bauman conducts research on bullying, cyberbullying, and peer victimization, and teacher responses to bullying. She is a frequent presenter on these topics at local, state, national, and international conferences. She is the author or first author of five books and third author of one other book, and has over 60 publications in peer-reviewed journals, many book chapters, three training DVDs, and numerous other publications.

About the Authors

Kaito Abe is Secretary at Teens Online Japan and a Master's student at the Graduate School of Education with a specialization in school psychology at Osaka University of Education. He holds a BA in Government from Wesleyan University. He has facilitated discussions among youth on online risks and opportunities for more than 4 years. His research interests include problems of child victimization, cyberbullying, and child help seeking behavior. E-mail: kaito.katuo@gmail.com

Alan Barnes, PhD is a Senior Lecturer at the University of South Australia. His career has focused on the emancipatory possibilities of digital technologies in Indigenous affairs, education and more recently, youth engagement with the Internet. His research has included studying peer relations, Internet-enabled cooperative work, student voice, contemporary learning environments, internetted communities, and cyberbullying. His current interests are iPad use in kindergarten, online gaming and cyberbullying, and learning analytics and pedagogy. His teaching courses include quantitative methods, leading with learning technologies and digital citizenship. Dr. Barnes's long-term goal is for digital technologies to improve the human condition. E-mail: alan.barnes@unisa.edu.au

Amy Barnes, BA(Hons), MPH, is a Research Support Officer with the Telethon Kids Institute, University of Western Australia. Her research interests include the social and psychological bases of health behavior, gendered aspects of young people's wellbeing, and the prevention of bullying and cyberbullying behavior in primary and secondary schools. E-mail: amy.barnes@telethonkids.org.au

Des Butler is a Professor of Law at the Faculty of Law, Queensland University of Technology, where he served as Assistant Dean, Research (1997–2002). He was awarded his doctorate in 1996 for his thesis on liability for psychiatric injury, and is the author or coauthor of 23 books and numerous articles on topics including cyberbullying, media and entertainment law, psychiatric injury caused by negligence, contract law, and legal education. He has been a chief investigator on several Australian Research Council grants on topics including cyberbullying and teachers' duties to report suspected child abuse. He is an Australian Learning and Teaching Fellow and a Senior Fellow of the United Kingdom Higher Education Academy. E-mail: d.butler@qut.edu.au

Patricia Cardoso is a Lecturer in the School of Medical and Health Science at Edith Cowan University (ECU) in Australia. She currently teaches health promotion planning and administration, and child and adolescent health. She received an Inspiring Minds' scholarship to undertake a PhD at Edith Cowan University. The aim of this research is a rich exploration of electronic image sharing from the perspectives of young people (13–14 years), and their adults explored primarily through the use of a Design Thinking process. Patricia's research interests are grounded in creating opportunities that authentically engage young people in research and intervention development and implementation. E-mail: p.cardoso@ecu.edu.au

Jose A. Casas, PhD is Assistant Professor in the Department of Psychology at the University of Cordoba (Spain), and member of the Laboratory of Studies on Convivencia and Violence Prevention (laecovi.com). His main lines of investigation are about cyberconvivencia, cyberbullying and, more recently, sexting. He is the author of over twenty research articles on cyberbullying and other risks associated with the use of virtual environments. E-mail: jacasas@uco.es

Donna Cross, BEd, EdD, is a Professor with the Faculty of Medicine, Dentistry and Health Sciences at the University of Western Australia and Telethon Kids Institute, and an Adjunct Professor at Edith Cowan University. Her research focuses on the development and implementation of school and community-based interventions to improve mental health and wellbeing among children and adolescents, particularly in relation to bullying, cyberbullying, and chronic illness/disability. E-mail: donna.cross@telethonkids.org.au

Francine Dehue, PhD and **Trijntje Völlink, PhD** are working at the Faculty of Psychology and Educational Sciences at the Open University of the Netherlands. Their main research focuses on determinants, coping strategies and parenting styles in relation to cyberbullying, and the effectiveness and dissemination of (eHealth) interventions to prevent and combat cyberbullying. They were guest editors of a special issue for the *Journal of Community and Applied Social Psychology* concerning Antisocial behavior in online communities (2013) and editors of the book titled *Cyberbullying: from theory to intervention* (2016). From 2008 to 2012, they were members of the management committee of a European network for researchers concerning cyberbullying (COST Cyberbullying: IS0801). E-mail: Francine.Dehue@ou.nl; Trijntje.Vollink@ou.nl

Douglas Deiss, PhD teaches in the Department of Communication and World Languages at Glendale Community College in Arizona. He teaches intercultural communication, interpersonal communication, and communication theory. His research background includes numerous studies on cyberbullying and the effects of negative and positive emotions on our health and communication. He is also a third-party facilitator and has lead numerous discussions on the topic of diversity on college campuses. E-mail: Douglas.deiss@gccaz.edu

Jen Eden, received her Ph.D. from the Hugh Downs School of Human Communication at Arizona State University in 2010. Currently she is an associate professor in the Communication Department at Marist College in Poughkeepsie, New York. Her research interests include the dark side of communication in close relationships, social influence, and health communication. E-mail: jeneden@gmail.com

Elizabeth Kandel Englander is a Professor of Psychology and the founder and Director of the Massachusetts Aggression Reduction Center at Bridgewater State University, a Center that delivers programs, resources, and research for the state of Massachusetts and nationwide. She is a nationally recognized researcher and expert in the area of bullying and cyberbullying, childhood causes of aggression and abuse, and children's use of technology. She was named Most Valuable Educator of 2013 by the Boston Red Sox because of her work in technological aggression and how it interacts with peer abusiveness in general. Dr. Englander was a Nominee for the 2015 National Crime Victims' Service

Award and is the Chair of the Cyberbullying Workgroup for the Institute of Child Development and Digital Media, collaborating with the National Academy of Sciences. Each year Dr. Englander trains and supervises graduate and undergraduate students and collaborates with multiple agencies around the State of Massachusetts and across the nation. E-mail: eenglander@bridgew.edu

Philip Fine, PhD is Senior Lecturer in Psychology at the University of Buckingham. Philip's main research interests are applied cognitive psychology. In addition to working in the area of cyberbullying and online risk perception, he is currently researching factors contributing to problem-solving expertise (specifically cryptic crossword solving), creativity and insight, music psychology, and aspects relating to time perception and time-related behaviors. Philip is a director of the Centre for Research in Expertise Acquisition, Training and Excellence (CREATE) at the University of Buckingham. Outside of psychology, Philip is a keen actor, singer, and pianist. E-mail: philip.fine@buckingham.ac.uk

Petra Gradinger, Mag. Dr. Psychologist, Senior Researcher at the Platform for Intercultural Competencies, University of Applied Sciences Upper Austria, Linz, Austria. Her main research area is on social relationships (e.g., bullying, cyberbullying, and discriminatory bullying) among adolescents and competencies (e.g., intercultural competencies, self-regulated learning, and learning with new media) among university students. E-mail: petra.gradinger@fh-linz.at

Coosje Griffiths works as Manager—Complex Learning and Wellbeing for the Department of Education Western Australia. She has worked in public education as a classroom teacher, school psychologist, and senior school psychologist, and is a registered psychologist (AHPRA). Coosje works collaboratively with researchers on numerous research projects and publications on a range of topics including bullying, violence, school safety, and alternative education. She conducted an international study on bullying in schools as a Churchill Fellowship recipient and has instigated and managed numerous initiatives on a range of topics including bullying, positive psychology, mindfulness, alternative education, school climate, and social and emotional learning (SEL). Coosje is on the National Centre Against Bullying (NCAB) board and national cross jurisdiction committee (SSSC) to counteract bullying and violence, the executive of the School Psychologists' Association WA, and the national body Australian Psychologists and Counsellors in Schools (APACS), and past General Secretary, International School Psychology Association. E-mail: Coosje.Griffiths@education.wa.edu.au

Nicole Gunther is working at the Faculty of Psychology and Educational Sciences at the Open University of the Netherlands. Her main research interests include internet-based mental health interventions, risk and protective factors for adolescents' mental health and cyberbullying involvement, and mental, physical and behavioral negative outcomes of cyberbullying. E-mail: Nicole.Gunther@ou.nl

Kate Hadwen, PhD is Principal of Presbyterian Ladies' College, Perth (WA). Kate's background includes teaching and leadership roles in junior, middle, and senior schools, research and lecturing in the tertiary sector, and National project management of school-based pastoral care programs. Kate is an honorary fellow at the Telethon

Kids Institute and is an ambassador for Australia's Biggest Mental Health Check-In. Her publications to date focus on boarding students and families, and cyberbullying. Kate is particularly interested in the mental wellbeing of young people with a focus on prevention, early intervention, and the development of evidence-based programs for schools. E-mail: Kate.Hadwen@plc.wa.edu.au

Sanna Herkama is a Communication Scholar currently working as a Senior Researcher Fellow in the Division of Psychology, University of Turku, Finland. Her research focuses on development and implementation of intervention programs as well as to school bullying and the communication and cognitive processes connected to it. She has been involved in the development of pilot trials of the KiVa antibullying program in various countries. She is also a certified KiVa trainer. E-mail: sanna.herkama@utu.fi

Niels Jacobs, PhD was working at the Faculty of Psychology and Educational Sciences at the Open University of the Netherlands from April 2011 till December 2015. He developed an online tailored intervention for victims of cyberbullying according to the Intervention Mapping method. The intervention aimed to teach victims how to cope with cyberbullying and the negative effects of cyberbullying via insights in their thoughts and feelings caused by the event. They learned to replace irrational thoughts and ineffective coping strategies into rational thoughts and effective coping strategies. The intervention was based on cognitive behavioral therapy (the Rational Emotive Behavioral Therapy (REBT)) and methods from the social cognitive theory of Bandura (1986). E-mail: ncl.jacobs@gmail.com

Meghan K. McCoy, EdD, is the Manager of Programs at the Massachusetts Aggression Reduction Center, at Bridgewater State University. Dr. McCoy is also a Part-time Instructor of Psychology at BSU. She has a BA in Psychology, an MEd in School Counseling 5-12, and an EdD in Curriculum, Teaching, Learning, and Leadership from Northeastern University. Her work focuses on adult learning, adolescent emotional development, bullying, and digital use of children and teens. Dr. McCoy works with and trains K-12, undergraduate, and graduate students and consults in K-12 education. E-mail: megatmarc@gmail.com

Lian McGuire, MEd, MA, is a Research Fellow at the National Anti-Bullying Research and Resource Centre located at DCU Institute of Education, Ireland. She has obtained a Master's in Aggression Studies from Trinity College Dublin and a Master's in Psychology from Manchester Metropolitan University. She has coordinated a number of EU-funded projects and has previously published on bullying in higher education. E-mail: lian.mcguire@dcu.ie

Ersilia Menesini is Full Professor in Developmental Psychology, University of Florence. Her research activity has been focused on knowledge and intervention related to violence and aggressive behavior in adolescence and childhood, specifically school bullying, peer rejection, dating aggression, cyberbullying and risk behaviors in virtual contexts. E-mail: ersilia.menesini@unifi.it

Motoko Miyake is Associate Professor of Okayama University. She holds a B.A. in Education from Okayama University and PhD in Psychology from Hiroshima

University. Within training course for school teachers, she currently teaches classes in prevention education and psychology. Her research interest includes evaluation of prevention education, and schoolchild and adolescent development of identity and social interaction. E-mail: miyake@okayama-u.ac.jp

James O'Higgins Norman, EdD, PhD is a Senior Lecturer in Sociology and Director of the National Anti-Bullying Research and Resource Centre at Dublin City University. He is best known for his research on homophobic bullying in second-level schools in Ireland, which has drawn international media attention and was referenced in parliamentary proceedings in Ireland and at the EU Commission. Other research interests include gender and cyberbullying, and diversity and bullying in schools. He has worked on a number of EU-funded projects and presented his work at conferences in Ireland, the USA, UK, Scandinavia, Australia, and Italy. E-mail: james.ohigginsnorman@dcu.ie

Isabelle Ouellet-Morin, PhD investigates the biological, cognitive, and socioemotional mechanisms by which early adversity and victimization (e.g., bullying, maltreatment) affect long-term trajectories of mental health problems and antisocial behavior. She holds a PhD in clinical psychology (Laval University, Canada) and was a postdoctoral fellow at the MRC Social, Genetic, and Developmental Psychiatry Centre (King's College, UK). Dr. Ouellet-Morin is now Associate Professor at the University of Montreal (Canada) and holds a CIHR New Investigator Award. E-mail: isabelle.ouellet-morin@umontreal.ca

Benedetta E. Palladino obtained her doctorate in Psychology and Neuroscience in 2014. She is currently a postdoctoral researcher at the University of Florence. Her main research interests are on bullying, cyberbullying, the impact of new technologies on youth development, and the evaluation of efficacy of evidence-based interventions. E-mail: benedetta.palladino@gmail.com

Katalin Parti has a PhD in criminal justice, and an MA in media and communication sociology. She is a senior research fellow with the National Institute of Criminology Hungary with research fields in cybercrime, cyberdeviances, policing virtual realities, online sexual abuse, media and society, sexual violence, and society. She is a member of the editorial board at Infocommunication and Law, peer reviewer with the Masaryk University *Journal of Law and Technology*, and reviewer of evaluation of applications at the Slovenian Research Agency. She was a Fulbright visiting scholar (2013/14) with the Massachusetts Aggression Reduction Center, Bridgewater State University, MA. She is a member of the Cyberbullying Workgroup for the Institute of Child Development and Digital Media, collaborating with the National Academy of Sciences and cowriter of the White Paper on Cyberbullying aiming to define the nation's research agenda regarding children and digital technology. E-mail: partikat@gmail.com

Maša Popovac, PhD is a Lecturer in Psychology at the University of Buckingham. Maša's research focuses on cyberbullying, cyberaggression, online risk behaviors such as sexting, and risk perception of adolescents. She has also conducted research focusing on parents and their online mediation strategies. Maša has developed and teaches the Cyberpsychology module at the University of Buckingham. Apart from her work on cyberbullying, she is also currently researching gaming, online dating, and health-related online behaviors. E-mail: masa.popovac@buckingham.ac.uk

Rosario Del Rey, PhD is Associate Professor in the Department of Developmental and Educational Psychology of the Faculty of Educational Sciences at the University of Seville (Spain) and member of the IASED research group (Interpersonal Aggression and Socio-Emotional Development). Her main lines of investigation are about convivencia, bullying and cyberbullying and, more recently, sexting and other risks associated to virtual environments. At scientific and informative level, she has published several books and articles and has intervened in international congresses. She is currently leading the R&D Project named "Sexting, Ciber-bullying and Emerging Risks on the Internet: Keys for their Comprehension and Educational Response." E-mail: delrey@us.es

Ken Rigby, PhD is an Adjunct Professor in the School of Education at the University of South Australia. He has a Postgraduate Certificate in Education (Leicester University) and a PhD in Psychology (Adelaide University). He was employed as a school teacher in primary and secondary schools in England and in Australia over a ten-year period before being appointed lecturer in psychology and research methods at the South Australian Institute of Technology. Since 1990, he has specialized in researching and writing about issues of school bullying. He has published over 100 papers on school bullying and authored or coauthored 20 books on the subject. He has been employed as consultant to the Victorian and Queensland Education Departments. His more recent books include *Bullying Interventions in schools: six basic approaches* (published by Wiley in 2012), *The Method of Shared Concern: a positive approach to bullying in schools* (ACER, 2011), and *Children and Bullying: How parents and educators can reduce bullying in schools* (Blackwell/Wiley, 2008). Website: www.kenrigby.net; E-mail: Ken.Rigby@unisa.edu.au

Anthony J. Roberto (Ph.D., Michigan State University) is a Professor in the Hugh Downs School of Human Communication at Arizona State University. His primary teaching and research interests are in the areas of social influence and health communication, and he has received over 20 awards from a variety of local, national, and international venues for his teaching, research, and service in these areas. E-mail: Anthony.Roberto@asu.edu

Marie-Pier Robitaille holds a Master Degree in criminology and is about to obtain a PhD in the same field (University of Montreal). She specializes in the investigation of sex differences in antisocial behavior, from childhood to early adulthood. Part of Dr. Ouellet-Morin's team since 2012, she is the research coordinator behind the development of +Fort, a mobile application for youth victim of bullying. Mrs. Robitaille is now a postdoctoral fellow in psychiatry at the Research Centre of the Montreal University Institute for Mental Health, where she investigates the childhood precursors of mental health problems and criminality. E-mail: mp.robitaille.4@gmail.com

Rosario Ortega-Ruiz, PhD is Professor of Psychology at the University of Córdoba. She has more than 25 years of research experience in interpersonal relations and development of social and emotional competences. She is expert on children's play and social knowledge construction, bullying and cyberbullying, as well as dating violence.

She is Principal Investigator of the Laboratory of Studies on Convivencia and Violence Prevention (laecovi.com) and Vice President of the International Observatory on School Violence. She has published more than one hundred and fifty scientific articles and other peer-reviewed publications. E-mail: ortegaruiz@uco.es

Leslie Ramos Salazar (PhD, Arizona State University) is an Assistant Professor of business communication and decision management at the College of Business at West Texas A&M University. Her teaching areas include current issues in management communication, business communication for health care managers, business communication, and statistics for business and economics. Her research specializes in health communication, cyberbullying, business communication, and interpersonal communication. E-mail: lsalazar@wtamu.edu

Christina Salmivalli, PhD is a Professor of Psychology at the University of Turku, Finland. She has led the development of the KiVa antibullying program, with funding from the Finnish Ministry of Education and Culture. The KiVa program has been awarded both nationally and internationally, and is widely implemented in Finland and elsewhere. Salmivalli has published numerous widely cited articles, book chapters, and books on children's peer relations and school bullying. Her current research interests include different approaches to tackle bullying and their effectiveness, the sustainability of the implementation of prevention programs, and mediating mechanisms of program effects. E-mail: Tiina.salmivalli@utu.fi

Matthew Savage (Ph.D., 2012, Arizona State University) is an Assistant Professor in the School of Communication at San Diego State University whose research interests focus on the intersection of health and interpersonal communication. Dr. Savage's scholarship is conducted within the context of creating and supporting health communication campaigns aimed to deter risky behaviors among young adults. Many of his research projects are community embedded. Currently, he is working to address important topics including adolescent bullying/cyberbullying, dangerous drinking behavior, and intimate partner violence. E-mail: matthewsavage@uky.edu

Herbert Scheithauer is Professor for Developmental and Clinical Psychology at Freie Universität Berlin and Head of the Unit "Developmental Science and Applied Developmental Psychology." His research interests are on bullying, cyberbullying, and the development and evaluation of preventive interventions. E-mail: herbert.scheithauer@fu-berlin.de

Anja Schultze-Krumbholz is a Postdoctoral Research Associate at the Department of Educational Psychology at Technische Universität Berlin. Her research interests focus on the nature of cyberbullying and its determinants, aggression and bullying in school, and social competence and its promotion. E-mail: anja.schultze-krumbholz@tu-berlin.de

Thérèse Shaw is a Statistician with over 20 years' research experience, in particular in school-based health promotion research, including bullying prevention and mental health promotion research. Her expertise lies in study design, instrument development and testing, intervention implementation measurement, and statistical evaluations of intervention trials. Her research focus is the methodological strength of quantitative health program evaluations and related statistical analyses. E-mail: Therese.Shaw@telethonkids.org.au

Phillip T. Slee is a Professor in Human Development, School of Education, Flinders University, Adelaide. He is a trained teacher and registered psychologist. His research interest include, child & adolescent mental health, childhood bullying/aggression. His particular interest is in the practical and policy implications of his research. He has presented nationally and internationally in workshops and lectures. His web site is http://www.caper.com.au. He is the director of the Flinders Centre for "Student Wellbeing & Prevention of Violence" (SWAPv) (http://www.flinders.edu.au/ehl/educationalfutures/groups-and-centres/swapv/). His publications include over 100 refereed papers, 25 book chapters, and 15 books including "Child Development Theories and critical Perspectives." E-mail: phillip.slee@flinders.edu.au

Peter K. Smith was Chair of COST Action IS0801 on Cyberbullying, 2008-2012, and PI of Bullying, Cyberbullying, and Pupil Safety and Wellbeing, financed by the Indian-European Research Networking in the Social Sciences, 2012-2015. He is currently co-PI (with M. Samara and others) of Comparative study of cyberbullying in Qatar and the UK: risk factors, impact on health and solutions, financed by the Qatar National Research Fund. In 2015 he was awarded the William Thierry Preyer award for Excellence in Research on Human Development, by the European Society for Developmental Psychology. He is author of Understanding School Bullying: Its Nature and Prevention Strategies (Sage Publications, 2014). E-mail: p.smith@gold.ac.uk

Barbara A. Spears, PhD is Associate Professor in Education, at the University of South Australia. She is recognized nationally and internationally for work on youth voice, cyber/bullying, sexting, mental health, wellbeing, and the role of technology in young people's social relationships. With a particular interest in preservice teacher education and the translation of research to policy and practice, she has led the following projects: review of the National Safe Schools Framework; A Public Health Approach to Sexting; Youth Exposure to and Management of Cyber-Bullying Incidents in Australia; and the Safe and Well Online Study: Young and Well Co-operative Research Centre. E-mail: barbara.spears@unisa.edu.au

Dagmar Strohmeier, FH-Prof. PD, Dr. is Professor for Intercultural Competence at the University of Applied Sciences Upper Austria, Linz. Her main research area is on peer relations among adolescents with a crosscultural and crossnational perspective and a special focus on immigrant youth. She has developed, implemented, and evaluated the ViSC Program to foster social and intercultural competencies in Austrian, Romanian, Cypriot, and Turkish schools. E-mail: dagmar.strohmeier@fh-linz.at

Carmel Taddeo, PhD is a Lecturer at the University of South Australia. Carmel has expertise in technology initiatives in schools and has been involved in the education sector for over 20 years, both as a practitioner in the primary and tertiary sectors and as a researcher. Carmel's research interests include online research methods and design, change processes, wellbeing of young people and the potential of technology to facilitate positive outcomes, both in learning settings and broader life contexts. E-mail: carmel.taddeo@unisa.edu.au

Kazuo Takeuchi is Associate Professor at the School of Human Science and Culture, University of Hyogo, and the executive coordinator of Smartphone Summit Program. Takeuchi taught at public junior high schools for 20 years and served Neyagawa City Board of Education for 5 years before assuming his current position. As an educator, he frequently appears on TV programs and advocate for collaborative rule making between children and adults. He was a Visiting Fellow at the University of Vienna, Austria, in 2013. He is the recipient of Yomiuri Prize for Education in 2008. E-mail: takekaz0205@shse.u-hyogo.ac.jp

İbrahim Tanrikulu, PhD is an Assistant Professor in Psychological Counseling and Guidance Department/Faculty of Education, Gaziantep University, in Gaziantep/Turkey. He earned his PhD in Psychological Counseling and Guidance at Middle East Technical University, Ankara, Turkey. His interests include prevention research on bullying, cyberbullying, sibling bullying as well online applications in counseling profession. Currently, he is working on editing the first book on cyberbullying in Turkish. In addition to the primary, middle, and high-school students and university students, he conducts research on bullying prevention in preschool level. E-mail: ibrahimtanrikulu@gmail.com

Yuichi Toda is Professor of Osaka Kyoiku University (Osaka University of Education). He received his B.A. and M.A. at University of Tokyo, and then he studied at the doctoral course of University of Tokyo. He was a visiting fellow at Goldsmiths College, University of London, during March 1998-January 1999, and a short-time visiting professor of University of Vienna in summer time from 2007 till 2010. He has written several English language articles on bullying/ijime. His research with Dr. Dagmar Strohmeier has received den Hauptpreis des Bank Austria Preises zur Förderung innovativer Forschungsprojekte 2008. E-mail: toda@cc.osaka-kyoiku.ac.jp

Cigdem Topcu-Uzer, PhD is an Assistant Professor of psychological counseling and guidance at Sinop University, Sinop, Turkey. She received her PhD in Psychological Counseling and Guidance at Middle East Technical University, Ankara, Turkey. Her research interests include interaction between difficult life events and emotional and cognitive development (e.g., empathy, emotion regulation, rumination) among children and adolescents as well as bullying, cyberbullying, and violence among adolescents and children. Her other research interests include close relationships, sacrifice in dating and marital relationships, and quantitative data analysis methods. E-mail: cigdemtopcu@gmail.com

Pavle Zagorscak is a Research Associate at the Division of Clinical Psychological Intervention at Freie Universität Berlin. His research interests include effect mechanisms of online therapy and online counseling for anxiety and affective disorders, and determinants and prevention of cyberbullying in the school context. E-mail: p.zagorscak@fu-berlin.de

Valentina Zambuto is a PhD student at the Department of Educational Sciences and Psychology at the University of Florence. Her main research interests are on bullying, cyberbullying, and on the application of peer-led models (peer education/peer support) in anti-(cyber)bullying programs. E-mail: valentina.zambuto@live.it

Part One

General Strategies

Cyberbullying: Definition, consequences, prevalence

1

Marilyn Campbell[*], *Sheri Bauman*[†]
[*]Queensland University of Technology (QUT), Brisbane, QLD, Australia, [†]University of Arizona, Tucson, AZ, United States

Introduction

This chapter will set the stage for the remainder of the chapters in the book. Although our focus is on evidence-based solutions to problems associated with cyberbullying, and programs designed to prevent or reduce cyberbullying, we think it is necessary to first provide an overview of what we have learned from cyberbullying research in the last two decades. Although cyberbullying is often described to as a recent phenomenon, a large and growing body of literature has investigated the problem: a Google Scholar search yielded 36,600 hits on the term "cyberbullying" (15,400 having been published since 2013).

Although there is now a sizable body of research on many aspects of cyberbullying, what is missing is investigations of promising programs designed to reduce it. This book is an attempt to remedy that deficit and provide readers with information about programs that have at least preliminary evidence of efficacy or effectiveness. While the study of the motivations, mechanisms, and dynamics of cyberbullying is ongoing, we want to bring attention here to successful efforts to do something about the problem. We also want to be sure that adults have accurate information about cyberbullying. Adults often think that there is an epidemic of cyberbullying and believe it is more common than data show it to be. In fact, cyberbullying occurs much less frequently than traditional forms. Furthermore, adults may also mistakenly believe the students are more upset by incidents of cyberbullying than students report being (Compton, Campbell, & Mergler, 2014).

Cyberbullying definition

Cyberbullying has been defined as intentional harmful behavior carried out by a group or individuals, repeated over time, using modern digital technology to aggress against a victim who is unable to defend him/herself (Juvonen & Gross, 2008; Konig, Gollwitzer, & Steffgen, 2010; Smith et al., 2008). Smith, del Barrio, and Tokunaga (2013) add that the aggressor is more powerful in some way than the target. This definition parallels the definition of traditional bullying, essentially adding "digital technology" as the mechanism by which the harm is inflicted.

In addition to the traditional criteria of intention, repetition, and power imbalance, some researchers have suggested that "anonymity" and "publicity" are additional

Reducing Cyberbullying in Schools. https://doi.org/10.1016/B978-0-12-811423-0.00001-8

features that define cyberbullying (Nocentini et al., 2010). For example, Sticca and Perren (2013) found that middle-school children rated public and anonymous cyberbullying as worse than incidents that were private or when the perpetrator was known. While we know these features are important, we disagree with making these qualities defining attributes because anonymity, while definitely easier to accomplish when cyberbullying, is not always the case, and cyberbullies can use private as well as public channels. However, it is important to keep in mind that other unique features of the digital environment may increase risks for cyberbullying. These are: the huge size of the potential audience; the continuous access; the permanence of online content; the ease of copying material and distributing it widely; and the lack of oversight of online behavior. In addition, the inability to view the emotional reactions of the target keeps perpetrators from having empathy for the target. The advent of sexting—sending explicit images or text using digital channels—has created a particularly dangerous opportunity for perpetrators to take images intended for an intimate relationship and broadcast them (without the knowledge or the consent of the target) in order to humiliate the target and damage his/her social relationships.

Historically, cyberbullying was first noticed late last century. Bill Belsey, a Canadian, is widely credited with coining the term *cyberbullying* on his website, although the earliest use was actually in 1995 in a *New York Times* article (Bauman, 2011). Although there is still some debate about the definition and whether it is the best term to use to describe the behaviors of interest (cf. Bauman, Underwood, & Card, 2013), the term is so widely accepted in both scholarly and public contexts that we continue to use it here. Since the term is an extension of the term "bullying," we include a discussion of that definition next.

Bullying definition

Smith and Slonje (2010) define bullying as "an aggressive, intentional act or behaviour that is carried out by a group or an individual repeatedly over time against a victim who cannot easily defend him or herself" (p. 147). This definition is based on Olweus' (1993) original premise that bullying is a subset of aggression with three main characteristics. These are the intention of the perpetrator to hurt, that the behavior is repeated, and the defining characteristic, that there is a power imbalance in the relationship. Three main types of bullying have been identified: physical (hitting, kicking, etc.), verbal (malicious teasing, threatening), and relational (social exclusion, rumor spreading). One of the points of contention is that it is impossible to unambiguously know someone's intent. In an effort to resolve differences about this, a consensus view has been proposed by Langos (2012), who suggested that bullying should be considered as intentional harm if a "reasonable person" thinks it would be harmful. This is a standard often used in legal cases to determine culpability for an action.

The concept of repetition in defining bullying is probably the most widely debated. Most bullying is low in severity but relentless, meeting that criterion. However, some have argued that one serious incident of aggression may be sufficient to call it bullying (Naylor, Cowie, Cossin, Bettencourt, & Lemme, 2006). Most researchers agree that if the definition says usually repeated that it captures both of these views. Recently, the

American organization, the Center for Disease Control (CDC) revised its official definition to say that the action must either be repeated or be "highly likely to be repeated" (Center for Disease Control (CDC), 2016).

The third characteristic—the imbalance of power, the key defining feature, is also the most contentious. The debate about this concept is more divided along European and North American lines. European scholars see the imbalance of power as integral in distinguishing this subset of aggression from fighting and other forms of aggression. Many studies have tried to operationalize the imbalance of power by physical size, psychological strength, or the number of students involved in bullying one person. Researchers in the USA, such as Justin Patchin and Sameer Hinduja (Hinduja & Patchin, 2015, p. 11) do not see the imbalance of power as a key concept in bullying, especially in cyberbullying, mainly because it is difficult to define this concept precisely enough that laws can be clear, i.e., that the legal, school community, and research definitions may vary according to the contexts and requirements. No single definition of bullying is currently able to meet all needs, and it is for this reason that academic, education, and wider community members engaged in these discussions are encouraged to clearly detail the definition they are referring to or drawing from when making comments or claims about these matters (Department of Education & Training, 2015).

However, we believe that using Olweus' (1993) original explanation of the imbalance of power, which is that the student being victimized feels powerless as s/he cannot get the bullying to stop or cannot escape the damage (Menesini, Nocentini, & Camodeca, 2013) is helpful to clarify what is meant by that criterion. Some consensus has now been reached by the United States Center for Disease Control defining bullying as "any unwanted aggressive behaviour(s) by another youth or group of youths who are not siblings or current dating partners that involves an observed or perceived power imbalance and is repeated multiple times or is highly likely to be repeated" (Gladden, Vivolo-Kantor, Hamburger, & Lumpkin, 2014, p. 7). The Australian Research Alliance for Children & Youth (ARACY) also proposed a definition of school-based bullying as "a systematic abuse of power in a relationship formed at school characterized by: (1) Aggressive acts directed (by one or more individuals) towards victims that a reasonable person would avoid; (2) Acts which usually occur repeatedly over a period of time; and (3) Acts in which there is an actual or perceived power imbalance between perpetrators and victims, with victims often being unable to defend themselves effectively from perpetrators" (Hemphill, Heerde, & Gomo, 2014, p. 3). In a study of preservice teachers in the US, Bauman and Del Rio (2006) found that only 6 percent of participants, asked to provide a definition of bullying mentioned repetition, and 28 percent alluded to the imbalance of power.

Is cyberbullying a form of bullying, or something different entirely?

The initial response to the proliferation of cyberbullying from the media and scholars was that this was an entirely new and distinct form of bullying. However, there has been vigorous debate over the last ten years as to whether cyberbullying is a form of bullying or a discrete form of aggression (Dooley, Pyżalski, & Cross, 2009). This matters to practitioners because if cyberbullying is a form of bullying, then antibullying programs designed for traditional bullying should have an effect, whereas if it is a unique phenomenon, then it is likely that unique and new programs will have to be developed.

The argument for considering cyberbullying to be a type of bullying is that most victimized students are both traditionally and cyberbullied (as high as 93% according to Hase, Goldberg, Smith, Stuck, & Campain, 2015) and that common predictors have been identified for both forms (e.g., strain, low self-esteem, negative relationships with family and peers; Kim, Song, & Jennings, 2016); that cyberbullying meets the criteria of bullying but is manifested in different ways and has similar outcomes to face-to-face bullying (Thomas, Connor, & Scott, 2015). Recent research has found that both forms lead to negative consequences for involved youth, and both are associated with low self-control on the part of the cyberbullies (Kim et al., 2016). However, the proportion of bully-victims (those who both bully and are bullied) is much greater for cyberbullying than for traditional bullying (Festl, Vogelgesang, Scharkow, & Quandt, 2017). Furthermore, very few adolescents report only being cyberbullied; of those who reported victimization in a large US study, only about 5% were only cyberbullied while more than half said they were victimized in physical, verbal, relational, and cyber ways (Waasdorp & Bradshaw, 2015). Those who contend that cyberbullying is not a form of bullying point to studies that show that negative outcomes are more severe than those found for traditional bullying (e.g., Bonanno & Hymel, 2013; Campbell, Spears, Slee, Butler, & Kift, 2012; Perren, Dooley, Shaw, & Cross, 2010), although other studies have not found this additional degree of harm. Moreover, imbalance of power is not necessarily obvious in cyberbullying (although some believe that technological advantage may be just that); that it may happen only once (although it can be distributed many times after the initial event) and that it can be anonymous (Dooley et al., 2009). There are also features, noted earlier, of cyberbullying that distinguish this phenomenon from bullying (24/7 access, enormous audience, permanence of content, perception of anonymity, tendency for more vicious attacks due to the online disinhibition effect (Suler, 2004). On balance most people now think that cyberbullying is a form of bullying.

Why is the meaning of the word *cyberbullying* important?

Words mean different things to different people. We live in a society, which appropriates words that describe psychological disorders and applies them in our everyday speech. For instance, we often say we are "depressed" when we are sad; that we have the "flu" and not just a cold; that someone who is neat and tidy has OCD (Obsessive-Compulsive Disorder). The words bullying and cyberbullying seem to be so carelessly used now, so broadly defined that they can refer to anybody being mean, or even a supervisor using legitimate power, to appropriately reprimand a supervisee, being called a bully.

Studies have shown that different people understand the word bullying differently. In one study teachers, parents, and students said it was an imbalance of power that distinguished bullying from fighting, but none mentioned repetition. Parents disagreed with teachers about the intention to harm, with parents saying that students who bully might not know they are harming, while teachers said students who bullied always knew they were harming (Compton et al., 2014). Younger children also understand bullying differently from older children (Currie, Zanotti, Morgan, & Currie, 2012; Smith, Cowie, Olafsson, & Liefooghe, 2002) with people from different cultures also having varying ways of interpreting the term (Jacobson, Hood, & van Buren, 2014).

Practitioners cannot prevent and intervene in a behavior without a common understanding of what the behavior is. This is especially true of managing any form of bullying. If two students are fighting, then we usually punish them and teach them to solve their differences more constructively. If one student is bullying the other, it would be unfair to punish both, as the victimized student was already suffering unjustified aggression from a peer. Mediation is also not appropriate to encourage the two students to solve their differences when one does not want to stop and the other feels powerless. We all experience conflict in our lives, which can be functional or dysfunctional, but bullying is always dysfunctional for all involved. Schools are likely to have explicit policies for bullying and cyberbullying, spelling out consequences (but often lacking a definition of the behaviors). This leads to complaints that other forms of aggression are ignored or that someone is being unfairly punished.

Some researchers, tired of trying to tease out what cyberbullying is, call for all forms of aggression using technology to be investigated using the term cyberaggression (Bauman et al., 2013). However, there are two reasons to disagree with this view. First, students who are cyberbullied have more negative consequences than those who are involved in cyber fighting (Ybarra, Boyd, Korchmaros, & Oppenheim, 2012). This could be because of the fear engendered by the imbalance of power and the worry about repetition in cyberbullying as opposed to cyber fighting. Second, as in the playground, cyberbullying needs a different solution from cyber fighting because cyberbullying implies the victim is unable to make it stop, whereas with cyber fighting both parties are equally powerful.

Types of cyberbullying

While all cyberbullying uses digital technology, there are various actions than can be employed to hurt a target. Youth report that the distress they experience varies among the types. Some perpetrators find ways to obtain the passwords of the target, and then send or post messages or content that the target would never actually send, embarrassing the target and forcing them to convince those who received the message that they had not been the sender. Sending anonymous texts or posting anonymously on a website can generate considerable fear on the part of the recipient because they do not know who the source is. They can find themselves suspecting everyone, thus damaging relationships. Of course, sometimes cyberbullying is quite direct: mean, insulting, rude, or offensive content can be sent or posted directly to the target. A more indirect strategy is to spread rumors or slander the target, usually distributing the information widely. The target often learns what has happened only after many people have seen it, and someone alerts him or her. Sending or distributing sexual images was the most upsetting type of cyberbullying experienced by college students (Bauman & Newman, 2013). Other researchers found that denigration, outing and trickery (getting someone to reveal secrets and then sharing those with others), exclusion, and impersonation were the most distressing (Staude-Müller, Hansen, & Voss, 2012). Using the *Cyber Experiences Survey,* Bauman and Baldasare (2015) found that college students were most distressed by unwanted contact, followed by malice (mean and hurtful content) and humiliation.

Prevalence of cyberbullying

There are extremely wide variations in the reported prevalence of cyberbullying among youth. Although prevalence is generally measured by student self-report (Frisen et al., 2013) the wide range in findings is due to many differences in the way participants are recruited, how the data are collected, and the kind of measures used (Espinoza & Juvonen, 2013). Several differences are important to note. The first issue is whether a survey provides a researcher's definition of bullying or not. Providing a definition of the word bully results in a more accurate response (Ybarra et al., 2012). The second issue is whether cyberbullying is measured by global questions such as "Have you been cyber bullied?" or behavioral questions such as "Have you been sent a mean text message?" Behavioral questions elicit more bullying responses than global questions (Huang & Cornell, 2015) mainly because students do not consider some of the specific behaviors to be bullying. The third issue is how often the behavior has to occur for it to be considered cyberbullying; some researchers consider two or three times a month to constitute bullying, while others may consider anything other than "never" as evidence of cyberbullying, while others use the same cutoff for both. Kubiszewski, Fontaine, Potard, and Auzoult (2015) studied both traditional and cyberbullying in their study, but used different cutoffs for classifying bullying. For traditional bullying, participants were considered a bully or victim if they reported being involved at least two to three times a month, while the cutoff for cyberbullying was once. The researchers argued that even one instance of cyberbullying can be seen multiple times by multiple people, and that the number of viewers can increase the longer the item remains accessible to others. The fourth issue is the reference time period selected: whether the cyberbullying happened in the last couple of months (about a school term), or the past year, or ever. The age range of the students has also varied, as are the different countries in which the studies are conducted. Furthermore, how the students are recruited (schools vs. websites) also influences the findings. In one US study, differences were found by ethnicity, with White students being more involved in cyberbullying as both perpetrators and victims than Hispanic students (Kupczynski, Mundy, & Green, 2013).

These differences of course make it extremely difficult to compare studies to ascertain prevalence rates. Spears, Keeley, Bates, and Katz (2014) in their report to the Australian government, reviewed eight major studies, which had collectively surveyed over 50,000 young people in Australia between the years 2007–2013, about their experiences of cyberbullying, drawing attention to the difficulty in synthesizing an accurate picture of the prevalence of cyberbullying because of the different ways each study collected and organized its data, and how the definition of bullying and/or cyberbullying was operationalized for measurement. A conservative estimate, extrapolated from all frequencies, timeframes, methodological approaches and definitions, was that approximately 20% of Australian minors had experienced cyberbullying over the course of a year.

To address that problem, one study included both bullying and cyberbullying at the same time, and found that almost half of the sample of 1225 secondary students in the US had been traditionally bullied at least two or three times in the previous month, compared to about 16% were victimized by cyberbullying (Hase et al., 2015). Ninety-three percent of those who had experienced traditional victimization also reported being cyberbullied; the correlation between bullying and cyberbullying was quite high. There were also gender differences in the findings: cyberbullying was associated with psychological symptoms more strongly for males than females. Reviewing the literature on cyberbullying, Kowalski, Giumetti, Schroeder, and Lattanner (2014) estimate that the majority of studies have found cybervictimization rates to be between 10% and 40%, with higher rates reported in the US than in Australia and Europe.

In a recent meta-analysis of 80 international studies in English, the researchers found that 15% of students admitted to cyberbullying others, compared to 35% who reported bullying using traditional means. For victimization, the rates were similar (15% and 36%, respectively). The two forms of bullying were strongly correlated for both perpetration and victimization (Modecki, Minchin, Harbaugh, Guerra, & Runions, 2014). In Australia 10% of students in grades 4–9 reported being cyberbullied in the previous term (Cross et al., 2009). In a more recent Australian longitudinal study, there were 21% of traditional victims, 15% of cyber victims, and 7% of students victimized in both ways (Hemphill et al., 2012). Student reports of being a cyber perpetrator are much lower than those reporting victimization. In the US, a meta-analysis of 81 papers found a range of perpetration from 1% to 41%, of cybervictimization from 3% to 72%, and both perpetration and victimization from 2.3% to 16.7%. These ranges reflect the concern regarding the wide variation in how the studies are conducted (Selkie, Fales, & Moreno, 2016). These researchers also performed a quality assessment of the 81 studies included in their analysis, and found that out of a possible 42 points, the range of scores was from 12 to 37, so we must always consider findings, even in scholarly journals, with a critical lens.

Consequences of cyberbullying

The experiences of students who have been cyberbullied are frequently associated with increased depression, anxiety, and social difficulties (Campbell et al., 2012), substance abuse (Mitchell, Ybarra, & Finkelhor, 2007), conduct, and peer problems (Dooley et al., 2009), and decreased self-esteem (Chang et al., 2013). Large-scale studies have also illustrated that cyberbullying perpetration by students is linked with higher levels of stress symptoms (Cross et al., 2009), social difficulties, depression, and anxiety (Campbell, Slee, Spears, Butler, & Kift, 2013), and also aggression and rule-breaking behavior (Ybarra & Mitchell, 2007). Compared to the negative outcomes of traditional bullying, those associated with cyberbullying are thought to be more negative, with higher levels of anxiety, depression, and social difficulties reported by students who have been cyberbullied (Perren et al., 2010; Sticca & Perren, 2013). Cyberbullying has also been more strongly association with suicidal behavior (thoughts, plans, and attempts) than traditional bullying in some studies (Bonanno & Hymel, 2013; Klomek, Sourander, & Gould, 2011). Kowalski and Limber (2013) found that those who were both cyberbullies and cybervictims had the worst scores on measures of physical and psychological health and academic performance. Spears et al. (2016) reported that across four studies (2011–2015), cyberbully-victims were consistently less socially connected, demonstrated lower levels of respect for others, and were more anxious, depressed, and stressed than those with no experience of cyberbullying.

A theory that attempts to explain why online bullying seems to often be more cruel and damaging has been proposed. Suler (2004) suggested that *online disinhibition* occurs when people get behind the screen and ignore the usual social conventions about how we treat one another. Perpetrators often say things online they would never say to the target in person. Cyberbullying can reach much larger and more distant audiences with perpetrators remaining anonymous, as bullying through electronic means has no geographic boundaries and can expand beyond the school into the family home (Mishna, Saini, & Solomon, 2009) and indeed into one's pocket. These characteristics are considered by some to account for the increased psychological harm that has been detected with cyberbullying.

Overlap of forms of bullying

While we refer to physical, verbal, social/relational, and cyberbullying, as if they were separate, it has been found that most students (87%) who are victimized by technological means are also bullied in other ways (Cross et al., 2009; Kubiszewski et al., 2015). Additionally, those students who bullied others (77%) by technology also bullied face-to-face (Cross et al., 2009). In a study of 28,104 teens in US high schools, 25.6% reported they had been victimized. Of those, about half said they had been victimized by physical, verbal, relational, and cyber methods, while only 4.6% reported being bullied only by cyber methods. Those who were cyberbullied had greater reported psychological symptoms than those who were bullied in other ways (Waasdorp & Bradshaw, 2015). These findings are similar to those from a Canadian study of 2186 students in an urban area, in which 49.5% reported being bullied online and 33.7% acknowledged bullying others online (Mishna, Cook, Gadalla, Daciuk, & Solomon, 2010). This study also found that only 11% of participants did not know who did the online bullying; 36% of respondents said the perpetrator was a friend. Half of participants said the most common experience was being called names online.

Some researchers believe that victims of school bullying may retaliate against their traditional bullies using cybermethods (Kubiszewski et al., 2015). This phenomenon has been reported in other studies as well (Dehue, Bolman, Vollink, & Pouwelse, 2012; Klomek et al., 2011; Olweus, 2012; Sourander et al., 2010; Smith, 2011; Smith & Slonje, 2010; Sticca, Ruggieri, Alsaker, & Perren, 2013; Waasdorp & Bradshaw, 2015). Holfeld and Grabe (2012) found that those middle-school students who were traditional victims were nearly 10 times as likely to be cybervictims, while being a traditional bully increased the chances of being a cyberbully by seven times (Monks, Robinson, & Worlidge, 2012).

An interesting study conducted in Spain found that while involvement in cyberbullying could be predicted by previous involvement in traditional bullying, the reverse was not the case. That is, cyberbullying involvement did not predict involvement in traditional bullying (Del Rey, Elipe, & Ortega-Ruiz, 2012).

Another type of overlap is also important, which is the overlap between cyberbullying and cybervictimization. In traditional bullying, young people who are both perpetrators and victims are called bully/victims, and usually represent a small proportion of the sample. In cyberbullying, however, we find that the overlap is significantly higher (e.g., Bauman, 2010; Bauman & Pero, 2011; Del Rey et al., 2012).

The implication is that no matter what form bullying takes, prevention efforts need to focus on all forms, including cyberbullying. Teaching strategies for preventing cyberbullying need to include not only technological means, but need to address it as part of the relationship problem which is bullying. As shown later in the book, prevention programs addressing traditional bullying also reduce cyberbullying.

Readers should keep this general information about cyberbullying in mind as they read about the various programs that have shown some success in addressing this global problem that affects youth. It is important to realize that the technology is continually changing, with new devices and applications being developed at an astonishing rate. We cannot create programs for each individual innovation, because we will always be behind, and trends are in constant flux. The focus of prevention needs to be on more underlying commonalities in the technology and in the relationship dynamics that are involved.

References

Bauman, S. (2010). Cyberbullying in a rural intermediate school: An exploratory study. *Journal of Early Adolescence*, *30*, 803–833.

Bauman, S. (2011). *Cyberbullying: What counselors need to know*. Alexandria, VA: American Counseling Association.

Bauman, S., & Baldasare, A. (2015). Cyber aggression among college students: demographic differences, predictors of distress, and the role of the university. *Journal of College Student Development*, *56*, 317–330. https://doi.org/10.1353/csd.2015.0039.

Bauman, S., & Del Rio, A. (2006). Pre-service teachers' response to bullying scenarios: Comparing physical, verbal, and relational bullying. *Journal of Educational Psychology*, *98*, 219–231. https://doi.org/10.1037/0022-0663.98.1.219.

Bauman, S., & Newman, M. L. (2013). Testing assumptions about cyberbullying: Perceived distress associated with acts of conventional and cyber bullying. *Psychology of Violence*, *3*(1), 27. https://doi.org/10.1037/a002986.

Bauman, S., & Pero, H. (2011). Bullying and cyberbullying among deaf students and their hearing peers: An exploratory study. *Journal of Deaf Studies and Deaf Education*, *16*, 236–253. https://doi.org/10.1093/deafed/enq043.

Bauman, S., Underwood, M., & Card, N. (2013). Definitions: Another perspective and a proposal for beginning with cyberaggression. In S. Bauman, D. Cross, & J. Walker (Eds.), *Principles of cyberbullying research: Definitions, measures, and methodology* (pp. 41–46). New York: Routledge.

Bonanno, R. A., & Hymel, S. (2013). Cyber bullying and internalizing difficulties: Above and beyond the impact of traditional forms of bullying. *Journal of Youth and Adolescence*, *42*, 685–697. https://doi.org/10.1007/s10964-013-9937-1.

Campbell, M. A., Slee, P. T., Spears, B., Butler, D., & Kift, S. (2013). Do cyberbullies suffer too? Cyberbullies' perceptions of the harm they cause to others and to their own mental health. *School Psychology International*, *34*, 613–629. https://doi.org/10.1177/0143034313479698.

Campbell, M. A., Spears, B., Slee, P., Butler, D., & Kift, S. (2012). Victims' perceptions of traditional and cyberbullying, and the psychosocial correlates of their victimisation. *Emotional and Behavioural Difficulties*, *17*, 389–401. https://doi.org/10.1080/13632752.2012.704316.

Center for Disease Control (CDC), (2016). *Youth bullying: What does the research say?* Retrieved from https://www.cdc.gov/violenceprevention/youthviolence/bullyingresearch/index.html?s_cid=cs_951.

Chang, F. C., Lee, C. M., Chiu, C. H., Hsi, W. Y., Huang, T. F., & Pan, Y. C. (2013). Relationships among cyberbullying, school bullying, and mental health in Taiwanese adolescents. *Journal of School Health*, *83*, 454–462. https://doi.org/10.1111/josh.12050.

Compton, L., Campbell, M. A., & Mergler, A. (2014). Teacher, parent and student perceptions of the motives of cyberbullies. *Social Psychology of Education*, *17*, 383–400. https://doi.org/10.1007/s11218-014-9254-x.

Cross, D., Shaw, T., Hearn, L., Epstein, M., Monks, H., Lester, L., & Thomas, L. (2009). *Australian covert bullying prevalence study (ACBPS)*. Western Australia: Report prepared for the Department of Education, Employment and Workplace Relations (DEEWR).

Currie, C., Zanotti, C., Morgan, A., & Currie, D. (2012). *Social determinants of health and well-being among young people*. Geneva, Switzerland: World Health Organisation.

Dehue, F., Bolman, C., Vollink, T., & Pouwelse, M. (2012). Cyberbullying and traditional bullying in relation with adolescents' perceptions of parenting. *Journal of CyberTherapy and Rehabilitation*, *5*(1), 25–34.

Del Rey, R., Elipe, P., & Ortega-Ruiz, R. (2012). Bullying and cyberbullying: Overlapping and predictive value of the co-occurrence. *Psicothema*, *24*, 608–613.

Department of Education and Training. (2015). *A review of literature (2010–2014) on student bullying* by Australia's Safe and Supportive School Communities Working Group. Retrieved from https://bullyingnoway.gov.au/UnderstandingBullying/Documents/review-of-literature2010-2014.pdf.

Dooley, J., Pyżalski, J., & Cross, D. (2009). Cyberbullying versus face-to-face bullying: A theoretical and conceptual review. *Journal of Psychology*, *217*, 182–188. https://doi.org/10.1027/0044-3409.217.4.182.

Espinoza, G., & Juvonen, J. (2013). Methods used in cyberbullying research. In S. Bauman, D. Cross, & J. Walker (Eds.), *Principles of cyberbullying research: Definitions, measures, and methodology* (pp. 112–124). New York: Routledge.

Festl, R., Vogelgesang, J., Scharkow, M., & Quandt, T. (2017). Longitudinal patterns of involvement in cyberbullying: Results from a latent transition analysis. *Computers in Human Behaviour, 66*, 7–15. https://doi.org/10.1016/j.chb.2016.09.027.

Frisen, A., Berne, S., Schultze-Krumbholz, A., Scheithauer, H., Naruskove, K., Zukauskiene, R., et al. (2013). Measurement issues: A systematic review of cyberbullying instruments. In P. K. Smith & G. Steffgen (Eds.), *Cyberbullying through the new media: Findings from an international network* (pp. 37–62). London: Psychology Press.

Gladden, R. M., Vivolo-Kantor, A. M., Hamburger, M. E., & Lumpkin, C. D. (2014). *Bullying surveillance among youths: Uniform definitions for public health and recommended data elements, Version 1.0.* Atlanta, GA: National Center for Injury Prevention and Control, Centers for Disease Control and Prevention, and U. S. Department of Education.

Hase, C. N., Goldberg, S. B., Smith, D., Stuck, A., & Campain, J. (2015). Impacts of traditional bullying and cyberbullying on the mental health of middle school and high school students. *Psychology in the Schools, 52*, 607–617. https://doi.org/10.1002/pits.21841.

Hemphill, S. A., Heerde, J. A., & Gomo, R. (2014). *A conceptual definition of school-based bullying for the Australian research and academic community*. Canberra: Australian Research Alliance for Children and Youth.

Hemphill, S. A., Kotevski, A., Tollit, M., Smith, R., Herrenkohl, T. I., Toumbourou, J. W., & Catalano, R. F. (2012). Longitudinal predictors of cyber and traditional bullying perpetration in Australian secondary school students. *Journal of Adolescent Health, 51*(1), 59–65. https://doi.org/10.1016/j.jadohealth.2011.11.019.

Hinduja, S., & Patchin, J. W. (2015). *Bullying beyond the schoolyard: Preventing and responding to cyberbullying*. Thousand Oaks, CA: Sage.

Holfeld, B., & Grabe, M. (2012). Middle school students' perceptions of and responses to cyber bullying. *Journal of Educational Computing Research, 46*(4), 395–413.

Huang, F. L., & Cornell, D. G. (2015). The impact of definition and question order on the prevalence of bullying victimization using student self-reports. *Psychological Assessment, 27*, 1484–1493. https://doi.org/10.1037/pas0000149.

Jacobson, K. J. L., Hood, J. N., & van Buren, H. J. (2014). Workplace bullying across cultures: A research agenda. *Journal of Cross Cultural Management, 14*, 47–65.

Juvonen, J., & Gross, E. F. (2008). Extending the school grounds? Bullying experiences in cyberspace. *Journal of School Health, 78*, 496–505. https://doi.org/10.1111/j.1746-1561.2008.00335.x.

Kim, J., Song, H., & Jennings, W. G. (2016). A distinct form of deviance or a variation of bullying? Examining the developmental pathways and motives of cyberbullying compared with traditional bullying in South Korea. *Crime & Delinquency*, 1–26. https://doi.org/10.1177/0011128716675358. online first.

Klomek, A. B., Sourander, A., & Gould, M. S. (2011). Bullying and suicide: Detection and intervention. *Psychiatric Times, 28*(2), 27–31.

Konig, A., Gollwitzer, M., & Steffgen, G. (2010). Cyberbullying as an act of revenge? *Australian Journal of Guidance and Counselling, 20*, 210–224. https://doi.org/10.1375/ajgc.20.2.210.

Kowalski, R. M., & Limber, S. P. (2013). Psychological, physical, and academic correlates of cyberbullying and traditional bullying. *Journal of Adolescent Health, 53*(1), S13–S20.

Kowalski, R. M., Giumetti, G. W., Schroeder, A. N., & Lattanner, M. R. (2014). *Bullying in the digital age: A critical review and meta-analysis of cyberbullying research among youth.* https://doi.org/10.1037/a0035618.

Kubiszewski, V., Fontaine, R., Potard, C., & Auzoult, L. (2015). Does cyberbullying overlap with school bullying when taking modality of involvement into account? *Computers in Human Behaviour, 43*, 49–57. https://doi.org/10.1016/j.chb.2014.10.049.

Kupczynski, L., Mundy, M. A., & Green, M. E. (2013). The prevalence of cyberbullying among ethnic groups of high school students. *International Journal of Educational Research*, *1*(2), 48–53.

Langos, C. (2012). Cyberbullying: The challenge to define. *Cyberpsychology, Behaviour, and Social Networking*, *15*, 285–289. https://doi.org/10.1089/cyber.2011.0588.

Menesini, E., Nocentini, A., & Camodeca, M. (2013). Morality, values, traditional bullying, and cyberbullying in adolescence. *British Journal of Developmental Psychology*, *31*(1), 1–14. https://doi.org/10.1111/j.2044-835X.2011.02066.x.

Mishna, F., Cook, C., Gadalla, T., Daciuk, J., & Solomon, S. (2010). Cyber bullying behaviors among middle and high school students. *American Journal of Orthopsychiatry*, *80*(3), 362–374.

Mishna, F., Saini, M., & Solomon, S. (2009). Ongoing and online: Children and youth's perceptions of cyber bullying. *Children and Youth Services Review*, *31*, 1222–1228. https://doi.org/10.1016/j.childyouth.2009.05.004.

Mitchell, K. J., Ybarra, M., & Finkelhor, D. (2007). The relative importance of online victimization in understanding depression, delinquency, and substance use. *Child Maltreatment*, *12*, 314–324.

Modecki, K. L., Minchin, J., Harbaugh, A. G., Guerra, N. G., & Runions, K. C. (2014). Bullying prevalence across contexts: A meta-analysis measuring cyber and traditional bullying. *Journal of Adolescent Health*, *55*, 602–611. https://doi.org/10.1016/j.jadohealth.2014.06.007.

Monks, C. P., Robinson, S., & Worlidge, P. (2012). The emergence of cyberbullying: A survey of primary school pupils' perceptions and experiences. *School Psychology International*, *33*, 477–491. https://doi.org/10.1177/0143034312445242.

Naylor, P., Cowie, H., Cossin, F., Bettencourt, R., & Lemme, F. (2006). Teachers' and pupils' definitions of bullying. *British Journal of Educational Psychology*, *76*, 553–576. https://doi.org/10.1348/000709905X52229.

Nocentini, A., Calmaestra, J., Schultz-Krumbholz, A., Scheithauer, H., Ortega, R., & Menesini, E. (2010). Cyberbullying: Labels, behaviours and definition in three European countries. *Australian Journal of Guidance and Counselling*, *20*, 129–142. https://doi.org/10.1375/ajgc.20.2.129.

Olweus, D. (1993). *Bullying at school: What we know and what we can do*. Cambridge, MA: Blackwell.

Olweus, D. (2012). Cyberbullying: An overrated phenomenon? *European Journal of Developmental Psychology*, *9*(5), 520–538.

Perren, S., Dooley, J., Shaw, T., & Cross, D. (2010). Bullying in school and cyberspace: Associations with depressive symptoms in Swiss and Australian adolescents. *Child and Adolescent Psychiatry and Mental Health*, *4*(1), 1–10. https://doi.org/10.1186/1753-2000-4-28.

Selkie, E. M., Fales, J. L., & Moreno, M. A. (2016). Cyberbullying prevalence among US middle and high school-aged adolescents: A systematic review and quality assessment. *Journal of Adolescent Health*, *58*, 125–133. https://doi.org/10.1016/j.jadohealth.2015.09.026.

Smith, P. K. (2011). Why interventions to reduce bullying and violence in school may (or may not) succeed: Comments on the special section. *International Journal of Behavioural Development*, *35*, 419–423. https://doi.org/10.1177/0165025411407459.

Smith, P. K., Cowie, H., Olafsson, R. F., & Liefooghe, A. P. D. (2002). Definitions of bullying: A comparison of terms used, and age and gender differences, in a fourteen-country international comparison. *Child Development*, *73*, 1119–1133.

Smith, P. K., del Barrio, C., & Tokunaga, R. S. (2013). Definitions of bullying and cyberbullying: How useful are the terms? In S. Bauman, D. Cross, & J. Walker (Eds.), *Principles of cyberbullying research: Definitions, measures, and methodology* (pp. 26–40). New York: Routledge.

Smith, P. K., Mahdavi, J., Carvalho, M., Fisher, S., Russell, S., & Tippett, N. (2008). Cyberbullying: Its nature and impact in secondary school pupils. *Journal of Child Psychology and Psychiatry*, *49*, 376–385. https://doi.org/10.1111/j.1469-7610.2007.01846.x.

Smith, P. K., & Slonje, R. (2010). Cyberbullying: The nature and extent of a new kind of bullying, in and out of school. In S. R. Jimerson, S. M. Swearer, & D. Espelage (Eds.), *Handbook of bullying in schools: An international perspective* (pp. 249–262). New York: Routledge.

Sourander, A., Klomek, A. B., Ikonen, M., Lindroos, J., Luntamo, T., Koskelainen, M., et al. (2010). Psychosocial risk factors associated with cyberbullying among adolescents: A population-based study. *Archives of general psychiatry*, *67*(7), 720–728.

Spears, B., Keeley, M., Bates, S., & Katz, I. (2014). *Research on youth exposure to, and management of, cyberbullying incidents in Australia: Part A—Literature review on the estimated prevalence of cyberbullying involving Australian minors (SPRC Report 9/2014)*. Sydney: Social Policy Research Centre, UNSW Australia. Retrieved from https://www.communications.gov.au/search?search_api_views_fulltext=cyberbullying.

Spears, B., Taddeo, C., Collin, P., Swist, T., Razzell, M., Borbone, V., & Drennan, J. (2016). *Safe and Well Online: Learnings from four social marketing campaigns for youth wellbeing*. Melbourne: Young and Well Co-operative Research Centre. Retrieved from http://search.ror.unisa.edu.au/media/researcharchive/open/9916073608201831/53133988560001831.

Staude-Müller, F., Hansen, B., & Voss, M. (2012). How stressful is online victimization? Effects of victim's personality and properties of the incident. *European Journal of Developmental Psychology*, *9*, 260–274. https://doi.org/10.1080/17405629.2011.643170.

Sticca, F., & Perren, S. (2013). Is cyberbullying worse than traditional bullying? Examining the differential roles of medium, publicity, and anonymity for the perceived severity of bullying. *Journal of Youth and Adolescence*, *42*, 739–750. https://doi.org/10.1007/s10964-012-9867-3.

Sticca, F., Ruggieri, S., Alsaker, F., & Perren, S. (2013). Longitudinal risk factors for cyberbullying in adolescence. *Journal of Community and Applied Social Psychology*, *23*, 52–67. https://doi.org/10.1002/casp.2136.

Suler, J. (2004). The online disinhibition effect. *Cyberpsychology & Behaviour*, *7*, 321–326. https://doi.org/10.1089/1094931041291295.

Thomas, H. J., Connor, J. P., & Scott, J. G. (2015). Integrating traditional bullying and cyberbullying: Challenges of definition and measurement in adolescents—A review. *Educational Psychology Review*, *27*, 135–152. https://doi.org/10.1007/s10648-014-9261-7.

Waasdorp, T. E., & Bradshaw, C. P. (2015). The overlap between cyberbullying and traditional bullying. *Journal of Adolescent Health*, *56*, 483–488. https://doi.org/10.1016/j.jadohealth.2014.12.002.

Ybarra, M. L., Boyd, D., Korchmaros, J. D., & Oppenheim, J. K. (2012). Defining and measuring cyberbullying within the larger context of bullying victimization. *Journal of Adolescent Health*, *51*, 53–58. https://doi.org/10.1016/j.jadohealth.2011.12.031.

Ybarra, M. L., & Mitchell, K. J. (2007). Prevalence and frequency of Internet harassment instigation: Implications for adolescent health. *Journal of Adolescent Health*, *41*, 189–195. https://doi.org/10.1016/j.jadohealth.2007.03.005.

Further reading

Archer, J., & Coyne, S. M. (2005). An integrated review of indirect, relational, and social aggression. *Personality and Social Psychology Review*, *9*, 212–230. https://doi.org/10.1207/s15327957pspr0903_2.

Berkowitz, L. (1993). *Aggression: Its causes, consequences and control*. New York: McGraw-Hill.

Bradshaw, C. P., Waasdorp, T. E., & Johnson, S. L. (2015). Overlapping verbal, relational, physical, and electronic forms of bullying in adolescence: Influence of school context. *Journal of Clinical Child and Adolescent Psychology*, *44*, 494–508. https://doi.org/10.1080/15374416.2014.893516.

Chen, L. M., Liu, K. S., & Cheng, Y. Y. (2012). Validation of the perceived school bullying severity scale. *Educational Psychology*, *32*, 169–182. https://doi.org/10.1080/01443410.2011.633495.

Craig, W. M., Henderson, K., & Murphy, J. G. (2000). Prospective teachers' attitudes toward bullying and victimization. *School Psychology International*, *21*, 5–21.

Humphrey, G., & Crisp, B. R. (2008). Bullying affects us too: Parental responses to bullying at kindergarten. *Australian Journal of Early Childhood*, *33*(1), 45–49.

Maunder, R., Harrop, A., & Tattersall, A. (2010). Pupil and staff perceptions of bullying in secondary schools: Comparing behavioural definitions and their perceived seriousness. *Educational Research*, *52*, 263–282. https://doi.org/10.1080/00131881.2010.504062.

Menesini, E., Nocentini, A., Palladino, B. E., Frisén, A., Berne, S., Ortega-Ruiz, R.…Naruskov, K. (2012). Cyberbullying definition among adolescents: A comparison across six European countries. *Cyberpsychology, Behaviour, and Social Networking*, *15*, 455–463. https://doi.org/10.1089/cyber.2012.0040.

Rigby, K., & Bagshaw, D. (2003). Prospects of adolescent students collaborating with teachers in addressing issues of bullying and conflict in schools. *Educational Psychology*, *23*, 535–546. https://doi.org/10.1080/0144341032000123787.

Slonje, R., & Smith, P. K. (2008). Cyberbullying: Another main type of bullying? *Scandinavian Journal of Psychology*, *49*, 147–154. https://doi.org/10.1111/j.1467-9450.2007.00611.x.

Spears, B., Slee, P., Owens, L., & Johnson, B. (2009). Behind the scenes and screens: Insights into the human dimension of covert and cyberbullying. *Journal of Psychology*, *217*, 189–196. https://doi.org/10.1027/0044-3409.217.4.189.

Thomas, H. J., Chan, G., Scott, J., Connor, J., Kelly, A., & Williams, J. (2016). Association of different forms of bullying victimisation with adolescents' psychological distress and reduced emotional wellbeing. *Australian and New Zealand Journal of Psychiatry*, *50*, 371–379. https://doi.org/10.1177/0004867415600076.

Underwood, M. K. (2002). Sticks and stones and social exclusion: Aggression among girls and boys. In P. K. Smith & C. H. Hart (Eds.), *Blackwell handbook of childhood social development* (pp. 533–548). Oxford: Blackwell.

Addressing traditional school-based bullying more effectively

2

Ken Rigby, Coosje Griffiths*†

*University of South Australia, Adelaide, SA, Australia, †Department of Education, East Perth, WA, Australia

Introduction

The case for action to reduce bullying in schools is indisputable. Over the last 20 years evidence-based knowledge of the prevalence of bullying in schools around the world has been continually increasing, together with evidence of associated serious negative mental and physical conditions among peer-victimized students (Arseneault, Bowes, & Shakoor, 2010; Bogart et al., 2014; Rigby, 2003). Over this period, modest reductions in bullying prevalence in a number of countries have been achieved (Rigby & Smith, 2011). The prevalence of bullying in its various forms continues to be considered unacceptable and requiring continued sustained effort to reduce it.

There is evidence that bullying in schools can be reduced. According to leading researchers in the field of bullying in schools, Farrington and Ttofi (2009), antibullying programs can be effective in reducing bullying and victimization (being bullied). Their meta-analysis of outcomes from 44 published studies indicated that on average bullying behavior decreased by 20%–23%, and being victimized by 17%–20%.

Interventions: proactive and reactive

Interventions have been categorized as proactive or reactive. By proactive is meant taking action in order to *prevent* the occurrence of bullying behavior. Reactive intervention implies taking action when cases of bullying have been identified in order to prevent the bullying from continuing and causing harm. The two forms of intervention are best conceived as complementary and may act in tandem. Insofar as proactive steps are effective in reducing the number of cases of bullying that occur, resources can be concentrated on addressing the fewer cases that are not prevented. Moreover, effectively dealing reactively with actual cases of bullying, especially when the intervention results in improved relationships among those involved, can help to produce a social environment in which bullying is less likely to occur. Both proactive and reactive approaches to bullying are needed, each increasing the potential effectiveness of the other.

This view that both proactive and reactive approaches are required in countering bullying in schools is reflected in various frameworks and programs that have been

Reducing Cyberbullying in Schools. https://doi.org/10.1016/B978-0-12-811423-0.00002-X

developed and utilized in schools. Examples include Australia's National Safe Schools Framework in Australia, which recommends a multitiered approach to addressing bullying (Ministerial Council on Education, Early Childhood Development and Youth Affairs (2004/2011). The Positive Behavioural Interventions and Supports (PBIS) initiative (Bradshaw, Pas, Debnam, & Johnson, 2015) and the Friendly School Plus program (Cross, Thompson, & Erceg, 2013, Cross, Waters, & Thompson, 2014) provide practical applications of how schools can employ a comprehensive approach to tackling bullying, both traditional and cyber (Slee, Spears, Campbell, & Cross, 2011). More recently, the *Handbook of Australian School Psychology* (Thiekling & Tergesen, 2017) has provided advice and instruction on the integration of international research, practice, and policy in addressing school bullying (Nickersen & Rigby, 2017).

Griffiths and Weatherilt (2012) demonstrate how the creation and implementation of well-thought through and connected antibullying strategies can provide the basis for student support and well-being (Fig. 2.1).

Differences arise over what particular intervention strategies in addressing bullying are most appropriate and effective. These relate as much to ideology or philosophy as to evidence. For example, some educators have taken a legalistic stance arguing that that undesirable behavior needs to be punished and may serve as an effective deterrent. Others with a more humanistic approach emphasize the importance of understanding the motivation of the perpetrator(s) and encouraging them to act positively in their relations with others. Neither approach has been shown unequivocally to produce better results.

One study conducted in Finland compared the effectiveness of the two approaches in addressing cases of bullying (Garandeau, Poskiparta, & Salmivalli, 2014). Schools were randomly allocated to one condition in which a confronting (legalistic) approach

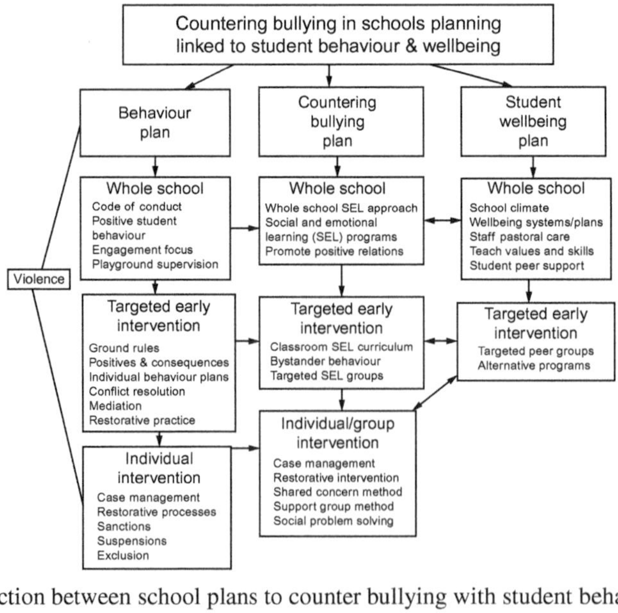

Fig. 2.1 Interaction between school plans to counter bullying with student behavior and well-being.

was employed, while other schools employed a nonconfronting (humanistic) approach. The researchers reported that the two approaches produced similar outcomes. It is unclear, however, whether this conclusion would apply in culturally diverse countries.

What is sometimes ignored in generalizing about the comparative effectiveness of interventions is that bullying can differ widely in nature and severity. Thus, one case of bullying may involve relatively mild and occasional disparagement of another student, and another severe and sustained physical abuse. Bullying may be provoked or unprovoked. Bullying may involve groups of students picking on one student or only a single perpetrator and target. Children may be targeted using cyber technology and/ or traditional means. Arguably different forms of intervention may be applied depending on the actual case. Similarly, what can be done proactively may differ from school to school, depending upon the school context and resources, including, lesson time available to the teacher. Hence, it is considered doubtful whether any one intervention method is appropriate and effective in all cases and in all schools.

The idea that there is more than one way of dealing with bullying runs counter to what may be called the traditional approach to bullying in schools. This may be illustrated by reference to the well-known novel *Tom Brown's School Days* (Hughes, 1857; Rigby, 1997). This book is centered on the school days of Tom Brown at an English public school where as a new boy he was continually bullied, both verbally and physically, by a senior boy known as Flashman. The preface to the book discusses at length the public outcry that followed and examines the views expressed as to what should be done to deal with the bullying. The prevailing view was that sadistic children like Flashman should be taught a lesson. Bullying was seen as a consequence of an individual's personality. Very little attention (if any) was given to school climate, which might conceivably give rise to such behavior. The answer to the problem was seen as lying in the administration of harsh discipline or, in some cases, the valorous actions of those children who decided not to take it anymore. In the story the problem is solved by Tom and his friend, East, goaded beyond measure, one day rushing at the malevolent Flashman and knocking him out! The moral of the story was that that you must meet force with force—and in reality the bully is a coward.

In recent years, the understanding of bullying behavior and how it can be addressed has changed radically. It is now generally recognized that given the social nature of bullying and the complex interactive factors, it is vital to take account of the student's unique individual and the socioecological factors involved in being persistently bullied. It is expected that interventions and support needs are tailored to meet the unique needs of those students and their family, as well as the peer dynamic involved in the bullying. The promotion of positive bystander and peer support is an element in such a multitiered approach (Bradshaw, 2015; Swearer, Wang, Berry, & Myers, 2014).

The use of disciplinary action as the stock response to bullying has become much less accepted (Bradshaw, 2015). As noted, bullying is now widely understood to be the result of a complex interplay between individual, relationships, community, family, and societal factors (Cornell & Bradshaw, 2015; Espelage & Swearer, 2004; Farrington & Ttofi, 2009; Schott & Søndergaard, 2014). Accordingly, attention is commonly directed toward developing a sociocultural climate in which students are no longer motivated to bully one another. In practice, this requires teachers, administrative, and counseling staff to work with children, especially, but not exclusively, in classrooms to inculcate desirable social attitudes and healthy prosocial behavior. How this can be done has become the subject of numerous proposals and an important component of many antibullying programs, each of which makes use of both proactive and reactive strategies.

Proactive interventions

1. **Working with students**
   One of the earliest educationalists to recognize the importance of influencing the way students relate to each other was Swedish psychologist, Olweus (1993). He advocated regular classroom meetings between teachers and students to discuss issues relating to bullying. He proposed that teachers invite students to discuss the sort of rules they saw as important in governing the way they treated each other, and to provide an agreed-upon list that could be used to remind themselves of how they felt they should behave. Examples of the kinds of rules that might be agreed upon included: we will not bully other students; we will try to help students who are being bullied; we will try to include students who are left out. Importantly, the rules were to be generated through student discussion rather than imposed by teachers.
   Subsequently, numerous strategies have been developed and utilized by schools to engage students constructively in promoting antibullying initiatives. These have included the creation of antibullying committees in which students and teachers can meet to share ideas on how they can work together (Petersen & Rigby, 1999). Various peer-support schemes have been developed and implemented, in some schools taking the form of student to student mentoring and befriending, advice-giving, peer mediation, and counseling (Smith & Thompson, 2014). Central to such schemes has been the need to provide student-helpers with basic skills such as active listening, empathy, problem-solving, and supportiveness and also to provide ongoing supervision and support. Peer-support schemes are thought to contribute to the quality of the school climate and to promote positive relationships that are incompatible with bullying behavior. According to results from the evaluation of such a scheme in England, this approach can raise the self-esteem of peer-supporters and impact upon the perceptions of bullying in a school. Less clearly, however, is its effectiveness in changing the prevalence of actual bullying behavior (Houlston & Smith, 2009).
2. **Promoting positive bystander behavior**
   A further strategy designed to reduce the likelihood of bullying in a school is the encouragement of students to become positive rather than ineffective as bystanders when bullying is taking place. It is known that student bystanders are usually present when bullying occurs at school, especially when it is in the playground (Pepler & Craig, 1995). Evidence suggests that students are less likely to bully if bystanders object to what is happening. Unfortunately, student bystanders are often reluctant to speak up to try to stop the bullying or to intervene. The problem is to motivate students to take positive action, without putting themselves at risk. The KiVa antibullying program employed in 90% of schools in Finland has provided a demonstration of how this can be done (Garandeau et al., 2014). Through classroom work, teachers seek to promote greater affective empathy for victims of bullying and inculcate antibullying attitudes. It is further recognized that student bystander behavior is strongly influenced by perceived beliefs about bullying held by teachers and students. Hence, the need for teachers to act as role models in relation to bullying and also to raise awareness of the positive actions that students are actually taking to discourage bullying. In a longitudinal

study conducted in Finland, decreases in both self and peer-reported bullying perpetration were related to improvements in student attitudes toward bullying and to positive appraisals of how teachers and students were seen as acting to discourage bullying (Saarento, Boulton, & Salmivalli, 2015).

The Finnish study emphasized the need for schools to influence the attitudes held by individual students as well as the way students in general view how their peers behave. Whether students are more strongly influenced as bystanders, by teachers, or by peers may vary across cultures. In Australia, for instance, student reports suggest that the views and actions of other students carry more weight (Rigby & Johnson, 2005). These researchers have argued that the direct influence by teachers through *telling* students how they ought to behave as bystanders is likely to be relatively ineffective. Enabling students to discuss how they think they should act as bystanders in hypothetical situations and the listening to their suggestions was seen as much more likely to lead to positive bystander action. The use of scenarios as a tool for students and their peers to provide opportunities to problem solve in order to establish appropriate and comfortable ways to respond as bystanders was seen as much more likely to lead to positive bystander action.

3. **Promoting Social and Emotional Learning (SEL)**

The promotion of social and emotional learning (SEL) has been seen as an effective way of developing so-called life skills among schoolchildren and in countering school bullying. According to the Collaborative for Academic, Social, and Emotional Learning (CASEL), the peak body supporting evidence-based SEL programs in schools, SEL is a process through which students can acquire and effectively apply the knowledge, attitudes, and skills necessary to understand and manage emotions, set and achieve positive goals, feel and show empathy for others, establish and maintain positive relationships, and make responsible decisions (see http://www.casel.org). Many schools have been persuaded to include content in their curricula consistent with this approach. For example, within the Australian Curriculum it is stated that expectations are that "personal and social capability skills are addressed in all learning areas and at every stage of a student's schooling." These include the ability "to understand themselves and others, and manage their relationships, lives, work and learning more effectively" including their ability to "resolve conflict and reach positive outcomes" (ACARA, 2013, p. 2).

It has been claimed that the application of the Social and Emotional Learning (SEL) programs significantly reduces bullying (Smith & Low, 2013). Given the importance that has been ascribed to this initiative, it is desirable to examine the available evidence critically. Three studies have examined possible links between social and emotional learning and bullying as distinct from antisocial behavior or delinquency. A randomized controlled trial of the effects of a SEL program was undertaken with 1296 students attending 33 elementary schools in the United States (Brown, Low, Smith, & Haggerty, 2011). Significant reductions in physical bullying perpetration were found; however, no changes were found for non-physical bullying perpetration, or for being victimized. A similar outcome was reported by Espelage, Low, and Polanin (2015) following a SEL program applied to 47 middle-school students with disabilities; that is, bullying perpetration reduced but victimization did not. A further relevant study has been reported by Espelage, Rose, and Polanin (2015) in an evaluation of the Second Step program. This was undertaken in 36 schools drawing on results of an intervention with 3658 students in Years 6 and 7. Over a 3-year period, no direct effects on either bullying perpetration or being victimized were found. There was, however, a reported reduction in delinquent behavior, which in turn was related to reduced bullying This suggests that SEL programs can have some significant effect on bullying behavior, of a delinquent kind: that is involving criminal behavior, which makes up a relatively small proportion of bullying. In the UK, evaluations of the SEAL program (a British adaptation of SEL) in secondary schools undertaken by Humphrey, Lendrum, and Wigelsworth (2010), one of the assessed outcomes was "behavior problems." On this broad category of behavior, which included bullying, no significant effect was found. Explanations have been suggested for the limited success of SEL in its impact on bullying. These include inadequate involvement on the part of school leadership, a failure to employ programs and content best suited the local context, an absence of whole school planning and a lack of appropriate training for teachers (Durlak, Weissberg, Dymnicki, Taylor, & Schellinger, 2011; Humphrey, 2013; Polanin, Espelage, & Pigott, 2012). Schools may be assisted in selecting and applying an appropriate SEL program by following step-by-step process detailed by the Australian Department of Education (2016).

Critics of the use of SEL and similar programs in schools have suggested that, based on psychotherapeutic conjecture, their content is inappropriate and cannot be taught effectively by teachers who are untrained in the area, and that its inclusion in school curricula comes at the expense of more relevant academic content (Ecclestone & Hayes, 2008). Whether SEL or similar programs will remain an orthodox approach to preventing bullying in schools is currently uncertain. Further evidence on how this approach can be implemented effectively is needed.

4. **Circle time**

   Circle time refers to meetings held periodically with students in class time in which the participants are enabled by the teacher to share and discuss experiences or matters of personal concern. Circle time can be used as a means of improving the classroom climate, promoting mutual respect between students, and providing opportunities for group problem-solving (Collins, 2013). If done well, this strategy can help prevent conflict from festering and potentially restore relationships that have started to break down (Costello, Wachtel, & Wachtel, 2010). However, if the process is not handled well by the facilitator, the process can also have an underlying retributive element (Leach & Lewis, 2013). More research is needed to ascertain its scope and the extent of its effectiveness as an antibullying strategy (Glazzard, 2016).

Reactive interventions

What has sometimes been understood as "reactive" is the application of sanctions or punishments designed to deter perpetrators of bullying or would-be perpetrators. This view of reactive interventions is still held by some educators. However, this is not the only way in which a school may react to cases of bullying. In fact, there is now a wide range of reactive strategies that may be used, sometimes in conjunction with a proactive approach. Typically, they are embedded in a whole school approach and are considered more effective within a school climate that fosters dialog about relationships and gives students the confidence to seek help from teachers when it is needed (Perren et al., 2012) The following is a summary of various intervention strategies developed to address identified cases of peer victimization in schools. Some schools may make use of more than one method.

1. **The use of direct sanctions**

   Direct sanctions involve the use of negative sanctions imposed on the perpetrator(s) of bullying. Typically, schools outline in their plans that bullying behavior is unacceptable and contrary to school rules. Depending on the severity of the incident, an appropriate form of sanction is applied, for example, a verbal reprimand, withdrawal of privileges, detention, internal exclusion in a special room, school community service, meetings with parents, suspension or exclusion from school. The rationale given is that the application of sanctions is likely to reduce the likelihood of further victimization being committed by the offender, as well as by others who have become aware of the actions taken by the school. Its effectiveness depends, in part, on whether the offender (and others) believes that subsequent acts of bullying will be detected by the school authorities and that the possible consequences will be severe and that this will act as a deterrent. To be effective, schools need to be consistent rather than arbitrary so that they avoid generating anger and resentment among students. Employing this intervention method requires careful monitoring of its effectiveness, a task that can be difficult to achieve.

In some schools, elected students have been involved in deciding upon what action should be taken in dealing with cases of bullying. These students are constituted as a tribunal or "bully court." They are empowered to hear evidence and to advise the school on appropriate sanctions or punishments. At one secondary school community in England, this method was seen as effective in reducing bullying (Mahdavi & Smith, 2002). Arguably, judgments made by fellow students may be more acceptable to other students than those made by school authorities. At the same time, misgivings may be raised as to whether members of the bully courts have sufficient maturity and detachment to make appropriate decisions, especially in cases of severe forms of bullying.

2. **Strengthening the victim**

   This approach aims at strengthening the victimized student so that he or she is able resist or cope with the bullying behavior. Training may involve instruction in physical skills such as martial arts or, more commonly, in the use of appropriate social skills, including assertiveness training and techniques such as "fogging" (Rigby, 2011). The technique can be taught to some students. It aims at discouraging would-be aggressors by adopting a nonchalant attitude, agreeing that they may believe what they are saying without showing any particular concern. Its use is limited to low-level forms of verbal bullying for which there are reasonable expectations that the targeted child can acquire and employ the necessary social skills through the help of a school psychologist or counselor (Smith & Thompson, 2014). These methods need to be used judiciously, depending on the skills and aptitudes of the student and the type of bullying involved.

3. **Mediation**

   Mediation involves a meeting facilitated by a mediator—a staff member or trained student—with students who have agreed to be present to see if the conflict in which they are involved can be resolved to their mutual satisfaction. Importantly, this process requires the unforced cooperation of all concerned; at any stage individuals are free to leave. A difficulty in applying this method is that schools are generally committed to taking action to stop cases of bullying from continuing, especially bullying that is considered severe. Allowing bullying to continue may be seen as not an option. At the same time, if a mediator can help students to come to a negotiated agreement that leads to a cessation of the bullying, the outcome is likely to be more sustained than would be obtained through an imposed solution (Tyrrell, 2002).

4. **Restorative practice**

   Restorative Practice is an approach for dealing with "offenders," which seeks to resolve a problem by leading the perpetrator of the bullying to reflect upon his or her unacceptable behavior, experience a sense of remorse, and act to restore a damaged relationship. Its application may take place at a meeting arranged by the practitioner with the identified perpetrator(s) and targeted student(s). In some cases, the method is employed by practitioners working with a group or class of students or at a "community conference" attended by those involved in the bullying plus significant others such as parents. It is considered important to enable a sense of genuine remorse in the perpetrator to arise without undue pressure or consequent stigmatization, and to make it possible for the "offender" to become reintegrated in the school community (Sullivan, 2012).

5. **The support group method**
This is a nonpunitive approach to bullying developed in England by Robinson and Maines (2008). The target of the bullying is interviewed first to discover what has been happening, what effects the bullying has had, and who have been responsible. Next the perpetrators are confronted at a group meeting with and provided with evidence of the target's distress. Those present at the meeting also include a number of students who have been selected because they are expected to be supportive. The targeted students are generally not present. It is impressed upon everyone that they have a responsibility to help. Each student is required to say what he or she is prepared to do. The practitioner continues to monitor the situation and keep in touch with group members. This approach has been combined with Solution-Focused Brief Therapy (SBFT), which focuses on personal strengths and successes as well as providing and strengthening peer support for victims of bullying (Kvarme, Aabo, & Saeteeren, 2013).

6. **The method of shared concern**
This is also a nonpunitive approach, sometimes known as the Pikas Method after its originator (Pikas, 2002; Rigby, 2011). It is used for working with groups of students who are suspected of bullying someone. The process involves a number of stages. It begins with the identification of a number of students who are suspected of bullying someone. The practitioner interviews each of these students in turn and shares a concern over how the target may be feeling, and elicits suggestions on how things may be improved. Having secured some commitment on what actions the suspected bullies are prepared to take, the targeted student is then interviewed to discover his or her perception of what has been happening. At this meeting, the possibility is raised that the target may have provoked the bullying. Progress is then monitored through further meetings with individual students. Once it has been ascertained that some positive actions have taken to support the target, a meeting is held with the suspected bullies as a group to plan how the problem might be permanently resolved. Finally a joint meeting is held, including the targeted student, at which the practitioner helps to bring about a mediated and sustainable solution. As this method can be time consuming, it is generally justified only in cases of at least moderate severity in which groups of students are involved. Some applications of the Method dispense with group meetings after individual suspected bullies have promised to be cooperative. This shortening of the process greatly weakens its effectiveness, which depends largely on practitioners engaging with groups of students, that is, not solely with individuals (Rigby & Griffiths, 2011).

7. **Motivational interviewing**
Motivational interviewing (MI) as a tool for working with resistant clients to address behavioral and health issues is a promising approach in being applied to reduce or stop persistent bullying behavior (Juhnke et al., 2013). Motivational interviewing involves three phases:
   1. Expressing empathy: by allowing students who bully to talk without condemnation.
   2. Rolling with resistance: by having ongoing conversations about the topic (of bullying others) with no judgment so that the student feels understood.
   3. Developing discrepancy: by asking questions, active listening, and providing opportunities for students to identify their own reasons for change and the necessary support to make those changes (Juhnke et al., 2013).

   Further research on this approach is underway by the Telethon Kids Institute in Western Australia on the efficacy of MI as a tool for reducing bullying through a project entitled *Beyond Bullying: Testing a comprehensive targeted intervention to reduce student bullying* (www.telethonkids.org.au).

A note on interventions in cases of cyberbullying

A distinction is often made between traditional and nontraditional bullying, by which is meant bullying that makes use of electronic technology: in other words, cyberbullying. Advice on what to do about cyberbullying has become increasingly available as the prevalence and harmfulness of this practice has become more widely recognized. For example, in Australia, the Office of the Children's eSafety Commissioner's website (https://www.esafety.gov.au/about-the-office) provides information on resources and a complaints system to help children when they experience cyberbullying. It is sometimes presumed that nontraditional cyberbullying needs to be addressed exclusively using nontraditional methods, as distinct from the methods described and discussed here. Certainly there are technological means of preventing some cyberbullying, for example, by blocking messages from known perpetrators. Also knowledge of how to be safer in using cyber technology can be taught to reduce the number of potential victims. However, it has been found that to a considerable extent the students involved in cyberbullying are also the ones that are involved in what has been called traditional bullying (Cross et al., 2009; Levy et al., 2012). Both forms of bullying can usefully be viewed as relationship problems that typically manifest in both cyber and noncyber space (Olweus, 2012). In Australia, some 77% of students who reported engaging in cyberbullying also reported engaging in face-to-face bullying (Cross et al., 2009) Whatever can be done to change behavior in one area of interaction is likely to affect behavior in another. Hence, traditional forms of intervention can be relevant to addressing cyberbullying. In terms of perpetration, the proportion of students in an Australian study who reported they cyberbullied others and also bullied face-to-face was 77% (Cross et al., 2009); in a US study by Raskauskas and Stoltz (2007) the corresponding figure was 94%. This high level of behavior transfer strongly suggests that Information and Communication Technology provides another means to experience/deliver "virtually" the same types of bullying behavior. Thus, if schools and families have effective strategies in place to prevent and manage young people's face-to-face bullying, these may also be effective to reduce the likelihood of cyberbullying behaviors.

A feature that sets cyberbullying apart from other forms is that there can often be ignorance or uncertainty of who the perpetrators are. Sometimes there are suspicions only. However, in a large number of cases, it is possible to identify the *probable* perpetrators of the bullying. When this is done, schools can be informed and investigations proceed, leading to the identification of individuals who are engaged in traditional bullying at school as well as cyberbullying. The application of one or more of the methods of intervention employed in face-to-face meetings can then be undertaken.

An important question is whether schools are prepared to accept some responsibility for addressing cases of cyberbullying. Commonly, the bullying behavior is initiated from outside the school in nonschool time. It is not always the case that students who are being victimized in this way are being bullied by children from their own school. Arguably, schools can wash their hands of it, claiming that it none of their business. However, many schools do feel motivated to act when a case of cyberbullying is reported to them. In an Australian survey of 25 government schools, 24 indicated that they encourage students to report to them if they experience cyberbullying (Rigby & Johnson, 2016).

The question may be raised as to which of the methods of intervention should be used when cyberbullying is involved. This may differ according to legal requirements in different places. If the law says that offences regarded as cyber crimes are to be subject to prosecution, then nonpunitive forms of intervention may be difficult, or impossible, to apply. However, there is some evidence that cases of cyberbullying can be effectively handled by nonpunitive approaches; for example, the Method of Shared Concern has been successfully applied in resolving a case of cyberbullying to the satisfaction of the students involved and the parents of the victimized student (Rigby & Griffiths, 2011). The extensive review of online bullying research funded by the Australian Government (Keeley, Katz, Bates, & Wong, 2014) did not nominate specific appropriate approaches, instead highlighting the need to consider a response appropriate to each situation. Prevailing circumstances, the policy and practices of the school, and the attitudes of stakeholders such as parents may play a crucial part in deciding what steps may be taken. However, knowledge of the options that are available for addressing cases of bullying, including cyberbullying, may determine precisely what is done and how effectively a case is tackled.

Discussion

As indicated, a variety of methods of intervention have been developed and applied by schools in seeking to prevent bullying and/or stop cases from continuing. Generally it is agreed that a whole school approach is needed to maximize the chances of success in reducing bullying and that both proactive and reactive methods should be employed in a complementary manner. As yet there is limited agreement on the effectiveness of particular methods of intervention. For instance, although the use of SEL programs is regarded as the current orthodoxy (Humphrey, 2013), the limited success of their use in repeated studies in reducing peer victimization suggests that improvements, especially in the implementation, of such programs is needed.

Much has been said and written about the importance of schools employing only "evidence-based" intervention methods. There is an assumption here that some methods are "evidence-based" and others are not, and that an examination of the peer-reviewed literature enables one to make an informed decision. In practice, it is often not possible to identify precisely what actions taken by a school have led to significant changes in bullying behavior. For example, the best known antibullying program employed in schools in the United States, the Olweus Bullying Prevention Program, is sometimes regarded as effective because of its use of rules and direct sanctions to deter bullying behavior. However, as noted earlier, it also includes other important features designed to promote student engagement in proactive peer-related behavior. Further, while considerable success in the use of this program has been reported in studies in some countries, for example, in Norway, failures have been reported in evaluative studies of the program in the United States and elsewhere (Bradshaw, 2015). Generalizations about the effectiveness of methods may ignore the crucial role of social or cultural context.

Where evaluations of methods are concerned with how successfully cases of bullying are addressed, as distinct from changes in bullying prevalence, conclusions may be more focused and arguably more reliable, although even here their success or otherwise may be due to what else is being done. Comparisons between the effectiveness of intervention methods have been reported with respect to (i) the use of sanctions (ii) restorative practice and (iii) the support group method based on reports provided by schools in England by Thompson and Smith (2011), as in Table 2.1.

Results in Table 2.1 suggest that the use of direct sanctions may be the least successful way of stopping cases of bullying from continuing. Notably, the least commonly used approach, the Support Group Method, appears to be the most successful, especially in primary schools. In a similar study conducted by Rigby and Johnson (2016) in Australian schools ($N=23$) using a 5-point rating scale from very negative to very positive, Restorative Practice with those directly involved in the bullying was rated highest (mean = 4.14) followed by the Support Group Method (mean = 3.92) and Direct Sanctions (mean = 3.77). These findings suggest that direct sanctions, though successful in reportedly stopping bullying in more than half the cases, are not more effective than other nonpunitive approaches. It should however be recognized that sometimes more than one method of intervention is employed by a school and that the choice of method may depend on the nature and severity of the case.

It is emphasized that the results showing the percentage success rates in Table 2.1 are as perceived by schools and largely reflect teacher judgments. Reports from students tend to provide lower estimates of the percentages of cases that are stopped as a result of school interventions. For example, results obtained from 331 students in the Australian study indicated that a much lower success rate of 29.3%.

It is clear from school reports in the English and Australian studies that some methods are used much less frequently than others. For instance, Thompson and Smith reported the Support Group was used in around 10% of schools in England and the Method of Shared Concern in less than 5% of schools. Empirical evidence regarding the effectiveness of the Method of Shared Concern suggests that this method may be greatly underused (Rigby, 2012; Rigby & Griffiths, 2011). One popular way of tackling cases of bullying is to seek to strengthen the victim. In the 23 schools surveyed in the Australian study, all of them used this method of intervention and rated it positively (mean rating 4.04). As well, all the schools claimed to be using "mediation."

Table 2.1 Percentage of success rate in England in stopping the bullying from continuing, according to reports from schools

	Schools		
Method	**Primary**	**Secondary**	**Total**
Direct sanctions	58 (74)	65 (69)	62 (122)
Restorative practices	68 (24)	77 (86)	73 (110)
Support group method	80 (15)	71 (14)	76 (29)

Note: In brackets are the numbers of cases in which the intervention was used.
Adapted from Thompson, F., & Smith, P. K. (2011). *The use and effectiveness of anti-bullying strategies in schools.* Research Report DFE-RR098. London: HMSO.

Understanding of this term varied, with some schools in the study believing that mediation could be made compulsory.

It is evident that there is no one best practice supported by empirical studies that schools should use to counter bullying. Various factors may determine the choice of method. These include the following:

1. *Whether the school is familiar with the proposed methods.* There is evidence that many schools are not aware of the nature, rationale, and reported effectiveness of some methods of intervention, including some that have been shown to achieve a substantial degree of success. These include the Support Group Method and the Method of Shared Concern. Most teachers in the Australian study reported that they received very limited relevant preservice instruction or training in the use of these methods.
2. *Whether the school community approves of their use.* Where less familiar methods are considered by schools—and by parents—schools may err on the conservative side and be averse to employing methods that may produce controversy. As many educators have pointed out, a whole school approach is vital to the success of an antibullying policy.
3. *Whether the school is sufficiently resourced and has the necessary expertise.* Some methods of intervention, whether proactive or reactive, require considerable time and effort devoted to training. Generally, relevant antibullying education must be provided through sessions organized within staff time.
4. *Whether the strategy used is the most appropriate for the case in point.* It is not enough to know about the methods of intervention and how they can be implemented. The choice of method needs to be appropriate to particular cases. These may provide different challenges; some cases are severe or criminal; some relatively mild; some involving groups of students as perpetrators, others involving single individuals; some a consequence of provocation; some perpetrated by students who become genuinely remorseful; some are strongly resistant to change. It is therefore unreasonable to prioritize any one method. It is better for schools to consider what they believe would provide the best course of action for each case.

Conclusion

A variety of alternative and supplementary methods of intervention are being employed in schools with a dual aim: proactively, to prevent cases of bullying from actually occurring, and reactively to stop cases of bullying from continuing. These can operate in a complementary manner. Until relatively recently, the emphasis has been on reacting to cases of identified bullying, typically through the use of direct sanctions. Currently, proactive methods of addressing school bullying are prioritized through the use of a school curriculum that promotes social and emotional learning and encourages prosocial behavior, such as peer support and positive bystander action. Cases of bullying are currently being addressed using a range of approaches, most commonly through the use of direct sanctions and restorative practices. At the same time, schools may seek to assist targeted students in acquiring relevant social skills to cope more effectively and employ nonpunitive methods of changing the behavior of students who bully others. These include the Support Group Method and the Method of Shared Concern. Empirical studies suggest that the different kinds of intervention methods can achieve some success in preventing bullying from continuing. Such success may depend upon how well the chosen method matches the case to which it is applied and the knowledge and skill of the practitioners.

Finally, it is vital that schools have sound systems of support in place across the whole school, targeted groups, and individual cases. Although there is emerging research pointing to more restorative approaches to counter bullying, the more severe cases may require disciplinary measures. Schools need systems in place to ensure that a staff member is assigned to incidents of bullying to ensure that the best outcome possible can be achieved for all parties involved in bullying incidents. Cases of bullying can become an opportunity for schools to review their plans, increase preventative measures, and for students to restore and improve relationships.

References

Australian Curriculum, Assessment and Reporting Authority (ACARA), 2013. General capabilities in the Australian curriculum. Retrieved from http://v7-5.australiancurriculum.edu.au/GeneralCapabilities/Pdf/Personal-and-social-capability.

Arseneault, L., Bowes, L., & Shakoor, S. (2010). Bullying victimization in youths and mental health problems: 'Much ado about nothing'? *Psychological Medicine*, *40*(5), 717–729.

Bogart, L. M., Elliott, M. N., Klcin, D. J., Tortolcro, S. R., Mrug, S., Peskin, M. F., Davies, S. L., Schink, E. T., & Schuster, M. A. (2014). Peer victimization in fifth grade and health in tenth grade. *Pediatrics*, *133*(3), 440–447.

Bradshaw, C. P. (2015). Translating research to practice in bullying prevention programs. *American Psychologist*, *70*(4), 322–332.

Bradshaw, C. P., Pas, E. T., Debnam, K. J., & Johnson, S. L. (2015). A focus on implementation of positive behavioral interventions and supports (PBIS) in high schools: Associations with bullying and other indicators of school disorder. *School Psychology Review*, *44*(4), 480–498.

Brown, E. C., Low, S., Smith, B. H., & Haggerty, K. P. (2011). Outcomes from a school-randomized controlled trial of steps to respect: a bullying prevention program. *Psychology Review*, *40*(3), 423–443.

Collins, B. (2013). Empowerment of children through circle time: Myth or reality? *Irish Educational Studies*, *32*(4), 421–436. https://doi.org/10.1080/03323315.2013.854459.

Cornell, C., & Bradshaw, C. P. (2015). From a culture of bullying to a climate of support: the evolution of bullying prevention and research. *School Psychology Review*, *44*(4), 499–503.

Costello, B., Wachtel, J., & Wachtel, T. (2010). *Restorative circles in schools: Building community and enhancing learning*. Bethlehem, PA: International Institute for Restorative Practices.

Cross, D., Shaw, T., Hearn, L., Epstein, M., Monks, H., Dooley, J., & Hearn, L. (2009). *Cyberbullying in Australia: Is school context related to cyberbullying behaviour?* Australia: Child Health Promotion Research Centre, Edith Cowan University. Retrieved 26th October 2016, from http://www.utas.edu.au/__data/assets/pdf_file/0008/532772/Cyberbullying_in_Australia-donna-cross.pdf.

Cross, D., Thompson, S., & Erceg, E. (2013). *Friendly Schools Plus*. Moorabbin, Victoria: Hawker Brownlow Education.

Cross, D., Waters, S., & Thompson, S. (2014). *Evidence for practice: A comprehensive guide to the implementation of friendly school plus*. Moorabbin, AU: Hawker Brownlow Education.

Department of Education and Training, (2016). Bullying. No Way! STEPS decision-making framework, from Bullying. No Way! https://bullyingnoway.gov.au.

Durlak, J. A., Weissberg, R. P., Dymnicki, A. B., Taylor, R. D., & Schellinger, K. B. (2011). The impact of enhancing students' social and emotional learning: A meta-analysis of school-based universal interventions. *Child Development*, *82*, 405–432.

Ecclestone, K., & Hayes, D. (2008). *The dangerous rise of therapeutic education*. London: Routledge.

Espelage, D. L., Low, S., & Polanin, J. R. (2015). Clinical trial of second step middle-school program: impact on aggression and victimization. *Journal of Applied Developmental Psychology*, *37*, 52–63.

Espelage, D. L., Rose, C. A., & Polanin, J. R. (2015). Social-emotional learning program to reduce bullying, fighting, and victimization among middle school students with disabilities. *Remedial and Special Education*, 1–13.

Espelage, D. L., & Swearer, S. M. (2004). *Bullying in American schools: A socio-ecological perspective on prevention and intervention*. New Jersey: Lawrence Erlbaum.

Farrington, D. P., & Ttofi, M. M. (2009). *School-based programs to reduce bullying and victimization. Campbelll systematic reviews*. Oslo: Campbell Collaboration.

Garandeau, C. F., Poskiparta, E., & Salmivalli, C. J. (2014). Tackling acute cases of school bullying in the KiVa anti-bullying program: A comparison of two approaches. *Abnormal Child Psychology*, *42*, 981–991.

Glazzard, J. (2016). The value of circle time as an intervention strategy. *Journal of Educational and Developmental Psychology*, *6*(2), 207–214.

Griffiths, C., & Weatherilt, T. (2012). *Shared concern method (SCm) for dealing with bullying incidents: Training manual and CD Rom*. Perth: Western Australia, Education Department.

Houlston, C., & Smith, P. K. (2009). The impact of a peer counselling scheme to address bullying in an all-girl London secondary school: a short-term longitudinal study. *British Journal of Educational Psychology*, *79*(Pt 1), 69–86.

Hughes, T. (1857). *Tom Brown's school days* (6th ed.). London, UK: Macmillan.

Humphrey, N. (2013). *Social and emotional learning: A critical appraisal*. London: Sage.

Humphrey, N., Lendrum, A., & Wigelsworth, M. (2010). Social and emotional aspects of learning (SEAL) programme in secondary schools. *National Evaluation Research Report, DFE, RRO49*. London: Department for Education.

Juhnke, B. A., Juhnke, G. A., Curtis, R. C., Thompson, E. H., Coll, K. M., Fangzhou, Y., Moyer, M. S., & Mullett, A. (2013). Using motivational interviewing with school-age bullies: A new use for a proven, evidence-based intervention. *Journal of School Counseling*, *11*(14), 1–27.

Keeley, M., Katz, I., Bates, S., & Wong, M. (2014). *Research on youth exposure to, and management of, cyberbullying incidents in Australia: Part B—Cyberbullying incidents involving Australian minors, the nature of the incidents and how they are currently being dealt with*. Retrieved 19 August 2014 from http://www.communications.gov.au/__data/assets/pdf_file/0005/242537/Cyberbullying_Research_Report_-_Part_B.pdf.

Kvarme, L. G., Aabo, L. S., & Saeteeren, B. (2013). "I feel I mean something to someone": Solution-focused brief therapy support groups for bullied school children. *Educational Psychology in Practice*, *29*(4), 416–431.

Leach, T., & Lewis, E. (2013). Children's experiences during circletime: A call for research-informed debate. *Pastoral Care in Education*, *31*(1), 43–52. https://doi.org/10.1080/02643944.2012.702781.

Levy, N., Cortesi, S., Gasser, U., Crowley, E., Beaton, M., Casey, J., et al. (2012). *Kinder & Braver world project: Research series bullying in a networked era: A literature review*. Publication No. 2012–17, September 2012 The Berkman Center for Internet & Society Research Publication Series.

Mahdavi, J., & Smith, P. K. (2002). The operation of a bully court and perceptions of its success: A case study. *School Psychology International, 23*, 327–341.

Ministerial Council on Education, Early Childhood Development and Youth Affairs. (2004). *National safe schools framework (Revised in 2011)*. Melbourne: Education Services Australia.

Nickersen, A., & Rigby, K. (2017). Understanding and responding to bullying in the school setting. In M. Thiekling & M. D. Tergesen (Eds.), *Handbook of Australia school psychology: integrating international research, practice, and policy* (pp. 521–536). Switzerland: Springer.

Olweus, D. (1993). *Bullying at school: What we know and what we can do*. Cambridge: Blackwell.

Olweus, D. (2012). Cyberbullying: An overrated phenomenon? *European Journal of Developmental Psychology, 9*(5), 520–538.

Pepler, D. J., & Craig, W. M. (1995). A peek behind the fence: naturalistic observations of aggressive children with remote audiovisual recording. *Developmental Psychology, 31*(4), 548–553.

Perren, S., Corcoran, L., Cowie, H., Dehue, F. M., Garcia, D. J., McGuckin, C., et al. (2012). *Coping with cyberbullying: A systematic literature review*. Bibliothek der Universität Konstanz.

Petersen, L., & Rigby, K. (1999). Countering bullying at an Australian secondary school. *Journal of Adolescence, 22*(4), 481–492.

Pikas, A. (2002). New developments of the shared concern method. *School Psychology International, 23*, 307–336.

Polanin, J. R., Espelage, D. L., & Pigott, T. D. (2012). A meta-analysis of school-based bullying prevention programs' effects on bystander intervention behavior. *School Psychology Review, 41*, 47–65.

Raskauskas, J., & Stoltz, A. D. (2007). Involvement in traditional and electronic bullying among adolescents. *Developmental Psychology, 43*, 564–575.

Rigby, K. (1997). Reflections on Tom Brown's Schooldays and the problem of bullying today. *Australian Journal of Social Science, 4*(1), 85–96.

Rigby, K. (2003). Consequences of bullying in schools. *The Canadian Journal of Psychiatry, 48*(9), 583–590.

Rigby, K. (2011). *The method of shared concern: A positive approach to bullying*. Camberwell, Vic.: ACER.

Rigby, K. (2012). *Bullying interventions in schools: Six basic approaches*. Boston: Wiley. American edition.

Rigby, K., & Griffiths, C. (2011). Addressing cases of bullying through the method of shared concern. *School Psychology International, 32*, 345–357.

Rigby, K., & Johnson, B. (2005). Student bystanders in Australian schools. *Pastoral Care in Education, 23*(2), 10–16.

Rigby, K., & Johnson, K. (2016). *The Prevalence and effectiveness of approaches to counter bullying in Australian schools*. Canberra: Australian Department of Education and Training. Accessed through http://www.unisa.edu.au/Education-Arts-and-Social-Sciences/school-of-education/News-and-Events/News/the-prevalence-and-effectiveness/.

Rigby, K., & Smith, P. K. (2011). Is school bullying really on the rise? *Social Psychology of Education, 14*(4), 441–455.

Robinson, G., & Maines, B. (2008). *Bullying: A complete guide to the support group method*. London: Sage.

Saarento, S., Boulton, A. J., & Salmivalli, C. (2015). Reducing bullying and victimization: Student- and classroom-level mechanisms of change. *Journal of Abnormal Child Psychology, 43*(1), 61–76.

Schott, R. M., & Søndergaard, D. M. (2014). *School bullying: New theories in context.* Retrieved from http://QUT.eblib.com.au/patron/FullRecord.aspx?p=1578906.
Slee, P., Spears, B., Campbell, M., & Cross, D. (2011). *Addressing bullying and cyberbullying in schools: Translating theory to practice.* Centre for Strategic Education Occasional Paper.
Smith, B., & Low, S. (2013). the role of social-emotional learning in bullying prevention efforts. *Theory Into Practice, 52*(4), 280–287.
Smith, P. K., & Thompson, F. (2014). *What works best to help stop bullying in schools? The Conversation.* Retrieved from: http://theconversation.com/what-works-best-tohelp-stop-bullying-in-schools-28865.
Sullivan, K. (2012). *The Anti-Bullying Handbook* (2nd ed.). Los Angeles, London, New Delhi, Singapore, and Washington DC: Sage Publications. https://uk.sagepub.com/en-gb/eur/the-anti-bullying-handbook/book234440.
Swearer, S. M., Wang, C., Berry, B., & Myers, Z. R. (2014). Reducing bullying: application of social cognitive theory. *Theory Into Practice, 53*, 271–277.
Thiekling, M. & Tergesen, M. D. (Eds.), (2017). *Handbook of Australia school psychology: Integrating international research, practice, and policy.* Switzerland: Springer.
Thompson, F., & Smith, P. K. (2011). The use and effectiveness of anti-bullying strategies in schools. *Research Report DFE-RR098.* London: HMSO.
Tyrrell, J. (2002). *Peer mediation: A process for primary schools.* London: Souvenir Press.

Further reading

Australian Government, Office of the Children's eSafety Commissioner (2017a). https://esafety.gov.au/complaints-and-reporting/offensive-and-illegal-content-complaints.
Australian Government, Office of the Children's eSafety Commissioner (2017b). https://esafety.gov.au/complaints-and-reporting/offensive-and-illegal-content-complaints.
OK Cross, D., Shaw, T., Hearn, L., Epstein, M., Monks, H., Lester, L., & Thomas, L. (2009). *Australian covert bullying prevalence study (ACBPS).* Perth: Child Health Promotion Research Centre, Edith Cowan University.

Technological solutions for cyberbullying

3

Cigdem Topcu-Uzer, İbrahim Tanrıkulu*[†]
[*]Sinop University, Sinop, Turkey, [†]Gaziantep University, Gaziantep, Turkey

Introduction

Conceptualization of cyberbullying

The definitional criteria of cyberbullying proposed by the extant literature are intentionality, power imbalance, anonymity, repetition, and publicity (e.g., Langos, 2012; Menesini et al., 2012). Each of these criteria appears to be related to the affordances of ICTs. For example, individuals may be aware that ICTs afford personal photos, videos, messages, addresses, or contact numbers, which can be used to actualize cyberbullying intentions. Or, if individuals believe the reason for their cybervictimization experiences is that they are physically weak, they may resort to targeting their bullies online. Such individuals can also be anonymous, either by being completely unknown or by hiding behind fake identities while bullying others online. In terms of publicity and repetition, ICTs enable cyberbullies to share the cyberbullying material with an infinite audience in a reiterative fashion.

Mobile phones, social networking websites, instant messaging, and web pages were reported as the most frequently used ICTs to harm others online (Tanrikulu, Altun, Baker, & Guneri, 2015). A number of ICT affordances used for cyberbullying were listed by the victims being targeted on social-networking websites (Dredge, Gleeson, & de la Piedad Garcia, 2014) such as sending emails, posting messages, uploading images or videos, obtaining personal information by scanning the previous posts, hacking an account, signing up an account with another person's name, and excluding or unfriending others. In fact, school children expressed pessimistic opinions about decreasing cyberbullying because of the facilities ICTs afford (Smith et al., 2008). Accordingly, school children reported that stopping cyberbullying is difficult since (a) identifying the cyberbully is almost impossible if they are anonymous, (b) there are an unlimited number of people who could potentially witness the incident, and (c) the incident can be repeatedly viewed and is often permanent.

Some researchers explain cyberbullying as a relational problem (e.g., Williams & Merten, 2011). According to this view, cyberbullying is a subtype of traditional school bullying (Del-Rey, Elipe, & Ortega-Ruiz, 2012). However, the characteristics of the cyber environment lead some other researchers to conceptualize cyberbullying as a product of the advanced technology (e.g., Ashktorab & Vitak, 2016). Therefore, researchers seem lacking a comprehensive conceptualization about cyberbullying. The supporters of the "cyberbullying is a relational/psychological problem view" argue that mitigation or prevention of cyberbullying is possible only

Reducing Cyberbullying in Schools. https://doi.org/10.1016/B978-0-12-811423-0.00003-1

through equipping the users with preventive psychological characteristics, rather than restricting them from the access of technology. In line with this view, Erdur-Baker (2010) reported that the frequent and the risky users of technology are more at risk of being a cyberbully. Furthermore, others supported this view by providing evidence demonstrating that the intrapersonal motives such as personality factors (Tanrikulu, 2015; Van Geel, Goemans, Toprak, & Vedder, 2016), negative emotion regulation (Den Hamer & Konjin, 2016) and interpersonal factors like lack of social competence (Romera, Cano, Garcia-Fernandez, & Ortega-Ruiz, 2016) are the motives for cyberbullying. Hence, according to this view, the risky usage as well as the interpersonal and intrapersonal factors appear to be related to cyberbullying, rather than the ICTs themselves.

The second view conceptualizes cyberbullying as a technological problem, and the theoretical framework of this view is rooted in *Theory of Affordances* (Gibson, 1979). According to Gibson (1979), the affordances offered by an object are constant, and do not change with the needs of the observer or the user. An object can be treated as many affordances as it offers. The determinative factor in use of an object for a specific goal is the affordances it provides. The use of an object for a particular aim suggests that the object is able to allow affordances for this specific purpose. The relationship between the affordances an object supplies and the intention of the user identify the ways this object can be used. In accordance with their needs, the observers or the users determine how to make use of the affordances an object makes possible.

Cyberbullying can be conceptualized by the principles of *Theory of Affordances*. ICTs offer several affordances to the users. ICT users, mostly children and young people, decide on how to use these affordances, and one possible aim is to bully someone online. Thus, cyberbullying can be considered as a problem emerging from the relation between the affordances that the ICTs enable and the ICT users' intentions. Young cyberbullies confirm this conceptualization by portraying themselves as very skillful and knowledgeable in harnessing the various ICT affordances (Vandebosch & Van Cleemput, 2008; Ybarra & Mitchell, 2004). In this respect, the main reason why bullying behaviors in physical settings transfer to the online platforms may be the ICT affordances provided to the traditional bullies. Hence, cyberbullying appears to be a technological problem caused by the ICT affordances, according to the perspective presented by the *Theory of Affordances*.

In short, while the psychological view claims that cyberbullying is a relational problem to be handled by fostering the relational capabilities of the young individuals, the technological view asserts that technological solutions are necessary to eliminate cyberbullying. The aim of the present chapter is specifically to investigate the technological solutions to prevent and intervene in cyberbullying.

Technological solutions

Some of the technological tools mentioned later could be considered as either supporting the relational or the technological view of cyberbullying. However, each of the technological tools is placed under only one heading to avoid confusion.

Solutions of the social media companies

We examined the policies of the social media companies regarding solution strategies for cyberbullying; *Facebook, Twitter, Instagram, Snapchat, Foursquare, Linkedin, Google+, Pinterest, Tumblr, Flickr, Reddit, and YouTube*. According to our examination, all of these social media tools have a policy against bullying and harassment, although the word "cyberbullying" is not used at all times. The Safety Centers of these social media tools share some common policies. They consist of brief information on what bullying is and provide the users with the examples of bullying acts (e.g., saying mean things, spreading rumors, posting inappropriate photos, and bothering someone). Then, the information is provided concerning the procedures to follow if a user is bullied, if a user witnesses a bullying incident, or if a user acts as a bully. Additionally, all the aforementioned social media companies publish *Community Standards/ Guidelines*, which clearly explain the appropriate and the inappropriate content.

The prevention and intervention strategies listed by the Safety Centers include both nontechnological (e.g., staying calm, telling someone trusted, avoiding retaliation, and deciding to help the user who is targeted by a bully) and technological solutions (e.g., reporting the bullying act, unfriending/unfollowing the person or leaving the conversation with the bully, and blocking the person). In addition, Safety Centers aim to increase awareness among the community and empower the users, parents, and educators by listing strategies such as becoming an expert, helping educate the community and being an advocate, securing the account to keep identity and personal info safe, being responsible, not retaliating, and not supporting the cyberbully. These efforts target parents and educators as well as children and adolescents because these tools require an age restriction that is mostly 13 (for some of them it is 18 and 13 is accepted only with parent permission) to own an account. Those underage users are expected to be monitored by their parents because there are significant numbers of users under 18. For some of the social media tools, a restricted or filtered account that can be created by parents is available.

Solutions of the internet service providers

Internet service providers (ISPs) are companies (e.g., ComCast, Cox, Sky Broadband, Spirit Telecom, Ttnet) delivering access to the Internet through wireless access, a broadband connection (cabled or DSL) or via a phone line (dial-up) (Wikipedia, 2016). The safety solutions of the ISPs related to cyberbullying seem to be mostly determined by the censorship policy of the country in which the ISP company is located. In case of complaints related to cyberbullying, the censorship policy of a country is used to prevent or manage cyberbullying. In some countries, social media sites, which are one of the most prevalent platforms for cyberbullying, are not allowed.

Apart from the country's censorship policy, ISPs aim to assist families to keep their children away from adult content (such as pornography or violence) by offering family-friendly plans, parental controls, and device-level or network-level filters. Beside these solutions, ISPs' precautions may be stricter such as blocking some social media sites. Parental controls, family-friendly options to Internet access, and filters are fee paying by some of the ISPs whereas these services are free by other ISPs.

Solutions of email service providers

Email service providers (ESPs) are organizations and/or companies that host messages in their servers and allow the information to be sent, received, or stored either free or paid (Wikipedia, 2016). Emails are among the tools that can be used to cyberbully someone (e.g., Slonje & Smith, 2008). Based on the findings of a web page (toptenreviews.com), the top three free ESPs by January 22nd, 2016 are Gmail (Google), Microsoft Outlook, and Yahoo. Therefore, these three ESPs were examined. When the help centers of those ESPs are investigated, three main prevention strategies were found. First, ESPs have their own filter, and they aim to block the messages including offensive, threatening, or harassing content before they are delivered. Second, ESPs present their users with information about ethical and respectful use of their services. As an example, Yahoo lists what they want their users to do to be safe online (be respectful, be a good citizen, moderate your content, share, use your tools to limit the exposure to the unwanted content), what they want their users not to do (don't use hate speech, don't bully or harass members of the community, don't forget the children and teens, don't be obscene, and don't behave maliciously), and what Yahoo will do (review the content, remove it if found harmful, deactivate the account if necessary) in case of violation of their Community Guidelines. Third, ESPs provide their users with email addresses such as abuse@hotmail.com (Microsoft) or report links/pages to inform the host company about the emails that contain offensive, harassing, and/or threatening words. For instance, Gmail has a help page that asks users about the details of a questionable message to enable users to report this message.

Solutions of instant-messaging apps

WhatsApp, Viber, Tango, Skype, Google Hangout, Facebook Messenger, WeChat, KiK, Snapchat, Instagram Direct were inspected as the popular instant-messaging apps. According to the policy documentations, the minimum age is 13 to use these apps. All the instant-messaging apps have a detailed written policy declaring that bullying, harassing, threatening, denigrating, hateful, and offensive content is not permitted. Moreover, blocking, reporting complaints to an official email address, and unfollowing/removing are the common and mostly suggested strategies offered by the instant-messaging apps against cyberbullying, *WhatsApp, KiK,* and *Instagram* provide an inside-app function to report cyberbullying incidents. A help/support/safety center where information and strategies about online safety is also offered by *WhatsApp, Google Hangout*, and *Snapchat*. In the case of cyberbullying, the suggestions provided by the instant-messaging apps can be listed as (a) solving the problem with the person/s who perpetrate/s, (b) offering help to the victim/s if any incident is witnessed, (c) no retaliation, (d) rethinking before sending/posting a harmful content, (e) getting in contact with the local authorities or law enforcement, (f) acquiring more information from other online resources including stopbullyingnow.hrsa.gov, ncpc.org/cyberbullying, cyberbullying.us, connectsafely.org, cyberbullying.org, and stopbullying.gov, (g) asking for support and guidance from trusted people.

Apps for cyberbullying prevention and intervention

Application software programs, or apps, can be defined as "a computer program designed to perform a group of coordinated functions, tasks, or activities for the benefit of the user" (Wikipedia, 2016). Although the apps can be used in all computer systems, they appear to be more popular with tablets or smartphones. Apps for cyberbullying aim to increase awareness and to guide young people in how to prevent and intervene in cyberbullying.

Following certain criteria, the authors of this current chapter have examined the cyberbullying apps currently in use to help the reader understand the roles and functions of the apps in cyberbullying prevention and intervention. First, App Store, Google Play, and Microsoft Store were checked for the cyberbullying apps. The scan was done throughout the week between December 12 and December 16, 2016. Second, the apps indirectly related to cyberbullying such as parental monitoring, Internet safety, or secure/responsible ICT usage were discarded. Only the apps directly related to cyberbullying awareness, prevention, or intervention were therefore considered in this study. Another criterion for inclusion was that satisfactory explanation about the app had to be provided in English. The details concerning the apps included in this research are presented in Table 3.1.

As can be seen in Table 3.1, 16 apps were identified. While 11 of them aimed to enhance awareness about the nature and prevention methods of cyberbullying, four of them provided young people and their parents information about how to behave in case of a cyberbullying incident, and one of them intended to prevent cyberbullying incidents before they happen. Considering the content of the apps, 11 of them directly provided practical information about the nature and the prevention and intervention strategies, and one of them incorporated the relevant information into a story. On the other hand, four of the apps function without supplying such information. The apps for cyberbullying employed different strategies. The most preferred strategies were online games ($n=5$) and gaining knowledge by reading ($n=4$). Additionally, blocking, reporting, evidence saving/sharing and rethinking strategies besides video clips, quizzes, and comics were employed by the apps. The majority of the apps were preventative ($n=11$), whereas four apps were interventions, and one app was designed for both preventative and intervention. Some apps for youth and adolescents have been developed; an excellent sources of current information about these is: http://www.parents.com/kids/safety/internet/best-apps-prevent-cyberbullying/.

Evidence regarding the effectiveness of technological solutions

The authors of this chapter examined the studies reporting scientific evidence about the effectiveness of social media companies, ISPs, ESPs, instant-messaging apps, and apps for cyberbullying in cyberbullying prevention and intervention. They conducted an in-depth search on Academic Search Complete, Ebscohost, Google Scholar, Sciencedirect, and Ulakbim databases. The search was carried out between December 6th and December 16th, 2016. Keywords used in the search were "cyberbullying + type of the technological tool (such as social media companies or ESPs)" or "apps for

Table 3.1 Details of the apps for cyberbullying prevention

Name	Aim	Content	Strategy	Preventive or interventional
Back Off Bullies	Providing awareness about cyberbullying	Information about the nature and prevention methods of cyberbullying	- Playing an online game, which provides information about cyberbullying	Preventive
BeCybersafe Game	Providing awareness about cyberbullying	Information about the nature and prevention methods of cyberbullying	- Playing an online game, which provides information about cyberbullying	Preventive
Bully Block	Saving the cyberbullying-related materials and blocking the cyberbullies	No specific content is provided	- Blocking a phone number used for cyberbullying purposes - Blocking a phone call of a cyberbully by aborting a call, making the cyberbully listen a busy signal or an automatic voice message - Blocking an SMS with cyberbullying content and sending automatic text message respond to the cyberbully - Recording the cyberbullies' voice during the cyberbullying calls besides in real-life situations - Creating and saving a file for audio, video, photo, or written cyberbullying materials to be used as evidence - Sending the audio, video, photo, or written records to the necessary authorities	Interventional
Bully Mysteries	Providing awareness about cyberbullying	A short story about a cyberbullying incident	- Solving the mystery provided in the story	Preventive

Name	Aim	Content	Strategy	Preventive or interventional
Clear Cyberbullying	Providing awareness about solutions to cyberbullying	Information about the nature and prevention methods of cyberbullying	- Playing online games, which provide information about cyberbullying	Preventive
Cyberbullying By Grey Lab	Providing awareness about cyberbullying	Information about the nature and prevention methods of cyberbullying	- Reading about functional information about cyberbullying	Preventive
Cyberbullying By Maple Tree	Providing awareness about cyberbullying	Information regarding the definition, the nature, the impacts, the signs and the avoiding strategies of cyberbullying	- Reading about functional information about cyberbullying	Preventive
Cyberbullying First-Aid	Giving information about the tactics to fight against cyberbullying	Behavioral tips, encouragement, legal aspects, web links to counseling centers, instructions about reporting, blocking or deleting cyberbullying materials	- Watching the short video clips	Interventional
Cyberbully Hotline	Helping the students and parents anonymously report cyberbullying incidents in a safe setting	No specific content is provided	- Setting up an online system by using schools' phone numbers - Reporting cyberbullying incidents via text or voice messages - Enabling the school managers take care and respond to the cyberbullying incidents without knowing who reported the incidents	Interventional

Continued

Table 3.1 Continued

Name	Aim	Content	Strategy	Preventive or interventional
Cyberbully Zombies Attack	Providing awareness about cyberbullying	Information about the nature and prevention methods of cyberbullying	- Playing online games, which provide information about cyberbullying	Preventive
Cybersafe	Giving information about the tactics to fight against cyberbullying	Information about how to save the evidence in cyberbullying incidents, how to keep online accounts safe from cyberbullies and the advices against cyberbullying	- Playing online games which provide information about cyberbullying	Preventive
Delete Cyberbullying	Providing awareness about cyberbullying	Information about the nature and prevention methods of cyberbullying	- Solving quizzes - Watching a short video clip - Asking for direct help in case of cyberbullying incidents	Preventive and interventional
Guardian Angel	Providing awareness about cyberbullying	No specific content is provided	- Reporting photos or the screenshots of the cyberbullying incidents to the related school counselor	Interventional
Professor Garfield Cyberbullying	Providing awareness about cyberbullying	Information about the nature and prevention methods of cyberbullying	- Reading comics - Solving quizzes	Preventive
Put an End to Cyberbullying	Providing awareness about cyberbullying	Information about the nature and prevention methods of cyberbullying	- Reading about functional information about cyberbullying	Preventive
ReThink	Preventing cyberbullying before it occurs	No specific content is provided	- Warning the users to stop and think again before sending a text message with cyberbullying content	Preventive

cyberbullying + effectiveness." However, the search did not yield any research reports presenting evidence about the effectiveness or of the solutions offered by the aforementioned technological tools in cyberbullying prevention and intervention.

Other technological solutions for cyberbullying

Most research on technological solutions is based on the detection of the cyberbullying incidents in online settings. The mechanism of these cyberbullying detection systems simply works as (a) introducing the cyberbullying-related keywords as input to the system, (b) identifying the cyberbullying incident by filtering the keywords. To detect cyberbullying in digital platforms, the following themes have been effectively used so far: text-based detection (Dinakar, Reichart, & Lieberman, 2011; Soundar & Ponesakki, 2016), participant-vocabulary consistency (Raisi & Huang, 2016), morphosemantic patterns (Ptaszynski et al., 2016), text-stream detection (Nahar, Li, Zhang, & Pang, 2014), content-driven detection (Zhong et al., 2016), data labeling (Hosseinmardi et al., 2015), analysis on the content of the comments (Galan-Garcia, De La Puerta, Gomez, Santos, & Bringas, 2016), support vector machine classifier algorithm (Shree, Vinutha, & Deepashree, 2016), a hybrid system involving expert system and supervised machine-learning model (Dadvar, Trieschnigg, & de Jong, 2014), gender information (Dadvar, de Jong, Ordelman, & Trieschnigg, 2012), user context (Dadvar, Trieschnigg, Ordelman, & de Jong, 2013), online harassment classification and username detection (Bretschneider & Peter, 2016), latent semantic indexing (Bigelow & Edwards, 2016), and a model constructed on the ICT features (Al-garadi, Varathan, & Ravana, 2016). It is important to note that all of the research cited here has provided data demonstrating that these detection systems are effective to detect cyberbullying incidents in online settings. These detection systems were tested on the data obtained from various popular social networking websites such as Ask.fm, Instagram, MySpace, Twitter, or YouTube. The accuracy rates of these detection systems ranged from 68.55% (Zhong et al., 2016) to 87% (Hosseinmardi et al., 2015) and to 93.33% (Bretschneider & Peter, 2016).

In addition to the detection systems, two more technological solution strategies exist for preventing cyberbullying. The first strategy is the *ReThink* app for mobile phones developed by teenager Trisha Prabhu (2014); however, there is no evidence about its effectiveness to date. However, Prabhu tested with 1500 users aged 12–18 and reported that <5% of the sample would publish or post the negative content.

The second strategy is the impact of a video film of cyberbullying behaviors and sad face photos on bystanders (Szuster, Barlinska, & Kozubal, 2015). These researchers aimed to increase empathy with the help of the sad face photos and a short movie demonstrating the negative experiences of a cybervictim. There were two experimental groups and a control group. While the first experimental group was shown a total of 14 sad faces to initiate empathy, the second experimental group watched a movie of a cyber victim to elicit empathy. The control group did not receive any treatment. Following these activities, the participants were directed to a web application, which comprised cyberbullying-related content in text form. According to the scenario, the cyberbullying text was prepared and sent to the participant by a friend, so the participants took the role of a cyberbullying bystander. The participants were to either send the cyberbullying-related content to a friend or delete it. The results revealed that, compared to the control group (23.7%), viewing sad faces (14.3%) and watching a short video of a cyber victim (8.2%) decreased the frequency of cyberbullying perpetration. The results also indicated that the probability of engaging in cyberbullying was lower for participants in the experimental groups. Thus, the individuals in the two experimental groups behaved more empathetically and avoided cyberbullying someone.

Discussion

Social media companies, ISPs, ESPs, instant-messaging apps, apps for cyberbullying, and other technological solutions were examined to understand solutions for cyberbullying that are available.

This review showed that technology providers do not use "cyberbullying" as a technical term, but they use "bullying" or "harassment" instead. Using "bullying" and "harassment" may depreciate the effects of cyberbullying acts, and such an inconsistency possibly creates confusion to users. Considering the evidence about the complexity of the definition of cyberbullying (Dredge et al., 2014) as well as the importance of the parents in cyberbullying prevention (Perren et al., 2012), children, adolescents, and especially parents might not clearly decide on whether the incident they experienced is cyberbullying. To be able to carry out effective preventive and intervention solutions, having a clear definition about the cyberbullying behaviors is a fundamental necessity. Thus, technology providers, researchers, and implementers need to use cyberbullying as a unanimously and internationally agreed term in order to reduce cyberbullying.

Our findings demonstrate that technological tools offer several strategies including filtering, blocking, or reporting to prevent or intervene in cyberbullying incidents. Research validates that these strategies are actively used by children and adolescents (Muller, Skues, & Wise, 2017). In addition, this implies that the technology providers are aware of the possible negative impacts of the current technological tools, and are eager to find solutions for cyberbullying. This research also contributes to the conceptualization of cyberbullying in *Theory of Affordances*, implying that cyberbullying has a technological side, and technological solutions are required to combat cyberbullying. Moreover, technology providers seem to be benefitting from the solutions suggested by existing cyberbullying research. For example, telling someone trusted, avoiding retaliation, reporting the bullying act or offering help to the victims are some of the prevention and intervention strategies in line with the cyberbullying research (e.g., Perren et al., 2012). This fact suggests that the strategies offered by researchers have been considered and used by technology providers. Therefore, future studies focusing on creating effective solutions for cyberbullying seem to be welcomed by the technology providers.

Another interesting finding demonstrating that the existing cyberbullying research is utilized by the technology providers is the online cyberbullying resources. Instant-messaging apps guide their users to the online cyberbullying resources including ncpc.org/cyberbullying, cyberbullying.us, or cyberbullying.org. This points out that such online resources are taken into consideration by the technology providers, and online resources provide information to the technology providers regarding cyberbullying prevention and intervention. Hence, the information given by the online resources should be accurate. Considering their importance, developing more online resources for different age groups and in different languages could be helpful in providing information about the prevention and intervention solutions for cyberbullying. Yet, as emphasized by Ahlfors (2010), the effectiveness of online cyberbullying resources awaits future research.

Technology providers seem oblivious to using strategies with scientific evidence because no evidence about the effectiveness or ineffectiveness of their solutions has been provided to date. In fact, technology providers do not explain how they test the effectiveness of the anticyberbullying strategies they provide to users (Milosevic, 2016). Yet, convincing evidence is available indicating that cyberbullying detection mechanisms (e.g., Soundar & Ponesakki, 2016), the *ReThink* software (Prabhu, 2014), as well as increasing empathy (Szuster, et al., 2015) are empirically effective in tackling cyberbullying. This shows that a bidirectional collaboration is essential in the future between technology providers and the researchers. While the technology providers should cooperate with the researchers in supplying evidence for their cyberbullying prevention and intervention strategies, the researchers should spend energy to test the effectiveness of the solutions proposed by the technological tools.

As can be seen in Table 3.1, apps targeting cyberbullying prevention and intervention are numerous. Efforts to develop such apps are valuable, but delivering those apps to children and adolescents may not be easy. Considering the developmental characteristics of childhood and adolescence, expecting them to be responsible technology users by themselves or leaving the decision to keep themselves safe online may not be realistic. Instead, social media tools and ISPs can have plug-ins, such as the *ReThink software,* giving information about cyberbullying or warning the users whenever an inappropriate content is about to be posted.

Technology providers seem reluctant to collaborate with researchers about the utilization of evidence-based cyberbullying prevention and intervention strategies. This issue is examined by Milosevic (2016) who investigated the cyberbullying policies of 14 social media companies and presented the findings of the interviews conducted with these social media companies' representatives. As reported by the interviewees cyberbullying incidents are not crystal clear at all times, as it is not always easy for the moderator of the social media tool to analyze if a reported incident is a cyberbullying case. Moreover, well-known companies, such as Facebook, prefer not to use a cyberbullying detection program because cyberbullying is mostly context dependent, and using an automated detection tool will not be 100% successful. However, an error made by the automatic cyberbullying detection system could be more desirable than a cybervictimization experience, which leads victims to suffer. Although an error caused by the automatic cyberbullying detection system can be corrected, the possible negative outcomes that a cybervictim experience cannot be reversed. Hence, the risk of the possible errors in cyberbullying detection should not prevent the technology providers from using well-evidenced technological strategies. Furthermore, according to Milosevic (2016), how well the technological solutions of social media companies are working is also not known since the users do not know how long it will take to receive feedback on a reported act or how many of the reported cases are solved. Therefore, the main concern regarding the effectiveness of the technological solutions is the lack of evidence about the effectiveness of the prevention and intervention strategies.

Limitations of the study

The present review is not free of limitations. First, only the tools that aim to prevent or intervene cyberbullying directly were investigated. However, cyberbullying prevention is possible indirectly through parental monitoring or parental control tools. Second, ICTs are alive, they are born, live, and die. So, the examined ICTs in the current study are limited to the tools alive in the present day. Facebook, Twitter, Instagram, etc. were examined as they are the most popular social media tools of today. As new technological tools appear and become popular, it would be better to repeat this study to update the cyberbullying prevention and intervention policies of these new tools.

Conclusion

Although it is not yet apparent whether cyberbullying should be conceptualized as a relational or a technological problem, cyberbullying partially seems a problem caused by the affordances online technologies provide. In this present chapter, the up-to-date technological solutions to prevent and intervene in cyberbullying are examined by investigating social media companies, ISPs, ESPs, instant-messaging apps, apps for cyberbullying, and other technological solutions. Though several preventative and intervention strategies for cyberbullying are offered by technological tools, a serious dearth of scientific evidence is present about their effectiveness. Except for the online cyberbullying detection systems, the *ReThink* software, and a research study analyzing the impact of human face and a video film to enhance empathy for cyberbullying, no scientific evidence on their effectiveness or ineffectiveness exists for any of the solutions provided by the current technological tools. While the technology providers appear to be highly skeptical about benefitting from the limited number of evidence-based technological solutions for cyberbullying, researchers continue to generate evidence-based but nontechnological solutions for cyberbullying (Chaux, Velasquez, Schultze-Krumbholz, & Scheithauer, 2016; Kärnä et al., 2013; Williford et al., 2013). Therefore, technology providers, researchers, and other stakeholders should work together to be able to carry out a more effective action plan to prevent and intervene in cyberbullying.

Acknowledgments

Cigdem thanks her husband Cengiz, and Ibrahim thanks his wife Nurhan for their patience and support during this project.

References

Ahlfors, R. (2010). Many sources, one theme: Analysis of cyberbullying prevention and intervention websites. *Journal of Social Sciences*, *6*, 515–522.

Al-garadi, M. A., Varathan, K. D., & Ravana, S. D. (2016). Cybercrime detection in online communications: The experimental case of cyberbullying detection in the Twitter network. *Computers in Human Behavior*, *63*, 433–443. https://doi.org/10.1016/j.chb.2016.05.051.

Application software (2016). In *Wikipedia*. Retrieved from https://en.wikipedia.org/wiki/Application_software.

Ashktorab, Z., & Vitak, J. (2016). *Designing cyberbullying mitigation and prevention solutions through participatory design with teenagers.* In *Proceedings of the CHI conference on human factors in computing systems, (pp. 3895-3905). Santa Clara, California.*

Bigelow, J. L., & Edwards, L. (2016). *Detecting cyberbullying using latent semantic indexing.* In *Proceedings of the first international workshop on computational methods for cyber-safety (pp. 11-14). Indianapolis, USA.*

Bretschneider, U., & Peters, R. (2016). Detecting cyberbullying in online communities. Research Papers, Paper 61.

Chaux, E., Velasquez, A. M., Schultze-Krumbholz, A., & Scheithauer, H. (2016). Effects of the cyberbullying prevention program media heroes (Medienhelden) on traditional bullying. *Aggressive Behavior*, *42*, 157–165. https://doi.org/10.1002/ab.21637.

Dadvar, M., de Jong, F., Ordelman, R., & Trieschnigg, D. (2012). *Improved cyberbullying detection using gender information.* In: *Proceedings of the twelfth Dutch-Belgian information retrieval workshop, (pp. 23–25). Ghent, Belgium.*

Dadvar, M., Trieschnigg, D., & de Jong, F. (2014). *Experts and machines against bullies: A hybrid approach to detect cyberbullies.* In: *Paper presented at Canadian conference on artificial intelligence, Victoria, Canada.*

Dadvar, M., Trieschnigg, D., Ordelman, R., & de Jong, F. (2013). *Improving cyberbullying detection with user context.* In: *Paper presented at European conference on information retrieval (pp. 693–696). Moscow, Russia.*

Del-Rey, R., Elipe, P., & Ortega-Ruiz, R. (2012). Bullying and cyberbullying: Overlapping and predictive value of the co-occurrence. *Psicothema*, *24*(4), 608–613.

Den Hamer, A. H., & Konjin, E. A. (2016). Can emotion regulation serve as a tool in combating cyberbullying? *Personality and Individual Differences*, *102*, 1–6. https://doi.org/10.1016/j.paid.2016.06.033.

Dinakar, K., Reichart, R., & Lieberman, H. (2011). Modeling the detection of textual cyberbullying. *The Social Mobile Web*, *11*(02), 11–17.

Dredge, R., Gleeson, J., & de la Piedad Garcia, X. (2014). Cyberbullying in social networking sites: An adolescent victim's perspective. *Computers in Human Behavior*, *36*, 13–20. https://doi.org/10.1016/j.chb.2014.03.026.

E-mail service providers (marketing) (2016). In *Wikipedia*. Retrieved from https://en.wikipedia.org/wiki/Email_service_provider_(marketing).

Erdur-Baker, Ö. (2010). Cyberbullying and its correlation to traditional bullying, gender and frequent and risky usage of Internet-mediated communication tools. *New Media & Society*, *12*, 109–125. https://doi.org/10.1177/1461444809341260.

Galán-García, P., De La Puerta, J. G., Gómez, C. L., Santos, I., & Bringas, P. G. (2016). Supervised machine learning for the detection of troll profiles in twitter social network: Application to a real case of cyberbullying. *Logic Journal of IGPL*, 42–53.

Gibson, J. J. (1979). The theory of affordances. In J. J. Gibson (Ed.), *The ecological approach to visual perception*. New Jersey: Lawrance Erlbaum Associates, Inc. pp. 127–143.

Hosseinmardi, H., Mattson, S. A., Rafiq, R. I., Han, R., Lv, Q., & Mishra, S. (2015). *Detection of cyberbullying incidents on the instagram social network*. Association for the Advancement of Artificial Intelligence.

Internet service providers (2016). In *Wikipedia*. Retrieved from https://en.wikipedia.org/wiki/Internet_service_provider.

Kärnä, A., Voeten, M., Little, T. D., Alanen, E., Poskiparta, E., & Salmivalli, C. (2013). Effectiveness of the KiVa antibullying program: Grades 1–3 and 7–9. *Journal of Educational Psychology*, *105*, 535–551. https://doi.org/10.1037/a0030417.

Langos, C. (2012). Cyberbullying: The challenge to define. *Cyberpsychology, Behavior and Social Networking*, *15*, 285–289. https://doi.org/10.1089/cyber.2011.0588.

Menesini, E., Nocentini, A., Palladino, B. E., Frisen, A., Berne, S., Ortega-Ruiz, R., et al. (2012). Cyberbullying definition among adolescents: A comparison across six European countries. *Cyberpsychology, Behavior and Social Networking*, *15*, 455–463. https://doi.org/10.1089/cyber.2012.0040.

Milosevic, T. (2016). Social media companies' cyberbullying policies. *International Journal of Communication*, *10*, 5164–5185.

Muller, R. D., Skues, J. L., & Wise, L. Z. (2017). Cyberbullying in Australian primary schools: How victims differ in attachment, locus of control, self-esteem, and coping styles compared to non-victims. *Journal of Psychologists and Counsellors in Schools*, *27*, 1–20. https://doi.org/10.1017/jgc.2016.5.

Nahar, V., Li, X., Zhang, H. L., & Pang, C. (2014). Detecting cyberbullying in social networks using multi-agent system. *Web Intelligence and Agent Systems: An International Journal*, *12*, 375–388. https://doi.org/10.3233/WIA-140301.

Perren, S., Corcoran, L., Cowie, H., Dehue, F., Mc Guckin, C., Sevcikova, A., et al. (2012). Tackling cyberbullying: Review of empirical evidence regarding successful responses by students, parents, and schools. *International Journal of Conflict and Violence*, *6*, 283. https://doi.org/ 0070-ijcv-2012211O.

Prabhu, T. (2014). *Rethink: An effective way to prevent cyber bullying*. Retrieved from http://goo.gl/cpVB6k.

Ptaszynski, M., Masui, F., Nakajima, Y., Kimura, Y., Rzepka, R., & Araki, K. (2016). *Detectingcyberbullying with morphosemantic patterns*. In *Paper presented at joint 8th international conference on soft computing and intelligent systems and 17th international symposium on advanced intelligent systems, Sapporo, Hokkaido, Japan*.

Raisi, E., & Huang, B. (2016). *Cyberbullying identification using participant-vocabulary consistency*. In: *Paper presented at 2016 ICML workshop on #Data4Good:Machine learning in social good applications, New York, USA*.

Romera, E. M., Cano, J. J., Garcia-Fernandez, C. M., & Ortega-Ruiz, R. (2016). Cyberbullying: Social competence, motivation and peer relationships. *Media Education Research Journal*, *24*, 71–79. https://doi.org/10.3916/C48-2016-07.

Shree, D., Vinutha, H., & Deepashree, N. S. (2016). An effective system to improve the cyberbullying. *International Journal of Innovative Technology and Research*, *4*(3), 3002–3006.

Slonje, R., & Smith, P. K. (2008). Cyberbullying: Another main type of bullying? *Scandinavian Journal of Psychology*, *49*, 147–154. https://doi.org/10.1111/j.1467-9450.2007.00611.x.

Smith, P. K., Mahdavi, J., Carvalho, M., Fisher, S., Russell, S., & Tippett, N. (2008). Cyberbullying: Its nature and impact in secondary school pupils. *Journal of Child Psychology and Psychiatry*, *49*, 376–385. https://doi.org/10.1111/j.1469-7610.2007.01846.x.

Soundar, K. R., & Ponesakki, P. (2016). Cyberbullying detection based on text representation. *International Journal of Engineering Science*, *6*(10), 2776–2785.

Szuster, A., Barlinska, J., & Kozubal, M. (2015). In search of a simple method: Is a human face an effective, automatic filter inhibiting cyberbullying? In M. F. Wright (Ed.), *A social-ecological approach to cyberbullying* (pp. 379–402). New York: Nova Science Publishers.

Tanrıkulu, İ. (2015). *The relationships between cyber bullying perpetration motives and personality traits: Testing uses and gratifications theory (Unpublished doctoral dissertation).* Ankara, Turkey: Middle East Technical University.

Tanrıkulu, İ., Altun, S. A., Baker, Ö.E., & Güneri, O. Y. (2015). Misuse of ICTs among Turkish children and youth: A study on newspaper reports. *Journal of Human Sciences*, *12*(1), 1230–1243.

Van Geel, M., Goemans, A., Toprak, F., & Vedder, P. (2016). Which personality traits are related to traditional bullying and cyberbullying? A study with the Big five, dark triad and sadism. *Personality and Individual Differences*, https://doi.org/10.1016/j.paid.2016.10.063.

Vandebosch, H., & Van Cleemput, K. (2008). Defining cyberbullying: A qualitative research into the perceptions of youngsters. *CyberPsychology & Behavior*, *11*, 499–503. https://doi.org/10.1089/cpb.2007.0042.

Williams, A. L., & Merten, M. J. (2011). iFamily: Internet and social media technology in the family context. *Family and Consumer Sciences Research Journal*, *40*, 150–170. https://doi.org/10.1111/j.1552-3934.2011.02101.x.

Williford, A., Elledge, L. C., Boulton, A. J., DePaolis, K. J., Little, T. D., & Salmivalli, C. (2013). Effects of the KiVa antibullying program on cyberbullying and cybervictimization frequency among Finnish youth. *Journal of Clinical Child & Adolescent Psychology*, *42*, 820–833. https://doi.org/10.1080/15374416.2013.787623.

Ybarra, M. L., & Mitchell, K. J. (2004). Online aggressor/targets, aggressors, and targets: A comparison of associated youth characteristics. *Journal of Child Psychology and Psychiatry*, *45*, 1308–1316. https://doi.org/10.1111/j.1469-7610.2004.00328.x.

Zhong, H., Li, H., Squicciarini, A., Rajtmajer, S., Griffin, C., Miller, D., et al. (2016). *Content-driven detection of cyberbullying on the Instagram social network.* In: *Paper presented at 25th international joint conference on artificial intelligence, New York, USA.*

Cyberbullying and the law: Parameters for effective interventions?

4

Des Butler
Queensland University of Technology (QUT), Brisbane, QLD, Australia

Introduction

In May 2011, 14-year-old Alex Boston's arrival at her school was accompanied by nasty looks and harsh words from her fellow students. She later discovered that a phony Facebook page had been created by two of her classmates using her name and information, and which featured a profile picture that had been altered to make her face appear bloated. The page also ascribed a range of obnoxious behavior to her, including the suggestion that she smoked marijuana, spoke a pseudo language called "Retardish," had left obscene comments on friends' pages, made frequent sexual references, and posted a racist video. When Alex and her parents complained to school officials and police, they were told that there was nothing that could be done because the website had been created off the school campus. Further, repeated requests to Facebook to have the site taken down went unanswered (Bluestein & Turner, 2012).

Experiences like Alex Burton's are becoming increasingly common among young people. Technology has become an essential companion of modern living. For example, recent research in Australia showed that 95% of the 8- to 11-year-olds and 100% of 16- to 17-year-olds accessed the internet, while 67% of 12- to 13-year-olds, 87% of 14- to 15-year-olds and 94% of 16- to 17-year-olds owned their own smartphone (A.C.M.A., 2012). Such technology is a double-edged sword: while it may be a conduit of good it may also present ready means for aggressive behavior amounting to cyberbullying. Studies of cyberbullying have identified varying rates of incidence of this behavior. For example, a 2006 study across countries including the United States, Canada, the United Kingdom, and Australia found that almost 30% of respondents had been victims of cyberbullying, which was defined as being ignored, disrespected, threatening, picked on, or made fun of, or having had rumors spread by others (Patchin & Hinduja, 2006), while a 2014 study estimated the prevalence of cyberbullying among Australian children aged 8–17 to be in the vicinity of 20%, or around 463,000 children (Katz et al., 2014). The same report noted that part of the difficulty associated with determining prevalence is differing definitions of cyber bullying and "other assumptions made when extrapolating from survey samples" (Katz et al., 2014, p. 2).

While researchers may differ in their precise definitions of cyberbullying, they generally agree that it shares certain attributes with traditional forms of bullying, namely a repeated exploitation of a real or perceived power imbalance with an intention to

Reducing Cyberbullying in Schools. https://doi.org/10.1016/B978-0-12-811423-0.00004-3

cause harm (Patchin & Hinduja, 2006). However, important differences remain. For example, whereas traditional bullying may be restricted to face-to-face encounters, such as in the schoolyard or on the way to or from school, cyberbullying has the capacity to reach the target 24h a day, 7 days a week: even the target's home is no longer a safe haven from the behavior. Further, while traditional bullying may inflict physical and/or psychological harm, cyberbullying tends only to result in psychological harm, although in some cases this may lead to physical consequences including suicide (see, e.g., Meredith, 2010).

Faced with an imbalance of power, some targets may seek the assistance of others to redress that imbalance. To that end some, like Alex Boston, may seek the help of not only school authorities but also the law, although as noted, in her case she received no satisfaction from either due to the prevailing situation in her jurisdiction, the American State of Georgia. It is worthwhile, therefore, to examine the current attitude of the law to cyberbullying, and in particular the expectations (if any) that the law places on school authorities when it comes to responding to cyberbullying and the parameters that may thereby be set for school interventions. The law can be a powerful driver for behavior when it is understood that acting or failing to act in a certain way may result in liability to pay monetary compensation (Keeton, 1984, p. 25).

For the purposes of this examination, the position in three countries will be compared: Australia and the United Kingdom (where the law is similar), and the United States. While all three follow a "common law" system of jurisprudence, comprising case precedents and statutes created by elected legislatures, distinct differences exist, which have significant implications for targets of cyberbullying. In the United Kingdom, the highest court in the country (the House of Lords, now known as the Supreme Court) determines the common law, and the Parliament in Westminster enacts legislation, which applies throughout the country. In Australia, the highest court (the High Court of Australia) determines the common law that applies throughout the country while under the Federal system the Commonwealth Parliament and State/Territory Parliaments enact laws within their respective constitutional jurisdictions, which have differences in some respects but which are for the most part consistent. By comparison, in the United States, the highest court (the Supreme Court of the United States) only determines federal laws and constitutional rulings that apply throughout the country, with the Supreme Courts (or equivalents) in each of the 50 States determining the common law for their respective States, and States' legislatures enacting legislation that can often differ substantially in their terms.

Australia/United Kingdom

There are no statutes in Australia or the United Kingdom that specifically prohibit cyberbullying and only one statute in New South Wales, the *Crimes Act 1900*, that outlaws bullying. However, this law is limited to someone who "assaults, stalks, harasses or intimidates" any school staff or student while attending the school. None of these terms is specifically defined, but by their natural meaning they might capture cyberbullying. Significantly, however, that statute only applies if the target was on, entering or leaving school premises for the purpose of school work or for before or after school care. Otherwise cyberbullying may constitute an offence under laws of more general application such as, in Australia, the Commonwealth *Criminal Code Act 1995* section 474.17 (misuse of telecommunication services) or State stalking laws (Kift, Campbell, & Butler, 2010; Langos, 2014) and, in the United Kingdom, the *Malicious Communications Act of 1998* section 1 and *Communications Act of 2003* section 127 (both of which deal with improper use of electronic communications) and the *Protection From Harassment Act of 1997* (which covers stalking and harassment). None of these laws, however, allow for the target of cyberbullying to recover monetary compensation or any other remedy for the behavior.

The target of cyberbullying may choose to commence legal action against the perpetrator of the behavior based on one or more causes of action, such as defamation, breach of confidence, assault, intentional infliction of harm in the form of psychiatric damage (if such should be caused), or (in the United Kingdom only) invasion of privacy (Butler, Kift, & Campbell, 2010). However, such actions have one overriding disadvantage: if the perpetrator is another child, he or she may have no financial resources to pay any compensation so that any judgment in favor of the target may be a pyrrhic victory. Moreover, in Australia and the United Kingdom, parents cannot be held liable for the wrongful acts of their children unless they in some way participated in, directed, or ratified the wrongdoing or provided the occasion for the wrongdoing (McHale v. Watson, 1964, p. 386–387). It would be difficult to argue that, for example, merely providing a child with a computer or smartphone amounted to "providing the occasion" for cyberbullying (Butler et al., 2010).

Instead a target may choose to seek to ascribe legal responsibility to the relevant school authority for failure to prevent the cyberbullying (Butler et al., 2010). That school authority may be the government (in case of public schools) or the company, trust, church diocese, or other entity running the school (in the case of private schools), and liability might be based on breach of its own common law duty or its "vicarious" liability as employer of a teacher who has breached his or her own common law duty of care. In other words, the question will depend upon whether the alleged failing was at an institution level or by an individual(s). In the case of private schools, it might alternatively be based on a breach of the contract entered into with the school, depending on the exact terms of the contract. To succeed based on the common law, it is necessary to show (a) a duty of care toward the target (b) breach of that duty and (c) damage that was caused by that breach of duty. There has yet to be a case involving a claim against the school for preventing cyberbullying in either country, but there have been cases involving traditional bullying, which are nonetheless instructive. From the outset, it is worth bearing one point in mind: as an English judge remarked "there is no magic in the term bullying" (Bradford-Smart v. West Sussex County Council, 2002). In other words, the focus is on the objectionable behavior rather than any definition. One consequence is that in Australia and the United Kingdom in some circumstances failure to prevent a one-off act of aggression may be regarded as constituting a breach of duty, even though for researchers it may not be regarded as constituting cyberbullying due to the lack of repetition. It is also worth noting that neither country has specific legislation that imposes obligations on schools in relation to bullying or cyberbullying.

Duty of care

Both Australia and the United Kingdom recognize that certain relationships give rise to so-called nondelegable duties of care. The relationship of school authority/teacher and pupil is one such relationship (Commonwealth v. Introvigne, 1982). This means that while responsibility for taking precautions against harm may, as a matter of fact, be delegated (for example by a school authority to a school principal), the school authority remains ultimately responsible as a matter of law and cannot escape liability simply by saying any breach was by its delegate and not by it. This duty extends to taking reasonable precautions against both physical and psychiatric injury (Cox v. New South Wales, 2007; Phelps v. Hillingdon London Borough Council, 2000).

While the existence of the duty of care is well recognized, greater uncertainty attends the exact scope of that duty, both in a geographical and temporal sense. Significantly for cyberbullying, which not infrequently happens away from school and out-of-school hours, it would appear that in both Australia and the United Kingdom, a school's responsibility can extend beyond the schoolyard and before and after the school bell. An English appellant judge observed, "One can think of circumstances where [the duty] might go beyond [the school gates], for example if it were reasonable for a teacher to intervene when he saw one pupil attacking another immediately outside the school gates" (Bradford-Smart v. West Sussex County Council, 2002). In the High Court of Australia case *Geyer v. Downs* (1977), it was held that the scope of a school's duty of care could extend to before and after school hours and depended upon "whether in the particular circumstances the relationship of school teacher and pupil was or was not then in existence." In another Australian case, a school was held liable where it knew that young students from a primary school and older students from a high school were gathering at the same bus stop after school and as a result of tensions between the groups a 12-year-old from the former group was struck in the eye with a stick thrown by a student from the latter group. The New South Wales Court of Appeal held that the extent and nature of the duty of a teacher was dictated by the particular circumstances, rather than the ring of the school bell or the closing the school gate, and here the school authority had breached its common law duty because it ought to have known of the mischief that was likely when children of different ages and from different schools mix without adequate supervision (Trustees of the Roman Catholic Church for the Diocese of Bathurst v. Koffman, 1996). The court went so far as to suggest that depending on the circumstances the common law duty of care could extend to students on a journey on a bus or while they were walking to or from school if the school authority were aware that "on that particular journey of the children habitually and violently bullied younger children" (Trustees of the Roman Catholic Church for the Diocese of Bathurst v. Koffman, 1996, p. 63, 597). The court thought that such a duty would be founded in the relationship of teacher and pupil and that in such case may well extend as far as to require the school to take preventative steps or to warn parents.

The significance of these cases lies in recognition that a school's duty of care toward its students is not limited to occurrences on school grounds and during school hours. Depending on the circumstances, it may extend to off-campus behavior by its students, particularly in the case of Australia where the relationship of teacher in pupil is in existence. That might, for example, mean that a duty of care may arise in relation to cyberbullying where the school has policies, which seek to dictate what may be regarded as acceptable behavior by its students both on and off school grounds and inside and outside of school hours.

However, a further layer of complexity arises in the case of psychiatric injury, which will generally be the kind of harm resulting from cyberbullying. In addition to the recognized duty of care owed by schools and teachers, targets need to show that it was reasonably foreseeable that a person of "normal fortitude" would suffer that type of injury in their circumstances, although different jurisdictions take different approaches to this consideration (Butler et al., 2010). Thus, in most Australian jurisdictions the "normal fortitude" test is a precondition to liability by virtue of the *Civil Liability Act* in those jurisdictions, while under the common law in Queensland and the Northern Territory the "normal fortitude" issue is merely only one of the range of matters to be taken into account when considering whether harm was reasonably foreseeable in the circumstances (Tame v. New South Wales, 2002). In the United Kingdom, there are differing views whether "normal fortitude" is a precondition or merely a relevant consideration (United Kingdom Law Commission, 1998). In any event, in as much as society is made up of people with varying susceptibilities to trauma (Chadwick v. British Railways Board, 1967), a "normal fortitude" test has no medical legitimacy: there is no such thing as a "normal" person, even less a "normal" child. At best, therefore, the test can be no more than a matter of impression in any given case rather than a question of science.

Breach of duty

Merely because a school owes its students a duty of care does not mean that the school authority is an insurer of its students. Instead it is a duty to take reasonable steps to protect the student against risks of injury, which are reasonably foreseeable (Richards v. Victoria, 1969). Under the common law in the United Kingdom and now under the *Civil Liability Act* in each Australian State and Territory, this in turn raises two issues: (1) whether the risk of injury was reasonably foreseeable in the circumstances, and (2) what precautions (if any) a reasonable person would have taken to avoid that risk in the circumstances, taking into account the probability that harm would occur absent care, the likely seriousness of that harm, the burden of taking precautions, and any social utility of the risk creating activity. The risk of harm arising from bullying is now well known in school settings (Oyston v. St Patricks College, 2013), with most cases instead turning on whether in the circumstances reasonable precautions were taken to avoid that harm from arising. The same will likely be the case with cyberbullying.

When addressing the second question, courts in the United Kingdom adopt the so-called *Bolam* rule, which requires a standard of care that is in accordance with a responsible body of opinion, even if others differ in opinion (Bolam v. Friern Hospital Management Committee, 1957). All six of Australia's States (but not the two Territories) adopted this test by requiring the court to defer to a "reasonable body of opinion" but added the caveat "unless no reasonable court would do so" in their *Civil Liability Acts*, although Western Australia limited this test to medical professionals. In other words, when deciding whether the school authority or teacher was in breach of the duty of care, the question will be whether the response was in accordance “with that which might have been acceptable at the time by reasonable members of the teaching profession” (Gower v. London Borough of Bromley, 1999, p. 359). Decisions in cases involving face-to-face bullying provide guidance concerning what may be reasonably expected of a teacher and school. At an institutional level, schools would be expected to have antibullying policies (Smith, 2008; Stoltz, 2007). Such policies should specifically refer to cyberbullying, as an important measure to address the attitude of some students that behavior amounting to cyberbullying is merely a matter of having fun (Butler et al., 2011). The policies must be unambiguous in their terms and well disseminated among students, staff, and parents (Faulkner v. London Borough of Enfield and Lea Valley High School, 2003; Oyston v. St Patrick's College, 2013). At an individual level, complaints must be handled strictly in accordance with school policies rather than, for example, by an exercise of discretion (Oyston v. St Patrick's College, 2013). That will include taking complaints seriously, and properly documenting and investigating them (Cox v. New South Wales, 2007; Scott v. Lothian Regional Council, 1998). In addition, where the circumstances warrant remedial action, it must be taken in a manner, which is consistent, or students who cyberbully may regard any policy as merely words without substance (Butler et al., 2011). As already noted, the law places no significance on labels or the definitions applied by researchers. Accordingly, in some circumstances, it may regard a failure to appropriately deal with a one-off incident as amounting to a breach of the duty of care.

Some measures may not yet be sufficiently widespread as to reflect accepted teaching practices, such as banning the use of smartphones at school (Butler et al., 2011). Apart from anything else, banning phones at school would not prevent them being used to bully out-of-school hours (Grigg, 2010). However, that is not to suggest that over time a new practice cannot come to be widely accepted and thereby be regarded as representing part of an expected response to the risk.

Damage

There must be a causal connection between the breach of duty and the injury suffered (Faulkner v. London Borough of Enfield and Lea Valley High School, 2003). In other words, the breach of duty must have caused the harm in the sense that it would not have occurred “but for” the breach, or alternatively the breach “materially contributed” to the harm. This can be an important consideration when dealing with claims of cyberbullying of students since many of these symptoms associated with psychiatric injury such as mood swings, depression, anxiety, and poor academic results may be attributable to other causes associated with growing up, or as a result of unrelated difficulties in the family situation (Kift et al., 2010). That said, if the failure to prevent cyberbullying by the school authority or teacher is judged to have contributed to the harm suffered, that will be sufficient (Butler et al., 2010).

United States

While in the United States it is possible to sue a parent for the wrongs of his or her child, a target of cyberbullying may still be inclined to sue a school for negligence based on the perception that a school may have greater financial resources than a parent to pay any compensation awarded by a court. A claim based on a common law duty of care in the United States must establish similar elements, namely that a duty was owed to the claimant, breach of that duty in the form of a failure to exercise reasonable care to avoid or minimize the risk of harm and that that breach was the "substantial factor" in bringing about the harm or alternatively that the harm would not have occurred "but for" the breach (Fenn, 2013). However, a target of cyberbullying is confronted by several obstacles in asserting such a claim against a school based on a common law duty of care that do not arise in either Australia or the United Kingdom.

Common law duty of care and sovereign immunity

The United States does not recognize a nondelegable duty owed by a school to its students as such. Instead it must be shown that the school owed a duty of care to the particular student who has been bullied. Generally speaking, absent a special relationship, there is no obligation on a person to prevent another person being injured by a third person (Burns v. Gagnon, 2012). Further, also absent a special relationship the "public duty" rule provides that government entities (like public schools) and their employees act for the public at large rather than owe a duty to specific individuals (Burns v. Gagnon, 2012). However, in some States, it has been recognized that at common law a special relationship exists between a school district and a student, which results in a duty on the school district to take all reasonable steps to protect its students, either because of the compulsory nature of education and the right of students to an environment fit for learning (Rodrigues v. Inglewood Unified School District, 1986) or because the school has custody of the student while at school (Burns v. Gagnon, 2012). Alternatively, the special relationship may arise by virtue of a statute, in which case its scope depends upon the specific wording of the statue. Indeed, in some States, it has been held that no such special relationship can arise via common law and must instead be imposed by statute (e.g., Silano v. Board of Education, 2011).

Nevertheless, a further difficulty arises in the form of a doctrine known as "government immunity" (or "sovereign immunity"), which holds that school districts, principals, and teachers are generally entitled to immunity from personal liability in tort for discretionary acts or omissions in the course of their employment (Albers v. Breen, 2004). For example, the way a principal responds to a complaint of cyberbullying may be regarded as a discretionary act because it involves balancing competing interests, including confidentiality and the appropriate punishment (Albers v. Breen, 2004). Different States take different approaches to this immunity, ranging from Georgia, which provides that it can only be waived by way of a statute enacted by the legislature, to States which provide that that immunity applies provided the legislature has not expressly denied it, and those that apply the immunity subject to exceptional cases such as where the failure to act would subject a specific person to imminent harm (Fenn, 2013).

Statutory intervention

Publicity given to numerous incidents of bullying and their tragic consequences has resulted in public pressure on lawmakers to respond, spawning what Fenn (2013) described as a "national boom" in antibullying legislation. Statutes dealing with bullying exist at both State and local levels, but vary widely in their terms (Beckstrom, 2008), creating a "complex, varied spectrum of State statutory schemes" (Fenn, 2013, p. 2753). For example, as at January 2016, only 23 States expressly included "cyberbullying" in their legislation, although 48 referred to electronic harassment, which may include bullying using electronic means (Hinduja & Patchin, n.d.).

Some States have enacted very detailed provisions. For example, Florida passed the *Jeffrey Johnson Stand up for All Students Act* that prohibits bullying, which is expressly defined as including cyberbullying (which is itself extensively defined), of any student or employee. It includes cyberbullying on campus, during school-sponsored activities, through technology accessed via a computer within the school or at a nonschool-related location or using nonschool equipment if the communication "substantially interferes with" the victim's ability to participate or benefit from services, activities, or opportunities offered by the school or substantially disrupts the "education process or orderly operation of the school." It also requires all public schools to adopt and review at least every 3 years an antibullying policy in conformity with the Department of Education's model policy, and that contains certain minimum components such as:

- a prohibition of bullying;
- the consequences for a student who bullies;
- a procedure for receiving reports (including provisions permitting a person to anonymously report an act);
- procedures providing for prompt investigation of a report of bullying, immediate notification to parents of the victim and for regularly reporting to parents on actions taken to protect the victim;
- referencing of victims and perpetrators to counseling;
- programs of education concerning bullying for students, parents, teachers, school administrators, and counseling staff; and
- procedures for publicizing the policy.

Other states have differing levels of detail in their statutes. Indeed only 14 states extend the school's power to discipline students for off campus behavior (Hinduja & Patchin, n.d.). The State of Montana is the only State that currently has no statutory requirement for schools to have antibullying policies at all.

One significance of statutes such as that in Florida is that, depending upon the words of the legislation, investigation of complaints of bullying can no longer be characterized as a discretionary act, so that the government immunity no longer applies (Fenn, 2013). Further, depending upon the exact wording of the statute, it may prescribe a more specific kind of duty than the general common law standard of care noted earlier. In such a case some courts allow the plaintiff to show breach of duty merely by showing that the statute was contravened, while others allow contravention of the statute to be relied upon as evidence of breach of duty (Fenn, 2013).

First amendment obstacles

A further complication arises by virtue of the First Amendment guarantee of freedom of speech, which by the Fourteenth Amendment also applies to state laws. In other words, a law such as that enacted in Florida, which prohibits cyberbullying may be seen as infringing the cyberbully's freedom of expression and for that reason be deemed to be invalid (King, 2010; Sumrall, 2016). It has been held that students do not "shed their constitutional rights to freedom of speech or expression at the schoolhouse gate" (*Tinker v. Des Moines Independent Community School District*, 1969, p. 506).

There has yet to be a United States Supreme Court ruling on the constitutional validity of cyberbullying laws (Sumrall, 2016). Until there is such a ruling, lower courts that are called upon to consider the question only have a quartet of Supreme Court decisions concerning the exercise of free speech in a school context in other circumstances to guide them. The most influential decision, *Tinker v. Des Moines Independent Community School District* (1969), held that the suspension of several students from school after wearing black armbands to protest the Vietnam War contrary to a school's policy against wearing armbands infringed their First Amendment rights. This was because wearing the armbands did not "materially and substantially" interfere with the requirements of appropriate discipline at the school, and did not invade the rights of other students. This ruling has since been described as the "magna carta of students' expression rights" (McCarthy, 2007, p. 15).

By contrast, in *Bethel School District v. Fraser* (1986), the Court upheld the suspension of a student who, when delivering a speech at a school assembly nominating a fellow student for Student Body Vice President, referred to the candidate in terms of an "elaborate, graphic and explicit sexual metaphor." The Court distinguished these facts from those in *Tinker* because the speech here involved more than passive, undisruptive conduct but instead could have been seriously damaging for an immature audience since it glorified male sexuality and insulted teenage girls. It held that public schools had a responsibility to instill fundamental values of "habits and manners of civility" upon their students. Similarly, in *Hazelwood School District v. Kuhlmeier* (1988), the Court upheld the acts of a principal who refused to allow students to include an article on teen pregnancy and another on divorce in the school newspaper on the ground that they were topics that were not appropriate for younger students and his concern that the students and their parents who were referred to in the articles, while not named, could nevertheless be identified from their contexts. Rather than apply the *Tinker* standard, the Court noted that the newspaper was published as part of the school curriculum, largely controlled by the school and designed as part of the student's training and held that public schools could prohibit students' speech in such a school-sponsored activity if the restriction was "reasonably related to legitimate pedagogical concerns." Finally, in *Morse v. Frederick* (2007), the Court held that a school was entitled to suspend a student for holding up a banner promoting illegal drug use at a school-sponsored trip to watch the Olympic torch relay. Rather than review the *Tinker* standard, as some scholars thought the Court was going to do (e.g., McCarthy, 2007), it simply noted that *Fraser* had shown that the *Tinker* standard was not absolute and that in light of the dangers of drug usage and the prevalence of drugs schools have the right to prevent speech that could be viewed as promoting illegal drug use.

This sum effect of these cases is that lower courts in the United States have no clear direction when dealing with First Amendment arguments in cases involving action taken against cyberbullies. For example, as Beckstrom (2008) noted, some courts have found that websites created using home computers that make derogatory comments about other students and/or teachers have a sufficient nexus with the school campus to qualify it as speech occurring on campus, and have found that they had caused substantial disruption of school operations due to the emotional toll on staff, disciplinary problems among students caused by them accessing the sites and/or (in one case) the shutdown of the computer system to student access, which prevented them from using the computers for school intended purposes. By contrast, other courts have held that such off-campus behavior did not cause substantial or material disruption on campus because the websites in issue may have been crude and juvenile but were not obscene, were created on home computers outside of school hours and/or were not shown to have interfered with teachers' ability to teach or control their classes.

Accordingly, schools in the United States face what has been described as a "lose-lose" situation (Schultz, 2011): they may face being liable to targets of cyberbullying when they do not act sufficiently aggressively to prevent it, and being liable to off-campus cyberbullies' issue if a court decides that the school has violated their First Amendment rights (Fenn, 2013). As Fenn (2013) noted, with the threat of legal liability looming as an incentivising force, it is little wonder that when schools are pushed in both directions—to take action or not to take action—some suggest the best advice is "don't do nothing, don't do too much" (Schultz, 2011). How exactly that translates in practice as a guideline for responding to particular circumstances is far from clear.

Conclusion

Cyberbullying is a scourge of the digital age. Technology has placed in the hands of bullies a potent tool that enables them to reach their targets any day or the week, wherever they may be. It is only natural, therefore, for targets such as Alex Boston to turn to a greater power in the form of the law as a means of addressing the power imbalance that they endure.

The threat of legal liability can be a powerful motivator for action. The circumstances in which a school can be held liable can provide guidance for expected parameters for interventions. However, an examination of the current positions in the Australia, the United Kingdom, and the United States shows a stark contrast in approaches. In Australia and the United Kingdom there is yet to be a reported case dealing specifically with cyberbullying, although cases dealing with traditional forms of bullying are instructive. It is clear that a school's duty of care is not restricted to behavior on school grounds and during school hours. While the exact geographical and temporal scope is not certain, the duty attaches when the relationship of teacher and pupil is in existence. It may be argued that school policies that dictate off-campus behavior that may affect the school may constitute such a relationship. The question will then be whether the school's response met the requisite standard of care, in most places reflecting the accepted standards of reasonable members of the teaching profession.

This will include such matters as developing antibullying policies that specifically extend to cyberbullying, disseminating, and promoting those policies, and proper investigation and documentation of, and responses to, complaints of bullying.

The position is much less clear in the United States. High-profile cases of cyberbullying have led to public pressure that has resulted in lawmakers in some states enacting statutes that detail the responses expected from schools and which set clear parameters for the kinds of interventions to be implemented. Other states have been much less proactive and have either no such legislation or less demanding requirements. However, until there is a clear consideration of cyberbullying in the context of the First Amendment by the Supreme Court of the United States, State legislatures and schools are left in a state of confusion concerning how aggressively the law requires them to respond to this form of objectionable behavior. The result is an uneven patchwork of inconsistent responses to the correct application of the *Tinker* standard of the effect of the behavior on the operations of the school in the particular circumstances arising, hardly a useful guide for educators grappling with this modern phenomenon.

References

Albers v. Breen, 806 N.E. 2d. 667 (Ill. App. Ct. 2004).

Australian Communications and Media Authority (ACMA). (2012). *Communications Report 2011-2012*. Melbourne: Commonwealth of Australia.

Beckstrom, D. C. (2008). State legislation mandating school cyberbullying policies and the potential threat to students' free speech rights. *Vermont Law Review*, *33*, 283–321.

Bethel School District v. Fraser, 478 U.S. 675 (U.S.S.C. 1986).

Bluestein, G. & Turner, D. (2012) Victims of cyberbullying fight back in lawsuits. Huffington Post 26th April. Retrieved from http://www.huffingtonpost.com/huff-wires/20120426/us-cyberbullying-lawsuit/.

Bolam v. Friern Hospital Management Corporation, 1 W.L.R. 582 (Q.B.D. 1957).

Bradford-Smart v. West Sussex County Council, L.G.R. 489 (Q.B.D. 2002).

Burns v. Gagnon 727 S.E. 2d. 634 (Va. S.C. 2012).

Butler, D., Kift, S., & Campbell, M. (2010). Cyber bullying in schools and the law: Is there an effective means of addressing the power imbalance? *eLaw Journal: Murdoch University Electronic Journal of Law*, *16*(1), 84–114.

Butler, D., Kift, S., Campbell, M., Slee, P., & Spears, B. (2011). School policy responses to cyberbullying: A legal perspective. *International Journal of Law and Education*, *16*(2), 7–28.

Chadwick v. British Railways Board, 1 W.L.R. 912 (Q.B.D. 1967).

Commonwealth v. Introvigne, 150 C.L.R. 258 (H.C.A. 1982).

Cox v. New South Wales, 71 N.S.W.L.R. 225 (N.S.W.S.C. 2007).

Faulkner v. London Borough of Enfield and Lea Valley High School, E.L.R. 426 (Q.B.D. 2003).

Fenn, M. (2013). A web of liability: Does new cyber bullying legislation put public schools in a sticky situation? *Fordham Law Review*, *81*(5), 2729–2768.

Geyer v. Downs, 138 C.L.R. 91 (H.C.A. 1977).

Gower v. London Borough of Bromley, E.L.R. 356 (E.W.C.A. 1999).

Grigg, D. (2010). Cyber-aggression: Definition and concept of cyberbullying. *Australian Journal of Guidance and Counselling*, *20*, 143–156.

Hazelwood School District v. Kuhlmeier, 484 U.S. 260 (U.S.S.C. 1988).

Hinduja, S. & Patchin, J.W. (n.d.) State cyberbullying laws: A brief review of state cyberbullying laws and policies Retrieved October 10, 2016 from http://cyberbullying.org/Bullying-and-Cyberbullying-Laws.pdf.
Katz, I., Keeley, M., Spears, B., Taddeo, C., Swirski, T., & Bates, S. (2014). *Research on youth exposure to, and management of, cyberbullying incidents in Australia: Synthesis report (SPRC Report 16/2014)*. Sydney: Social Policy Research Centre, UNSW Australia.
Keeton, W. P. (1984). *Prosser and Keeton on the law of torts* (5th ed.). St. Paul: West Publishing.
Kift, S., Campbell, M., & Butler, D. (2010). Cyberbullying in social networking sites and blogs: Legal issues for young people and schools. *Journal of Law, Information and Science*, *20*(2), 61–106.
King, A. V. (2010). Constitutionality of cyberbullying laws: Keeping the online playground safe for both teams and free speech. *Vanderbilt Law Review*, *63*, 845–884.
Langos, C. (2014). Regulating cyberbullying: A South Australian perspective. *Flinders Law Journal*, *16*, 73–109.
Mccarthy, M. (2007). Student expression rights: Is a new standard on the horizon? *Education Law Report*, *216*, 15–34.
McHale v. Watson, 111 C.L.R. 384 (H.C.A 1964).
Meredith, J. (2010). Combating cyberbullying: Emphasizing education over criminalization. *Federal Communications Law Journal*, *63*, 312–339.
Morse v. Frederick, 551 U.S. 393 (U.S.S.C. 2007).
Oyston v. St Patrick's College, (2013) N.S.W.C.A. 135.
Patchin, J. W., & Hinduja, S. (2006). Bullies move beyond the schoolyard: A preliminary look at cyberbullying. *Youth Violence and Juvenile Justice*, *4*(2), 148–169.
Phelps v. Hillingdon London Borough Council, 3 W.L.R. 776 (H.L. 2000).
Richards v. Victoria, V.R. 136 (V.S.C. 1969).
Rodriguez v. Inglewood Unified School District, 186 Cal. App. 3d. 707 (Cal. Ct. App. 1986).
Schultz, K. (2011). Free to be mean? What are the first amendment rights of bullies? Leadership insider, August 2011. Cited in Fenn, M. (2013). A web of liability: Does new cyber bullying legislation put public schools in a sticky situation? *Fordham Law Review*, *81*(5), 2729–2768.
Scott v. Lothian Regional Council, Outer House Cases. 29 September 1998 (Sco. Ct. Sess. 1998).
Silano v. Board of Education, 52 Conn. Supp. 42 (Conn. Super. Ct. 2011).
Smith, P. (2008). Cyberbullying: Its nature and impact in secondary school pupils. *Journal of Child Psychology and Psychiatry*, *49*, 376–385.
Stoltz, A. (2007). Involvement in traditional and electronic bullying among adolescents. *Developmental Psychology*, *43*, 564–575.
Sumrall, T. (2016). Lethal words: The harmful impact of cyber bullying and the need for people criminalization. *Houston Law Review*, *53*, 1475–1501.
Tame v. New South Wales, 211 C.L.R. 317 (H.C.A. 2002).
Tinker v. Des Moines Independent Community School District, 393 U.S. 503 (U.S.S.C. 1969).
Trustees of the Roman Catholic Church for the Diocese of Bathurst v. Koffman, Aust Torts Reports 81-399 (N.S.W.C.A. 1996).
United Kingdom Law Commission. (1998) Liability for psychiatric illness. Report 249. London: The Stationary Office.

Further reading

J.S. ex rel. H.S. v. Bethlehem Area School District, 807 A. 2d. 847 (Pa. Sup. Ct. 2002).
M.W. v. Panama Buena Vista Union School District, 1 Cal. Rptr. 3d. 673 (Cal. Ct. App. 2003).

Parents coping with cyberbullying: A bioecological analysis

5

*Lian McGuire**, *James O'Higgins Norman*†
*National Anti-Bullying Research and Resource Centre, DCU Institute of Education, Dublin, Ireland, †National Anti-Bullying Research and Resource Centre, Dublin City University, Dublin, Ireland

Introduction

Compared to even 20 years ago, technology has transformed both the pace of our daily lives and the way parents interact with others and the wider world. It has advanced and expanded parents' horizons, enhancing their access to knowledge and allowing them to communicate and "interact" with others well beyond their personal, social, and community networks. Nowhere is this more clearly demonstrated than among children and adolescents, whose home, educational, and social lives are saturated with technological resources. With each passing year, as Internet access becomes increasingly ubiquitous across the globe, parents and their children are more and more heavily involved in the online and social networking world. This world can convey great educational and social benefits but, unless properly prepared, can also leave the user potentially more exposed to the kinds of negative behaviors that can arise online, including cyberbullying (Patchin & Hinduja, 2010).

Cyberbullying is often an extension of traditional forms of bullying that make their way from the classroom and school yard to cyberspace (Gleeson, 2014; Li, 2007). However, despite this link to traditional forms of bullying, it is also a significantly different and insidious way to abuse others (O'Moore, 2012) that is ultimately linked to issues of personal development, self-esteem, and gender identity (Ging & O'Higgins Norman, 2016; Patchin & Hinduja, 2010). With cyberbullying, parents' role in creating safe spaces is under renewed pressure to adapt to the digital world.

A multisystemic issue

Bronfenbrenner's theory of human development (1977) is valuable in framing the complex interactions of individuals with the world around them in relation to bullying and cyberbullying (Cross et al., 2015). The theory recognizes that risks to individuals from bullying behaviors are not direct, linear outcomes of individual behaviors, but result instead from the multisystemic interactions between an individual and the environment in which they live (Espelage et al., 2012).

This bioecological approach contextualizes human emotional, cognitive, and social development into five nested environmental systems surrounding the individual with

Reducing Cyberbullying in Schools. https://doi.org/10.1016/B978-0-12-811423-0.00005-5

bidirectional influences within and among the systems, all of which influence the individual's relationship with the outside world. These are:

1. *The Microsystem*—the immediate environment surrounding the child, e.g., parents, siblings, peers, and school, who can influence and reinforce attitudes and behaviors.
2. *The Mesosystem*—e.g., two microsystems interact (e.g., a parent interacts with a child's school and teachers
3. *The Exosystem*—social/environmental settings that indirectly influences the individual, e.g., a parent's experience at work influencing the child at home.
4. *The Macrosystem*—the culture the individual lives in, and the larger societal values and identity they share.
5. *The Chronosystem*—time-oriented events over an individual's lifespan that affect development, e.g., deaths, divorce, upswing in economy over time providing greater opportunity for employment(Bronfenbrenner, 1994)

Espelage's review of bullying research (2014) lays out both the protective and risk factors in each of these five systems that impact the development of or protection against bullying behavior. But with the advent of the Internet, a further complex set of overarching interactions has come into play.

The pervasive influence of the Internet across all systems underlines the challenge that faces society in dealing with cyberbullying. Easy access to and influence of the Internet in all of these areas beyond the individual's control makes challenging and reducing risk itself a complex task (Hasebrink et al., 2011). For example (at macrosystemic level), it is no longer just the culture of the society in which the individual lives that impact the individual, but the culture and norms of whatever society or group they are encountering on the Internet from anywhere around the world.

However, at child/adolescent level within Bronfenbrenner's model, there is arguably one factor, which holds greater influence than any other in relation to cyberbullying and online risk—parents.

Parents—a unique role

According to Espelage (2014), protective/risk factors involving parents and their children in regards to the prevention or enabling of bullying include the levels of parental monitoring in a child's life; the presence of active/supportive parental involvement in a child's life; and the amount of exposure children have to parents' aggressive or retaliatory behaviors. When it comes to examining cyberbullying, we must add two more protective/risk factors.

Firstly, parents are overwhelmingly both the most prominent enablers of and safeguards against children being exposed to cyberbullying, through the simple provision of access to technology and the Internet itself (Merrill & Hanson, 2016). Children rely on the use of technological hardware such as computers, iPads, and phones and, in general, privately funded phone or Internet accounts in order to access the online world. These are almost universally provided by parents who as a result retain a greater degree of control over their use than any other group in a child's life.

Parents therefore, for the most part, retain the right to monitor and restrict usage as they deem fit. They also bear more of the responsibility for this monitoring and usage of their children. Coupled with the way previously "safe" spaces like home are invaded via online bullying behavior, this means much more of the onus in discovering a child being bullied, or being a bully, is placed on parents than in traditional bullying situations. Far more often in cyberbullying situations, parents find that they must be the initiator in alerting schools. Often they must deal with it entirely themselves if the schools feel the issue does not involve them, or in cases of cyberbullying incidents that do not involve children from the same schools or even locality (Perren et al., 2012).

This brings us to the second protective/risk factor. As a result of this increased onus, parents' own complex experience with the Internet has a significant impact on the child/adolescent in relation to cyberbullying. For example, what parents understand of cyberbullying coupled with their knowledge/ability with computers/cyberspace (*microsystemic influence*), their (*exosystemic*) experiences or lack thereof in dealing with Internet/phone providers, as well as their (*mesosystemic*) relationship with their child's schools/teachers will affect how they choose to approach or deal with cyberbullying.

Parents then have even more of a key role to play in dealing with cyberbullying than in traditional forms. Their Internet usage/facility, perceptions of their own ability, and awareness of online dangers including cyberbullying are absolutely crucial in influencing the education of their children about interactions with others on the Internet, and informing their own confidence as parents in coping with cyberbullying issues as they arise (McGuire, 2016). And their perceptions, correct or incorrect, of their child's technological ability may influence how much and in what way they may be willing to interact and intervene with them.

This in turn can have profound implications for what a child may be exposed online as well as what might be done to better guide parents in protecting their children. Yet while there is a growing body of data on children's Internet use, experiences, and perceptions of online dangers like cyberbullying (e.g., Hamm et al., 2015), there is a relative paucity of international research literature focusing directly on parent's perceived competence with and perceptions of dangers.

A digital divide?

The most commonly accepted perception of adult technological/Internet competence, and one that has often been the starting point for practitioners dealing with parents, is that parents are less technologically sophisticated than their children and are lax in educating their children in keeping safe (Ey & Cupit, 2011; Mishna et al., 2009; NetRatings, 2005; Perren et al., 2012; Stacey, 2009). However, the corroboration of this digital divide is garnered chiefly from research on students, and as Smith et al. (2008) point out in their study on cyberbullying and middle/high schools, this perception is in effect as yet unsubstantiated by parental research. And even without research into parent's capability online, the notion of the digital divide neglects the bioecological effect of the passing of time, and the increasing familiarity each subsequent generation of parents may have with the Internet.

Given the central role and increased responsibility of parents in cyberbullying, it seems to be essential that we know more about parent's Internet experience and practice, in order to better facilitate their approach to their children in regards to cyberbullying. Yet what research exists on parent Internet facility and their competency in dealing with cyberbullying risk is in general drawn from studies of parent-child pairs. Such studies tend to gather more information from students than parents.

Mesch's (2009) US study of teens aged 12-17 years, evaluated parental restrictive mediation use (*e.g., limits placed on the child's use of the Internet including imposed time limits, installing filters, monitoring websites*), vs educative mediation (*e.g., discussion of online risks, joint creation of rules around Internet use, and the placing of computers in common areas*) and found that restrictive parental mediation was used far more than educative mediation unless a child had experienced cyberbullying. However, educative mediation actions were found to be far more effective than restrictive measures in reducing a child's risk of victimization online.

This pronounced preference of parents for setting rules rather than engaging in educative mediation was also found in Dehue et al.'s study (2008) of Dutch teens who found that more than half of the parents always or usually set restrictive rules for their children in regards to their use of the Internet but did not frequently engage in educative evaluative mediation.

Dehue et al.'s (2008) study also found a disparity between child reports on their engagement in risky online behavior and parent's reports, with parents consistently underestimating their child's involvement, a result echoed in the Byrne et al. (2014) study of 456 parent-child pairs in the US Byrne et al.'s results showed that a variety of variables including a permissive parenting style, difficulty communicating about online risks, and allowing prolonged access to the Internet were associated with an underestimation of risky social interactions that their children encountered and experienced online.

The propensity for parents to overestimate the safety of their children online and underestimate their child's Internet interactions involvement highlights possible limitations to joint parent-child studies. These are discussed by Livingstone and Haddon (2009) in the EU Kids Online Study. They point out parents in studies using parent-child pairs may be influenced by the parent's knowledge that their child is also being surveyed, which may lead them to a more socially acceptable style of answering. These type of studies neglect to take into account the adult's skills in supervision and coping. As a result, the second E.U. Kids Online Study (Hasebrink et al., 2011), though also a child-parent study, attempted to collect some data on parent's confidence in regards to the Internet. Results countered previous perceptions about parents with 85% saying they are confident about their role in helping a child if they have problems on the Internet and 79% indicate they were confident in their child's ability to cope.

With the limited, fragmented, and somewhat contradictory evidence available on parents, it was apparent that more research needed to be done on parental facility and confidence levels in regards to the Internet, as well the nature of their knowledge of their child's Internet facility and coping skills, and the manner in which parents understand and approach preventing and intervening in online bullying.

ParentNets' study

As part of an E.U. Erasmus + project, *ParentNets*, the Anti-Bullying Centre in Dublin City University (ABC), undertook an evaluation of 908 Irish parents' experiences of the Internet. The aim was to analyze parental online facility, perceived confidence, and interactions with their children in regards to Internet use and cyberbullying. Specifically, it wanted to examine how parents approach cyberbullying and cyber safety, and how that might inform future practice of helping to better guide and educate parents (O'Higgins Norman & McGuire, 2016).

The study also looked at usage and understanding of social networks, as a prime conduit for cyberbullying. Only the parents of children with an age range of 9-16 years were asked to participate, both in accordance with prevailing knowledge on the more widespread use of the Internet among children from the age of 9 years, and also to meet the age demographic of the wider European project. The survey was distributed through a number of online contacts and national networks resulting in a total of 908 parents completing the online questionnaire (O'Higgins Norman & McGuire, 2016).

The majority of respondent parents were between 41 – 45 years of age (40%, n=362), followed by those between 46 and 50 years of age (26%, n=237), with the third highest grouping being 36–40 year olds (18%, n=163). Those over 50 comprised just 7% (n=61), and those between 31 – 35 years, 6% (n=58). Those identifying as between 25 and 30 years of age (.8%) and those under 25 years of age (1.3%) made up just 2% of respondents combined (n=19). Of the 908 respondents, 802 (88.6%) were identified as female. This would tend to corroborate the prevailing view of the mother as the primary caregiver in the home and in dealing with the school in relation to their children's safety in school and in relation to bullying issues (O'Higgins Norman & McGuire, 2016).

Parents' internet facility & new digital divide

A previous study on adult Internet use reported parent's Internet use in general to be significantly higher than the general adult population (Duggan et al., 2015). This is reflected in the ABC study, which found that Internet use by Irish parents in the home was 94%, This was an increase from the 83% previously reported usage by Irish parents in another study by O'Neill and Dinh (2011), and a strong increase from the 56% of Irish adults reported at the start of the century in a report by the European Commission (2002).

This increase in use relates to a number of factors such as a demand for access from their children, accompanied by the individual parent's need to nurture/monitor their children, in conjunction with exosystemic factors such as the rise of the Internet in the parent's workplace and their own social lives. Furthermore, devices have become more widely available and less expensive over this time period. This steady rise in online usage among parents seems to perfectly illustrate the chronosystemic changes that are outlined here within Bronfenbrenner's bioecological theory.

This gradual increase of parental usage over time appears to be reflected in increasing confidence, with almost 80% of respondents in the ABC study stating they felt confident in coping with an online risk to their children and 75% feeling they were sufficiently engaged in preventing online dangers to their children. There was also a strong degree of parental confidence in their children's knowledge about/ability to detect risky situations, though only 30% in the ABC study felt that their children would know how to protect themselves from online dangers.

These findings more closely match the high confidence levels of perceived parental facility suggested in Hasebrink et al. (2011) than they do the "weak parent" of Briggs and Hawkins (1997) and other studies. And they are supported by research on Irish children's perceptions of their parent's confidence with the Internet, with children reporting their parents growing ability to help them online (O'Briain & Nitting-Fulin, 2009).

Any "Digital Divide" then in regards to parent's confidence and facility with computers and the Internet vs their children's seems to be dwindling with each passing year. Instead, the ABC study highlighted that the divide appears now to occur in regards to *where* both groups are *active* on the Internet.

The parents reported a high level of familiarity/usage in regards to texting and certain social networks (SNS) such as Facebook but quite low levels of familiarity/usage in regards to other networks such as Instagram and Twitter. The usage level of Irish parents is very much in line with that found in the Pew Research Centre's studies on Parents & Social Media (Duggan et al., 2015), and yet (as can be seen in Fig. 5.1) when compared with Pew's teen SNS usage studies (Lenhart, 2015) it highlights a significant disparity in regards to the use of apps and networks between parents and children.

As illustrated in Fig. 5.1, types of social networks and online communication (i.e., Facebook, WhatsApp) favored by parents indicate that they do not always frequent the same networks and websites more widely favored by their children, e.g., Instagram, Twitter, Snapchat. In fact, further research shows a very different pattern of use of networks by children, and a constant migration of children away from where their parents are on the net (Cassada-Lohman, 2016).

Parental awareness of child's activities' online

Despite this evidence of a desire on the part of children to be apart and private from their parents online, three-quarters of parents were confident they knew about their children's actions on the Internet. Yet, when asked about the nature of their knowledge of their child's Internet use and how they knew what social networks, websites, and downloads their children used, in almost every case respondents stated that they more heavily relied on their *children telling them what they did online* than on any monitoring activities (e.g., supervision, parental blocks, etc.) they applied themselves.

Furthermore, three-quarters of respondents were also confident that their *children would inform them quickly* if they had a problem online. This high level of trust/faith placed in their children unfortunately runs contrary to what we know from research on child Internet use, where children confess to engaging in online activities they are not likely to tell their parents about, *e.g., signing up for networks underage, hi jacking others' accounts, posting negative comments* (Nominet, 2014), and from research on child reporting of cyberbullying where of those children who do tell, less than half will tell their parents (Livingstone et al., 2011).

In reviewing this dichotomy, it may well point to the kind of propensity shown in both Dehue et al. (2008) and Byrne et al.'s (2014) studies for parents to overestimate the safety of their children online. Alternatively, could it be that these newly

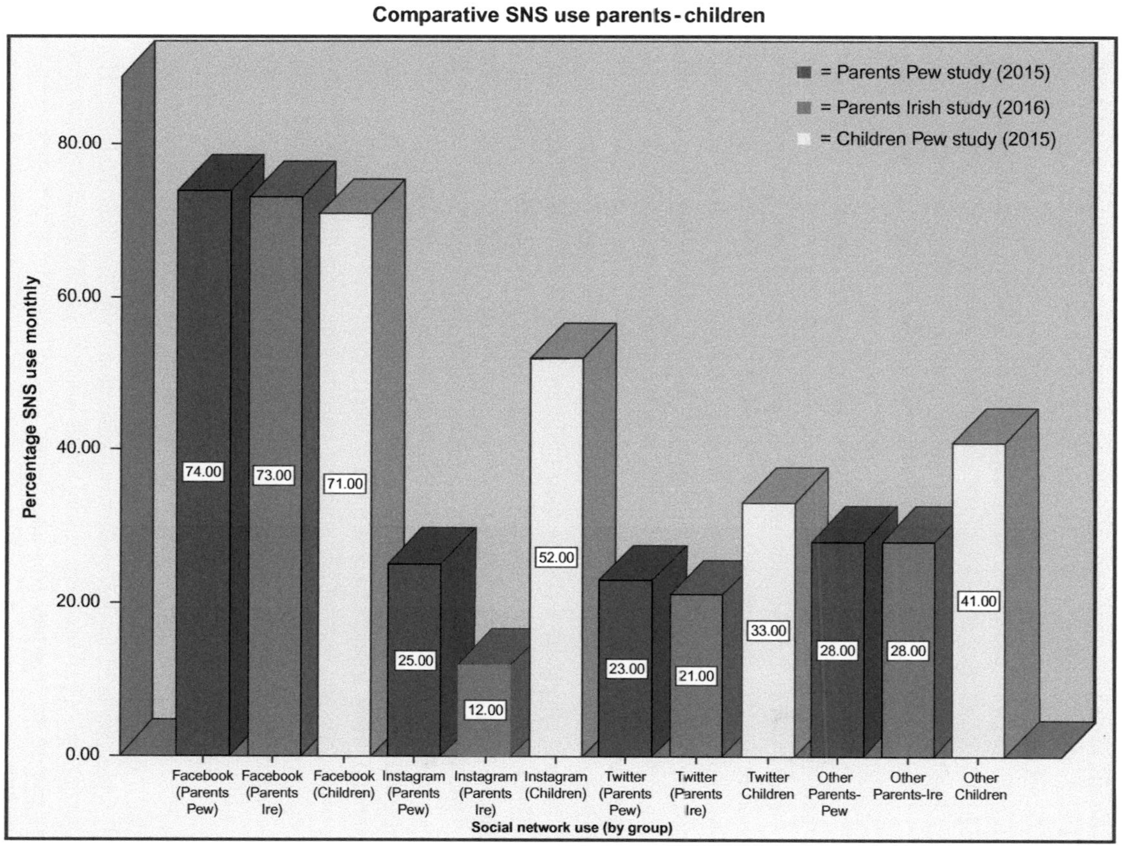

Fig. 5.1 Comparative SNS use parents—children.

Internet-savvy parents have established a working rapport about cyberbullying and online risk with their children that has increased their trust?

Trust or uncertainty?

It is difficult to directly compare outcomes of the different studies of parents' interactions with their children about the net, because of the aforementioned fragmented nature of pre-existing parent research and reporting of results. No specific figures are given for the rates of use of the more effective educative interaction in these studies, though in both cases they are stated to be consistently lower than restrictive approaches. In that respect, it is encouraging that two-thirds of Irish parents surveyed had often spoken to their children about the danger of cyberbullying, and over half have spoken often about how to interact with others online. However, it should be kept in mind that 17% ($n=128$) and 20% ($n=166$) of parents, respectively, had never spoken to their children about these issues at all. Crucially, it should be noted that when asked if they knew exactly *what cyberbullying is*, almost half of parents reported being unsure about what it was and report that they are still fearful of their child's exposure to online bullying, which must give rise to concerns about parents' education on the issue and place a possible caveat on the quality and effectiveness of the educative interaction in such cases.

In regards to active *in-house* restrictive prevention measures/monitoring, the use of Internet timetabling by Irish parents (30%) is far less common than that shown by parents in either the Mesch (66%) or Dehue et al. (60%) studies. Similarly, lower rates of Irish parents check the websites their children visit (46%) than those in the Mesch study (66%), and online filters of any kind were utilized at consistently lower rates by Irish parents than in the Mesch study (56%). In addition, almost half the respondents in the ABC study allowed the use of the Internet by their children in rooms with the door closed, only half applied control/limit of use of webcams and less than a third applied a timetable to their children's Internet use.

In general, there appears to be a more marked reluctance to implement direct monitoring measures, and very small negative correlations were discovered between parent's perceptions that they knew most of the dangers on the Internet, and their use of specific restrictive prevention tools. These occurred almost exclusively in the items that would be considered most easily and directly applicable by parents, e.g., the use of Internet timetabling, control of webcams, use of blocking passwords, visiting websites to educate oneself about risks, and researching websites their child visited.

When it came to more indirect measures, the vast majority of respondents (88%, $n=598$) were prepared to use restrictive prevention tools for their children. However, more than a third of parents were unsure about where to get information about prevention tools for use on the Internet. This uncertainty was reflected in their responses in regards to what restrictive prevention tools they either used or were aware of. About half had restricted privacy levels on social networks, researched websites before allowing access, and checked software permits before allowing games to be installed. However, half of respondents did not know how to utilize passwords to block screens or downloads to computers, while two-thirds had no idea how to verify a website or use filters in browsers, and over half no idea how to apply them in regards to social networks and operating systems.

Discussion and conclusion

Despite the increase in parental confidence and online facility, results of the ABC study appear to mirror the findings of Byrne et al.'s (2014) earlier study, which found that a main risk for parents was their inclination to underestimate the dangers in their child's interactions online. A permissive parenting style leads to difficulty in effectively communicating about online risks such as cyberbullying, and allowing children prolonged access to the Internet (O'Higgins Norman & McGuire, 2016). This type of permissive parenting does not always reflect how parents interact with their children in offline life. Consequently, we would argue that parents need to transfer some conventional parenting practices to their approach to online environments.

Within a bioecological framework, it may be that as parent confidence in their knowledge of the Internet has grown, they are better able to understand and rate the facility of their children's Internet use, but may be mistaking effective and confident utilization for safe interaction or knowledge for wisdom. This may result in parent's overestimation of their knowledge of their child's Internet interactions, which impacts at the microsystemic level by reducing their perceived need to directly monitor and interact with their children in regards to the net. This may inadvertently result in exposing their children to risks.

It could also be the case that parents do not wish to be seen to be directly "interfering" with their children or doubting them, This reluctance to be seen to be as intrusive would certainly be reflected in the low use of many direct measures, e.g., timetabling, blocking apps, use of passwords.

If increased Internet facility is feeding into a sense of confidence and hands off approach to monitoring or if it cannot overcome a reluctance on the part of some parents to be seen as intrusive in their interventions, then it is apparent that a perceived knowledge of the Internet alone on the part of parents is not enough to reduce risk.

It is also seems likely that in many cases it is merely *perceived* knowledge on the part of parents. There are definite gaps in parent's knowledge in regards to the use or even existence of certain preventative tools such as the use of privacy filters, website certificates, and blocking apps and downloads, and perhaps more alarmingly from a practitioner perspective in their lack of knowledge about what constitutes cyberbullying itself.

As the ABC study drew from a predefined European survey on online risk, there was also no way to discover if a parent's child had ever been exposed to any risk. It may be that the extent of their child's exposure influenced their responses, especially in regard to educative vs restrictive intervention, and the utilization of preventative measures.

Moreover, there is disproportionate representation of women in comparison to men in the samples, with 89% (n=808) of the parents being female in the ABC study. This could be indicative of women as the traditional point of initial contact with their children (and subsequently with schools, etc.) when it comes to difficulties, and research indicates children perceive mothers to know more about Internet than fathers and are the ones they speak to about what they do online (O'Briain & Nitting-Fulin, 2009).

In dealing with bullying and cyberbullying, as with other issues, research informs practice. This is all the more essential in cyberbullying, as it is often parents who have to educate and model good behavior to their children in regards to the Internet. They often handle a cyberbullying situation alone once it is brought to their attention. It is obvious that more comprehensive and focused research into parental knowledge and experience of cyberbullying, the Internet, and facility with preventative tools, is still necessary to more fully assess parent's strengths, weaknesses, and needs in coping with the issue, in order to more effectively help them on a practical level.

With that in mind, the provision of specific information pages/courses on the types of preventative tools (e.g., filters) available to should, be a focused outcome for practitioners.

In establishing areas of difficulties parents have (which may vary from region to region, and alter over time), practitioners can work with ICT partners (i.e., ISP providers, Facebook, Instagram, Twitter, etc.) as well as Internet safety experts to create the kind of specific, up-to-date, organic, and interactive (and therefore supportive) help sites for parents. In taking actions like this, one may see bioecological theory continuously at work. Practitioners working with and better educating themselves as to the actual needs of parents at the mesosystemic level, and working with ICT organizations at the exosystemic level, could potentially influence these organizations' approach to better safety/learning and working with parents around cyberbullying, which will over time return to influence parents at the microsystemic level, with their learning passed on to their children.

Going forward it seems crucial for practitioners working in the area of anticyberbullying and/or inclusion to embark on a campaign that highlight the risks of the permissive style of parenting. Such a campaign should advocate and provides means toward parental self-education in the area of ICT, and concentrate on teaching parents the value of educative mediation techniques of talking and listening to their child. Such an approach has demonstrated to be both a more effective tool for reducing risk and a method that is overall less intrusive.

Taking part in bidirectional communication, parents can not only advise from their own life skills but also listen to what their child thinks; then work with them to make rules, set boundaries on both sides, while making the child more responsible for their actions.

For ultimately, within that crucial microsystem surrounding parent and child, where the parents' own experiences and knowledge are key to what they impart, the child can only learn from the parent as much as the parent themselves know.

References

Briggs, F., & Hawkins, R. (1997). *Child protection: A guide for teachers and child care professionals*. Crows Nest: Allen & Unwin.

Bronfenbrenner, U. (1977). Toward an experimental ecology of human development. *American Psychologist*, *32*, 513–531. http://cac.dept.uncg.edu/hdf/facultystaff/Tudge/Bronfenbrenner%201977.pdf.

Bronfenbrenner, U. (1994). *Vol. 3. Ecological models of human development. International Encyclopaedia of Education*. (2nd ed.). Oxford: Elsevier.Reprinted in: Gauvain, M. & Cole, M. (Eds.), Readings on the development of children, 2nd ed. (1993, pp. 37–43). NY: Freeman. http://www.psy.cmu.edu/~siegler/35bronfebrenner94.pdf.

Byrne, S., Katz, S. J., Lee, T., Linz, D., & McIlrath, M. (2014). Peers, predators, and porn: Predicting parental underestimation of children's risky online experiences. *Journal of Computer-Mediated Communication, 19*, 215–231. https://doi.org/10.1111/jcc4.12040.

Cassada-Lohman, R. (2016). Top five social networking sites used by teens: The pros and cons of popular social networking sites by teens. *Psychology Today*, https://www.psychologytoday.com/blog/teen-angst/201601/top-five-social-networking-sites-used-teens.

Cross, D., Barnes, A., Papageorgiou, A., Hadwen, K., Hearn, L., & Lester, L. (2015). A social-ecological framework for understanding and reducing cyberbullying behaviours. *Aggression and Violent Behaviour, 23*, 109–117. https://doi.org/10.1016/j.avb.2015.05.016.

Dehue, F., Bolman, C., & Vollink, T. (2008). Cyberbullying: Youngsters' experiences and parental perception. *CyberPsychology & Behaviour, 11*, 217–223. https://doi.org/10.1089/cpb.2007.0008.

Duggan, M., Lenhart, A., Lampe, C., & Ellison, N. B. (2015). *Parents and social media.* Pew Research Centre. July http://www.pewInternet.org/2015/07/16/parents-and-social-media/.

Espelage, D. L. (2014). Ecological theory: Preventing youth bullying, aggression, and victimization. *Theory Into Practice, 53*, 257–264. https://doi.org/10.1080/00405841.2014.947216.

Espelage, D. L., Rao, M. A., & Craven, R. G. (2012). Theories of cyberbullying. In S. Bauman, D. Cross, & J. Walker (Eds.), *Principles of cyberbullying research: Definitions, measures, and methodology* (pp. 49–67). New York: Routledge.

European Commission. (2002). *Flash Eurobarometer 112: Internet and the public at large.* Brussels: DG Press.

Ey, L. A., & Cupit, C. G. (2011). Exploring young children's understanding of risks associated with Internet usage and their concepts of management strategies. *Journal of Early Childhood Research, 9*(1), 53–65. https://doi.org/10.1177/1476718X10367471.

Ging, D., & O'Higgins Norman, J. (2016). Cyberbullying, conflict management or just messing? Teenage girls understanding of gender, friendship and conflict on Facebook. *Feminist Media Studies*, 1–17. https://doi.org/10.1080/14680777.2015.1137959.

Gleeson, H. (2014). *The prevalence and impact of bullying linked to social media on the mental health and suicidal behaviour among young people.* Report to Health & Safety Executive for Suicide Prevention and Department of Education and Skills. Department of Education & Skills, Ireland. https://www.education.ie/en/Publications/Education-Reports/The-Prevalence-and-Impact-of-Bullying-linked-to-Social-Media-on-the-Mental-Health-and-Suicidal-Behaviuor-Among-Young-People-Briefing-Note.pdf.

Hamm, M. P., Newton, A. S., Chisholm, A., Shulhan, J., Milne, A., Sundar, P., et al. (2015). Prevalence and effect of cyberbullying on children and young people: A scoping review of social media studies. *JAMA Paediatrics, 169*(8), 770–777. https://doi.org/10.1001/jamapediatrics.2015.0944.

Hasebrink, U., Görzig, A., Haddon, L., Kalmus, V., & Livingstone, S. (2011). *Patterns of risk and safety online. In-depth analyses from the EU Kids Online survey of 9–16 year olds and their parents in 25 countries.* LSE, London: EU Kids Online.

Lenhart, A. (2015). *Teen, social media and technology overview.* Pew Research Centre. http://www.pewInternet.org/files/2015/04/PI_TeensandTech_Update2015_0409151.pdf.

Li, Q. (2007). Bullying in the new playground: Research into cyberbullying and cybervictimisation. *Australasian Journal of Educational Technology, 23*(4), 435–454. https://doi.org/10.14742/ajet.1245.

Livingstone, S., & Haddon, L. (2009). *EU Kids Online: Final report.* London: LSE, EU Kids Online (EC Safer Internet Plus Programme Deliverable D6.5). http://www.lse.ac.uk/media@lse/research/EUKidsOnline/EU%20Kids%20I%20(2006-9)/EU%20Kids%20Online%20I%20Reports/EUKidsOnlineFinalReport.pdf.

Livingstone, S., Haddon, L., Görzig, A., & Ólafsson, K. (2011). *Risks and safety on the Internet: The perspective of European children: Full findings and policy implications from the EU Kids Online survey of 9–16 year olds and their parents in 25 countries*. http://www.lse.ac.uk/media%40lse/research/EUKidsOnline/EU%20Kids%20II%20(2009-11)/EUKidsOnlineIIReports/D4FullFindings.pdf.

McGuire, L. (2016). *Towards preventing cyberbullying: Can Irish parent's online facility and perceptions help inform practice? A quantitative study*. Unpublished Master of Psychology thesis Manchester Metropolitan University.

Merrill, R. M., & Hanson, C. L. (2016). Risk and protective factors associated with being bullied on school property compared with cyberbullied. *BMC Public Health*, *16*, 145.

Mesch, G. S. (2009). Parental mediation, online activities, and cyberbullying. *Cyber Psychology & Behaviour*, *12*(4), 387–393. https://doi.org/10.1089/cpb.2009.0068.

Mishna, F., Saini, M., & Solomon, S. (2009). Ongoing and online: Children and youth's perceptions of cyber bullying. *Children and Youth Services Review*, *31*(12), 1222–1228. https://doi.org/10.1016/j.childyouth.2009.05.004.

NetRatings Australia. (2005). *Kidsonline@home: Internet use in Australian homes*. Sydney: Australian Broadcasting Authority and NetAlert Limited.

Nominet. (2014). The social age study. *Know the Net*. http://www.nominet.uk/kids-not-equipped-for-coming-of-digital-age/.

O'Briain, E., & Nitting-Fulin, S. (2009). *Webwise: Survey of children's use of the Internet*. Report prepared by Ipsos MORI on behalf of the National Centre for Technology in Education. http://www.Internetsafety.ie/website/ois/oisweb.nsf/page/DPCY-7R5JG51514315-en/$File/webwise-2008-survey-of-childrens-use-of-the-Internet-in-ireland.pdf.

O'Higgins Norman, J., & McGuire, L. (2016). *Cyberbullying in Ireland: A survey of parents internet knowledge and usage*. Dublin: National Anti-Bullying Research and Resource Centre.

O'Moore, M. (2012). Cyber-bullying: The situation in Ireland. *Pastoral Care in Education*, *30*(3), 209–223. https://doi.org/10.1080/02643944.2012.688065.

O'Neill, B., & Dinh, T. (2011). Irish kids online: Comparing youth and parent perspectives. Digital Childhoods Working Paper Series No. 1. *EU Kids Online*, . http://www.dit.ie/cser/media/ditcser/digitalchildhoods/Short%20Report%20IRL%20Feb%207.pdf.

Patchin, J. W., & Hinduja, S. (2010). Cyberbullying and self-esteem. *Journal of School Health*, *80*, 614–621. https://doi.org/10.1111/j.1746-1561.2010.00548.x.

Perren, S., Corcoran, L., Cowie, H., Dehue, F., D'Jamila, G., McGuckin, C., et al. (2012). Tackling cyberbullying: Review of empirical evidence regarding successful responses by students, parents, and schools. *International Journal of Conflict & Violence*, *6*(2), 283–293. https://doi.org/10.4119/UNIBI/ijcv.244.

Smith, P. K., Mahdavi, J., Carvalho, M., Fisher, S., Russell, S., & Tippett, N. (2008). Cyberbullying: Its nature and impact in secondary school pupils. *Journal of Child Psychology and Psychiatry*, *49*, 376–385. https://doi.org/10.1111/j.1469-7610.2007.01846.x.

Stacey, E. (2009). Research into cyberbullying: Student perspectives on Cybersafe learning environments. *Informatics in Education*, *8*, 115–130. https://www.mii.lt/informatics_in_education/pdf/INFE136.pdf.

Further reading

Department for Children, Schools and Families. (2007). *Cyberbullying: Safe to Learn: Embedding anti-bullying work in schools*http://www.digizen.org/downloads/cyberbullying.pdf.

Part Two

Programs

Online social marketing approaches to inform cyber/bullying prevention and intervention: What have we learnt?

6

Barbara A. Spears, Carmel Taddeo, Alan Barnes
University of South Australia, Adelaide, SA, Australia

Name of program: Safe and Well Online
Type of program: Online Social Marketing Approaches
Suitable for ages: 12–18 years

School bullying and cyberbullying are social relationship, aggression-oriented problems, which involve proactive, deliberate intent, some aspect of repetition, and power differentials between the parties. To date, most prevention and intervention approaches have traditionally targeted the individual, class, and the whole school community. Findings from research on the efficacy of such school-based cyber/bullying interventions have been mixed (e.g., Barlett, 2017; Menesini & Salmivalli, 2017; Ttofi & Farrington, 2011). Digital communication, however, forms an integral component of young people's in-school and out-of-school lives and contributes to their emerging social identity development (Spears & Kofoed, 2013). The digital setting also is increasingly cross-platform, personalized, mobile and social in nature, raising the question as to how the "always on" environment might be utilized effectively to inform cyber/bullying prevention and intervention strategies, and support student well-being and mental health.

Traditionally, marketing is an advertising mechanism aimed at consumers and is concerned with reach and impact, *viz.* how many people (X) are influenced to do/buy (Y). Effective marketing *reaches* the target audience, *influences* their opinions, and ultimately, *affects* their (consumer/buying) behavior. *Social* marketing, however, does not "sell products," but rather seeks to influence social behaviors through promoting ideas, attitudes, and behaviors with the aim of benefitting the target audience and society in general. Public health programs such as antismoking and drug education campaigns are examples of such approaches, which regularly have been employed nationally and internationally to influence individual attitudes and behaviors for positive social good (Spears & Zeederberg, 2013). Recently, there has been a shift away from solely focusing on the "message," toward focusing on what is happening "upstream": to consider causal pathways and contributing conditions of ill/health (VicHealth, 2016). How such approaches might *promote protective* well-being factors to young

Reducing Cyberbullying in Schools. https://doi.org/10.1016/B978-0-12-811423-0.00006-7

people: such as respect for self and others, social connectedness, and help seeking; while also *addressing risk factors* such as attitudes and beliefs in relation to aggression, cyber/bullying, and violence are considered in this chapter.

This chapter explores the potential of online social marketing-styled campaigns to contribute to, and move beyond, school-based prevention and intervention initiatives through operating in the digital setting and capitalizing on existing youth online practices. Four sequentially developed, online social marketing case studies from the Safe and Well Online Study[1] (2011–2016; Spears, Taddeo, Collin, et al., 2016), which investigated the role of technology in supporting and potentially improving, the mental health and well-being of young Australians, are considered. Specifically, the chapter outlines what we have learnt about employing this approach and how it may be best used to inform the prevention and reduction of cyber/bullying behaviors moving forward.

Why consider online social marketing as a strategy?

A plethora of strategies to date have: focused on all levels of schooling (the individual, class, and whole school); encompassed proactive, reactive and peer-support and mentoring strategies; targeted different cyber/bullying participant roles (bully, victim, bystander); employed curriculum, inclusion and whole school/multidisciplinary approaches; and explicitly taught social skills to individuals and peers (Polanin, Espelage, & Pigott, 2012; Smith, Schneider, Smith, & Ananiadou, 2004; Thompson & Smith, 2011; Ttofi & Farrington, 2011; Vreeman & Carroll, 2007; Yeager, Fong, Lee, & Espelage, 2015). Often, however, what might appear to work in one context/setting is not transferable or scalable in another (Evans, Fraser, & Cotter, 2014; Vreeman & Carroll, 2007), highlighting the difficulty in determining efficacy across sociocultural contexts and over time and place.

With the advent of cyberbullying in the early 2000s, a new sense of school-related time and place emerged: that which occurs *beyond* the school day, gate, and jurisdiction. While there is recognized overlap and interplay between what happens in school settings between peers and what happens online (Cross et al., 2009; Smith, 2014; Spears et al., 2008, 2009; Waasdorp & Bradshaw, 2015), to date, prevention and intervention strategies for bullying and cyberbullying have been predominantly school- or class-based, with many drawing on traditional bullying approaches to attempt to reduce cyberbullying. It is relevant therefore to reflect on the efficacy of school-based bullying interventions first.

[1] Funded by the Australian Government Young and Well Co-operative Research Centre (http://www.youngandwellcrc.org.au/), this chapter acknowledges the contributions of the teams from: the University of South Australia; the Western Sydney University; the Queensland University of Technology and *Zuni*, a Digital Strategy company and key partner.

What do meta-analyses of school-based cyber/bullying intervention research tell us?

Research on traditional antibullying programs is significant, but there is a paucity of evaluative research on cyberbullying interventions. Both, however, report mixed results in terms of efficacy. Merrell, Gueldner, Ross, and Isava (2008) found some evidence from 16 intervention studies reviewed from a 25-year period, which supported the interventions in enhancing students' social competence, self-esteem, and peer acceptance; in enhancing teachers' knowledge of effective practices, feelings of efficacy regarding intervention skills, and actual behavior in responding to incidences of bullying at school. They concluded however that interventions were likely to influence knowledge, attitudes, and self-perceptions, *rather than actual bullying behaviors.*Cook, Williams, Guerra, Kim, and Sadek (2010) in their meta-analysis of the predictors of bullying and victimization concluded that intervening simultaneously at multiple levels (individual, peer ecology, and broader aggression contexts) was the most promising. Ttofi and Farrington (2011) rigorously reviewed the effectiveness of 44 school-based programs to reduce bullying finding that overall, school-based antibullying programs were found to be effective in decreasing bullying and victimization by 20-23% and 17-20%, respectively Only certain elements however were found to be having the effect, and they further argued that "work with peers" should not be used, as it was associated with an *increase* in victimization, (2011, p. 44). Smith, Salmivalli, and Cowie (2012) challenged this arguing that abandoning work with peers, could undermine existing successful, integrated whole school approaches. This view also does not take account of the importance of *youth voice*: an enabling and empowering approach to youth-centered, codesigned approaches to cyberbullying, which have evolved from an understanding of children's rights (United Nations General Assembly, 1989; Spears, Slee, Campbell, & Cross, 2011), and most notably of late, children's *digital* rights (Third, Bellerose, Dawkins, Keltie, & Pihl, 2014; Spears & Kofoed, 2013).

Ttofi and Farrington (2011) also noted that effects were highest in age-cohort designs and weakest when more stringent designs (randomized controlled trials) were employed. This highlights the complexities of working and measuring impact in real-world contexts such as schools, where manipulation and control of variables, and establishing implementation fidelity may be problematic, and suggests that research design for these settings, may need consideration as to the most appropriate approach for the context. Polanin et al. (2012) suggested that overall, the reviewed programs were successful, at both a practical and statistically significant level, but found that there were differential effects for high school samples, suggesting that the programs were not as effective for this older age group. In an holistic approach to improving well-being, Durlak, Weissberg, Dymnicki, Taylor, and Schellinger (2011) in their meta-analysis of 213 school-based universal social and emotional learning (SEL) programs found that, compared to controls, SEL participants demonstrated significantly improved social and emotional skills, attitudes and behaviors, and academic performance. This supports a strategic role for promoting holistic protective and preventative attitudinal factors, such as respect for self and others, among all children and youth, as distinct from specifically targeting cyber/bullying and victimization behaviors. Evans et al. (2014) extended Ttofi and Farrington's meta-analyses, and reported that up to 45% of the 22 studies examined (controlled trials published from June 2009 to April 2013) had no demonstrated program effects for bullying perpetration, and 30% showed no program effects on victimization. More recently, Yeager et al. (2015) found that antibullying programs may not be effective beyond 8th grade, and that "aging-up" existing materials to be used with older adolescents may be a waste or even misuse of resources, supporting findings by Polanin et al. (2012). Yeager et al. also noted that there have been important advances in psychological theory and improvements to behavior-change techniques, which are underutilized in existing intervention programs.

Jiménez-Barbero, Ruiz-Hernández, Llor-Zaragoza, Pérez-García, and Llor-Esteban (2016) conducted a meta-analysis of 14 high-quality random clinical trials (RCTs) cautiously finding that there were beneficial, but discrete outcomes for schools with regard to victimization, warning, similar to Merrell et al. (2008) that "most of the mean effect sizes were too weak to be considered significant" (2016, p. 173).

Yet, Rigby and Smith (2011) noted that there had been decreases in the prevalence of reported bullying in many countries, consistent with the small reductions in peer victimization following the implementation of antibullying programs. Thompson and Smith (2011; 2012) reviewed the use and effectiveness of antibullying strategies employed in the UK, finding there was much variation across individuals and contexts with regard to the proactive, reactive, and peer-support strategies employed within a whole school approach: specifically recommending, [that] a 'toolkit of strategies providing a range of interventions was fundamental (2011, p. 8). Rigby and Johnson (2016) similarly examined the prevalence and effectiveness of anti-bullying policies in a convenience sample of Australian schools. Intervention methods, reported by teachers, included: use of sanctions; strengthening the victim; mediation and restorative practices, and less frequently, specific methods such as the Support Group Method or Method of Shared Concern. Proactive approaches employed in the schools included having and using anti-bullying policies, classwork related to bullying, encouraging reporting of bullying, and peer-support initiatives. Reactive approaches were found to be inconsistent, with no single method preferred by schools. Parent responses suggested negative attitudes toward the school concerning how bullying had been dealt with. Alarmingly, students reported that after reporting being bullied to the school, in 70% of cases, it continued.

In sum, the findings from meta-analyses of bullying interventions across all levels of schooling point to many being trialed over time, with very limited effects overall. This has implications for cyberbullying interventions that are underpinned by these existing approaches.

Della Cioppa, O'Neil, and Craig (2015) reviewed 12 international cyberbullying intervention programs against criteria established by Craig, Pepler, and Shelley (2004), which emphasized scientific merit (e.g., control group, multiple informants; randomized assignment) and ease of implementation (e.g., availability of a manual, training, program maintenances, assessment, and who delivered the program) and found most studies lacked scientific merit and most met less than half the criteria, which were premised upon elements of traditional bullying interventions. Of note: *few programs were able to engage in a whole school approach; most prevention programs reviewed did not transcend the school* (e.g., to family, media), which is a problem when cyberbullying occurs via digital/social media; *and most programs targeted 12-13 year olds*, meaning that little understanding of program effectiveness is known beyond this age group, for particular time-points (school transitions). Four research-practice gaps were identified: (1) research and theory have been lacking; (2) there are few evidence-based programs tailored to diverse developmental stages; (3) few programs focus on relationships beyond peers and teachers; (4) there is lack of research on what works for whom and critical ingredients or processes for success, including deficits in knowledge about program implementation and processes of change.

If cyberbullying is a school-based problem as argued by Smith et al. (2008), then employing largely school-based prevention and intervention approaches is logical; however, on balance, existing school-based interventions have been shown to be limited in their program effects and cyberbullying is more than a school-based problem today; it is a worldwide societal and public health concern (Spears, Taddeo, Daly, et al., 2015).

Barlett (2017) noted the lack of theory-driven research involved in cyberbullying, and argued interventions, which are underpinned by theory, can be more successful. Citing various studies, e.g., Schultze-Krumbholz, Schultze, Zagorscak, Wölfer, and Scheithauer (2016) who had incorporated the Theory of Planned Behavior; Doane, Pearson, and Kelley (2014) (the Theory of Reasoned Action); Kowalski, Giumetti, Schroeder, and Lattanner (2014) (General Aggression Model); and Patchin and Hinduja (2011) (General Strain Theory), he suggested that these studies enabled broader psychological, aggression theories, and attitude-based theories to predict cyberbullying behavior. This does not necessarily mean however that these theories readily translate to the online setting.

Online social marketing (OSM) approaches are embedded in public health strategies (VicHealth, 2016) and are underpinned by contemporary psychological theories such as the Nudge Theory (Thaler & Sunstein, 2008) and other transtheoretical models of behavior change, such as those proposed by Prochaska and DiClemente (1983), Ajzen (1985, 1991), and Perugini and Bagozzi (2001).

Meta-analyses such as these, together with the changing online context that is never "off," highlight opportunities for moving beyond the school setting, and for extending evaluation techniques to: (1) include the online environment as the context in which young people socialize and operate, before, during, and after school; (2) cocreate, coresearch and codesign strategies with youth, so the programs closely resonate with the target audience and age contexts; (3) consider the methodological and ethical challenges of conducting randomized controlled studies with youth online, incorporating informed parental consent; and (4) advance thinking in relation to psychological theory as applied to online studies, such as Nudge Theory (Thaler & Sunstein, 2008) and Goal-Directed Behavior models (Perugini & Bagozzi, 2001).

These collective efficacy findings demonstrate that school-based approaches are necessary, but not universally successful and, while they may demonstrate some success at the individual level, it may not be sufficient especially in a climate of shifting digital and social media communications. Online social marketing (OSM) approaches specifically target attitudes and beliefs as a means of eventually leading to actual behavior change. They also work closely with end-users (in this case, youth) to ensure the relevance, age-appropriateness, credibility, and longevity of the campaigns and messages for maximum impact and reach. In other words, they are not adult driven or designed around adult conceptions of the problem, but are firmly oriented in a participatory codesign approach: with and by young people toward youth-identified issues. If bullying and cyberbullying are systemic group processes (Vreeman & Carroll, 2007), then intervention at only one level, even if that level is the whole school, is unlikely to create change, when their social environment includes the digital setting. Only focusing on schools does not take account of the breadth and depth of the blended on- and offline social interactions young people experience. If most reductions in bullying tend to be relatively small, and related to the children being victimized rather than those engaging in bullying, then it stands to reason that approaches that target broader social relationship issues, such as respect for self and others across all settings, may have merit.

The safe and well online study

The Safe and Well Online Study (2011–2016), a collaboration led by the University of South Australia with Western Sydney University; Queensland University of Technology; and Zuni, a Digital Marketing Agency, trialed and tested an online methodology to examine: (1) whether authentic online social marketing campaigns relevant to young people *(end-users)* could be successfully cocreated using a participatory design approach (Hagen et al., 2012); and (2) the extent to which safety and well-being messages could positively influence young people's attitudes and beliefs, and potentially behaviors, in online settings. To do this, innovative methods and measures, including an underpinning theoretical model (Model of Goal-Directed Behavior, Perugini & Bagozzi, 2001) and bespoke online data gathering techniques, which respected the ethical and privacy concerns of conducting online research involving young people, were required. The Model of Goal-Directed Behavior (Perugini and Bagozzi (2001) builds upon the Theory of Planned Behavior (Ajzen, 1991) and proposes that *attitudes, anticipated emotions, social norms, and perceived behavioral control* are mediated by the *desire* to perform a particular behavior (see Fig. 6.7). This model is explained briefly:

What did the program look like: four online social media campaigns

Using Bruner's notion of the Spiral Curriculum (1960) four sequentially developed, youth-centered, codesigned online campaigns were produced (*Keep It Tame!; Appreciate A Mate; Something Haunting You?* and *Goalzie)* as part of an inter-related, holistic preventative strategy/program: to nudge young people toward being considerate and respectful of self and others (see Fig. 6.1). The Spiral Curriculum is predicated on cognitive theory, and features revisiting a topic several times, with increasing complexity, so that new learning forms relationships with old learning and previous contexts. The benefits associated with this approach are that information is reinforced and solidified each time the content/message is revisited; there is a logical progression from simple to complex ideas; and early knowledge can be applied to later concepts.

Working closely with young people in a participatory codesign phase for each campaign (see Hagen et al., 2012), each process: (1) *identified the "problem"* from a youth perspective, which entailed reframing it so that it met their concerns (see Fig. 6.2); (2) *determined why it occurred, who it affected, and the magnitude of the problem* through a series of workshops; and subsequently (3) *codesigned the messaging and the look and feel of the campaign, considering what might work, and for whom* in conjunction with design and marketing experts, for delivery in the online space.

Campaign 1 *Keep It Tame!* (pilot study) (Spears, Taddeo, Barnes, Scrimgeour, et al., 2015) preparatory process *identified* that the *problem* with cyberbullying, from youth perspectives, was a *lack of respect for self and others.* This reframed cyberbullying for

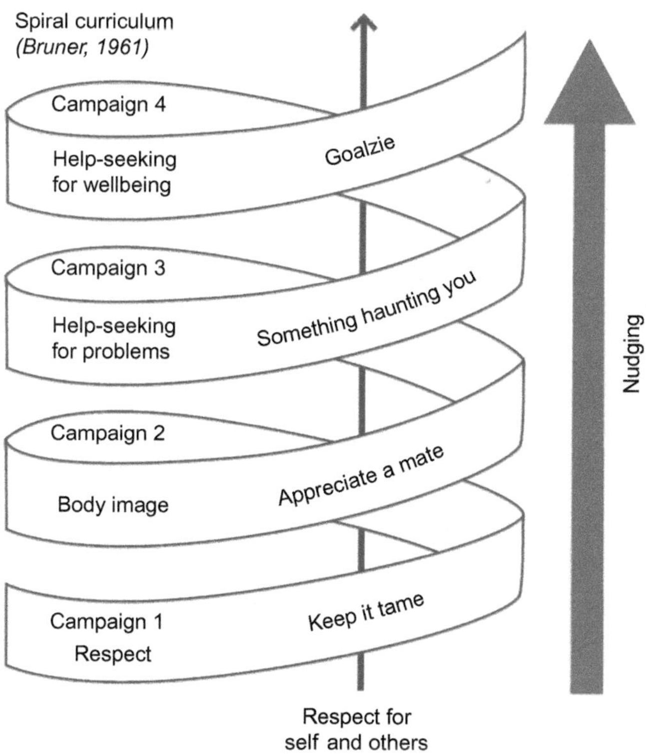

Fig. 6.1 The spiral curriculum approach to campaigns.
Adapted from Bruner, J. S. (2009). *The process of education.* Massachusetts: Harvard University Press.

Campaign themes reframed through participatory design

Theme identified by stakeholder groups	Theme reframed through participatory design with young people
Cyberbullying	Respect for self and others
Body image	Feeling good about yourself
Help-seeking for problems	Achievement by tackling everyday problems
Help-seeking for wellbeing	Goal Setting through fun peer interactions

Fig. 6.2 Campaign themes reframed through participatory design.

the purposes of campaign development from a problem behavior (*what not to do)*, to a positive, strengths-based behavior as a *preventative attitudinal* underpinning *(desired behavior: respect for self and others*), with the campaign challenge to *Keep It (their use of technology) Tame!* (see Fig. 6.3)

> *"You can use phones, tablets and computers to do awesome stuff. But things can turn nasty if you use them to disrespect each other. Treat each other with respect and KEEP IT TAME."*

Fig. 6.3 Keep it tame!

Fig. 6.4 *Appreciate a mate* graphics.

Campaign 2 *Appreciate A Mate* (Spears, Taddeo, Barnes, Collin, et al., 2015) built upon this theme by providing opportunity for *explicitly* showing respect for others, through distributing positive affirmations via a purpose-created and codesigned app (see Fig. 6.4). Youth rely on their peers for mutual acceptance, validation, and inspiration, which is underpinned by a desire to belong and be valued in their social contexts (Slee, Campbell, & Spears, 2012). Young people identified that image sharing was a problem related to cyberbullying, and determined that body image generally, and how others "saw" them off and online, was one of their most significant concerns (Ivancic, Perrens, Fildes, Perry, & Christensen, 2014). By mobilizing existing popular youth digital practices, such as "liking," to facilitate *desired* behaviors and attitudes, in this case, *positive* body image, self-esteem, and respect for self and others (see https://vimeo.com/94621287), young people could spread *positivity* through various social media sites, such as Instagram, Tumblr, Facebook, or Twitter.

Rather than tell young people not to cyberbully, *Appreciate A Mate* sought to reframe negativity in relation to image sharing and subsequent body image, through *promoting positive, youth-inspired, and designed affirmations as messages of support*

Don't Ever Change; You Rock! Virtual Hug!

In Campaign 3, *Something Haunting You?* (Spears et al., 2016a), young people identified that *reporting and reaching out for help* when facing difficult peer situations, such as bullying and cyberbullying, was challenging (Connolly, Hussey & Connolly, 2014; Cortes & Kochendorfer-Ladd, 2014; Smith, 2014; Spears et al., 2016a). Young people reframed *help seeking* from a negatively perceived, reactive response, to a positive, "ordinary" and "everyday" *action* for dealing with stressors, which can follow you around and *"haunt you like a Zombie"* (see Fig. 6.5). Through

Fig. 6.5 *Something haunting you?* graphics.

using dark, edgy humor and a cultural trope (the Zombie), together with graphics (enhanced comics), and existing digital practices (YouTube videos) relevant to the target audience of young men, young people were encouraged to practice help seeking (*Deal With It*) in various scenarios and to access a *Survival Guide*, an *ecosystem of support*, and online resources with links to reputable formal and informal evidence-informed supports (http://www.somethinghauntingyou.com/).

In Campaign 4, *Goalzie* (Spears et al., 2016b), young people identified that they needed to *practice helping themselves and others*, particularly in relation to supporting others when facing such peer difficulties as bullying and cyberbullying. *Goalzie* was codesigned to facilitate and enable rehearsing of *self-help*: *through setting goals and engaging with friends who can help you achieve those goals* (see Fig. 6.6). It gamified help seeking and encouraged fun, peer-to-peer interactions and goal setting, by giving players the opportunity to challenge friends and be challenged by them in fun ways: practicing and normalizing, setting and achieving goals, and seeking help in the process.

Fig. 6.6 *Goalzie* graphics.

How did we do it: methodology

Each campaign development and evaluation strategy comprised 5 components:

(1) A thematic, scoping *literature review* in consultation with key stakeholders, to identify current, key issues relevant to young people

(2) A *Participatory Design* (PD) study (Hagen et al., 2012) involving over 500 young people, researchers, digital strategists, key stakeholders, and creative agency professionals in focus groups, generative workshops, online discussions, and peer-research activities;

(3) An *Age-Cohort study* employing:

- **a.** pre-post experimental survey design using items related to each campaign theme; internet use and practices; social respect (user-designed scale); as well as measures of: mental health and well-being (Lovibond & Lovibond, 1995); social connectedness (adapted from Lee, Dean, & Jung, 2008; Lee, Draper, & Lee, 2001); help seeking (adapted from Rickwood, Deane, Wilson, & Ciarrochi, 2005); and cyberbullying experiences (Cross et al., 2009),
- **b.** random allocation to control and campaign exposure groups by employing coding during a short "contained" (prepublic release) research period
- **c.** the Model of Goal-Directed Behavior (Perugini & Bagozzi, 2001) to underpin prediction of attitude and behavioral change (see Fig. 6.7)
- **d.** a Unique ID assigned to each participant and mapped across the campaign platform and survey instrument to enable matching across pre-post surveys and campaign engagement analytics, with the Model of Goal-Directed Behavior (Perugini & Bagozzi, 2001).

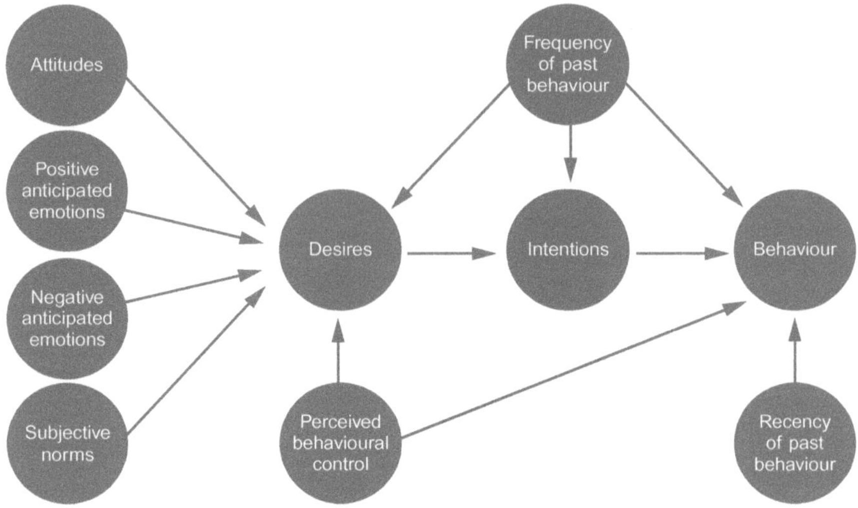

Fig. 6.7 Model of goal-directed behavior (Perugini & Bagozzi, 2001).

(4) a *Digital Data Collection* component, which progressively refined active and passive digital data collection methods over the four campaigns to explore campaign engagement; including the following innovations from Campaigns 3 & 4:
   a. capturing and matching young people's "real time" engagement, with the campaigns in the contained (prepublic release) research period, with survey responses at the individual (Unique ID) participant level;
   b. extending the passive (nonidentifiable) analytic data collection beyond the contained period, to "in the wild" (postpublic release) to explore organic campaign engagement in naturalistic settings
   c. linking of the Unique ID with self-report measures and Google Analytics (Campaigns 2 and 3) and a bespoke back-end database (Campaign 4), with time-stamped data touchpoints, to ascertain extent and nature of *individual engagement* with the campaigns.

(5) a postcampaign *qualitative study* exploring key messaging and outcomes through interviews, and or focus groups.

The *pilot cohort study* (Campaign 1) recruited participants (N=165) aged 12-18 years (M=14.53, SD=1.44, n =163; 2 missing) from South Australian schools, and trialed and tested the validity of instruments and scales when employed in online surveys; and the efficacy of employing the Model of Goal-Directed Behavior (MGB) (Perugini & Bagozzi, 2001) in an online setting to predict attitude and behavioral change (Spears, Taddeo, Barnes, Scrimgeour, et al., 2015). Data gathered provided comparative evidence of online practices and the mental health and well-being context of this pilot group. Subsequent campaigns recruited young people via their parents, from dedicated online research panels, ensuring representative samples required to test the campaigns. Over the course of the Safe and Well Online Study (2011–2016), over 5000 young people participated with informed parental consent (see Table 6.1). In addition, 15 sector partners acted as key stakeholders, and 9 schools contributed to the user testing and participatory design workshops.

Table 6.1 Presurvey campaign sample by states/territories compared to parent population

Australian State/Territory	Campaign 4 Safe and well online study (N=1106)	Campaign 3 Safe and well online study (N=1695)	Campaign 2 Safe and well online study (N=2212)	Parent population (ABS, 2014)
New South Wales	33.27%	31.64%	24.4%	32.04%
Victoria	26.94%	26.09%	34.1%	24.95%
Queensland	18.81%	21.43%	19.0%	20.10%
South Australia	8.68%	9.73%	11.4%	7.15%
Western Australia	7.78%	6.75%	5.5%	10.91%
Tasmania	2.53%	2.45%	3.1%	2.18%
Northern Territory	0.54%	0.24%	0.5%	1.03%
Australian Capital Territory	1.45%	1.67%	2.0%	1.64%
	100.0%	100.0%	100.0%	100.0%

What did we find and what does it mean practically[2]?

Participatory Design: Campaign Development

Through the Participatory Design process (Hagen et al., 2012; Spears, Taddeo, Collin, et al., 2016) negative peer issues, such as cyberbullying, were reframed as positive messages for their peers, to *be respectful of self and others; be affirming; see help seeking as a positive, strengths-based action; and recognize that with practice, goal setting for help seeking is easier.* Collectively, this study found that shifting adult-defined and expert-driven practices of designing interventions *for* youth to those designed *with and by youth,* enabled young people to act as coresearchers alongside the adults, refining the project themes, aims, campaign concepts, development, production, and review together, so that meaning was shared, and knowledge transferred, further maximizing the likelihood of relevancy and currency in the messaging of the campaigns.

The Cohort Studies: The well-being context[3]

The contexts into which the four campaigns were delivered (2012–2016) demonstrated that young people were largely well and had a positive outlook on life; the majority were socially connected and within normal ranges for mental health. Those more likely to be socially connected, demonstrated respectful behavior and had a greater awareness of the norms around social respect. Approximately one in five however reported an absence of hope and lack of confidence in society. This was *particularly the case for cyber bully-victims, and females, who, demonstrated significantly poorer*

[2] Please see all peer-reviewed reports for details and findings relating to each study.

[3] Please see the peer-reviewed Project Reports for all statistical information, including effect sizes.

mental health than males. Nearly half the young people in the pilot cohort study accessed the internet after 11pm, with one-third of these reporting they did so more than four nights a week. *Higher levels of antisocial behavior online, and significantly higher levels of cybervictimization, were evident for those regularly online after 11pm than those who were not.* This finding suggests that it may not be how often young people go online that is a factor in cyberbullying, but *when* they do.

Three campaigns and three years later, using representative age cohort samples: (see Table 6.1) (Spears, Taddeo, Barnes, Collin, et al., 2015; Spears, Taddeo, Barnes, Scrimgeour, et al., 2015; Spears et al., 2016a, 2016b; Spears, Taddeo, Collin, et al., 2016) the contexts into which they were released had changed very little from the Pilot Study ($N=165$): most young people were still largely healthy and well; the majority felt socially connected on- and offline; and were respectful of others. Consistent across all campaigns, parents/carers continued to provide a primary source of support for young people on a daily basis and most young people were in the normal or mild range for depression, anxiety, and stress.

However, approximately one in five continued to experience severe to extremely severe depression and anxiety: One in 10 experienced severe or extremely severe stress; and *cyber bully-victims continued to be a highly vulnerable group, being significantly less socially connected and more anxious, stressed, and depressed than those with no experience of cyberbullying, and demonstrated significantly lower levels of respect for others* (Spears, Taddeo, Barnes, Collin, et al., 2015; Spears, Taddeo, Barnes, Scrimgeour, et al., 2015; Spears et al., 2016a, 2016b; Spears, Taddeo, Collin, et al., 2016).

Building new knowledge to inform cyberbullying interventions: Nudging and Entry points

"Reach" is about reaching the intended audience, and "impact" relates to the effect that interventions may have on people, organizations, or systems. In terms of reach, the videos (Campaigns 1 & 3) were viewed over 1.76 million times; over 85,500 messages of positivity and appreciation were created and shared (Campaign 2), and over 1100 challenges were created via Goalzie (Campaign 4) during the contained trial periods (prepublic release). Impact, however, is noted at several levels. At the individual level, and similar to other previously noted interventions in this field, change was not able to be established to any significant effect and further highlights the complexity of measuring actual change online where the setting is fluid, difficult to contain, viral, and freely networked.

Most importantly though this study's impact is at the broader system level and responds directly to the research-practice challenges highlighted by Della Cioppa et al. (2015) and noted previously: it has developed and trialed an innovative online research methodology, grounded in theory, which *has demonstrated* potential *entry points for interventions to maximize their impact and effect.* Careful consideration throughout was given to the methodology: sampling; tracking methods by Unique ID; approaches to operationalizing controlled experimental design in a contained online setting; and functionality and limitations of platforms.

To reiterate, the Model of Goal-Directed Behavior (MGB) (Perugini and Bagozzi (2001) proposed that *attitudes, anticipated emotions, social norms, and perceived behavioral control* are mediated by the *desire* to perform a particular behavior (see Fig. 6.7).

Investigations into relationships between key constructs of the model (MGB) (Perugini & Bagozzi, 2001) and campaign outcomes: *respect; helping others feel good about themselves; help seeking and goal setting*, demonstrated where *best* to target future initiatives and interventions, *viz. social norms, attitudes, and perceived control.* These were found to be key entry points necessary for *nudging attitudinal and behavioral change for young people's well-being, including cyberbullying.*

Desire, in turn, is a *determinant of intentions*, with *frequency and recency* of past behavior contributing either directly or indirectly to determining the behavior. The *desire* then in this case *to be respectful of self and others, to be affirming, to seek help and set goals, constitutes important motivators in the decision-making process to actually enact change.* Predicting behavioral change rests on being able to measure these constructs in relation to the desired behavioral and attitudinal outcomes over an appropriate timeframe in a controlled environment: a complex task in an online setting, where users employ different devices, platforms, and systems, and the viral and interconnected nature of the web is fundamental.

Social marketing, especially using digital media, holds enormous potential for engaging young people, and it may be that *nudging* behavior in less obvious, but positive ways is more realistic than determining actual behavioral change. Thaler and Sunstein (2008) defined Nudge Theory as "*any aspect of choice architecture that alters people's behavior in a predictable way, without forbidding any options or significantly changing their economic incentives... Putting fruit at eye level counts as a nudge. Banning junk food does not*" (p. 6).

Analytics engagement data from Campaign 3 demonstrated ongoing engagement with the messaging some years later, and passive data, obtained through real-time collection of data from users as they engaged with devices, websites, or Apps, generally demonstrated extensive engagement and reach, as noted at the beginning of this section. The nudge effect here thus relates to putting the youth-centered and driven campaign messaging online in engaging ways: metaphorically "*putting the fruit at [their online] eye level.*"

It is possible that these campaigns have "nudged" participants, as there is evidence to support return use and ongoing use of the campaign artifacts beyond the testing period: so-called in the wild, e.g., the videos and Appreciate a Mate messages are still being utilized, but since the project has finished, we are unable to continue to monitor uptake and spread.

Measures sensitive enough to capture shifts in attitudes in short time frames (the "nudge") are needed, particularly given that attitudinal and behavioral change is a long-term endeavor and the online campaign testing periods were relatively short, due to needing to "contain" the integrity of the controlled experimental design.

Given the majority of young people across all campaigns reported *positive attitudes and emotions toward behaving respectfully online, an appreciation of the social norms associated with respect, and feeling in control of their desire and intent to behave respectfully online,* it is reasonable to suggest that these are the entry points for online social marketing campaigns to successfully nudge young people toward actual change, without telling them directly what they need to do. Further to this, the *qualitative data* (Study 5) found that friends played a key role in motivating others to behave respectfully, including giving *disapproval for disrespectful behavior*, effecting "nudging" (Thaler & Sunstein, 2008) young people's behaviors in predictable ways.

Strengths, limitations, and conclusions

What have we learnt[4]*?*

Online social marketing approaches to intervention have merit, in that the affordances of social media are well suited to campaigns seeking to foster social connections as protective factors. They have reach far beyond the school settings, and can be revisited often, well beyond the initial release, reinforcing key messages over time, potentially *nudging young people toward the desired outcomes.* Campaigns that mirror youth language and behaviors (humor, "liking," posting, sharing) resonate well and increase the likelihood of uptake and reach. Constructing cyberbullying initiatives and interventions *with* young people is critical –the way forward cannot be mapped without their input and voice. Young people provided a new way of approaching cyberbullying initiatives by applying a positive, strengths-based lens to this serious youth problem, and reframed it into desirable behaviors to be addressed positively through the campaigns such as respect for others, help seeking, and making others feel good about themselves. Determining behavioral change online proved elusive, however, and therefore not dissimilar to many offline interventions. However, the key findings from this study suggest *key entry points for interventions to nudge young people toward change for well-being are addressing social norms, attitudes, and perceived control.*

The ethical, design, and technical challenges in evaluating campaigns in real time and in the public domain are substantial. The research methodology, which brought together self-report and engagement data and applied both sets of data to the Model of Goal-Directed Behavior with a nationally representative sample of young people aged 12–18, is promising, and future research should continue to develop and test these innovative techniques. Young people's engagement with campaigns, 2, 3, and 4 was mapped in real time; in naturalistic settings; at the individual level by unique ID; across relevant data touch points; then collected in databases and merged for analyses. This enabled campaign engagement data to be mapped against self-report data. In this way, data collection did not only rely on what young people told us, but also used passive data that provided a "real" indication of how young people were actually engaging with the campaigns.

There were however a number of project limitations, including the potential for self-selection bias, and ethical requirements restricting young people's engagement with the full functionality of some of the campaigns: Campaign 4 especially where young people were required to have a Facebook account in order to establish peer connections for the challenges. Importantly, as a series of age-cohort designs, claims about cause-and-effect relationships cannot be made.

However, the project does provide detailed insights into the well-being contexts into which each of the campaigns were delivered. Further, the project has contributed to understandings about the use, potential benefits and limitations of using social marketing to address cyberbullying with young people; proposed areas for ongoing

[4] Readers are directed to each of the five, peer reviewed, Safe and Well Online reports for all statistical analyses and detailed information: http://www.unisa.edu.au/Research/Centre-for-Research-in-Education/research-groups/Wellbeing-Research-Group/Wellbeing/

investigations, and highlighted the value of developing initiatives where youth participation and voice underpins intervention processes to maximize the potential reach and impact of cyberbullying initiatives.

Acknowledgments

This study was supported by the Australian Government Department of Innovation, Industry and Science through the Co-operative Research Centres Program: Young and Well Co-operative Research Centre, in partnership with young people, community, government, end users, research organizations, and the digital media industry.

The authors acknowledge the members of the extended research team: Philippa Collin; Teresa Swist; Judy Drennan; Phil Kavanagh; Jane Webb-Williams; Mike Zeederberg; Val Borbone; Mark Razzell; Gregory Yates; Margaret Scrimgeour; Tony Daly; and Cindy Brock.

The authors thank all the young people and their parents who gave their consent and their time to this project.

References

Ajzen, I. (1985). From intentions to actions: A theory of planned behavior. In J. Kuhl & J. Beckmann (Eds.), *Action control: From cognition to behavior* (pp. 11–39). New York: Springer-Verlag.

Ajzen, I. (1991). The theory of planned behavior. *Organizational Behavior and Human Decision Processes*, *50*, 179–211.

Australian Bureau of Statistics (ABS). (2014). http://www.abs.gov.au/AUSSTATS/abs@.nsf/latestmf/4102.0~99.

Barlett, C. P. (2017). From theory to practice: Cyberbullying theory and its application to intervention. *Computers in Human Behavior*, *72*, 269–275. https://doi.org/10.1016/j.chb.2017.02.060.

Cook, C. R., Williams, K. R., Guerra, N. G., Kim, T. E., & Sadek, S. (2010). Predictors of bullying and victimization in childhood and adolescence: a meta-analytic investigation. *School Psychology Quarterly*, *25*(2), 65–83. https://doi.org/10.1037/a0020149.

Connolly, J., Hussey, P., & Connolly, R. (2014). Technology-enabled bullying and adolescent resistance to report: the need to examine causal factors. *Interactive Technology and Smart Education*, *11*(2), 86–98.

Cortes, K. I., & Kochenderfer-Ladd, B. (2014). To tell or not to tell: what influences children's decisions to report bullying to their teachers? *School Psychology Quarterly*, *29*(3), 336.

Craig, W. M., Pepler, D. J., & Shelley, D. (2004). *Summary of interventions to address bullying problems at school.* Queen's Park: Ontario Ministry of Education.

Cross, D., Shaw, T., Hearn, L., Epstein, M., Monks, H., Lester, L., et al. (2009). *Australian covert bullying prevalence study (ACBPS).* Retrieved from http://www.deewr.gov.au/Schooling/NationalSafeSchools/Pages/research.aspx.

Della Cioppa, V., O'Neil, A., & Craig, W. (2015). Learning from traditional bullying interventions: A review of research on cyberbullying and best practice. *Aggression and Violent Behavior*, *23*, 61–68. https://doi.org/10.1016/j.avb.2015.05.009.

Doane, A. N., Pearson, M. R., & Kelley, M. L. (2014). Predictors of cyberbullying perpetration among college students: An application of the theory of reasoned action. *Computers in Human Behavior*, *36*, 154–162. https://doi.org/10.1016/j.chb.2014.03.051.

Durlak, J. A., Weissberg, R. P., Dymnicki, A. B., Taylor, R. D., & Schellinger, K. B. (2011). The impact of enhancing students' social and emotional learning: A meta-analysis of school-based universal interventions. *Child Development, 82,* 405–432. https://doi.org/10.1111/j.1467-8624.2010.01564.x.

Evans, C. B., Fraser, M. W., & Cotter, K. L. (2014). The effectiveness of school-based bullying prevention programs: A systematic review. *Aggression and Violent Behavior, 19,* 532–544. https://doi.org/10.1016/j.avb.2014.07.004.

Hagen, P., Collin, P., Metcalf, A., Nicholas, M., Rahilly, K., & Swainston, N. (2012). *Participatory design of evidence-based online youth mental health promotion, intervention and treatment.* Melbourne: Young and Well Cooperative Research Centre.

Ivancic, L., Perrens, B., Fildes, J., Perry, Y., & Christensen, H. (2014). *Youth mental health report.* Mission Australia and Black Dog Institute. Retrieved from http://www.mentalhealthcommission.gov.au/media-centre/news/youth-mental-health-report-released.aspx.

Jiménez-Barbero, J. A., Ruiz-Hernández, J. A., Llor-Zaragoza, L., Pérez-García, M., & Llor-Esteban, B. (2016). Effectiveness of anti-bullying school programs: A meta-analysis. *Children and Youth Services Review, 61,* 165–175. https://doi.org/10.1016/j.childyouth.2015.12.015.

Kowalski, R. M., Giumetti, G. W., Schroeder, A. N., & Lattanner, M. R. (2014). Bullying in the digital age: A critical review and meta-analysis of cyberbullying research among youth. *Psychological Bulletin, 140,* 1073–1137. https://doi.org/10.1037/a0035618.

Lee, R. M., Dean, B. L., & Jung, K. R. (2008). Social connectedness, extraversion, and subjective well-being: Testing a mediation model. *Personality and Individual Differences, 45,* 414–419. https://doi.org/10.1016/j.paid.2008.05.017.

Lee, R. M., Draper, M., & Lee, S. (2001). Social connectedness, dysfunctional interpersonal behaviors, and psychological distress: Testing a mediator model. *Journal of Counseling Psychology, 48,* 310–318.

Lovibond, S. H., & Lovibond, P. F. (1995). *Manual for the depression anxiety stress scales.* Sydney: The Psychology Foundation of Australia.

Menesini, E., & Salmivalli, C. (2017). Bullying in schools: The state of knowledge and effective interventions. *Psychology, Health & Medicine,* 1–14. https://doi.org/10.1080/13548506.2017.1279740.

Merrell, K. W., Gueldner, B. A., Ross, S. W., & Isava, D. M. (2008). How effective are school bullying intervention programs? A meta-analysis of intervention research. *School Psychology Quarterly, 23*(1), 26–42. https://doi.org/10.1037/1045-3830.23.1.26.

Patchin, J. W., & Hinduja, S. (2011). Traditional and nontraditional bullying among youth: A test of general strain theory. *Youth and Society, 43,* 727–751. https://doi.org/10.1177/0044118X10366951.

Perugini, M., & Bagozzi, R. P. (2001). The role of desires and anticipated emotions in goal-directed behaviors: Broadening and deepening the theory of planned behavior. *British Journal of Social Psychology, 40*(1), 79–98. https://doi.org/10.1348/014466601164704.

Polanin, J. R., Espelage, D. L., & Pigott, T. D. (2012). A meta-analysis of school-based bullying prevention programs' effects on bystander intervention behavior. *School Psychology Review, 41*(1), 47–65.

Prochaska, J., & DiClemente, C. (1983). Stages and processes of self-change in smoking: Toward an integrative model of change. *Journal of Consulting and Clinical Psychology, 5,* 390–395.

Rickwood, D., Deane, F. P., Wilson, C. J., & Ciarrochi, J. (2005). Young people's help-seeking for mental health problems. *Australian e-journal for the Advancement of Mental health, 4,* 218–251. https://doi.org/10.5172/jamh.4.3.218.

Rigby, K., & Johnson, K. (2016). *The prevalence and effectiveness of anti-bullying strategies employed in Australian Schools*. Adelaide: University of South Australia.

Rigby, K., & Smith, P. K. (2011). Is school bullying really on the rise? *Social Psychology of Education*, *14*, 441–455. https://doi.org/10.1007/s11218-011-9158-y.

Schultze-Krumbholz, A., Schultze, M., Zagorscak, P., Wölfer, R., & Scheithauer, H. (2016). Feeling cybervictims' pain—The effect of empathy training on cyberbullying. *Aggressive Behavior*, *42*, 147–156. https://doi.org/10.1002/ab.21613.

Slee, P. T., Campbell, M., & Spears, B. (Eds.), (2012). *Child, adolescent & family development*. (3rd ed.)Cambridge: Cambridge University Press.

Smith, P. K. (2014). *Understanding school bullying: Its nature and prevention strategies*. London: Sage.

Smith, P. K., Mahdavi, J., Carvalho, M., Fisher, S., Russell, S., & Tippett, N. (2008). Cyberbullying: Its nature and impact in secondary school pupils. *Journal of Child Psychology and Psychiatry*, *49*, 376–385. https://doi.org/10.1111/j.1469-7610.2007. 01846.x.

Smith, P. K., Salmivalli, C., & Cowie, H. (2012). Effectiveness of school-based programs to reduce bullying: A commentary. *Journal of Experimental Criminology*, *8*, 433–441. https://doi.org/10.1007/s11292-012-9142-3.

Smith, J. D., Schneider, B. H., Smith, P. K., & Ananiadou, K. (2004). The effectiveness of whole-school anti-bullying programs: A synthesis of evaluation research. *School Psychology Review*, *33*, 547–560.

Spears, B., & Kofoed, J. (2013). Transgressing research binaries: Youth as knowledge brokers in cyberbullying research. In P. Smith & G. Steffgen (Eds.), *Cyberbullying through the new media: Findings from an international network* (pp. 201–221). London: Psychology Press.

Spears, B., Slee, P., Campbell, M., & Cross, D. (2011). *Educational change and youth voice: Informing school action on cyberbullying*. Seminar Series 208 Melbourne: Centre for Strategic Education.

Spears, B. A., Slee, P. T., Owens, L., & Johnson, B. (2008). *Behind the scenes: Insights into the human dimension of covert bullying*. Canberra: Department of Education, Employment and Workplace relations. Retrieved from http://www.deewr.gov.au/Schooling/NationalSafeSchools/Pages/research.aspx.

Spears, B., Slee, P., Owens, L., & Johnson, B. (2009). Behind the scenes and screens: Insights into the human dimension of covert and cyberbullying. *Zeitschrift für Psychologie/Journal of Psychology*, *217*(4), 189–196. https://doi.org/10.1027/0044-3409.217.4.189.

Spears, B., Taddeo, C. M., Barnes, A., Collin, P., Swist, T., Borbone, V., et al. (2016a). *Something Haunting You? Reframing and promoting help-seeking for young men. The co-creation and evaluation of a social marketing campaign*. Melbourne: Young and Well Cooperative Research Centre.

Spears, B., Taddeo, C. M., Barnes, A., Collin, P., Swist, T., Borbone, V., et al. (2016b). *Connect. Challenge. Do. Design and evaluation of Goalzie: a goalsetting campaign to promote positive attitudes towards help-seeking for wellbeing*. Melbourne: Young and Well Cooperative Research Centre.

Spears, B., Taddeo, C., Barnes, A., Collin, P., Swist, T., & Razzell, M. (2015). *'Appreciate a Mate': Helping others to feel good about themselves*. Safe and Well Online: A Report on the Development and Evaluation of a Positive Messaging Social Marketing Campaign for Young People Melbourne: Young and Well Cooperative Research Centre.

Spears, B., Taddeo, C., Barnes, A., Scrimgeour, M., Collin, P., Drennan, J., et al. (2015). *Keep It Tame: Promoting respect online safe and well online pilot study: Evaluating the design, engagement and impact of a social marketing approach aimed at 12 to 18 year olds*. Melbourne: Young and Well Cooperative Research Centre.

Spears, B., Taddeo, C., Collin, P., Swist, T., Razzell, M., Borbone, V., et al. (2016). *Safe and Well Online: Learnings from four social marketing campaigns for youth wellbeing*. Melbourne: Young and Well Co-operative Research Centre.

Spears, B. A., Taddeo, C. M., Daly, A. L., Stretton, A., & Karklins, L. T. (2015). Cyberbullying, help-seeking and mental health in young Australians: Implications for public health. *International Journal of Public Health, 60*, 219–226. https://doi.org/10.1007/s00038-014-0642-y.

Spears, B. A., & Zeederberg, M. (2013). Emerging methodological strategies to address cyberbullying: Online social marketing and young people as co-researchers. In S. Bauman, D. Cross, & J. Walker (Eds.), *Principles of cyberbullying research: Definitions, measures and method* (pp. 273–285). New York: Routledge.

Thaler, R. H., & Sunstein, C. R. (2008). *Nudge: Improving decisions about health, wealth, and happiness*. New York, NY: Penguin.

Third, A., Bellerose, D., Dawkins, U., Keltie, E., & Pihl, K. (2014). *Children's rights in the digital age: A download from children around the world.* Melbourne: Young and Well Cooperative Research Centre.

Thompson, F., & Smith, P. K. (2011). *The use and effectiveness of anti-bullying strategies in schools*. Research Brief DFE-RR098. Retrieved online http://socialwelfare.bl.uk/subject-areas/services-activity/education-skills/departmentforeducation/131759DFE-RB098.pdf.

Thompson, F., & Smith, P. K. (2012). Anti-bullying strategies in schools: What is done and what works. *British Journal of Educational Psychology, 2*, 154–173. Retrieved from http://www.bullyingandcyber.net/media/cms_page_media/55/Thompson-Smith2.pdf.

Ttofi, M. M., & Farrington, D. P. (2011). Effectiveness of school-based programs to reduce bullying: A systematic and meta-analytic review. *Journal of Experimental Criminology, 7*(1), 27–56. https://doi.org/10.1007/s11292-010-9109-1.

United Nations General Assembly. (1989). *Convention on the rights of the child*. New York, NY: United Nations.

VicHealth. (2016). *Letter 42: The Changing face of social marketing*. Retrieved https://www.vichealth.vic.gov.au/media-and-resources/vichealth-letter.

Vreeman, R. C., & Carroll, A. E. (2007). A systematic review of school-based interventions to prevent bullying. *Archives of Pediatrics & Adolescent Medicine, 161*(1), 78–88. https://doi.org/10.1001/archpedi.161.1.78.

Waasdorp, T. E., & Bradshaw, C. P. (2015). The overlap between cyberbullying and traditional bullying. *Journal of Adolescent Health, 56*, 483–488. https://doi.org/10.1016/j.jadohealth.2014.12.002.

Yeager, D. S., Fong, C. J., Lee, H. Y., & Espelage, D. L. (2015). Declines in efficacy of anti-bullying programs among older adolescents: Theory and a three-level meta-analysis. *Journal of Applied Developmental Psychology, 37*, 36–51. https://doi.org/10.1016/j.appdev.2014.11.005.

Further reading

Bruner, J. S. (2009). *The process of education*. Massachusetts: Harvard University Press.

Fishbein, M., & Ajzen, I. (1975). *Belief, attitude, intention, and behavior: An introduction to theory and research*. Reading, MA: Addison-Wesley.

Cyber-Friendly Schools

7

Donna Cross,†, Amy Barnes*, Patricia Cardoso†, Kate Hadwen*, Thérèse Shaw*, Marilyn Campbell‡, Phillip T. Slee§*
*Telethon Kids Institute, The University of Western Australia, Perth, WA, Australia, †Edith Cowan University, Joondalup, WA, Australia, ‡Queensland University of Technology (QUT), Brisbane, QLD, Australia, §Flinders University, Bedford Park, SA, Australia

Name of program: Cyber-Friendly Schools
Type of program: Whole-school curriculum modules
Suitable for ages: Secondary school students, 13–18 years-old

What is the program and how is it delivered?

Multidimensional school-based programs with strategies targeting all levels of the school community are considered the most effective way to address peer bullying (Rigby & Slee, 2008; Ttofi & Farrington, 2011; Vreeman & Carroll, 2007) with some studies successfully using school-based interventions to reduce cyberbullying (Ortega-Ruiz, Del Rey, & Casas, 2012; Williford et al., 2013). However, there has been little empirical research in Australia on ways to address cyberbullying using a whole-school approach. Given the relative newness of this form of bullying and a lack of experience with technology, school staff often experience difficulty in defining, identifying, and knowing how to address cyberbullying behaviors (Bauman & Del Rio, 2006; Cassidy, Brown, & Jackson, 2012; DeSmet et al., 2015). In Australia, teachers are less likely to recognize instances of cyberbullying, and are more uncertain about how to address bullying involving technology, compared to other forms of bullying (Cross et al., 2009). Fewer than 10% of Australian secondary school staff report feeling very skilled to deal with cyberbullying, while 50% feel poorly or not at all skilled to do so (Barnes et al., 2012). There is a clear need for research on ways to enhance the ability of school staff to address cyberbullying among their students (DeSmet et al., 2015).

Multicomponent interventions targeting the whole-school environment are needed to prevent bullying behavior (Ttofi & Farrington, 2009; Vreeman & Carroll, 2007) and are in line with the World Health Organization's health-promoting school model (World Health Organization, 2004). These interventions address all levels and members of the school community, with strategies targeting parents, students, and staff; the school's physical environment; the school curriculum; school policies and practice; school culture and ethos; and links with the wider community.

This chapter describes a whole-school approach to cyberbullying prevention that was developed in response to the need to enhance school capacity to address cyberbullying. Developed in Western Australia, the 2-year Cyber-Friendly Schools (CFS) project was one of the first to implement and evaluate a whole-school intervention

Reducing Cyberbullying in Schools. https://doi.org/10.1016/B978-0-12-811423-0.00007-9

that enhanced the capacity of secondary school staff, students, and families to prevent cyberbullying behavior, and students themselves were involved in its design and implementation.

The CFS program has three components, which target (1) the whole-school community, (2) students, and (3) parents. Each includes teaching and learning resources and a website resource for students, families, and teachers. Extensive training is also provided to staff and students.

Whole-school component

The whole-school component aims to help schools develop consistent understandings about cyberbullying, implement strategies to support students' social and emotional development, develop policy relating to technology use and cyberbullying, develop a positive school ethos and culture, encourage positive behavior management strategies, implement pastoral care initiatives, and strengthen links between school, home, and community. This involves working directly with two groups of participants: a school project team, appointed by the school principal, and a grade 10 student cyberleadership team (see later). These student leaders are old enough to act as mentors to the participating students (grades 8 and 9) without being restricted by the increased academic pressures on grade 11 and 12 students. School project teams are provided with the following resources:

- "Cyberbullying Update" booklet, containing information about definitions and prevalence; social and legal consequences; the role of bystanders; and strategies for responding. The booklet also provides information about other activities in which young people engage using Information and Communication Technology (ICT) such as social networking sites (e.g., Facebook), gaming sites, and text messaging.
- "Strategies for responding" booklet, providing strategies for school staff to employ when responding to cyberbullying situations including The Method of Shared Concern, Motivational Interviewing, and the Critical Thinking Line.
- "Policy to Practice" booklet, providing information, guidelines and strategies to engage schools in discussion and planning toward a whole-school response to bullying, with a key component being the development or revision of the school behavior management plan and bullying policy.
- Three newsletter items for schools to use containing information relating to students' online behaviors. The first discusses friend lists on social networking sites, the second digital reputations, and the third cybersafety and the law.

School project teams attend a full-day workshop with their cyberleaders. This workshop provides a rationale and overview for the CFS program, discusses skill development in a whole-school approach to the prevention and reduction of cyberbullying, and provides an opportunity for school teams to begin planning their CFS whole-school activities.

Student component

In each study year, the CFS student component provides students (grades 8 and 9; aged 13–15 years) with a curriculum of information and strategies to develop their provictim attitudes and discourage probullying attitudes; teach them assertive and adaptive responses to cyberbullying; build their capacity to help other students; and enhance their resilience, positive communication, self-management, and social responsibility skills. This curriculum is presented by class teachers and accompanied by an activity booklet (student worksheets).

For grade 8, the curriculum includes eight learning modules relevant to all forms of bullying and cyberbullying:

1. *What's This All About*: Students define and learn about different forms of bullying. They begin to think about the consequences of bullying and how they can help those who are bullied.
2. *In the Know—The Stats on Bullying*: Students are provided with accurate information about the prevalence and consequences of bullying to help them understand how other people of the same age feel about bullying.
3. *Flaming—Just Jokes*: Students are presented with situations to help them identify what flaming/teasing/joking is and how it can hurt others, and to recognize the difference between joking around with friends and bullying.
4. *Your Voice, Your Choice:* Students are taught strategies to assess and respond to bullying situations. They are given an opportunity to practice strategies and are asked to develop their own plan for action.
5. *Being a Good Mate (BFF):* Students identify the roles of those involved in bullying, and investigate the role of the bystander and the effect bystanders can have on a bullying situation.
6. *Playing Judge and Jury:* Students examine what it feels like to be left out of a group. They consider how easy it is to judge others, what influences our judgments, and how this may lead to exclusion and discrimination. Students consider how they could help an excluded peer.
7. *In or Out:* Students define social "power" and how people use power in positive and negative ways to influence others. They examine peer influence and explore the positive and negative aspects of peer groups.
8. *Reflection:* Students reflect on what they have learned and prepare a presentation for members of the school community (e.g., other students or parents).

In grade 9, the learning modules are expanded to increase the cohort's understanding of online environments and ways to address cyberbullying:

- *My Online Status*: Students learn techniques to search for information about themselves online, and think about why their digital reputation is important to manage. Students learn strategies to use if they find unwanted content about themselves online.
- *Connect, Extend, and Challenge*: Students learn how to set privacy settings in Facebook through a series of web-based instruction clips. Students are challenged to extend their thinking on how they use these spaces, and what they could do if they or someone else was bullied in these spaces.
- *Helping Me, Helping You*: Students learn how to access support if they are being cyberbullied. This module takes students through a number of clips, podcasts, and activities showing them what it is like when they connect with support agencies such as Kids Helpline.
- *Cyberclips:* Through a series of clips and activities, students examine relationship and communication skills, and are encouraged to reflect on their own emotions and how to manage their responses to emotive situations.
- *Reality Bites*: Students learn about offline consequences for online actions. Students learn about cyberbullying and the law, and read about court cases where young people had behaved inappropriately online. Students are also asked to consider how they engage with the Internet and how information they put online could be used.

- *Standing By*: Students consider their responses to bullying situations as bystanders. The Activity Sheet and learning resources aim to guide their thinking and provide them with realistic supportive choices as bystanders. Students create a poster that encourages others to take action to support those who are being bullied.
- *Who, Me? Couldn't Be!:* Students are challenged to think about prejudices they may have; how these are influenced by society, their families or peers; and how they affect decision making. Through a critical thinking game, students are encouraged to take time to think before responding or reacting to stimuli.
- *Taking Control:* Students have the opportunity to revise all they have learnt through the curriculum while considering how this information could be used to lead others toward safe and enjoyable online experiences. The activities include a series of quizzes and clips, which cover each of the topics and activities designed to guide leadership in cyberspace.

In each year, students have access to the CFS website, which offers students, parents, and teachers in intervention schools new insights into what young people, families, and other adults can do to reduce cyberbullying and support young people who engage in or are the victims of cyberbullying. The website contains information, tutorials, practical strategies, and resources about ICT, cyberbullying and cybersafety, as well as the latest research findings and articles regarding cyberbullying and cybersafety. Students receive a Family Quiz Activities booklet, linked to the CFS website, encouraging parents to visit the website to complete the activities. The booklet is designed for each student to work through the activities with a parent/caregiver at home, to extend their classroom work. Eight family quizzes are included, with topics including "what kids get up to online," how to report cyberbullying, and places to get help.

In each intervention year, intervention schools are encouraged to send one staff member to a "train the trainer" Curriculum Training workshop. After the workshop, each school staff member is responsible for training the other teachers in their school who will be delivering the CFS curriculum. The focus of the Curriculum Training is to introduce and discuss the use of the learning modules, student activity books, family activity books, and a teacher's log for staff to document their implementation of the grade 8 curriculum.

Student cyberleaders

Educational resources that aim to address cyberbullying often fail to engage young people as codevelopers and cofacilitators, despite the evidence that adolescents are often more knowledgeable than adults about new technologies and online behaviors (Cross, Lester, Barnes, Cardoso, & Hadwen, 2015). In addition, organizations like UNICEF have emphasized the need to maximize young people's participation in projects that target or concern them (Hart, 1992). This helps to ensure that resulting programs or resources will be relevant, appropriate, effective, and sustainable. When such programs are school-based, providing young people with opportunities to contribute to policy and decision making, students' attachments to school, personal agency, and problem solving and social skills are enhanced (Cross et al., 2015; Mitra, 2004).

The CFS program therefore recruits and trains grade 10 students (aged 15–16 years) to act as "cyberleaders" for their school communities (for a full description, see Cross et al., 2015). In each intervention year, a staff member who acts as the project coordinator for their school nominates four to six grade 10 students who are interested in technology and likely to be positive role models. These students need to be able to attend training events, design and facilitate activities intended to raise awareness of cyberbullying prevention among peers, families, and their wider school community, and assist their school in the implementation of the CFS program.

Each cyberleader completes 6–12 hours of training during school hours, in workshops facilitated by two researchers/teachers and a specialized youth leadership trainer. At least one staff member from each school accompanies the leaders and participates in the workshops. The training provides:

- Information about the cyberleadership role and expectations
- Information about activities cyberleaders would be asked to tailor or develop for their school
- Strategies to improve peer leadership skills
- Strategies to address factors that might enhance or prevent the successful implementation of desired activities.

Within their school groups and with the support of their school's staff member/s, the cyberleaders use a purpose-built website to tailor and implement at least three whole-school CFS activities (approximately one every 3 months). These activities need to encourage students' positive use of technology and help them, their schools and parents address antisocial online behaviors (Cross, Epstein, Hearn, & Waters, 2011). The cyberleaders are also given opportunities during the workshops to network and share ideas with cyberleaders from other schools.

Cyberleaders are provided with ongoing access to the CFS website and a cyberleadership workbook. The workbook is designed to assist them in planning, developing, and implementing activities in their school, and contains activities to help the leaders evaluate their own values, strengths, and interests to determine which leadership roles in their group would suit them best. The cyberleaders typically develop or adapt suggested whole-school activities (e.g., school assembly presentations, newsletter items) with the aim of helping their school review and renew policies, increasing staff and parent knowledge about technology used by students, increasing students' awareness of their rights and responsibilities online, encouraging bystanders to respond appropriately to cyberbullying incidents, and encouraging students to seek help if they are targeted online. A school staff version of the workbook is provided to help staff identify ways to enhance cyberleaders' engagement and success.

Parent component

The parent component aims to increase parents' awareness of young people's technology use and enhance their ability to help their children address cyberbullying incidents (e.g., how to get help and how to respond). Parents of students involved in the study have access to the CFS website, work with their children on the Family Quiz Activities booklet, and receive newsletter information from the school. They are encouraged to attend a Parent Workshop, conducted by the staff and cyberleaders at their child's school. Students and staff are provided with a series of PowerPoint slides and extensive notes to help them facilitate their presentations, which cover the following topics:

- Information on technology and the world today
- Definitions—bullying, cyberbullying
- Statistics—bullying, cyberbullying, and correlational data
- Forms of cyberbullying
- Online risks and information on social networking sites, popular teenage sites, instant messenger, chat rooms, and gaming
- Information on bystanders
- Cyberbullying and the law
- Parent responses to cyberbullying
- Preventative strategies
- Communicating with your child
- Working with your child's school

Evidence for effectiveness

The effectiveness of the CFS program was evaluated using a 3-year group randomized controlled trial (2010–12) in Perth, Western Australia. All metropolitan nongovernment secondary schools were invited to participate if they had at least 90 students in grade 8 (aged 13 years), and 35 schools were recruited. Nineteen schools were randomized to an intervention and 16 to a comparison group. School principals were advised of their school's allocated group and those in the comparison group were informed they would receive the intervention, training, and resources upon completion of the project in 2012. Each intervention principal nominated a school staff member to act as the project's coordinator for their school community.

Over 3000 grade 8 students consented, and received parental consent, to participate. These students were tracked for 2 years until they were in grade 10 (aged 15 years). The whole-school and curriculum intervention, including the involvement of "cyberleaders," was delivered in 2010 and 2011 to the intervention schools. The intervention materials were adapted and disseminated, with training, to the comparison schools in 2012.

The primary outcome objective was to reduce, over a 2-year period, the proportion of intervention compared to comparison students who reported being cyberbullied in the previous school term. Additionally, over a 2-year period the project aimed to:

- Reduce the likelihood of *frequent* cyberbullying behavior (cyberbullying others and/or being bullied every few weeks or more often) among intervention students, relative to comparison students.
- Reduce the likelihood of frequent *face-to-face* bullying behavior (bullying others and/or being bullied every few weeks or more often) among the intervention students, relative to comparison students.
- Increase the number of intervention students who reported positive perceptions of social support and satisfaction with peer relations, relative to comparison students.
- Increase the number of intervention students who felt connected to the school, relative to comparison students.
- Increase the number of intervention students who sought help from others if they were cyberbullied, relative to comparison students.

The project also aimed to improve the knowledge, attitudes, skills, and self-efficacy of intervention school staff, relative to comparison school staff, to implement strategies that reduce cyber- and other forms of bullying.

Instruments and data collection

Several qualitative and quantitative instruments were developed to collect data from participating students, teachers, and other school staff at baseline (2010), posttest 1 (2011), and posttest 2 (2012).

Students

Data were collected from the grade 8 student cohort using web-based surveys at baseline, posttest 1 and posttest 2, as shown in Table 7.1. These surveys collected demographic information (e.g., students' age and gender, parents' employment), and information about students' use of technology, involvement in cyberbullying as victims or perpetrators, how they responded to bullying incidents, and symptoms of psychological distress. Cyberbullying victimization and perpetration behavior were measured using two 11-item scales (adapted from Smith, Mahdavi, Carvalho, & Tippett, 2006), which provided definitions and descriptions of different forms of bullying. Students were provided with information about how to seek help if the survey raised any concerns for them.

Trained project personnel administered the surveys in the students' classrooms according to a strict procedural and verbal protocol. Students with parental consent to participate were given a unique login ID and password to enter into the online survey site. Students without parental consent were given alternative activities or asked to continue with other work provided by their class teacher. Teachers were asked to remain in the classroom to help with behavior management. Confidentiality was maintained by the use of identification numbers and teachers were asked not to look at students' responses. Student survey data were downloaded by the project coordinator at the end of the data collection process.

Cyberleaders

In each study year, students acting as cyberleaders were surveyed, while attending their training workshop, about their proposed activities and confidence in acting as a cyberleader ($n=87$ in 2010, $n=138$ in 2011, and $n=48$ in 2012). Cyberleaders also completed survey evaluations of the training activities at the end of the workshop.

Table 7.1 CSF student survey completion in each project year

Year	Completed student surveys (*n*)
2010 (Grade 8)	3382
2011 (Grade 9)	2940
2012 (Grade 10)	2874

At the end of each year, they were invited to participate in a brief telephone interview to measure their progress and any barriers to activity implementation. Interviews were scheduled with the assistance of the project coordinator at each school and took approximately 10 min to complete.

School staff

School project teams were asked to complete a baseline survey during the training workshop they attended. This collected demographic data and information about their understanding of bullying and cyberbullying behaviors, their skills and self-efficacy in reducing these behaviors, and their commitment to implementing the CFS program in their school. They also completed evaluations of the training activities.

Teaching staff nominated to deliver the curriculum were asked to complete baseline surveys prior to curriculum training in their school and to return these using a reply paid envelope (2010, $n=51$). Follow-up surveys were mailed to the nominated staff and returned to the project personnel at posttest 1 (2011, $n=78$). The surveys collected demographic information and asked about the teacher's role at school, the average time they spent dealing with bullying and cyberbullying issues, their knowledge about bullying and cyberbullying, self-efficacy and skills in reducing cyberbullying, and attitudes toward bullying and cyberbullying. Participating teaching staff also completed evaluation surveys of the curriculum resources and training.

Finally, the project co-coordinators in each school were interviewed about their whole-school planning and activities at baseline (2010, $n=28$) and at both posttests ($n=25$ in 2011 and $n=33$ in 2012). Interviews were conducted by trained project staff using a standardized protocol, and data were collected on the actions that had been implemented in the respondent's school and the impact of these activities; the priority the school had placed on preventing and responding to bullying, and encouraging safer use of technology among students; the extent to which students had been involved in facilitating this process; how information about bullying/cyberbullying had been communicated to students, parents and staff; whether any professional learning had been provided to staff; whether the school had implemented new policies in relation to technology and bullying/cyberbullying; changes to the school's physical environment and supervision; and efforts to encourage a school ethos that promoted prosocial behavior.

Findings

For all participating schools, the percentage of students who reported being involved in cyberbullying victimization was reduced in grade 9 compared to grade 8 (30% and 25%, respectively). Similarly, fewer students were involved in bullying perpetration in grade 9 compared to grade 8 (11% and 9%, respectively). However, the CFS program resulted in significantly greater declines in the occurrence of cybervictimization and cyberperpetration cases from grade 8 to grade 9 (Cross et al., 2016). This positive outcome indicates the potential for whole-school programs to effectively prevent cyberbullying.

The intervention did not appear to impact the likelihood of cases of cyberbullying for the period between grades 9 and 10, and did not have an impact on the frequency or severity of cyberbullying victimization/perpetration for students who were involved in cyberbullying behaviors (Cross et al., 2016). These students may need more targeted support to change their bullying perpetration behavior or reduce their likelihood of being victimized.

Some difficulties were experienced by teachers in finding time to fit the intervention into their usual teaching program, which is likely to have attenuated the effectiveness of the CFS program (Cross, Cardoso, Shaw, & Thomas, 2013; Cross et al., 2016). Only about one-third of the intervention was implemented by classroom teachers, indicating a need for more support and training for teachers in future evaluations (Cross et al., 2016).

Cyberleaders

Evaluation of the cyberleader program indicated it had a positive impact on leaders' feelings of agency, belonging, and competence, while allowing them to make important and relevant contributions to their schools' actions to prevent cyberbullying (for a full discussion, see Cross et al., 2015). Most cyberleaders reported that the training they received was useful (88%), and that after completing this training they felt able to discuss ways to prevent cyberbullying with students (94%), parents (89%), and teachers (86%); discuss safe and appropriate technology use with students (94%); support whole-school activities to reduce bullying/cyberbullying (88%); encourage students to help someone who is being bullied/cyberbullied (95%); overcome challenges when planning and conducting activities (91%); plan and conduct activities to reduce bullying/cyberbullying (91%); get support when planning activities (88%); and work with their cyberleader team to plan and conduct activities at their school (94%) (Cross et al., 2015).

The leaders also identified key supports and barriers to being an effective school cyberleader, as shown in Table 7.2. Further research is needed to determine how to enhance school capacity to support student leaders in the design and implementation of cyberbullying prevention strategies.

Table 7.2 Perceived supports and barriers to being a cyberleader (Cross et al., 2015)

Supports	Barriers
Being listened to, respected, and trusted by peers	Lack of interest from peers
Having a connection with teachers	School ICT staff not helping or supporting
Having recognition and authority from school	Failure of communication between different parties in the school
Support from staff and parents	Not having support from staff and parents
Having confidence and leadership skills	Lack of confidence
Having a cohesive group of cyberleaders	Peer pressure from students
Having times in school when everybody comes together, e.g., assemblies	Lack of time

Implications and future research

The CFS longitudinal intervention research project provided important insights into ways to engage young people in the development and implementation of cyberbullying prevention in secondary schools, and identified some whole-school evidence-based strategies that appear to have reduced this behavior.

While the program's impact was significant, the effects were small, most likely due to poor implementation by teachers. Only about a third of this program's learning activities were implemented with fidelity by the intervention teachers. Just over 40% of Australian teachers in a national prevalence study reported they did not feel sufficiently skilled to deal with students' cyberbullying behavior (Cross et al., 2009). To mitigate this risk, the grade 9 CFS program was designed to be delivered to students using an online enquiry-based format. Teachers were only required to facilitate the learning by providing classroom time and helping students interact with the program website. The students, based on their interest in each lesson, effectively "self-taught" the program to themselves through their interaction with the purpose-built CFS program website. However, many teachers reported not being able to find sufficient time in their teaching curriculum to complete the eight learning activities. Some teachers indicated they could find almost no implementation time, as the class curriculum did not include the teaching of cybersafety in its scope and sequence of learning; hence, this program took teaching time from that which was needed to address other curriculum priorities. This difficulty is associated with growing curriculum demands and complex student needs in classrooms (Leadbeater & Gladstone, 2016) and is likely to have a negative effect on intervention outcomes. Providing sufficient classroom time to deliver the necessary level of teaching required to change or support student behavior remains a significant challenge for the effective teaching of cyberbullying prevention. Schools may benefit from the distillation of key intervention components into fewer lessons, and advocating for the inclusion of cybersafety in national education curriculum frameworks will be an important step to encourage teachers to include this content in their teaching.

Apart from the challenges of finding sufficient time to teach the content and skills to encourage positive online behaviors, it is important to provide teachers with sufficient in-service and preservice training to build their own cybersafety capacity, to increase their interest in this area of prevention, and to effectively implement effective cyber-related teaching. Assisting teachers to develop their own personal cybersafety to keep themselves safe online is also needed.

A follow-up study conducted by the CFS research team, named "Cyber Strong," developed and tested online resources to build school staff capacity to teach positive cyberbehaviors and online safety (see http://www.friendlyschools.com.au/cyberstrong). These Cyber Strong resources were found to be particularly helpful for teachers who worked in rural and remote areas and are unable to easily access professional learning.

The types of behaviors and the places young people are visiting online are dynamic, making it difficult for teachers to know what young people are doing online and how to support them positively in this environment. The involvement of students in a school's response to online behaviors enables school staff to not only increase their knowledge of young people's behaviors but also to actively involve students in actions that may reduce negative outcomes from these online behaviors. The CFS project involved students in resource development in order to increase the relevance of the resource to students, and in addition encouraged cyberleaders to disseminate some of the program's whole-school policy and school engagement activities. Leaders were encouraged, for example, to lead parent and staff meetings by sharing their knowledge and ideas, especially to help younger students. In some schools, the leaders were engaged well. However, in other schools, students were not given the opportunities to show leadership but rather, had tokenistic leadership roles that were highly directed by teachers. Given school staff have traditionally controlled the teaching and learning provided to students, future research is needed to investigate ways to successfully support students to develop and support teaching in areas where they have expertise, such as in online environments. Moreover, it would be essential to prepare teachers for this change in student roles, allowing students to develop agency and contribute to their own and others' learning.

As teachers are often unaware of students' involvement in covert bullying behaviors like cyberbullying (Barnes et al., 2012; DeSmet et al., 2015), it is critical that interventions can train students to be proactive and take positive action as bystanders/witnesses if they observe someone being treated badly online. It appears that young people frequently witness cyberbullying but few intervene (Lenhart et al., 2011; O'Moore, 2012), with intervention depending on the online context, the severity of the bullying, the bystanders' relationship to those involved, and their gender (Bastiaensens et al., 2014; DeSmet et al., 2014). Some young people indicate they don't get involved for fear of also becoming a target of the bullying or because they don't know what action to take (DeSmet et al., 2014; Salmivalli, 2010). Since it is easier for bystanders to morally disengage when they witness negative behaviors online (Bussey, Fitzpatrick, & Raman, 2015; Runions & Bak, 2015), which in turn may erode their motivation to support targets in the online environment, it is important to include and test learning activities that aim to encourage and enable young people to assist when they witness cyberbullying (Bussey et al., 2015). Future research is needed to identify ways, such as involving student cyber/peer leaders, to help teachers more effectively identify and support students who are bullied in online environments.

Research to reduce cyberbullying must focus on actions that can be taken by families, those who work with young people, and the wider community, to prevent and reduce the harms from all forms of bullying, particularly given most cyberbullying behavior occurs outside school hours.

Finally, as young people are now using online environments (especially social networking sites such as Instagram) that encourage the exchange of images, it is important to investigate ways to prevent harm from image sharing online. In particular, previous research has identified that picture/video clip bullying can have a greater negative impact on young people than other forms of cyberbullying (Slonje & Smith, 2008). This is likely due to the large audience involved in such instances, the public nature of this form of bullying, and the possible depiction of young people in embarrassing or compromising situations (Slonje & Smith, 2008).

While the CFS research has many strengths, including its large longitudinal sample, prospective study design, random assignment to condition, appropriate control conditions, and analyses that adjusted for the clustering of individuals in schools, it has some limitations. First, the generalizability of these findings is limited as the sample comprised only nongovernment (private or independent) secondary schools. Second, the student data were self-reported and may have been subject to social desirability and other biases affecting accuracy (Cornell & Bandyopadhyay, 2010).

Nevertheless, this study demonstrates the potential for whole-school interventions like the CFS program to engage the whole-school community in the prevention of cyberbullying, with positive outcomes for students' well-being. The CFS program provides a means of empowering teachers, parents, and students to play an active role in the prevention and reduction of cyberbullying through user-friendly materials and accessible and effective training. With the increasing centrality of ICT in young people's lives and learning, Australian schools need to have the resources and capacity to prevent harmful and antisocial online behaviors among their students.

Acknowledgments

We thank the school staff, students, and families who participated in the CFS project. We also acknowledge the student and other stakeholder advisory committees and the research staff for their valuable contributions to the project, especially Dr Laura Thomas. The CFS research was supported by the Western Australian Health Promotion Foundation (Healthway; research grant 18940).

References

Barnes, A., Cross, D., Lester, L., Hearn, L., Epstein, M., & Monks, H. (2012). The invisibility of covert bullying among students: Challenges for school intervention. *Australian Journal of Guidance and Counselling*, *22*, 206–226. https://doi.org/10.1017/jgc.2012.27.

Bastiaensens, S., Vandebosch, H., Poels, K., Van Cleemput, K., Desmet, A., & De Bourdeaudhuij, I. (2014). Cyberbullying on social network sites. An experimental study into bystanders' behavioural intentions to help the victim or reinforce the bully. *Computers in Human Behavior*, *31*, 259–271. https://doi.org/10.1016/j.chb.2013.10.036.

Bauman, S., & Del Rio, A. (2006). Preservice teachers' responses to bullying scenarios: Comparing physical, verbal, and relational bullying. *Journal of Educational Psychology*, *98*, 219–231. https://doi.org/10.1037/0022-0663.98.1.219.

Bussey, K., Fitzpatrick, S., & Raman, A. (2015). The role of moral disengagement and self-efficacy in cyberbullying. *Journal of School Violence*, *14*, 30–46. https://doi.org/10.1080/15388220.2014.954045.

Cassidy, W., Brown, K., & Jackson, M. (2012). 'Under the radar': Educators and cyberbullying in schools. *School Psychology International*, *33*, 520–532. https://doi.org/10.1177/0143034312445245.

Cornell, D. G., & Bandyopadhyay, S. (2010). The assessment of bullying. In S. R. Jimerson, S. M. Swearer, & D. L. Espelage (Eds.), *Handbook of bullying in schools: An international perspective* (pp. 265–276). New York: Routledge, Taylor & Francis.

Cross, D., Cardoso, P., Shaw, T., & Thomas, L. (2013). *An empirical intervention to reduce cyberbullying in adolescentsFinal report to Healthway*. Perth, WA: Edith Cowan University, Child Health Promotion Research Centre.

Cross, D., Epstein, M., Hearn, L., & Waters, S. (2011). *Cyber friendly parents' project: Final report to the Telstra foundation*. Perth, WA: Edith Cowan University, Child Health Promotion Research Centre.

Cross, D., Lester, L., Barnes, A., Cardoso, P., & Hadwen, K. (2015). If it's about me, why do it without me? Genuine student engagement in school cyberbullying education. *The International Journal of Emotional Education*, *7*, 35–51.

Cross, D., Shaw, T., Hadwen, K., Cardoso, P., Slee, P., Roberts, C., et al. (2016). Longitudinal impact of the Cyber Friendly Schools program on adolescents' cyberbullying behavior. *Aggressive Behavior*, *42*, 166–180. https://doi.org/10.1002/ab.21609.

Cross, D., Shaw, T., Hearn, L., Epstein, M., Monks, H., Lester, L., et al. (2009). *Australian covert bullying prevalence study (ACBPS)*. Western Australia: Report Prepared for the Department of Education, Employment and Workplace Relations (DEEWR).

DeSmet, A., Aelterman, N., Bastiaensens, S., Van Cleemput, K., Poels, K., Vandebosch, H., et al. (2015). Secondary school educators' perceptions and practices in handling cyberbullying among adolescents: A cluster analysis. *Computers & Education*, *88*, 192–201. https://doi.org/10.1016/j.compedu.2015.05.006.

DeSmet, A., Veldeman, C., Poels, K., Bastiaensens, S., Van Cleemput, K., Vandebosch, H., et al. (2014). Determinants of self-reported bystander behavior in cyberbullying incidents amongst adolescents. *Cyberpsychology, Behavior and Social Networking*, *17*, 207–215. https://doi.org/10.1089/cyber.2013.0027.

Hart, R. A. (1992). *Children's participation: From Tokenism to citizenshipInnocenti Essays No. 4.*. Florence: NICEF International Child Development Centre.

Leadbeater, B. J., & Gladstone, E. J. (2016). Supporting schools for the widespread implementation of evidence-based mental health promotion programs. In R. Shute & P. T. Slee (Eds.), *Mental health and wellbeing through schools: The way forward* (pp. 27–39). London: Routledge.

Lenhart, A., Madden, M., Smith, A., Purcell, K., Zickuhr, K., & Rainie, L. (2011). *Teens, kindness and cruelty on social network sites: How American teens navigate the new world of digital citizenship*. Washington, DC: Pew Internet and American Life Project.

Mitra, D. L. (2004). The significance of students: Can increasing "student voice" in schools lead to gains in youth development? *Teachers College Record*, *106*, 651–688.

O'Moore, M. (2012). Cyber-bullying: The situation in Ireland. *Pastoral Care in Education*, *30*, 209–223. https://doi.org/10.1080/02643944.2012.688065.

Ortega-Ruiz, R., Del Rey, R., & Casas, J. A. (2012). Knowing, building and living together on internet and social networks: The ConRed cyberbullying prevention program. *International Journal of Conflict and Violence*, *6*, 302–312. https://doi.org/10.4119/UNIBI/ijcv.250.

Rigby, K., & Slee, P. (2008). Interventions to reduce bullying. *International Journal of Adolescent Medicine and Health*, *20*, 165–184. https://doi.org/10.1515/IJAMH.2008.20.2.165.

Runions, K. C., & Bak, M. (2015). Online moral disengagement, cyberbullying, and cyber-aggression. *Cyberpsychology, Behavior and Social Networking*, *18*, 400–405. https://doi.org/10.1089/cyber.2014.0670.

Salmivalli, C. (2010). Bullying and the peer group: A review. *Aggression and Violent Behavior*, *15*, 112–120. https://doi.org/10.1016/j.avb.2009.08.007.

Slonje, R., & Smith, P. K. (2008). Cyberbullying: Another main type of bullying? *Scandinavian Journal of Psychology*, *49*, 147–154. https://doi.org/10.1111/j.1467-9450.2007.00611.x.

Smith, P. K., Mahdavi, J., Carvalho, M., & Tippett, N. (2006). *An investigation into cyberbullying, its forms, awareness and impact, and the relationship between age and gender in cyberbullying*. London: DfES. Research Brief No. RBX03-06.

Ttofi, M., & Farrington, D. (2009). What works in preventing bullying: Effective elements of anti-bullying programmes. *Journal of Aggression, Conflict and Peace Research*, *1*(1), 13–24. https://doi.org/10.1108/17596599200900003.

Ttofi, M. M., & Farrington, D. P. (2011). Effectiveness of school-based programs to reduce bullying: A systematic and meta-analytic review. *Journal of Experimental Criminology*, *7*, 27–56. https://doi.org/10.1007/s11292-010-9109-1.

Vreeman, R. C., & Carroll, A. E. (2007). A systematic review of school-based interventions to prevent bullying. *Archives of Pediatrics & Adolescent Medicine*, *161*, 78–88. https://doi.org/10.1001/archpedi.161.1.78.

Williford, A., Elledge, L. C., Boulton, A. J., DePaolis, K. J., Little, T. D., & Salmivalli, C. (2013). Effects of the KiVa antibullying program on cyberbullying and cybervictimization frequency among Finnish youth. *Journal of Clinical Child & Adolescent Psychology*, *42*, 820–833. https://doi.org/10.1080/15374416.2013.787623.

World Health Organization. (2004). *The physical school environment: An essential element of a health-promoting school*. Geneva: World Health Organisation.

A model for providing bullying prevention programs to K-12 education while training future educators

8

Meghan K. McCoy, Elizabeth Kandel Englander*, Katalin Parti†*
*Bridgewater State University, Bridgewater, MA, United States, †National Institute of Criminology, Budapest, Hungary

Name of program: The Massachusetts Aggression Reduction Center
Type of program: Whole school approach
Suitable for ages: Kindergarten–Grade 12

The Massachusetts Aggression Reduction Center

In the United States and elsewhere, there are limited educational resources for programming and curricula that focus on the social and emotional needs of children and adolescents. In the face of this challenge, it seems wise to explore interventions that make use of existing and low-cost resources. These realities prompted Dr. Elizabeth Englander, a Professor of Psychology at Bridgewater State University, to develop the Massachusetts Aggression Reduction Center (MARC) in 2004. MARC is an academic center staffed by faculty and students, including graduate and undergraduate students in several fields. MARC faculty and staff bring education, training, research, curricula, and other resources to the primary and secondary education community and other stakeholders (e.g., pediatric physicians, social workers, attorneys, etc.), while providing graduate and undergraduate students with the opportunity to engage in supervised field work.

Center philosophy

It is the Center's mission to provide high-quality, evidence-based programming for students, faculty, administrators, and parents in K-12 education at little to no cost. The focus is on understanding and preventing social problems among children, with a particular emphasis on bullying, cyberbullying, and the central and complicated role that digital communications play in the social lives of children and teens today (Englander, 2013).

All of MARC's programs are based on the principles promoted by researcher Dan Olweus and his concept of the "whole-school" approach to bullying prevention (Olweus, 1993). When MARC works with a school, we train faculty, students, and

Reducing Cyberbullying in Schools. https://doi.org/10.1016/B978-0-12-811423-0.00008-0

administrators and provide education for parents and community members. The goal is to alter the school climate, i.e., behaviors, beliefs, and attitudes, from one that promotes bullying into a climate that discourages it—the only effective method uncovered by decades of research (Lumsden, 2002). MARC's whole-school program is also based on the body of research showing that bullying is a systemic problem (Atlas & Pepler, 1998), so the most successful programs involve *all school personnel and the entire student body as one community* (Cromwell, 1999; Hazler, 1998; Pepler, Craig, & Connolly, 1997).

Characteristics of MARC programming

First, all programming and curricula are grounded in ongoing, up-to-date research conducted with students from elementary, secondary, and postsecondary schools and developed with careful attention paid to the developmental needs and realities of children and teens.

Second, MARC focuses on educating and training all stakeholders. As others have emphasized for decades, MARC understands that in order to create lasting change, prevention efforts must be focused on the community as a whole (Bradshaw, 2015; Cromwell, 1999; Hazler, 1998; Olweus, 2005; Pepler et al., 1997; Swearer, Espelage, & Napolitano, 2009; Ttofi & Farrington, 2011; Letendre, Ostrander, & Mickens, 2016).

Third, programming for adults emphasizes the importance of building emotional connections with students. Adults are encouraged to talk to children on a regular basis, to offer advice and guidance based on their own experiences, to coach and support them when they are dealing with bullying situations, and to check back in with students after reports of bullying.

Fourth, MARC trains graduate and undergraduate students to work with Kindergarten through 12th grade students. University students, who receive course credits for their work in MARC, are powerful role models to younger students in a way that many older authority figures (such as parents and teachers) cannot be. Utilizing slightly older peers to work with younger students is called the *high-status peer model* and was chosen for a number of reasons. In addition to the benefits for younger students (Andreou, Vlachou, & Didaskalou, 2005; Cowie & Olafsson, 2000; Salmivalli, 2001), it allows MARC to train and educate future professionals. Many of the students who are involved with the center plan to work with children and teens, and this work provides them a unique internship-like opportunity while receiving course credit or tuition assistance for their graduate programs.

The program also offers peer mentor trainings for middle and high school students. Peer mentors are recruited and selected by the school staff, to be trained on the core problem of bullying and cyberbullying, how to early recognize and handle difficult situations among peers, and how to stand up for those who in need. Peer mentors are trained at the University campus. This training model is an effective way to teach students skills and strategies to resolve situations on their own (Cowie & Hutson, 2005; Wentzel & Caldwell, 1997).

Program description and delivery

Faculty trainings

Professional development opportunities for teachers are intended to increase awareness and knowledge about bullying and cyberbullying; provide adults with effective and practical intervention strategies; and introduce adults to cutting edge research about bullying and cyberbullying.

Content can always be tailored to a school's specific needs. For example, if a school is struggling with a recent type of problem (such as problems on social media), we address those issues in more detail.

Train the trainer

MARC has also developed a Train the Trainer Faculty Training program that prepares professionals to train their colleagues about bullying and cyberbullying prevention. This training is designed to deliver an even more in-depth understanding of bullying and cyberbullying than traditional faculty trainings.

Parent and community workshops

As part of the center's efforts to improve school culture, presentations for parents and other community groups have been developed. The emphasis of these presentations is on practical, concrete knowledge. Tips for parents are offered to assist them in having discussions with their children, approaching schools for help, and assisting school administrators to successfully resolve bullying situations. Programs can also be tailored to respond to specific concerns the parents or schools may have.

Student workshops and events

Student programming in MARC is distinctive in that it is delivered by older students and not by professionals, who can be viewed as authority figures. College students, in contrast, are more likely to be viewed as high-status peers (Hoff, Reese-Weber, Schneider, & Stagg, 2009; Levi, Kaplan, & Peter, 2004; Sasso & Rude, 1987; Shi & Xie, 2011).

In addition, these student programs cover negative behaviors but emphasize positive behaviors (i.e., they do not simply tell children not to bully others, but cover a variety of ways students can help themselves and others, and feature stories of similar age students who are actively engaging in positive bullying prevention activities). Although active participation and empowerment of students is always emphasized, all student programs are accompanied by follow-up guides for teachers and parents. These guides review the main points and provide discussion questions for teachers to use in the classroom as a follow-up.

Student programs are offered in the following formats: large group presentations (assemblies); interactive group presentations (assemblies); small group leadership training; student contests; and K-5, 6-12 Advisory, and High School Cyber Skills Curricula. Advisory periods seen in many US schools and are short periods of time designated for lessons and activities related to academic scaffolding and social and emotional learning. Because these periods are common in many schools, but are often no more than 20 or 30 min, MARC created a curriculum specifically designed to be implemented during Advisory periods.

Large group presentations and interactive assemblies

Large group student presentations are offered for students K-12. All presentations are developmentally appropriate, grade-specific, and discuss bullying and cyberbullying in practical ways. The focus is on helping students understand the issues, develop the skills necessary to combat bullying and cyberbullying, and how to treat their peers, even those who are not their friends, with respect and civility.

Presentations for kindergartners and first graders are about 20–25 min long and introduce students to the concept of bullying, better understood at this age as being mean to someone on purpose. The focus is also on how bullying can make people feel and exploring the difference between physical and verbal bullying. The idea of being mean online is briefly introduced. The presentation ends with a practical, concrete discussion of how to be a good friend to everyone, how to help victims of bullying, and how to get help from adults when necessary.

For older elementary aged students in grades 2–4, the presentation is about 30–35 min. This presentation builds on the ideas introduced to younger students with a more in-depth focus on cyberbullying and other digital behaviors. Students are provided with detailed information about how to tell the difference between bullying/cyberbullying and other common social problems like conflict, drama, and teasing. The different roles students play in bullying (i.e., bully, victim, bystander, and egger, a word used by MARC to describe students who may inadvertently support bullying by laughing along, spreading rumors, etc.) are identified and discussed. Tips for helping classmates and oneself are offered with a focus on the low risk strategies students can use to combat bullying.

Presentations for students in the 5th and 6th grades are about 45 min long and continue to build on concepts presented to younger students. Specifically, the presentation goes into great detail about digital aggression and cyberbullying in addition to general information about bullying and peer aggression. Students are introduced to the concept of relational aggression, peer behaviors designed to show contempt for others and create social problems and emotional distress for its victims. The negative consequences of these behaviors are discussed and emphasis is placed on understanding that these behaviors, while not considered bullying/cyberbullying, can have devastating impacts for students. The role of social media in students' lives and the importance of protecting privacy online are discussed. Students are provided concrete ways that they can use different avenues, e.g., the arts, athletics, and peer support, to combat bullying and offered tools and tips for helping themselves and others to deal with challenging peer behaviors online and in person.

Programs for older middle school and secondary students typically run about 55 min. Building on concepts introduced in earlier grades, these presentations go into great detail about cyberbullying and other digital problems. Common pitfalls of communicating online are discussed. Students are asked to think critically about the unique characteristics of digital communications and why they can lead to problems with peers. Misinterpretations, the use of anonymous apps, and the tricks our minds play to make us think online communication is private are presented with the use of real life examples. Students are asked to think deeply about how online behaviors can impact themselves and their classmates. Students in high school are pushed to think of the long-term impacts of online behaviors on their future opportunities. Sexting, the electronic distribution of nude or seminude images, is discussed. The rules and laws regarding these behaviors are introduced. Students are pushed to think about other negative consequences of these behaviors (i.e., negative emotional responses) and the reasons students report engaging in such behaviors (i.e., pressure from romantic partners). Rules and laws regarding bullying and cyberbullying in Massachusetts are presented. The presentation concludes with concrete, positive strategies for dealing with bullies at school and online.

Small group peer leadership training

For students in grades 5–12, MARC offers the option to have small student groups trained by experienced graduate and undergraduate students. These trainings are designed to help students identify and label what they view as the most important social issues going on in their schools, and to work with them to develop, and eventually implement, student-led programming in their own community. These sessions start by educating the student trainees and then these students, working in small groups facilitated by MARC students, are led through a process of identifying issues of concern, and then grouping and organizing their concerns into categories (e.g., people talking about each other, rumors being spread online, and people telling others' secrets could be reduced to "problems with rumors and gossip"). After the categories of problems are established, the groups then brainstorm about solutions and programs to address them. These solutions and programs are developed, chosen, and implemented by students, which is the source of their power. Ultimately, student groups leave with action plans that discuss what program they want to implement, the resources and possible obstacles to implementation, and the roles of the students and their faculty advisors. Some examples of programs include students creating presentations and plays to be delivered to younger peers; implementing "pay it forward" and "small acts of kindness" campaigns at their schools; and forming action-oriented student groups dedicated to combating bullying.

Student contests

In an effort to encourage the recognition and promotion of positive peer behaviors, the Center also runs annual contests for primary and secondary grade students. Contests for 3rd–5th grade students ask age-appropriate questions, and students respond by making posters or writing poems. Examples of questions asked are:

- Third Grade: Has a friend ever helped you when someone else was being mean, or just when you felt badly? How did they help you?
- Fourth Grade: How do teachers help kids who are being bullied? Does it help to talk to a teacher?
- Fifth Grade: How would you teach younger kids about the best and most positive ways to use social media? What mistakes would you advise them to avoid?

Secondary grades write, direct, film, and edit Public Service Announcements on a chosen topic. All entries are judged by MARC staff and students, and winners are invited to visit campus for Award Ceremonies (for younger students) and the Youth Summit (for older students). The Youth Summit also serves to recognize and celebrate the accomplishments of students all over Massachusetts in bullying and cyberbullying prevention.

Curricula for students

Finally, MARC has created curricula that are available to schools and educators for free upon request. Curricula are intended for use in the classroom for younger students (K-5) and in the classroom or during advisory periods for older students (6–12). All outcomes research establishing the efficacy of these curricula is posted on MARC's website (www.marccenter.org). Generally, these curricula address issues such as the lack of knowledge about bullying and cyberbullying behaviors; secrecy and shame surrounding all types of peer abuse; inadvertent and overt peer support for these behaviors; lack of understanding about the protective role of friendships; overuse of the terms bullying and cyberbullying; and commonly accepted myths, especially about online interactions (e.g., "it's no big deal if it's just online"). Topics for secondary students also include tagging and facial recognition, self-focus online, strong feelings and social media, fighting online, and anonymous apps. These curricula are simply requested through the website's request function, and then pdf versions of the curriculum are sent to the requester through secure download links. Trainings are held at the University for school staff and MARC staff are always available to answer questions or concerns that arise.

Among all the student programs and services offered by MARC, these curricula are the most often used beyond Massachusetts. They are requested by schools located in approximately half of the states in the United States and in several other countries.

Outcomes research

MARC is committed to ensuring the highest quality programming possible and we engage in ongoing outcomes research in order to achieve this goal. Qualitative and quantitative data are collected to assess how well programming is meeting needs, resulting in increased knowledge for participants. Research conducted at the center is primarily self-assessment and is helpful in ongoing efforts to improve program delivery. Research is conducted in the form of online surveys as well as anecdotally in the field, as described earlier. In addition, The Fulbright Foundation and the Hungarian Eötvös Scholarship funded a researcher to study MARC's programs during the 2013–14 school year. By the methods of pre- and post-tests, students and teachers' knowledge and improvement was assessed, testing the effectiveness of the student Assemblies and the Train the Trainer programs. Additional one-on-one semistructured qualitative interviews were conducted with teachers and school counselors who participated in In-service Faculty Trainings. This section will present both the qualitative and quantitative results from that year-long study as well as other data that has been collected.

Evaluating programming for faculty

Train the trainer

Eighty-four educators attended two separate "Train the Trainer" workshops in November and December 2013. The gender ratio of the participants at the training was 24%–76%, with female participants in the majority. Most participants were between 31 and 40 years old ($n = 34$; 42%); followed by the age group 41–50 years ($n = 17$; 21%), and then that of 51–65 years ($n = 15$; 18.5%).

Participants completed a questionnaire before and after the training (a within-subjects' pre- and post-test design), which enabled a comparison of expectations for the training to the achievement of those expectations. The posttest included semistructured questions that allowed for the gathering of qualitative data about participants' experiences.

Table 8.1 shows the results of the comparison between expectations and outcomes. Overall, the training modestly exceeded expectations, with subjects reporting they had gained knowledge beyond their initial expectations. The largest positive differences were for subjects who wanted to learn more about cyberbullying, to learn to differentiate between bullying and other behaviors, to learn information related to specific problems occurring in their schools, to learn how to recognize early signs of cyberbullying problems, and to learn how to help resolve problems. To varying degrees, the content did not meet expectations regarding information on helping parents deal with bullying, providing information on helping students resolve incidents of cyberbullying, understanding how cyberbullying impacts school climate, and learning how to help students make more mature decisions (see Table 8.1).

For 64% of respondents (53 out of 83), this was not their first experience with a bullying prevention program. Generally, MARC's training received excellent marks. Participants were generally much more satisfied with the training than they had been with past programs. The trainer's preparedness, organization of material, and quality of information provided received the highest ratings (see Table 8.2).

Interestingly, only 55% of the respondents believed that they were in general more prepared on the topic by the end of the workshop. This might be explained by the qualitative data gathered, including open-ended questions in the self-report questionnaire; notably, 22% of the participants felt they needed more time to digest the high volume of information they received at the training; 33% of the participants also reported a desire for even more practical content.

Table 8.1 Participant gains during training (expected vs. achieved)

Statement	Expected (*n*)	Gained (*n*)	How much the gains exceeded the expectations? (pre- and post-test of participants)
I am not particularly interested	1	1	0
I am generally interested	4	7	+3
…to learn information related to specific problems occurred in my school	32	44	+12
…to learn how (cyber) bullying influence school climate	65	64	−1
…to learn the side effects of (cyber) bullying and how pupils experience them	55	57	+2
…to learn how to avoid premature decisions	57	53	−4
…to be better able to help parents in understanding and solving	66	59	−7
…to learn how to help pupils solve (cyber) bullying more effectively	67	55	−12
…to learn what educators can do when confronting such problems	65	68	+3
…to learn to differentiate between bullying and other types of conflicts	61	77	+16
…to learn how to early recognize potential (cyber) bullying problems	67	74	+7
…to learn how to help resolve problems	65	72	+7
…to develop a better understanding of (cyber) bullying	65	80	+25
Mean (How much the gains exceeded the expectations?)			+3.6

In-service faculty training

MARC does its best to take advantage of the limited time available for teacher training, and many schools where we train teachers also engage MARC for periodic telephone consultation and support. Fortunately, even while teachers acknowledge their need for more ongoing training, they also report that the in-service trainings were relevant and useful. Qualitative information gathered has included the following comments:

Table 8.2 Participant satisfaction with training

How satisfied the participant was with the train-the-trainer workshop?						
	1 (Not satisfied at all)	**2 (Somewhat satisfied)**	**3 (Satisfied enough)**	**4 (Very much satisfied)**	**No answer**	**Total**
Was the program well organized?	0 (0.0%)	1 (1.2%)	10 (11.9%)	73 (86.9%)	0 (0.0%)	84 (100.0%)
Were the topics relevant?	0 (0.0%)	5 (6.%)	11 (13.1%)	68 (81.0%)	0 (0.0%)	84 (100.0%)
Was at least 25% of the material new or new perspective?	1 (1.2%)	9 (10.7%)	30 (35.7%)	44 (52.4%)	0 (0.0%)	84 (100.0%)
Were the trainers informative?	0 (0.0%)	1 (1.2%)	3 (3.6%)	80 (95.2%)	0 (0.0%)	84 (100.0%)
Were the trainers prepared?	0 (0.0%)	0 (0.0%)	2 (2.4%)	82 (97.6%)	0 (0.0%)	84 (100.0%)
Was the material presented in an understandable way?	0 (0.0%)	2 (2.4%)	8 (9.5%)	74 (88.1%)	0 (0.0%)	84 (100.0%)
Were the questions handled satisfactorily?	1 (1.2%)	3 (3.6%)	22 (26.2%)	58 (69.0%)	0 (0.0%)	84 (100.0%)
Was the room adequate?	1 (1.2%)	13 (15.5%)	36 (42.9%)	34 (40.5%)	0 (0.0%)	84 (100.0%)
Was the food adequate?	1 (1.2%)	3 (3.6%)	16 (19.0%)	64 (76.2%)	0 (0.0%)	84 (100.0%)
Were the starting and ending times convenient?	1 (1.2%)	0 (0.0%)	13 (15.5%)	70 (83.3%)	0 (0.0%)	84 (100.0%)
Was your registration handled smoothly?	1 (1.2%)	2 (2.4%)	5 (6.0%)	75 (89.3%)	1 (1.2%)	84 (100.0%)

The material is research-based with proven results and the program adapts to the needs of the target audience. I appreciate that the presentations incorporate the latest findings and are never perceived as canned.

It is notable that answers to open-ended questions tend to focus on the two distinctive characteristics of the MARC faculty training: the emphasis on data and research (versus unsubstantiated beliefs or abstract theory) and the practical strategies for dealing with antisocial behaviors. It seems that even though these are one-time trainings, they do appear to meet many (if not all) of the teachers' needs.

As part of other ongoing outcomes research, pre- and post-test data were collected from a group of 22 middle and high school teachers, nurses, and guidance counselors from a small secondary school in Massachusetts. They were trained during a professional development in-service in 2012. Questions for the pre- and post-test were created, based on the factual concepts in the training curriculum. Items were multiple choice and designed to detect increase in knowledge. Overall, data showed that knowledge about bullying and cyberbullying increased significantly after the faculty training, from a mean score of 7.09 on the pretest to a mean of 11.05 on the posttest. A paired t-test showed that the difference between conditions was significant ($t=10.89$, $df=21$, and $p<0.0001$). The difference showed that participants improved their scores by an average of four correct answers following the faculty training.

Evaluating programming for students

Large group presentations

In addition to the evaluation of faculty programs, we conducted an evaluation of several assemblies held for 6th & 7th graders at a middle school in Massachusetts. The school volunteered to participate in the evaluation, and the analysis involved anonymous, self-report, pre- and post-test questionnaires on the prevalence and patterns of students' online activities posing risk (e.g., having own cell phone, playing games online, using SNS sites, chat with people who they know and don't), whether they feel their school is responsive in helping to stop bullying and cyberbullying, if they ever experienced online embarrassing activities, who they spoke to about a bullying or cyberbullying incident, their perception of frequency of bullying and cyberbullying among their peers, whether they discussed online safety issues (such as being private online, predators online etc.) with adults, their practical knowledge on what students can do for each other in a bullying situation, their legal knowledge on activities widespread among the youth (e.g., video sharing and downloading), their perception of being safe in cyberspace (i.e., less likely be punished due to violation of law), and what they personally liked to see in an antibullying school program (Table 8.3).

Attrition was low between the pretest and posttest (only 12 out of 380 pretest subjects failed to complete the posttest). The posttest was conducted within 2–3 weeks after the assembly was held.

One interesting finding concerned students' preferences for reporting a bullying or cyberbullying incident. In a multiresponse question we asked "Have you ever spoken to someone about an incident of bullying and cyberbullying? If yes, indicate who

Table 8.3 Changes in attitudes among students

Statement	Do you agree with the statement? Pre-test (*n*, %)	Do you agree with the statement? Post-test (*n*, %)	Rate of development (pre- and post-test)
Bystanders CAN change bullying/cyberbullying incidents at all	220 (57.9%)	256 (69.6%)	+11.7%
Bullying is when a person/ group uses power to hurt another person repeatedly	343 (90.3%)	328 (89.1%)	−1.2%
Texting a lot when we are mad can make us feel worse	149 (39.2%)	91 (24.8%)	−14.5%
Bullying is sometimes criminal harassment or a civil rights violation	229 (60.3%)	308 (83.7%)	+23.4%
Once we post something online it could be there online forever, even if we "deleted" it	272 (71.6%)	305 (82.9%)	+11.3%
Passwords should be kept private (not to be shared and should be changed periodically)	179 (47.1%)	307 (83.4%)	+36.3%
We are less likely to be punished due to violation of law in cyberspace	28 (7.4%)	8 (2.1%)	+5.3%
Mean (How much is the development between pre- and post-test?)			+10.3%

you decided to speak with." The pretest revealed their marked preference for discussing bullying and cyberbullying incidents with their parents and peers, regardless of whether they were the target or a bystander. Students' roles were identified by asking whether they witnessed something written online or in a text message that may have been embarrassing to them or someone else. Almost two-thirds of targets and almost half of bystanders preferred discussions with parents, and more than half of targets and one-third of bystanders preferred discussions with peers.

Participants were somewhat less interested in reporting bullying and cyberbullying to other trusted adults (e.g., counselor, relative). In general, students indicated a stronger preference for talking to school adults when they were the target. The content of MARC student programming consistently emphasizes the positive actions that bystanders, witnesses, friends, and peers can take in reporting bullying and helping targets; possibly because of this, the posttest results detected change in reporting preferences. A few weeks after the assembly, the respondents indicated an increased willingness to discuss bullying and cyberbullying with all possible parties, especially when they were bystanders of cyberbullying incidents. The proportion of students

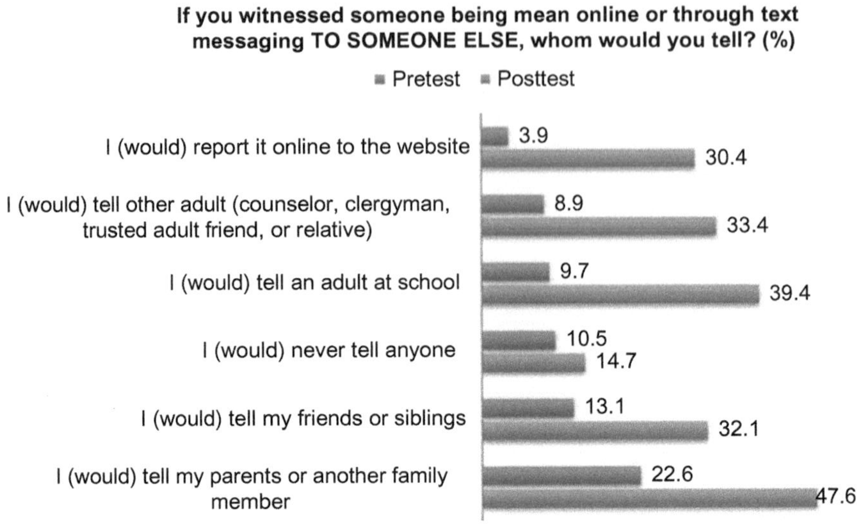

Fig. 8.1 Changes in willingness to report among students.

Table 8.4 Numbers of students participating in pre- and post-test evaluations

	Students participating in both test phases				
	Grade		**Gender**		
	6th Grade	**7th Grade**	**Boys**	**Girls**	**N.A.**
Pre-test phase	188 (49.5%)	192 (50.5%)	199 (52.4%)	178 (46.8%)	3 (0.8%)
Post-test phase	181 (33.3%)	187 (34.4%)	186 (50.5%)	182 (49.5%)	0 (0.0%)

agreeing that they would talk to parents, peers, and adults at school if they witnessed someone being mean online or through text messaging to someone else all increased between the pre- and post-test (Fig. 8.1).

Why did willingness to report increase, particularly to school personnel? MARC's trainers stress the importance of school climate and how significantly a bullying/cyberbullying incident can impact the entire community. In other words, they emphasize that the actual impact of such an incident or engaging in other negative peer behaviors can be very broad, despite the fact that it may only affect a few persons directly. It is possible that, after the presentation, students better understood the significance of involving other community members (such as teachers or other school staff) in the management of bullying and conflicts. Another possibility is that when students witness their teachers learning alongside with them during the programming, that co-learning experience may increase their comfort in reporting to them (Table 8.4).

Factors that showed little or no change included participants' understanding of the conceptual elements of bullying; however, there were high levels of understanding already present in the pretest ("bullying is when a person/group uses power to hurt another person repeatedly": +1.2%).

Qualitative data suggested that the program was met with a predominantly positive response. Not only did the students absorb new knowledge, but they were also successfully mobilized; MARC student presenters increased their interest in the topic and gave inspiring advice. The students seemed most appreciative of the detailed understanding they gained about digital behaviors and cyberbullying. They highlighted the easy-to-follow, practical advice as one of the most helpful parts of the presentation.

Some negatives were mentioned, notably, the methodological shortcomings of the student assembly, such as insufficient interactivity or group work, and that they wanted to hear more about how to stop bullying.

Students frequently referenced their gains in knowledge about how to best handle bullying and cyberbullying situations as they encounter them. Humorously, one student wrote, "I find this a refreshment from all those dumb strategies that only work in musicals." Another student said, "Finally, not some dumb, 'go be friends with the bully' presentation" [sic].

Advisory curriculum for grades 6–12

This curriculum is designed to be used in short periods of time, e.g., 20-min segments–herefore, it can be used during Advisory Periods (which vary in length but can be quite short). It is a discussion-based curriculum, where videos of older students bringing up social issues are then discussed among the class, with the use of a Teacher's Guide that underscores main points and poses helpful discussion questions. A pilot study of the curriculum was conducted between April and June 2013. Forty-eight schools in Massachusetts agreed to complete the Lesson Plans and record all required data. By the end of the pilot, 48 faculty and staff had taught 123 lessons. Almost two-thirds (64%) identified themselves as classroom teachers, and 18% were counseling staff. Other categories included administrators, librarians, resource officers, secretaries, and substitute teachers.

To measure efficacy, both students and teachers were asked if the students had learned something new during the lesson. In addition, teachers were asked how engaged the students were, and if the lesson plan had stimulated a vigorous discussion between students. Both students and teachers used a five-point rating system (from 1 "completely unengaged" to 5 "completely engaged"). Across all lessons, the curriculum scored highest for stimulating engagement and discussion (mean score was 3.65 out of 5 or 73%). The average scores for increased understanding and learning were somewhat lower (60.4% by the students, and 45% by the teachers). It is interesting that students regarded their own learning as greater relative to teachers' ratings. This gap underscores the difficulty in estimating learning when it comes to social and emotional concepts. More than one teacher in this study expressed surprise at how much the students felt they had learned through the class discussion.

High school cyberskills' curriculum

The premise of this Curriculum is that helping students understand how digital technology can filter or skew information can help them avoid inadvertent social conflict. Lesson plans also address related issues such as the impact of cyberbullying and what effective policies and interventions might look like. During the fall of 2010, a pilot program was launched to systematically evaluate the potential impact of the High School Cyberskills' Curriculum. This evaluation study used a within-subjects' pre- and post-test design. Students were tested on their knowledge prior to engaging with the Curriculum, and then retested afterward. The study sample consisted of 1444 children in grades 9–12 from five different schools who were given the lessons in one of their classes. This study directly measured any change in students' knowledge about digital information skills following the implementation of the curriculum.

Across grades 9–12, six general topics were examined: General knowledge about social networking; knowledge about privacy limitations within social networking; general knowledge about cyberbullying and cyberbehaviors; Internet-based scams, theft, and phishing; cookies, behavioral tracking, and targeted advertising; laws about making and using video/audio recordings. Every topic and grade level studied resulted in statistically significant differences between Time 1 (the pretest) and Time 2 (post-curriculum) levels. A few individual lessons showed no significant difference between the two times. Students significantly increased their general knowledge about social media, the limitations about privacy within social networking, the difference between cyberconflict versus cyberbullying, and ways to combat cyberbullying.

Discussion

This chapter discussed both quantitative and qualitative evaluations examining the efficacy of MARC programming and curricula for students and faculty. Overall, feedback highlighted the success of some of the centers' distinctive characteristics, notably the reliance on research findings, the focus on digital issues, the use of high-status peers, and the provision of practical strategies. Both quantitative and qualitative data suggest that these programs were largely successful, but some weaknesses were also identified. Both adults and students cite the need for ongoing, interactive programs, and while they endorsed practical strategies, always wanted more.

Findings presented suggest that programming at the center is received positively across stakeholders. Increased knowledge was seen among faculty and students. Willingness to talk about and intervene in bullying was seen in students. Attendees at the train the trainer indicate that trainings are informative and with subjects reporting they had gained knowledge beyond their initial expectations. Outcome research has been positive overall, but this pool of data has limitations.

Other outcomes studies are not reported in this chapter, although they are freely available on the MARC website. Overall, the outcomes research relied on within-subjects' research, qualitative comments and feedback, and quasiexperimental design. A more solid review would require random assignment to different conditions, including a control group, and a prospective longitudinal follow-up of subjects to ascertain behavioral and emotional changes. Still, there are advantages in the type of efficacy research undertaken. Pre- and post-test designs can certainly document change although such studies cannot pinpoint the cause of any change noted. Also, while qualitative data can provide only limited answers, it is extremely helpful given the fast-paced nature of changes in the digital realm. This means that by the time questions about particular behaviors or platforms make their way into research studies, trends may have changed. Open-ended surveys of students may be particularly useful in identifying areas that may be inadvertently neglected, e.g., new social media platforms and apps, common online behaviors that may not have entered the adult world like sexting, the use of terminology, etc. Often it is not a disregard for these issues that result in them being ignored, but more likely a result of adults' limited knowledge base (even those adults engaged in current research efforts).

Finally, while evidence-based programming is without a doubt the gold standard in the field, many programs offer evidence of efficacy that does not rise to the level of randomized controlled research. For example, the programs evaluated here did not include a comprehensive fidelity check. The programs offered by MARC should be considered within that context.

References

Andreou, E., Vlachou, A., & Didaskalou, E. (2005). The roles of self-efficacy, peer interactions and attitudes in bully-victim incidents: Implications for intervention policy-practices. *School Psychology International*, *26*(5), 545–562.

Atlas, R. S., & Pepler, D. J. (1998). Observations of bullying in a classroom. *Journal of Educational Research*, *92*(2), 86–99.

Bradshaw, C. P. (2015). Translating research to practice in bullying prevention. *American Psychologist*, *26*(4), 322–332.

Cowie, H., & Hutson, N. (2005). Peer support: A strategy to help bystanders challenge school bullying. *Pastoral Care in Education*, *23*, 40–44. https://doi.org/10.1111/j.0264-3944.2005.00331.x.

Cowie, H., & Olafsson, R. (2000). The role of peer support in helping the victims of bullying in a school with high levels of aggression. *School Psychology International*, *21*(1), 79–95. https://doi.org/10.1177/0143034300211006.

Cromwell, J. (1999). *Transmen and FTMs: Identities, bodies, genders, and sexualities.* University of Illinois Press.

Englander, E. (2013). *Bullying and cyberbullying: What every educator needs to know.* Cambridge, MA: Harvard Education Press.

Hazler, R. J. (1998). Promoting personal investment in systemic approaches to violence prevention. *Education*, *119*, 222–232.

Hoff, K. E., Reese-Weber, M., Schneider, W. J., & Stagg, J. W. (2009). The association between high status positions and aggressive behavior in early adolescence. *Journal of School Psychology*, *47*(6), 395–426. https://doi.org/10.1016/j.jsp.2009.07.003.

Letendre, J., Ostrander, J. A., & Mickens, A. (2016). Teacher and staff voices: Implementation of a positive behavior bullying prevention program in an urban school. *Children and Schools*, *38*(4), 1–9. https://doi.org/10.1093/cs/cdw032.

Levi, I., Kaplan, A., & Patrick, H. (2004). Early adolescents' achievement goals, social status, and attitudes towards cooperation with peers. *Social Psychology of Education*, *7*(2), 127–159. https://doi.org/10.1023/B:SPOE.0000018547.08294.b6.

Lumsden, L. (2002). *Preventing bullying. ERIC Digest.* Eugene, OR: ERIC Clearinghouse on Educational Management.

Olweus, D. (1993). *Bullying at school: What we know and what we can do*. New York, NY: Blackwell.
Olweus, D. (2005). A useful evaluation design, and effects of the Olweus Bullying Prevention Program. *Psychology Crime and Law*, *11*, 389–402.
Pepler, D. J., Craig, W. M., & Connolly, J. (1997). *Bullying and victimization: the problems and solutions for school-aged children*. Fact sheet prepared for the National Crime Prevention Council of Canada. Ottawa: National Crime Prevention Centre, Department of Justice.
Salmivalli, C. (2001). Peer-led intervention campaign against school bullying: who considered it useful, who benefited? *Educational Research*, *43*(3), 263–278.
Sasso, G. M., & Rude, H. A. (1987). Unprogrammed effects of training high status peers to interact with severely handicapped children. *Journal of Applied Behavior Analysis*, *20*(1), 35–44. https://doi.org/10.1901/jaba.1987.20-35.
Shi, B., & Xie, H. (2011). Socialization of physical and social aggression in early adolescents' peer groups: High -status peers, individual status and gender. *Social Development*, *20*(1), 170–194. https://doi.org/10.1111/j.1467-9507.2011.00621.x.
Swearer, S. M., Espelage, D. L., & Napolitano, S. A. (2009). *Bullying prevention & intervention: Realistic strategies for schools*. New York, NY: The Guilford Press.
Ttofi, M. M., & Farrington, D. P. (2011). Effectiveness of school-based programs to reduce bullying: A systematic meta-analytic review. *Journal of Experimental Criminology*, *7*, 27–56.
Wentzel, K. R., & Caldwell, K. A. (1997). Friendships, peer acceptance, and group membership: Relation to academic achievement in middle school. *Child Development*, *68*, 1198–1209.

Further reading

Coloroso, B. (2008). *The bully, the bullied, and the bystander: From preschool to high school: How parents and teachers can help break the cycle of violence*. New York: Collins Living.
Gini, G., Pozzoli, T., Borghi, F., & Franzoni, L. (2008). The role of bystanders in students' perception of bullying and sense of safety. *Journal of School Psychology*, *46*(6), 617–638. https://doi.org/10.1016/j.jsp.2008.02.001.
Pepler, D., Smith, P. K., & Rigby, K. (2004). Looking back and looking forward: Implications for making interventions work effectively. In P. K. Smith, D. Pepler, & K. Rigby (Eds.), *Bullying in schools: How successful can interventions be?* (pp. 307–324). Cambridge: Cambridge University Press.
Trach, J., Hymel, S., Waterhouse, T., & Neale, K. (2010). Bystander responses to school bullying: A cross-sectional investigation of grade and sex differences. *Canadian Journal of School Psychology*, *25*(1), 114–130. https://doi.org/10.1177/0829573509357553.

KiVa antibullying program

9

Sanna Herkama, Christina Salmivalli
University of Turku, Turku, Finland

What is the KiVa antibullying program?

Name of program: KiVa antibullying program
Type of program: Whole-school approach including manualized curriculum lessons and targeted intervention
Suitable for ages: 7–15 years old (Years 1–9)

KiVa is an evidence-based antibullying program developed at the University of Turku, Finland. The program was originally an answer to the demand to reduce bullying nationwide. In 2006, the Finnish Ministry of Education and Culture decided to allocate resources to the development and evaluation of a new intervention program aimed at preventing and reducing bullying. Nowadays, the KiVa program is widely implemented across Finnish basic education schools (grades 1–9, children aged 7–15). It has three main goals, which are to (1) prevent bullying, (2) effectively tackle acute cases of bullying, and (3) minimize the negative effects of bullying.

The KiVa antibullying program was originally evaluated during two consecutive school years. In 2007–08, its effects were tested in grades 4–6 (primary school, children aged 10–12) and 2008–09 in grades 1–3 (primary school, children aged 7–9) and 7–9 (secondary school, students aged 13–15). The broad roll-out took place in 2009 when each Finnish school providing compulsory education was informed about the possibility for implementing the program.

The KiVa antibullying program is based on the theoretical standpoint of bullying being a group phenomenon. This approach, translated into practical tools included in the program, stresses the fact that the whole peer group is part of the bullying problem—but also the solution to it. Even the name of the program reflects this idea. KiVa is an acronym and stands for Kiusaamista Vastaan, against bullying. Furthermore, the name carries another meaning. Precisely, the Finnish word "kiva" also means someone who is nice and kind to others.

Studies focusing on the participant roles (Salmivalli, Lagerspetz, Björkqvist, Österman, & Kaukiainen, 1996; Salmivalli, Voeten, & Poskiparta, 2011) shed light on the importance of the role peer bystanders have in bullying processes. Peers often provide support for the bully, for example, by laughing or joining in mean acts to harm the victimized student. Thus, they reward the student bullying others instead of, for instance, supporting the victim, and by doing so they maintain the bullying process.

The program consists of two integral elements, namely the universal and indicated actions (see Table 9.1). The universal actions focus on preventing bullying and they are targeted at all students in a KiVa school. The essential part of the universal actions are

Reducing Cyberbullying in Schools. https://doi.org/10.1016/B978-0-12-811423-0.00009-2

Table 9.1 Universal and indicated actions included in the KiVa antibullying program

Universal actions	Indicated actions
– KiVa student lessons and themes – KiVa online games – Staff meeting, KiVa kick-off, and back-to-school night materials – Parents' newsletter and guide – Visible symbols, such as posters, and vests – Annual KiVa online survey for both students and staff with feedback	– Tackling the bullying cases coming to attention – Series of discussions with the victim and the perpetrator/s effectuated by KiVa teams – A few high-status classmates are invited to provide support for the victimized peer – Parents are informed

the student lessons delivered (primary school) and themes presented (secondary school) by teachers during regular school hours. Their main aim is to raise awareness among the students regarding the various participant roles and the importance of bystander responses to bullying. Such an approach is needed because the core idea of the program is to have an influence on the whole the peer group, diminishing the rewards gained by the bullies.

In addition, there are KiVa online games available providing additional material to the student lessons and themes to deepen the students' understanding of the topics covered during the lessons. The online games can be played either during regular school hours or at home. Furthermore, the program includes materials for staff meetings, kick-off activities, and back-to-school night as well as a parents' guide and newsletters aimed at raising awareness about bullying in general and the KiVa antibullying program specifically. Visible symbols, such as posters and recess supervisors' vests, are provided to remind that the school is a KiVa school.

The annual KiVa online survey conducted at the end of each school year is an important part of the universal actions offering the schools valuable information on the outcomes obtained and the level of implementation of the KiVa program. Both students and key staff members are invited to participate and an automatically generated report is provided for schools. In practice, the schools have the opportunity to evaluate what they have done during the past school year in order to reduce bullying (e.g., what actions have been taken? reported by teachers and students) and to compare it with the results achieved (e.g., the prevalence of students who report being repeatedly bullied by others, or bullying others). Furthermore, the schools are able to follow their progress throughout the years and in comparison to other Finnish schools.

The indicated actions take place when acute cases of bullying are detected. Each school implementing the program has a KiVa team consisting of several (typically three) school staff members. The KiVa team is responsible for the handling of bullying cases by initiating a series of discussions with both the victimized students and their perpetrators. In addition, the classroom teacher is advised to select and encourage a few high-status peers to consider how they could support the victim for some time.

Overall, the program takes the position that although addressing social-emotional skills, group processes, and well-being in school in general are needed, it is also necessary to address the bullying problem directly in order to reduce it. Raising awareness and addressing questions connected to bullying specifically, such as recognizing bullying and not rewarding it, providing support for vulnerable peers, and being assertive when being bullied, is essential.

Implementation of the KiVa antibullying program

The KiVa antibullying program takes a whole-school approach to create a school culture where bullying is not tolerated. School staff and especially teachers are at the heart of the program. Many of the cornerstones of the program, such as KiVa lessons aimed at increasing students' bullying-related awareness and skills, are implemented by teachers.

Delivering KiVa lessons and themes and utilizing KiVa online games

The KiVa antibullying program includes three age-specific units. Unit 1 is designed for students between the ages of 7–9 and Unit 2 for students aged 10–12 years. These units consist of ten double lessons (2×45 min). Unit 3, targeted at secondary school students (13–15 years), is built upon four distinct themes which are (1) Interaction in a group, (2) Me and others, (3) Forms and mechanisms of bullying, and (4) Consequences and counterforces of bullying, rather than a series of lessons. There are also three age-specific KiVa online games, one for each unit, to support and deepen the key messages presented in the KiVa lessons and themes.

Teachers have the opportunity to plan their KiVa lessons and the presentation of themes to students. The manuals together with the KiVa online games, offer plenty of material to build a KiVa curriculum. The material is easy to use and the manuals cover everything needed for the preparation of the lessons and the presentation of themes. For example, research-based information connected to each topic is presented, along with various types of exercises described in a detailed fashion. Typically, a KiVa lesson would include group and small group discussions, watching short films, and various learning-by-doing activities.

The topics covered in the manuals are connected to basic social-emotional skills, such as emotions, respect, being in a group, and bullying specifically. Bullying is addressed from different points of view (e.g., bullying as group phenomenon, recognizing bullying, consequences of bullying, not joining in bullying, supporting those who are bullied). Ideally the Unit 1 and Unit 2 lessons would be delivered in the order they appear in the manual since they are inter-related and the previous topics are the core of several lessons following.

Addressing cyberbullying in the program

The leading idea in KiVa is that cyberbullying is not separate from more traditional, face-to-face bullying. Basically, this is reflected in the materials in three different ways. First, cyberbullying is taken into consideration when bullying as a phenomenon is being discussed in class. All of the units include contents concentrating on what is bullying and how to recognize it. Typically, it is stressed that also nasty and mean messages delivered, for example, via mobile phone or internet or posted in social media sites are bullying. Students might be asked to share their experiences or observations on bullying and cyberbullying or they are presented with fictional stories including a broad variety of forms to bully others.

Second, in Units 2 and 3, there are special sections devoted to cyberbullying. They include various exercises addressing specifically the manifestations, unique features, consequences, and ways of coping with cyberbullying. In Unit 2, for example, the students are asked to describe how they use mobile phones and the Internet (e.g., Which applications? How often? For what purpose?) to reflect what kind of communication, in their opinion, is respectful in this context. Short films on the topic are watched together in class and various forms of cyberbullying are discussed in connection to ways of responding to and coping with cyberbullying. In addition, the question of reporting and telling about cyberbullying to adults is brought up.

Third, to make the issue concrete, cyberbullying is illustrated in many ways in the KiVa material. Pictures, figures, short films, and tasks in KiVa's online games together with various learning-by-doing exercises aim to deepen the students' understanding of cyberbullying. For example, the KiVa Game 2 is designed to increase the knowledge (I KNOW—module of the game; participating in a Quiz, evaluating ways to respond to cyberbullying), strengthen the skills (I CAN—module of the game; practising to recognize cyberbullying), and create links to one's own everyday behavior with peers (I DO—module of the game; reporting to what extent one has been involved in cyberbullying or seen bullying taking place and receiving feedback). In general, the idea of the program is to introduce the concept of cyberbullying from different standpoints to students and to equip them to recognize it and to act in ways which could possibly solve the problem rather than fuel it.

Tackling acute cases of bullying: KiVa team discussions

In the KiVa program, school-based KiVa teams handle the ongoing cases of bullying. It is the school's responsibility to choose a few staff members to be part of the KiVa team. The adults are advised not to address the cases of bullying in class but rather to conduct a series of discussions with the students involved. Special attention is given to recognizing bullying and differentiating it from other problems in social relationships, such as quarrels, fights, conflicts, and disagreements. KiVa teams' priority is to focus on cases that fulfill the criteria of bullying.

It is emphasized that any repeated and continuing bullying behavior should be handled by the KiVa team no matter what the medium is. Dealing with cyberbullying does not differ from how other forms of bullying are addressed. Actually, various forms of bullying are usually intertwined and inseparable. Often the incidences taking place outside of school hours, for example, in social media, may be apparent the very next day at school among the peers involved. Being bullied online is often associated with being bullied in other ways (Salmivalli, Sainio, & Hodges, 2013; Waasdorp & Bradshaw, 2015). When KiVa teams take action, they are supposed to handle a bullying case as a whole, not a single bullying incident. This means that they need to discuss the overall situation of the victimized student and find a way to put an end to it.

Training model

During the broad roll-out of KiVa in Finland in 2009, two days of training were offered to schools starting to implement the program. School staff in key roles, that is, members of the KiVa team and teachers delivering the lessons, participated in the training. Later on, many more teachers had the opportunity to participate in further training organized by the KiVa development and research team at the University of Turku.

The preimplementation training included presentations aimed at raising awareness and providing knowledge on bullying as a phenomenon in general and as a group process specifically. Furthermore, time was allocated for preparing the participants to deliver the student lessons. The topics, contents, and exercise types were introduced. The indicated actions were demonstrated and practiced to familiarize the KiVa team members with them.

At the moment the KiVa antibullying program is being implemented in countries outside of Finland too. So far, trainers from 18 countries (including Finland) have participated in the training for trainers offered by the Turku University KiVa development and research team. Only certified KiVa trainers cooperating with the licensed partner institution or company at given region or country are allowed to offer training for the end-users and guide the implementation of the KiVa antibullying program at local schools.

Evidence of effects KiVa antibullying program has on cyberbullying

The effects of the KiVa antibullying program have been studied in a large randomized controlled trial in Finland in 2007–09 (Kärnä, Voeten, Little, Poskiparta, Kaljonen, et al., 2011; Kärnä et al., 2013) and during the broad roll-out (Kärnä, Voeten, Little, Poskiparta, Alanen, et al., 2011). The main findings have been reported elsewhere. Besides reducing bullying and victimization, KiVa had positive effects on several aspects of well-being and adjustment, such as increased school liking and academic motivation as well as reduced social anxiety (e.g., Salmivalli, Garandeau, & Veenstra, 2012; Williford et al., 2012). In addition, the KiVa team discussions have been found to be efficient in putting an end to bullying according to the reports offered by victimized student a few weeks after the first KiVa team meeting (Garandeau, Poskiparta, & Salmivalli, 2014).

During the randomized controlled trial, data were also collected on being targeted by, and bullying others by *different forms of bullying*. More specifically, the Olweus bully/victim questionnaire (OBVQ, Olweus, 1996) including nine different forms of bullying was used: verbal, social exclusion, physical, social manipulation, material (e.g., taking or destroying other's possessions), threatening, racial, sexual, and cyberbullying victimization.

The first study utilizing data on cyberbullying and victimization involved a sample of 5,651 students in grades three, four, and five (Salmivalli, Kärnä, & Poskiparta, 2011). During the intervention year, the students were in grades four, five, and six; these were the grade levels where KiVa was first evaluated in 2007–08. The baseline data were collected in May 2007, the implementation of KiVa started in August 2007 in the beginning of the new school year, and the post-test data were collected in May 2008, at the end of the school year. The 78 schools involved had been assigned to intervention (39 schools) and control (39 schools) conditions. The study focused on the prevalence changes of students who were targeted by different forms of bullying.

Identifying the victims was based on the recommendation of Solberg and Olweus (2003) to use the cut-point of "two or three times a month." In other words, the pre/post-test victims were students who reported, at the respective assessment points, that they had been bullied two to three times a month, every week, or several times a week, during the past couple of months.

The findings showed that when KiVa had been implemented in intervention schools for one school year, students in these schools were significantly less likely to be bullied online than students in control schools (Salmivalli, Kärnä, et al., 2011). The odds' ratio was 1.80 (confidence interval: 1.11–2.93), indicating that control school students were 1.8 times more likely to be identified as victims of online bullying after the intervention year than students from schools where KiVa had been implemented for one school year. In terms of percentage changes, there was a 36% reduction in the prevalence of cyber-victims in KiVa schools, as compared with the 14% *increase* in control schools: in other words, -50% change in favor of KiVa schools. The effects on cybervictimization were actually larger than the effects on many other forms. The average odds' ratio, across all nine forms, was 1.58, with a range from 1.32 (social exclusion) to 1.94 (physical victimization), whereas percentage changes varied between -21% and -63%.

To test the effects for students who were bullied even more frequently, that is, every week or several times a week, the authors reran the pretest–posttest analyses while categorizing only those students as victims (response alternatives "3 = every week" and "4 = several times a week" in the OBVQ). The effect of KiVa on cybervictimization became even larger, the odds' ratio now being 2.57. That is, the likelihood of a student being bullied online at least weekly was 2.57 times higher for a control school student than for a student in a KiVa school. This can be considered a large effect.

Williford et al. (2013) continued studying the effects of KiVa on cyberbullying, this time looking at both victimization and bullying perpetration. To our knowledge, this was the first study ever testing whether a school-based bullying prevention program can reduce cyberbullying perpetration. The data were, again, from the randomized controlled trial but it now included middle school students (grades 8 and 9 during the intervention year), in addition to students in grades four through six. Since some studies suggest that cyberbullying peaks in middle school (e.g., Williams & Guerra, 2007), this was considered an important extension of the prior investigation.

There were 9,914 students in the intervention schools and 8,498 students in the control schools. To examine subtle changes in cyberbullying and cybervictimization frequencies, Williford et al. (2013) used the entire ordinal scale from the OBVQ rather than categorizing students into online bullies, victims, and noninvolved, allowing a fine-grained analysis of KiVa's impact on cyberbullying and cybervictimization.

Furthermore, they examined potential moderating effects of age and gender on the effects of KiVa on cyberbullying and victimization.

The main findings were the following. KiVa significantly reduced the frequency of cybervictimization in the intervention schools, as compared with control schools (OR=1.29). This effect was not moderated by age or gender. The effect of KiVa on the frequency of bullying others online was, however, moderated by age. The authors tested, with a simple slopes analysis, the effect at three different values for age: (1) one standard deviation below the mean age of the students in the sample (11.30 years), (2) the mean age (12.88 years), and (3) one standard deviation above the mean (14.46 years). The effect of KiVa was clearly significant for students that were one standard deviation below the mean age (OR=1.69, CI [1.15, 2.48]), almost (but not quite) significant at the mean age (OR=1.34), CI [.99, 1.79]), and nonsignificant for students who were one standard deviation above the mean age (OR=1.06), CI [.77, 1.45]).

Since 2009, the annual KiVa online survey has been used to collect data from students in schools implementing KiVa. In this survey, only two general questions about bullying and victimization (one item for each) were included for the first five years, but in 2014 we added a question on cybervictimization in surveys filled in by students in grades four through nine (for younger students, the questionnaire was kept short and thus these questions were not included in their version). Every year, around 125,000 students from these grade levels respond to the survey.

During the three assessments since the cybervictimization question was included in the survey (from 2014 to 2016), the proportion of students who said they have been bullied online (2–3 times or more often during the past couple of months) decreased from 2.9% to 2.6%, representing a 10% reduction, while the proportion of students (in the same age group, i.e., grades 4 to 9) reporting being bullied in general (2–3 times a month or more often, no form of bullying specified) decreased from 8.9% to 8.0%, i.e., a 10% reduction. In other words, it seems that the prevalence of cybervictims is going down equally with the rate of being bullied in general. These data cannot be considered strong evidence of the effects of KiVa program, as there are no control schools—all schools responding to our annual survey are schools implementing the program. However, the results suggest that the prevalence of victims, including cybervictims, is decreasing in Finnish KiVa schools across the years.

Together, the findings from the randomized controlled trial and the data collected during nationwide implementation of the KiVa program show that cyberbullying and victimization can be reduced in the context of a general bullying prevention/intervention program.

Implications and future directions

Is there a need for distinct prevention strategies for cyberbullying?

On the basis of evidence available so far, we argue that cyberbullying should be addressed together with more traditional, offline forms, rather than having a program or policy for cyberbullying specifically. There are several reasons for this; we will outline them in the following.

First, online bullying is relatively rare, if we compare its prevalence with the rates of offline bullying. There are fewer targets as well as perpetrators. This means that a strong focus on cyberbullying might prevent policy makers, researchers, educators, and parents from realizing that most bullying takes place in face-to-face interactions—and thus from recognizing and intervening the most common forms of bullying. Also, the perception that "all bullying takes place online" may lead to a belief that schools can do little to tackle it.

Second, it seems that maintenance of peer relationships online and offline cannot be separated and therefore cyberbullying cannot be solved apart from face-to-face interaction. For example, the study by Mishna, Saini, and Solomon (2009) stressed the fact that cyberbullying may manifest itself in the peer group context. The qualitative reports of students indicated that cyberbullying may be anonymous in the sense that the identity of the perpetrator is unknown, but there are still witnesses online and the incidents are often situated within the peer context of the victimized student.

Third, being bullied online is almost always accompanied with being bullied offline. In a large dataset of 17,625 Finnish students from grades 3 to 8 (9–15 years of age), it was found that only 0.5% of the sample were targeted online but not offline (Salmivalli et al., 2013). Furthermore, as few as 1.4% were targeted both online and offline, whereas 11.6% were targeted only offline. The vast majority of the sample were not targeted by bullying at all (86.4%). Similarly, in a study by Waasdorp and Bradshaw (2015), 23% ($n=6379$) of adolescents in grades 9–12 (mean age: 15.93 years) in the US were bullied in some way, 25.6% of them were bullied online, but only 4.6% ($n=81$) of the students bullied online were bullied *only* online. As almost all students who are bullied online are also bullied offline, their situation needs a broad, comprehensive solution, rather than addressing cyberbullying, or any other form by which they are attacked, separately. Bullying taking place online is in most cases a signal of a child being bullied by several forms.

Fourth, bystanders are key actors with great potential to either fuel bullying or to put an end to it—this is true of online, as well as offline bullying. When bullying takes place in a social media site, the responses (e.g., "likes" and shares) by peers who have not posted the hurtful message themselves, are food for further insults. Addressing bystander responsibility in a prevention program is, in our view, more important than addressing the specific forms, or incidents of bullying. We believe that the mechanisms of bullying are similar, regardless the form or medium it takes, and the most important element in a prevention/intervention program is addressing the mechanisms underlying the problem.

Finally, the findings reported regarding the effects of KiVa on cyberbullying and –victimization suggest that a "general" bullying prevention program can reduce online bullying at least to an equal extent as it reduces other, more traditional forms. Considering the limited resources, it makes little sense to develop and implement separate prevention/intervention programs or strategies for separate kinds of bullying.

All this is not to say that online bullying should be *ignored* in antibullying programs: quite the contrary, it is one form of bullying with some unique features that together with other forms should be addressed within a program taking a wider perspective on bullying generally. Online bullying is not just an issue of internet safety or "netiquette." It is a matter of respect in relationships, and of bystanders' responsibility to react when they see abuse happening.

Future directions

KiVa does include some contents related to cyberbullying, but the data do not tell whether it is these specific components of KiVa that are responsible for the change, or whether it is the program overall. This should be examined in future studies.

The effectiveness findings also do not tell *what* in the KiVa antibullying led to reductions in cyberbullying perpetration and victimization or *how*. One study looked into the mediators of KiVa effects on bullying perpetration generally. The effects were found to be mediated by three factors; 1) students' antibullying attitudes increased, 2) students started to observe more constructive bystander responses (less reinforcing of the bullies; more defending of the victims), and 3) they gradually saw their teachers as less approving of bullying (Saarento, Boulton, & Salmivalli, 2015). It is likely, but so far not tested, that the same mechanisms are responsible for reductions in cyberbullying.

The extreme rapid development of social media and the vast amount of applications popular among children and youth has created a need to develop antibullying policies and practices to tackle bullying taking place online. Well-structured preventive/interventive programs with contemporary contents are likely to invite teachers to address issues connected to cyberbullying with students. In our understanding, this is not always easy for teachers, since they may feel the social reality including various social media applications, children and adolescents currently are involved with, are somewhat distanced from them. It is important to offer school personnel clear guidelines to also tackle cyberbullying and this can be done successfully within the framework of a general antibullying program.

References

Garandeau, C. F., Poskiparta, E., & Salmivalli, C. (2014). Tackling acute cases of school bullying in the KiVa anti-bullying program: A comparison of two approaches. *Journal of Abnormal Child Psychology*, *42*, 981–991. https://doi.org/10.1007/s10802-014-9861- 1.

Kärnä, A., Voeten, M., Little, T. D., Alanen, E., Poskiparta, E., & Salmivalli, C. (2013). Effectiveness of the KiVa antibullying program: Grades 1–3 and 7–9. *Journal of Educational Psychology*, *105*, 535–551. https://doi.org/10.1037/a0030417.

Kärnä, A., Voeten, M., Little, T. D., Poskiparta, E., Alanen, E., & Salmivalli, C. (2011). Going to scale: A nonrandomized nationwide trial of the KiVa antibullying program for grades 1–9. *Journal of Consulting and Clinical Psychology*, *79*, 796–805. https://doi.org/10.1037/a0025740.

Kärnä, A., Voeten, M., Little, T. D., Poskiparta, E., Kaljonen, A., & Salmivalli, C. (2011). A large-scale evaluation of the KiVa anti bullying program: Grades 4–6. *Child Development*, *82*, 311–330. https://doi.org/10.1111/j.1467-8624.2010.01557.x.

Mishna, F., Saini, M., & Solomon, S. (2009). Ongoing and online: Children and youth's perceptions of cyber bullying. *Children and Youth Services Review*, *31*, 1222–1228. https://doi.org/10.1016/j.childyouth.2009.05.004.

Olweus, D. (1996). The Revised Olweus Bully/Victim Questionnaire. *Research Center for Health Promotion (HEMIL Center)*. Norway: University of Bergen.

Saarento, S., Boulton, A. J., & Salmivalli, C. (2015). Reducing bullying and victimization: Student- and classroom-level mechanisms of change. *Journal of Abnormal Child Psychology*, *43*, 61–76. https://doi.org/10.1007/s10802-013-9841-x.

Salmivalli, C., Garandeau, C. F., & Veenstra, R. (2012). KiVa Anti-Bullying Program: Implications for school adjustment. In A. M. Ryan & G. W. Ladd (Eds.), *Peer relationships and adjustment at school* (pp. 279–307). Charlotte, NC: Information Age Publishing.

Salmivalli, C., Kärnä, A., & Poskiparta, E. (2011a). Counteracting bullying in Finland: The KiVa program and its effects on different forms of being bullied. *International Journal of Behavioral Development*, *35*, 405–411. https://doi.org/10.1177/0165025411407457.

Salmivalli, C., Lagerspetz, K., Björkqvist, K., Österman, K., & Kaukiainen, A. (1996). Bullying as a group process: Participant roles and their relations to social status within the group. *Aggressive Behavior*, *22*, 1–15. https://doi.org/10.1002/(SICI)1098-2337(1996)22:1<1::AID-AB1>3.0.CO;2-T.

Salmivalli, C., Sainio, M., & Hodges, E. V. E. (2013). Electronic victimization: Correlates, antecedents, and consequences among elementary and middle school students. *Journal of Clinical Child and Adolescent Psychology*, *42*, 442–453. https://doi.org/10.1080/15374416.2012.759228.

Salmivalli, C., Voeten, M., & Poskiparta, E. (2011b). Bystanders matter: Associations between reinforcing, defending, and the frequency of bullying behavior in classrooms. *Journal of Clinical Child and Adolescent Psychology*, *40*, 668–676. https://doi.org/10.1080/15374416.2011.597090.

Solberg, M. E., & Olweus, D. (2003). Prevalence estimation of school bullying with the Olweus bully/victim questionnaire. *Aggressive Behavior*, *29*, 239–268. https://doi.org/10.1002/ab.10047.

Waasdorp, T. E., & Bradshaw, C. P. (2015). The overlap between cyberbullying and traditional bullying. *Journal of Adolescent Health*, *56*, 483–488. https://doi.org/10.1016/j.jadohealth.2014.12.002.

Williams, K. R., & Guerra, N. G. (2007). Prevalence and predictors of Internet bullying. *Journal of Adolescent Health*, *41*, 14–21. https://doi.org/10.1016/j.jadohealth.2007.08.018.

Williford, A., Boulton, A., Noland, B., Little, T. D., Kärnä, A., & Salmivalli, C. (2012). Effects of the KiVa anti-bullying program on adolescents' depression, anxiety, and perception of peers. *Journal of Abnormal Child Psychology*, *40*, 289–300. https://doi.org/10.1007/s10802-011-9551-1.

Williford, A., Elledge, L. C., Boulton, A. J., Depaolis, K. J., Little, T. D., & Salmivalli, C. (2013). Effects of the KiVa antibullying program on cyberbullying and cybervictimization frequency among Finnish youth. *Journal of Clinical Child and Adolescent Psychology*, *42*, 820–833. https://doi.org/10.1080/15374416.2013.787623.

Online and school-based programs to prevent cyberbullying among Italian adolescents: What works, why, and under which circumstances

10

Ersilia Menesini, Valentina Zambuto, Benedetta E. Palladino
University of Florence, Florence, Italy

What is the *NoTrap!* program

Name of program: *NoTrap!*
Type of program: Whole school, online, peer-led
Suitable for ages: 7th–10th grade

NoTrap! (*Noncadiamointrappola!*, which means "Let's not fall into the trap!") is an Italian online school-based universal intervention for bullying and cyberbullying. It is designed for adolescents attending 7th–10th grades. It is a peer-led program, in which adolescents are, at the same time, the target and the agents of the intervention. The *NoTrap!* program development was started in 2008, and version by version, thanks to the findings of scientific evaluation, it has been improved in order to enhance its level of efficacy. This revision process led to the third edition (school year: 2011/2012) that is the final official version of *NoTrap!* program (Menesini, Palladino, & Nocentini, 2016) now implemented as an evidence-based intervention. Since then, some details have been changed in order to accommodate new aspects of the problem, but the core model remains the same.

NoTrap! is a theory-driven intervention, based on psychological scientific literature. Each phase has been conceived in order to address a specific aim, and to change specific mechanisms responsible for bullying and cyberbullying. In this regard, many authors (Pozzoli & Gini, 2013; Ttofi & Farrington, 2011) have underlined the social and group aspects of bullying; therefore, an ecological approach, targeting the multiple contexts that impact school-bullying, would seem to prove most effective in order to counteract these phenomena. Specifically, an antibullying intervention should address the whole school community, the peer group, and the individuals involved. Following this evidence, the *NoTrap!* program aims to involve the whole school and the community at different levels. Initially, there is teacher and staff training aimed to prepare the ground and activate all the resources. The program includes lessons for students and for teachers. Besides, thanks to the program webpage and communication mechanisms

Reducing Cyberbullying in Schools. https://doi.org/10.1016/B978-0-12-811423-0.00010-9

therein, the intervention could reach other adolescents in schools not participating in the program and potentially the whole community.

Another important theoretical framework underlying the development of the program is the social nature of bullying and cyberbullying. We know that in both the bullying and cyberbullying processes, bystanders have an important role, as they can reinforce the bully and increase the negative impact on the victim, or, conversely, they can stop the bullying and defend the victim (Allison & Bussey, 2016; DeSmet et al., 2016; Salmivalli, Lagerspetz, Björkqvist, Österman, & Kaukiainen, 1998). However, the majority of bystanders usually do not do anything when they see a bullying or cyberbullying episode. Many studies have tried to explain this passive behavior on the basis of the so-called bystander effect, a model developed by Latané and Darley (1970). According to these studies, failure to help the victim in school or online depends on the failure in one of the five phases of the model: (1) Noticing that something in going on; (2) interpreting the situation as an emergency; (3) feeling a certain degree of responsibility; (4) knowing the coping strategies in order to intervene; and (5) implementing the action choice. *NoTrap!* encourages bystanders' activation in each of the phases. In particular, in order to help adolescents to notice the episode, the program aims to increase their awareness of what is bullying and cyberbullying, helping youth know different typologies and criteria to recognize the problem as bullying or cyberbullying. In this way, they will be able to identify the phenomenon, and to distinguish it from other similar patterns of interaction between peers. In order to help them to interpret the situation as an emergency, in each phase of *NoTrap!*, we have worked on understanding the victim's point of view. Specifically we emphasize victim's emotions and the possible long-term effects of bullying. This allows the intervention to enhance the level of empathy toward the victim, and to recognize an emergency in a bullying or a cyberbullying episode. In order to increase the sense of responsibility, from the first awareness meeting, we stimulate reflection on the consequences of the bystanders' passive behavior. Students understand that if they do not do anything, they reinforce the bullies and increase the victim's suffering. Besides, thanks to the peer education model, and to students' role as agents of change in the class, we try to promote adolescents' sense of responsibility. Bystanders often do not intervene because they do not know what they can do. In order to decrease the feeling of powerlessness, and increase perceived competence, *NoTrap!* deals extensively with adaptive coping strategies in the case of bullying and cyberbullying phenomena. These strategies are focused on the victims' and bystanders' points of view. Then, thanks to a problem-solving technique, adolescents can explore the best strategy to intervene; they can develop a plan and evaluate whether it might work or not. Finally, another theoretical aspect addressed by the *NoTrap!* program is the importance of maintaining attention both to face-to-face and online contexts (Palladino, Nocentini, & Menesini, 2012).

How *NoTrap!* program is delivered

Before introducing how the *NoTrap!* program is delivered, it is useful to provide an overview of the Italian educational system, which is organized around three main stages:

- Primary education, lasting 5 years, for children between 6 and 11 years of age;
- Lower secondary school, lasting 3 years, for children between 11 and 14 years of age;
- Upper secondary school, lasting 5 years, for students from 14 to 19 years of age. This stage is divided among high schools, technical institutes, and vocational institutes.

For each school-stage, students are organized into groups called "classes." A class has a minimum of 15 and a maximum of 30 pupils. The classes' composition remains stable for all the years of the school stage. This means that classmates remain together throughout the school-day and are stable for several years. The school year begins in September and ends in the first week of June.

The *NoTrap!* program normally lasts 4 months. In Italy, on average, it is delivered from January to May. The program tools are the manual for teachers and for peer educators, the webpage and the Facebook page for students, peer educators, and the larger community.

The program can be implemented in three main phases:

Launch event and awareness meeting

We divide this phase into two meetings that are carried out in parallel: the first one is for teachers and the second for students.

Teachers meeting: For each grade (7–10), the program requests two representative teachers. At this stage, one training session with all the representative teachers of the schools, plus other teachers willing to take part, is organized. The meeting starts with an introduction on bullying and cyberbullying followed by an explanation of the *NoTrap!* program. In the second part of the meeting, teachers are invited to participate in some activities that peer educators will perform in class in the final phase of the program. In this way, teachers will be ready to help their students when they start to work in the group class. This means that teachers will assume a *scaffolding* role during the peer education phase. With the expression "scaffolding," we refer to the support that teacher can offer to their students during the intervention; this support is tailored to the needs of students and it is gradually removed in order to promote students' autonomy.

Students' meeting: In all classes involved, psychologists present the program and start raising awareness on bullying and cyberbullying by means of videos, discussions, and role play activities. In particular, the following topics are addressed:

(a) bullying and cyberbullying criteria and typologies. In this phase, we underline the continuity between the two phenomena, but also point out the differences implied by the specific contextual features of cyberbullying (e.g., anonymity, publicity) (Menesini et al., 2012). The defining criteria of the phenomena are emphasized to help students to clearly recognize a bullying or cyberbullying episode and to differentiate them from other similar situations (e.g., joke, fight);
(b) victims' emotions and long-term consequences of this situation. This aspect is useful to focus attention on the victim's suffering and to promote empathy toward the victims;
(c) bystanders' responsibility. We talk about bystander roles in face-to-face and online contexts. Through videos and scenarios, we stimulate awareness and ask why bullies often act in front of classmates, and why bystanders do not help the victims. Then, we encourage reflection on what could be the consequences of bystanders' passivity (i.e., to reinforce

bullying behavior and to aggravate the victim's pain and loneliness). We finally introduce some positive coping strategies useful for victims and bystanders to make students aware of their power when they see a bullying situation;

(d) ICT risks. We also focus on possible risks online and how we can prevent and cope with them.

At the end of this meeting, we explain what the *NoTrap!* program is and what it means to be a peer educator. We then request four or five students in each class to self-select as peer educators, assuming a more involved role in the further phases of the program.

Peer educators' training

In each school, peer educators attend a day-training (8 h) all together. We normally organize day-training of 20–25 peer educators. The training is designed to empower three areas of peer educators' competence. Each unit is composed of activities and practice (e.g., realization of posters, role play, games) and reflection. The three units of the training are:

(a) *Listening skills*: The activities and discussions of this unit are intended to help students understand what we have to do when we listen to someone face-to-face and online. Students gradually become more aware of nonverbal language to communicate listening and empathic attitudes. In particular, at the end of this unit, we introduce "the active listening" scheme and "the empathic feedback" concepts. Students try to put into practice what they have learned, by means of role plays and other practical activities;

(b) *Emotional competence and empathy*: The activities of this unit are devised to teach peer educators how to recognize and analyze a victim's emotion in depth, considering its causes, and behavioral and physiological reactions. Peer educators are stimulated to think about similarities and differences between emotions, and about the several emotional reactions that the same situation can elicit in different persons. Then we introduce the concept of "empathy." At the end of these activities, peer educators should understand that everyone feels emotions but there are several ways to live and experience an emotion. In addition, they should know that there are not right or wrong emotions, but simply some affective and behavioral reactions that are more functional than others. They should be aware that when the intensity level of an emotion is too high, we can lose control of our actions. Therefore, it is important to learn how to regulate our emotions. Finally, they should reflect on how the ability to understand others' emotions can improve our relationships;

(c) *Problem solving and coping strategies of bullying and cyberbullying*: This unit has three main aims. The first one is to deeply consider the effects and the long-term consequences of bullying and cyberbullying situations; then peer educators explore all possible strategies in order to cope with this problem and to avoid its detrimental long-term consequences. They should understand that there is not a unique solution that always works for all victims in all situations. At this point, we explain the problem solving technique: exploring deeply the advantages and disadvantages of all solutions, choosing the best one, then selecting the most appropriate plan for that specific problem and for that specific person.

At the end of the three units, there comes the so-called "online training": peer educators visit the program web page, http://www.notrap.it, and they can register in the community. The virtual community of the web page is an online space in which peer educators can offer a peer support service for all adolescents asking for help. The community is accessible to students below 18 years, and psychologists and adults normally moderate and supervise all the interactions in the community.

The workshops led by peer educators

After the training, the peer educators led two cooperative interventions in their group-class under their teachers' supervision. In particular, classmates are divided into four or five subgroups, each with a peer educator. In every subgroup, each student has a specific role to perform in order to cooperate and complete the activity. A short manual is available for peer educators, in order to help them lead the two workshops. In particular, peer educators suggest some training activities to their classmates.

Both workshops are focused on the victim and bystander points of view. The first one is aimed at thinking about which emotions can be elicited in a bullying or cyberbullying episode. Then the victim's emotions are explored deeply in order to promote empathic feelings toward the victims. The second workshop is focused on functional and positive coping strategies in order to counteract bullying and cyberbullying either as a victim or a bystander. The groups create posters, photos, and other products, all of which are published on the *NoTrap!* Facebook page. At the end of the activities, the students present their posters to the other classmates and the class discusses together the emotions they worked on and the solutions they found.

Evidence of the program's effectiveness

In order to test the efficacy of the program, we carried out two different trials of the same third revision of *NoTrap!* (Palladino, Nocentini, & Menesini, 2016) involving different participants, classes, and schools. In both trials, we paired schools who asked to participate as experimental schools with other control schools selected specifically for having classes with the same type of curriculum. For both trials, students in the control group did not receive any kind of intervention: they just completed the same questionnaires as the experimental group (pretest before the start of the intervention, posttest at the end, and follow-up in 6 months). In order to detect possible effects of the sampling, we checked the experimental and control group for pretest differences on the target variables such as victimization, bullying, cybervictimization, and cyberbullying, and other important variables such as attitudes toward victims, moral disengagement, and empathy: no differences between the two groups were found for any of these variables. All target variables were assessed by measures with good psychometric properties. In particular, we used the Florence Bullying and Victimization Scales (FBVSs), and the Florence Cyberbullying and Cybervictimization Scales (FCBCVSs) (Palladino, Nocentini, & Menesini, 2015). Each scale consists of items asking how often the respondent had experienced bullying and cyberbullying as both perpetrator and victim during the past couple of months. Each item covered a specific behavior, asking both for perpetration and victimization experiences (e.g., “I threatened someone” and “I beat and pushed someone” for bullying; “I was threatened” and “I was beaten and pushed" for victimization). Specifically, we compared the prevalence of bullying and cyberbullying in the experimental groups and in the control group. More details about the procedure, measures and results of the two trials are reported in Palladino et al. (2016). In summary, results clearly confirm the efficacy of the program. We found a significant decrease in bullying (−20%), victimization (−17%), cyberbullying (−28%), and cybervictimization (−25%) in the experimental group compared to the control group. In addition, these results remained stable after the end of the intervention according to the follow-up carried out 6 months later. This means that the program was efficacious, and the outcomes did not diminish over time.

NoTrap! also had another indirect effect: the decrease in cybervictimization, but not in traditional victimization, led to a significant decrease in internalizing symptoms. This result underlines the differential impact of bullying and cyberbullying on the victims and the necessity to keep the two kinds of bullying in mind for prevention.

Deepening what works, why, and for whom

A study by Palladino et al. (2012) showed that in the experimental group the program predicted an increase over time in seeking support, both on informational and instrumental aspects (distal advice) and on the more emotional way of getting help from people (close support). This increase is a mediational mechanism explaining how the program is able to decrease cybervictimization.

In a recent study (Zambuto, 2017) related to the implementation quality of the *NoTrap!* program (school year 2015/2016), we asked students to nominate the classmates who usually help victims of bullying and we found that the experimental classes showed a significant increase in the number of victims' defenders at the end of the year. The mechanisms of effectiveness are related to the increase of supporting and defending behaviors in the experimental classes.

Another important aspect of program and intervention evaluation is to investigate for whom *NoTrap!* program works. In order to answer this question, we explored two different relations. Our first question was whether *NoTrap!* works differently for males and females. Then, we evaluated possible gender moderation effects on the efficacy of the program in all the outcome variables (Palladino et al., 2016). We found that gender had no effects on the outcomes of the program. This means that both males and females benefit of the intervention at the same level, whereas in the control group males increased their level of bullying, and females remained stable or had a small decrease in bullying and cyberbullying behaviors.

Finally, we asked whether the effectiveness of the *Notrap!* program is moderated by the role students played in the program, when they were peer educators vs all the other students. Many studies have suggested that peer support systems and peer education can provide benefits to users of such schemes, to peer supporters, and to schools in general (Cowie, Naylor, Talamelli, Chauhan, & Smith, 2002; Menesini, & Nocentini, 2012). We found that, for victimization, students in the control condition increased their level of victimization, while "peer educators" and "all the other students in the experimental group " decreased it. Also in the case of cybervictimization, results were similar. Specifically, peer educators decreased their level of cybervictimization to a greater extent compared to all the others, thus showing that a model based on peer involvement for bullying and cyberbullying prevention can be effective at different levels for the entire classes, for peer educators, and for their classmates.

Conclusion and future research

These promising results suggest that, thanks to the direct and active involvement of adolescents as agents of change in their reference group, the *NoTrap!* program can be an effective means of intervention to counteract bullying and cyberbullying in secondary schools. As reported in the introduction, the program is composed of several phases, each one based on the scientific literature and on the role bystanders and students can have in bullying dynamics. The result is a theory-driven program able to decrease bullying, victimization, cyberbullying and cybervictimization, and internalizing symptoms at a significant level.

In this chapter, we explained how the program can work. In particular, thanks to the adoption of an ecological approach, *NoTrap!* has been able to activate a process of collective responsibility at class and school level. As a first step, the program is able to increase the awareness of bullying and cyberbullying, the ability to recognize these phenomena, and to interpret it as an emergency. In addition, the program actively works to enhance empathy toward the victim. This is a prerequisite of defending behaviors (Cappadocia, Pepler, Cummings, & Craig, 2012). The adoption of a peer education model and the implementation of activities aimed to promote the bystanders' involvement are useful to reinforce their sense of responsibility. Besides, thanks to this program, adolescents improved their coping strategies, so that they are able to cope with these phenomena in a functional way.

An important role is also played by the online component of the program. The web page http://www.notrap.it extends the coverage of the program, possibly involving adolescents that do not participate directly in the school context. The online peer support service is an appealing way to take advantage of the virtual environment.

In conclusion, we think that *NoTrap!* is effective because it builds on competencies and skills relevant for adolescents. Thanks to the peer education scheme and the creation of an adequate scaffolding structure, the program allows adolescents to translate their antibullying attitude into behaviors. This empowerment process is useful for the whole class, in order to change the group's dynamics, and to promote a group culture based on prosocial behavior. In this way, it is possible to break the so-called wall of silence often reported in classes where bullying is going on.

Future research should try to investigate the peer education component of the program more in depth. In particular, new directions of investigation can be related to understanding whether the type of recruitment of peer educators (as volunteers or nominated by peers) can make a difference in the results obtained. In conclusion *NoTrap!* can be defined as an evidence-based intervention developed on the basis of a translational approach that benefits from the integration of theoretical research and applied interventions. Within this approach, the model is "a work in progress" and can be further improved or innovated thanks to new and challenging studies addressing specific components or processes enhanced by the model.

Acknowledgments

The authors are grateful to all of the students, teachers, and schools for their participation in the several revisions of the program, and Portale Ragazzi and Province of Lucca for their collaboration in the study. The research was supported by Cassa di Risparmio Foundation of Lucca (2014–16) and by Ente Cassa di Risparmio of Florence (2015–16).

References

Allison, K. R., & Bussey, K. (2016). Cyber-bystanding in context: A review of the literature on witnesses' responses to cyberbullying. *Children and Youth Services Review*, *65*, 183–194. https://doi.org/10.1016/j.childyouth.2016.03.026.

Cappadocia, M. C., Pepler, D. J., Cummings, J. G., & Craig, W. (2012). Individual motivations and characteristics associated with bystander intervention during bullying episodes among children and youth. *Canadian Journal of School Psychology*, *27*, 201–216. https://doi.org/10.1177/0829573512450567.

Cowie, H., Naylor, L., Talamelli, L., Chauhan, P., & Smith, P. K. (2002). Knowledge, use of and attitudes towards peer support: A 2-year follow-up to the prince's trust survey. *Journal of Adolescence*, *25*, 453–467. https://doi.org/10.1006/jado.2002.0498.

DeSmet, A., Bastiaensens, S., Van Cleemput, K., Poels, K., Vandebosch, H., Cardon, G., et al. (2016). Deciding whether to look after them, to like it, or leave it: A multidimensional analysis of predictors of positive and negative bystander behavior in cyberbullying among adolescents. *Computers in Human Behavior*, *57*, 398–415. https://doi.org/10.1016/j.chb.2015.12.051.

Latané, B., & Darley, J. M. (1970). *The unresponsive bystander: Why doesn't he help?* New York, NY: Appleton-Century-Crofts. Inneed editors, The unresponsive bystander (pp. 1–67).

Menesini, E., & Nocentini, A. (2012). Peer education intervention: Face-to-face versus online. In A. Costabile & B. Spears (Eds.), *The impact of technology on relationships in educational settings* (pp. 139–150). London: Routledge.

Menesini, E., Nocentini, A., Palladino, B. E., Frisén, A., Berne, S., Ortega-Ruiz, R., et al. (2012). Cyberbullying definition among adolescents: A comparison across six European countries. *Cyberpsychology, Behavior and Social Networking*, *15*, 455–463. https://doi.org/10.1089/cyber.2012.0040.

Menesini, E., Palladino, B. E., & Nocentini, A. (2016). Online and school based intervention to prevent cyberbullying among adolescents. In T. Vollink, F. Dehue, & C. Mc Guckin (Eds.), *Cyberbullying: From theory to intervention* (pp. 56–175). London/New York, NY: Routledge/Taylor & Francis Group.

Palladino, B. E., Nocentini, A., & Menesini, E. (2012). Online and offline peer led models against bullying and cyberbullying. *Psicothema*, *24*, 634–639. Available at http://www.ncbi.nlm.nih.gov/pubmed/23079363.

Palladino, B. E., Nocentini, A., & Menesini, E. (2015). Psychometric properties of the florence cyberbullying-cybervictimization scales. *Cyberpsychology, Behavior and Social Networking*, *18*, 112–119. https://doi.org/10.1089/cyber.2014.0366.

Palladino, B. E., Nocentini, A., & Menesini, E. (2016). Evidence-based intervention against bullying and cyberbullying: Evaluation of the Noncadiamointrappola! Program through two independent trials. *Aggressive Behavior*, *42*, 194–206. https://doi.org/10.1002/ab.21636.

Pozzoli, T., & Gini, G. (2013). Why do bystanders of bullying help or not? A multi-dimensional model. *The Journal of Early Adolescence*, *33*, 315–340. https://doi.org/10.1177/0272431612440172.

Salmivalli, C., Lagerspetz, K., Björkqvist, K., Österman, K., & Kaukiainen, A. (1998). Bullying as a group process: Participant roles and their relations to social status within the group. *Aggressive Behavior*, *22*, 1–15.

Ttofi, M. M., & Farrington, D. P. (2011). Effectiveness of school-based programs to reduce bullying: A systematic and meta-analytic review. *Journal of Experimental Criminology*, *7*(1), 27–56. https://doi.org/10.1007/s11292-010-9109-1.

Zambuto, V. (2017). *How and why peer-led models can be effective in the anti-(cyber)bullying interventions*. University of Florence, Firenze, Italy: Unpublished doctoral dissertation.

Further reading

Maticka-Tyndale, E., & Barnett, J. (2010). Peer-led interventions to reduce HIV risk of youth: A review. *Evaluation and Program Planning*, *33*, 98–112. https://doi.org/10.1016/j.evalprogplan.2009.07.001.

Naylor, P., & Cowie, H. (1999). The effectiveness of peer support systems in challenging school bullying: The perspectives and experiences of teachers and pupils. *Journal of Adolescence*, *22*, 467–479.

Zambuto, V., Nocentini, A., Palladino, B. E., & Menesini, E. (2016). Is a peer led intervention against bullying and cyberbullying more or less effective for subgroups of participants? In *Oral symposium Preventive interventions for cyberbullying in schools and its impact in traditional bullying—24th Biennial meeting of the international society for the study of behavioural development (ISSBD), Vilnius, Lithuania.*

A school-based cyberbullying preventive intervention approach: The Media Heroes program*

11

Anja Schultze-Krumbholz, Pavle Zagorscak†, Herbert Scheithauer†*
*Technische Universität Berlin, Berlin, Germany, †Freie Universität Berlin, Berlin, Germany

Introduction

Name of program: The Media Heroes
Type of program: Manualised school program
Suitable for ages: Grades 7–10

Modern communication technologies provide a range of positive uses to all age groups. For children and adolescents, the internet is a vast resource of information for school, work, news, and any other topic of interest, and also for getting and staying in contact with friends and peers and for the exchange of views, ideas, and arguments. It facilitates the access to groups of like-minded people, for example, regarding hobbies or problems (e.g., online self-help groups). Platforms like social networking sites provide opportunities to test out identities and to present oneself to others. However, many of these opportunities can also pose a potential risk to children's and youths' psychological well-being. Harmful behavior, such as aggression or autoaggression (i.e., self-harm), may be reinforced by "meeting" others with similar harmful views or by different social mechanisms of digital communication. In Germany, cyberbullying has been found to be a serious problem with up to 22% reporting to have perpetrated cyberbullying and with up to 28% reporting to have become victims of cyberbullying sometimes or more often during the previous year (Festl & Quandt, 2016).

The present cyberbullying preventive intervention program "Media Heroes" (Schultze-Krumbholz, Zagorscak, Siebenbrock, & Scheithauer, 2012b) was developed in Germany as part of the more comprehensive European Cyberbullying Intervention Project (ECIP, www.bullyingandcyber.net). It was developed, implemented, and first evaluated in 2011. At the time, an overview of the then existing studies showed estimated prevalence rates of up to 43% for victims and 33% for bullies (Schultze-Krumbholz & Scheithauer, 2010), which were quite alarming numbers and emphasized the need for prevention strategies against cyberbullying. Up until then, no evaluated prevention programs targeting cyberbullying existed in Germany. "Media Heroes" was

*The original German title of the program is "Medienhelden". Further information and materials are available at www.media-heroes.info.

Reducing Cyberbullying in Schools. https://doi.org/10.1016/B978-0-12-811423-0.00011-0

one of the first German programs specifically designed to prevent cyberbullying, which was also empirically evaluated in a pre-post-follow-up waiting control group design.

The present program was awarded second place of the European Crime Prevention Award in 2015. Since cyberbullying has also been linked to media-specific risk factors such as risky self-disclosure, sharing of passwords, and deviant online behavior, the prevention of highly prevalent cyberbullying behaviors is also (online) crime prevention. "Media Heroes" is listed in the German "Grüne Liste Prävention" ("Green List of Prevention," Communities That Care; www.gruene-liste-praevention.de), which is a database that classifies prevention programs by the degree to which their effectiveness has been demonstrated to assist practitioners in their selection of interventions.

"Media Heroes" as it is presented here is thus far available in German language ("Medienhelden") and is tailored to the German school system. The program has already been implemented in other German-speaking EU states (e.g., Austria) and can also be implemented in countries with German-speaking minorities (e.g., in Belgium). A Spanish version with adaptations is currently being tested in Colombia (Chaux, Scheithauer, Schultze-Krumbholz, & Zagorscak, 2014). An English version with the respective tailoring to the different school systems is in preparation and will be available within the next 2 years.

What is the program and how is it delivered?

"Media Heroes" aims to prevent cyberbullying and to promote online self-protection and is suitable for students in Grades 7 to 10 (approx. ages 12–16), their teachers, and their parents. The program consists of a structured manual, which was published as a book in 2012. The first chapters offer theoretical knowledge on the phenomenon of cyberbullying, the scientific basis of the program, an overview of the most popular technological communication devices and channels, and the (preliminary) results of the evaluation study. The second part of the manual consists of recommendations and instructions for teachers on how to conduct the specific, consecutive, modularized sessions, including the respective teaching materials (on CD-ROM).

The present program is a universal preventive intervention targeting not only perpetrators and victims of cyberbullying, but also the noninvolved students to foster future intervention of peers. On the one hand, peers play a crucial role since adolescents prefer to turn to peers and friends for support instead of adults (Perren et al., 2012a; Stacey, 2009; Topçu, Erdur-Baker, & Çapa-Aydin, 2008). On the other hand, the involvement of the whole group of students is important in order to address the group dynamics that are maintaining (cyber-) bullying situations (Salmivalli, Lagerspetz, Björkqvist, Österman, & Kaukiainen, 1996).

After successful development and evaluation, a train-the-trainer approach (for school teachers, social workers, and school police officers) has been developed for the purpose of implementation and roll-out of the program. These training sessions introduce the participants to the program, its aims, and its methods. Participants can discuss open questions and practice the methods and exercises. Thereafter, the teachers and youth work professionals can carry out the program within their usual structured work settings (e.g., the classroom environment) with the help of the materials. They are then able to conduct the program on their own, which ensures sustainability over time and student cohorts. Utilizing external experts and additional monetary resources is not necessary with the structured and manualized "Media Heroes" program, although it is possible and is implemented thus by licensed partners, for example, in Austria (www.medienhelden.at). Meanwhile, a licensed, external German enterprise (stravio UG, Berlin) offers the train-the-trainer workshops for implementation of the program in schools.

The theoretical model behind the program

"Media Heroes" is based on knowledge about the association between cyberbullying and empathy and perspective taking. Previous research has shown empathy to be negatively related to cyberbullying perpetration (see Schultze-Krumbholz, Schultze, Zagorscak, Wölfer, & Scheithauer, 2016), i.e., perpetrators of cyberbullying display less empathic feelings generally and toward victims of cyberbullying. Moreover, 95% of perpetrators perceive their behavior to be harmless (Shapka, 2011). Therefore, "Media Heroes" addresses and trains students in empathy and perspective taking through different methods such as a film of a cyberbullying situation ("Let's fight it together", Childnet International (Producer), 2007) and role plays.

Overall the program relies on social learning and cognitive-behavioral theory. It thus incorporates methods like peer-to-peer and student-to-parent learning. The different sessions are clearly structured and offer an active learning environment that reinforces positive behaviors of students. On a more fine-grained perspective, "Media Heroes" is theoretically based on the Theory of Reasoned Action (Ajzen & Fishbein, 1980; Fishbein & Ajzen, 1975) and the Theory of Planned Behavior (Ajzen, 1991). A first empirical test showed the more parsimonious Theory of Reasoned Action (Madden, Ellen, & Ajzen, 1992) to be a fitting and valid theoretical framework for this program (Zagorscak, Schultze-Krumbholz, Wölfer, & Scheithauer, in preparation). Fig. 11.1 shows the process model that builds the basis of the present program. We hypothesized that education through the conveyance of potential negative impact for the victims and by promoting empathy with the victims influences attitudes in a positive way. Further, one exercise examines the legal situation and potential consequences for perpetrators of cyberbullying. This is implemented in a moral dilemma discussion (simulated court session), which additionally aims at moral reasoning. Cyberbullying can be viewed as immoral behavior because it affects the welfare and rights of the victims through intentional behavior (Bussey, Fitzpatrick, & Raman, 2015, p. 31). Previous studies showed a link between moral reasoning or moral disengagement, respectively, and cyberbullying. Moral disengagement allows people to selectively act immorally toward groups or individuals without violating their general moral standards through a number of cognitive justifications (see Bandura, 2002). Adolescents with higher scores on moral disengagement are more likely to engage in cyberbullying (Bussey et al., 2015; Gini, Pozzoli, & Hymel, 2014). Further, studies on traditional bullying also showed that some subgroups of bystanders (outsiders and unconcerned bystanders) are more morally disengaged than adolescents who support the victim by defending him or her, for example (Obermann, 2011). Working closely together with classmates in group

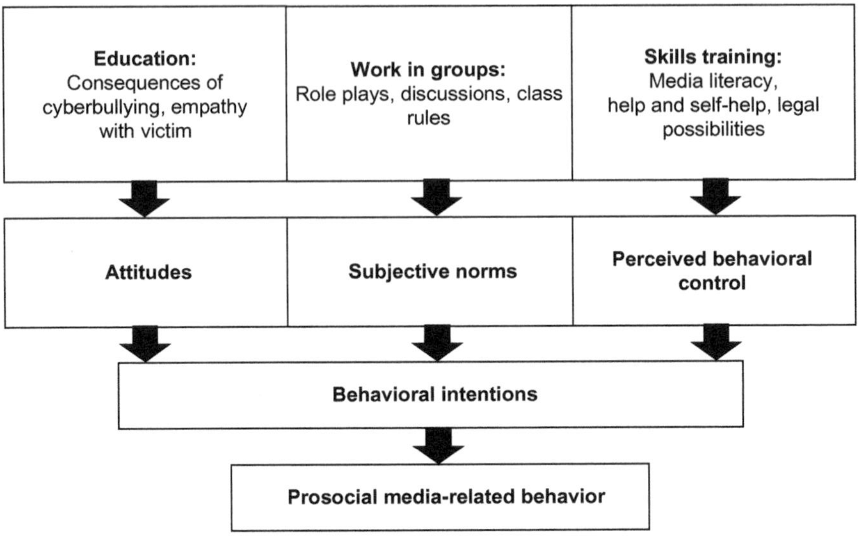

Fig. 11.1 Process model of "Media Heroes", based on Ajzen (1985) and Zagorscak, Schultze-Krumbholz, Siebenbrock, Wölfer, and Scheithauer (2011).

exercises such as role plays, discussions, and the formulation of class rules enables the adolescents to get a more realistic impression of their peers' actual norms regarding cyberbullying. Subjective norms, i.e., their beliefs of how others expect them to behave (Ajzen & Fishbein, 1980), may become more realistic as students learn that their peers do not actually expect them to bully others (for perpetrators) or that their peers expect them to intervene in cyberbullying incidents (for bystanders). Promoting social skills as well as media literacy and behavioral alternatives is expected to improve the perceived behavioral control, i.e., adolescents' perceptions regarding the extent to which they can actually influence a situation. Using peer-to-peer and student-to-parent approaches as well as role plays for practicing alternative behavior, we aim to improve self-efficacy and self-esteem, which is expected to further contribute to perceived behavioral control. Together, attitudes, subjective norms, and behavioral control are believed to influence behavioral intentions (for example, the intention not to post negative comments below possibly unfavorable pictures on social networks as tempting as this might be). According to Ajzen (1985), behavioral intentions directly influence actual behavior.

Different versions of the program for different needs

In accordance with different needs and resources of schools, administrations, and teachers, two versions of the program were developed representing different expenditure: an approximately 10-week program (also called "Media Heroes Curriculum") with 90 min per week, and a 1-day intervention (subsequently referred to as the "Media Heroes Project Day") consisting of four blocks of 90 min each. In the Curriculum, the weeks are further divided into steps. These two versions differ regarding elaborateness,

Table 11.1 Overview of the program versions' contents

Week	Content in ...		Description
	Curriculum	Project Day	
1. Introduction	Assets and dangers of communication technologies	Blocks I and II (condensed content)	Students are introduced to the program, its aims and contents
2. Awareness raising and education	Definition and consequences of cyberbullying		The phenomenon of "cyberbullying" and students' attitudes to it are addressed
3. Empathy training	Feelings and perspectives regarding cyberbullying		Students examine and experience different perspectives
4. Role plays	Social roles and opportunities for action in cyberbullying	–	Students test out different perspectives and behavioral alternatives
5.–6. Peer-to-Peer Tutoring	Protection strategies for oneself and others	Block III (condensed content)	"Expert" (supervised) students teach peers online protection strategies
7. Moral dilemma discussions	Information on the legal background	–	In a simulated court session, students reflect upon legal issues and consequences
8.–9. Student-to-Parent Tutoring	Preparation and implementation of a parents' evening	–	Students impart their insights on communication technologies and cyberbullying to their parents
10. Consolidation of knowledge	Reflection and quiz	Block IV	Students summarize and reflect upon the contents of the program

number, and intensity of the exercises. Also, not all topics of the Curriculum are also included in the Project Day. Table 11.1 gives an overview of the content of the sessions and the program versions. Generally, we recommend implementing the Curriculum, because it provides the duration and intensity needed for long-term change, as previous studies on traditional bullying prevention have found dose effects (e.g., Ttofi & Farrington, 2011). However, conducting the Project Day is still to be preferred over not implementing any intervention at all (as will be shown in the empirical evidence section) and the Project Day can also serve as a first introduction to the program and testing the responses toward the program.

Table 11.2 gives an example of a typical program session of the Curriculum.

Table 11.2 Example of a session of the "Media Heroes Curriculum" (condensed description; translated from Schultze-Krumbholz & Scheithauer, 2012, p. 217)

Step 3—Classifying cyberbullying incidents
1. Recapitulation: Throughout the program the students keep a reflection sheet with the core insights of each step. At the beginning of each step, a student reads out loud what he/she has recorded for the previous step and thus presents a summary of the most important contents. (Timeframe: 5 min) 2. Classifying incidents: In the previous step, students were assigned the homework to note down cyberbullying experiences. These are now collected, shuffled, and distributed. Subsequently, these experiences are classified on an opinion line with the endpoints "no cyberbullying" and "severe cyberbullying" according to the perceived severity. (Timeframe: 15–20 min) 3. Discussing impact: Some examples from the middle and both endpoints of the opinion line are selected and discussed in a group discussion using a chair circle regarding how the target might have felt and how the students themselves would feel in this situation. (Timeframe: 15–20 min) 4. Closing ritual and homework assignment: Using colored traffic-light-cards the students give an overview of their mood in a so-called flashlight. As homework, students record the core insights of the present step in two to three sentences in their reflection sheet. (Timeframe: 5 min)

The intervention levels of the program

"Media Heroes" addresses cyberbullying on different levels: the individual level, the classroom level, and the family level. On the *individual level*, students take part in the training of different individual social skills such as empathy and perspective-training. Through a simulated (classroom) court session, the individual's moral reasoning is challenged and sharpened to make students aware that there may be a freedom of speech, but that this does not automatically justify the denigration of others. Further, sessions in the computer lab where students teach each other (peer-to-peer approach) about privacy settings and other online self-protection strategies on their most popular (social networking) sites extend the repertoire of the individual's action strategies. The exercises on awareness raising and perspective taking further aim at an attitude change toward the acceptability of cyberbullying at the individual level. Also, the targeted change of adolescents' subjective norms takes place on the individual level.

At the *classroom level*, the program aims to raise awareness of the negative consequences of cyberbullying especially for the victims and to increase the motivation to intervene when peers become aware of cyberbullying incidents. Many of the exercises are designed to foster positive class norms and negative attitudes toward cyberbullying. Working on the topic as a class, students are expected to reach a social consensus and classroom norm not supporting cyberbullying behavior. This is an important aspect since the behavior of the so-called bystanders supports the social consensus (Quirk & Campbell, 2015). Letting students work together in groups and letting them prepare materials by themselves in groups (with supervision and guidance by the teacher) aim at promoting a positive class climate. At the classroom level, the teacher is also educated, for example through additional information and material in the theoretical background of the manual. Raising awareness and providing potential intervention and prevention strategies is an important aspect for teachers, because many campaigns and approaches recommend that students confide in teachers or adults in general. However, often teachers (and parents) are left on their own to deal with cyberbullying incidents when approached by students. If adults lack helpful advice and strategies once adolescents have mustered the courage to confide in them, students might feel even more isolated and disappointed afterward.

To include parents in the program on the *family level*, students prepare a parent evening (student-to-parent approach) in which they decide on the content and the forms of presentation and the teacher only assists them and monitors time management of the preparatory activities. Besides the repetition and reflection of the program's contents by the students on the individual level, this activity aims at educating parents on modern communication technologies, but also on their children's (newly acquired) skills in handling them. Parents' confidence is expected to increase when the students present them with their knowledge of online self-protection strategies (such as knowing where to change privacy settings). Students may also decide to plan a session where they actually teach their parents these strategies and repeat the respective sessions of the program with their parents thus specifically educating their parents in online safety. We also expect this parent evening to at least initiate communication between students and parents about the technology. Fig. 11.2 summarizes the different components of "Media Heroes" on the different intervention levels.

"Media Heroes" works at different stages of the prevention process, but it is not suitable as a direct intervention for a current severe cyberbullying incident. Perren et al. (2012b) applied the stages of prevention (Mrazek & Haggerty, 1994) to cyberbullying prevention. They allocated specific prevention approaches to these levels. Fig. 11.3 shows an adaptation of this categorization and includes the components also present in "Media Heroes." This program aims to reduce risks before cyberbullying takes place by including exercises on privacy settings (Weeks 5 and 6, see Table 11.1), for example. Empathy training and educating students on different perspectives and feelings is also suited for reducing risks. Including all students into the program, teaching noninvolved students about the consequences for victims, and providing them with behavioral alternatives, enables social support during and right after a cyberbullying incident from peers and friends, but also from teachers and parents through the awareness raising and education of these groups of adults. The same is applicable for emotional support from peers, friends, teachers, and parents after a cyberbullying incident to buffer potential negative impact on the victim.

Evidence for effectiveness to date

"Media Heroes" was one the first cyberbullying prevention programs to be evaluated empirically. Data were collected at three time points: before the intervention (January 2011), right after the conclusion of the intervention (April 2011), and about six months

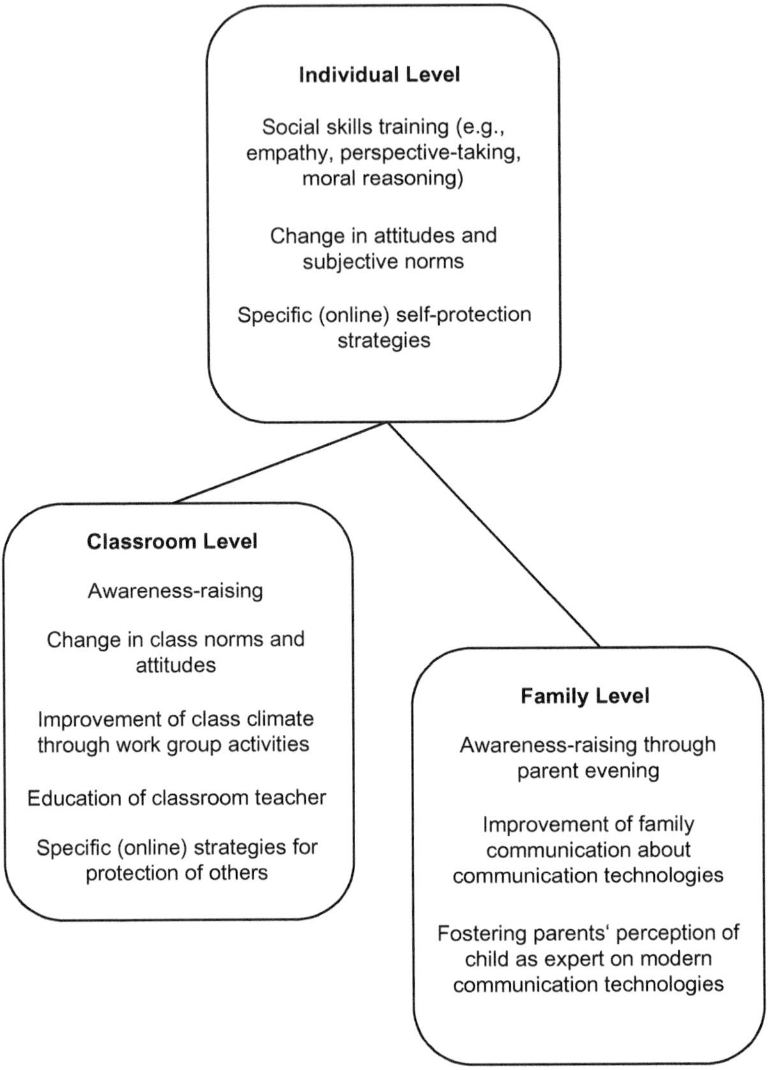

Fig. 11.2 Components of "Media Heroes" on the different intervention levels.

after the implementation of the program (November-December 2011). At the first data assessment, 897 students from 35 classes from five schools in a German major city (inhabitants > 1,000,000) participated in the first data assessment of the study. Students were from Grades 7 to 10 with an average age of 13.45 (SD = 1.07) years. Four-hundred-and-thirty-nine students were part of the nonintervention control group, 286 participated in the Curriculum, and 172 received the Project Day. This corresponds to 16 control group classes, 12 classes conducting the Curriculum, and 7 classes implementing the Project Day. Depending on the outcome variables that were examined in the different analyses, sample sizes differed due to different completion rates.

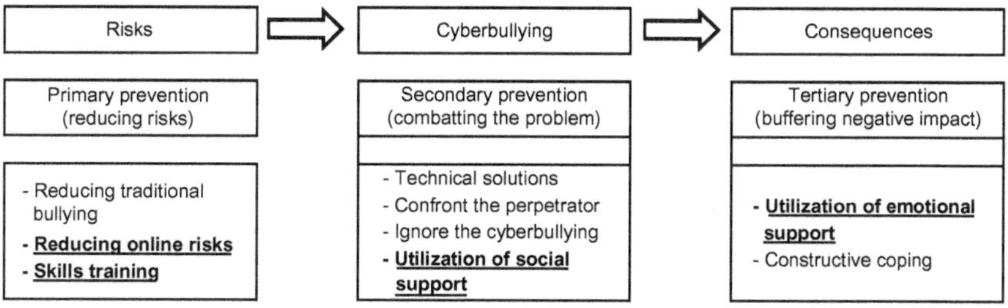

Fig. 11.3 Stages of cyberbullying prevention. Components that are present in "Media Heroes" are highlighted in bold and underlined text.
Adapted from Perren, S., Corcoran, L., Cowie, H., Dehue, F., Garcia, D. J., Mc Guckin, C., … Völlink, T. (2012b). Tackling cyberbullying: Review of empirical evidence regarding successful responses by students, parents, and schools. International Journal of Conflict and Violence, 6, 283–292.

One of the participating schools was a general high school while the other four schools were college-preparatory schools. The sample was a self-selective convenience sample. Schools were asked to provide waiting-control-group classes (i.e., classes that did not take part in the program while the evaluation study was still ongoing, but received training and the materials after the end of the study) along with intervention classes. Schools were asked to randomly assign their classes to the intervention and control conditions. Data were collected using standardized questionnaires during regular schools lessons. Questionnaires were also distributed to the teachers and parents.

Program acceptance

The questionnaire included questions on the program acceptance and perception. Further, teachers completed standardized protocol sheets after each session of the Curriculum or at the end of the Project Day, respectively, regarding feasibility, methods, contents, quality of the materials and instructions, and acceptance of each session.

Program acceptance among participants was very good overall and shows that "Media Heroes" is suited well for the school context. Of participating adolescents 46.4% liked the program much or very much. An additional 32.1% liked it at least partly. The most popular components of the Curriculum were the work with the movie "Let's fight it Together" (Childnet International (Producer), 2007), the exercises in the schools' computer labs, and the role plays. Regarding their subjective perception of whether "Media Heroes" led to a decrease in cyberbullying 38.6% of the students answered "much" or "very much" and 22.1% believed that this effect took place "partly." Among teachers, acceptance of the program was even higher than among the students: None of the teachers liked the program "a little" or "not at all"; 25% liked it partly and 75% liked it much or very much. Nearly two-thirds of the participating teachers believed that the program decreased cyberbullying "much" or "very much." Fig. 11.4 shows the results for these subjective perceptions of students and teachers. Analyses of the session protocols revealed that on average teachers judged the

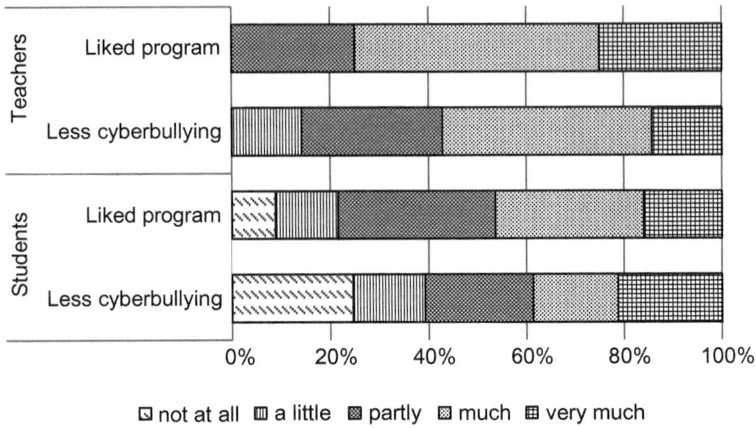

Fig. 11.4 Perceptions of the Curriculum and its effects.

materials and exercises as "satisfactory" or "very satisfactory" (Schultze-Krumbholz, Wölfer, Zagorscak, & Scheithauer, 2012a).

Program effectiveness

A number of analyses were conducted of various aspects and outcome variables based on standardized measures. The main focus was on the improvement of the social skills "empathy" and "perspective taking," personal well-being, and the perpetration of cyberbullying. In the following, we give a summary of the evaluation results that have been published to date.

Perpetration of cyberbullying increased over time in the control group, remained stable in the Project Day (short) intervention group, and decreased in the Curriculum (long) intervention group, which indicates a positive long-term effect on this behavior, i.e., a long-term decrease in cyberbullying perpetration (Schultze-Krumbholz, Zagorscak, Wölfer, & Scheithauer, 2014a; Schultze-Krumbholz, Zagorscak, Wölfer, & Scheithauer, 2014b). Students in the control group also generally displayed development-related increases in different forms of aggression, which were to be expected considering the developmental courses of aggression in this age group. However, these developments were not shown by participants of the intervention groups. "Media Heroes" seems to be able to attenuate development-related increases in aggression. We did not find any effects on *cyberbullying victimization* (Chaux, Velásquez, Schultze-Krumbholz, & Scheithauer, 2016). We believe this might be due to the specific characteristics of cyberbullying. While we can reach perpetrators of cyberbullying who attend the class in which the program is implemented, we cannot deliver the intervention to nonclassmate perpetrators. Students who are victimized by nonclassmates online therefore are not less victimized after the intervention. However, they might be more capable of buffering negative impact after "Media Heroes." This needs to be examined in further analyses.

Notably, *willingness* to participate in or initiate cyberbullying only decreased in the long intervention group while no significant changes could be found for the control and short intervention groups (Schultze-Krumbholz et al., 2014b). Willingness can be viewed as a behavioral readiness, which leads to behavioral intentions.

Adolescents in the control group showed a decrease in *empathy* over time, which is in accordance with previous studies (e.g., Van der Graaff et al., 2013), showing this to be normal at this developmental stage, especially for boys. Participants of both intervention groups did not show this decrease. Regarding *perspective taking*, both intervention groups showed improvements compared to the control group (Schultze-Krumbholz et al., 2014a). Multilevel analyses revealed that classes with high aggregated scores of perspective taking, showed stronger decreases in cyberbullying behavior, indicating a synergistic overall dynamic and emphasizing the importance of perspective-taking training within the framework of a program like "Media Heroes" (Wölfer et al., 2014). Another analysis further showed that the improvement in perspective taking in the long intervention group did not differ significantly from the control group, whereas the short intervention group differed significantly. The short intervention may be able to influence thoughts and cognitions, but not feelings regarding cyberbullying and was not able to reduce cyberbullying within the whole intervention group. However, the analyses showed that students who increased in their perspective taking, decreased their cyberbullying behavior. This indicates that this type of intervention is not suitable for every participant (Schultze-Krumbholz et al., 2016).

Regarding outcome variables related to personal well-being, we found that adolescents from the long intervention group showed increases in *self-esteem* and *subjective health* six months after termination of the intervention (Schultze-Krumbholz et al., 2014a).

In another analysis, we explored spillover effects of "Media Heroes" on *traditional bullying*. A significant effect on traditional bullying perpetration was found for the long intervention group: while initial nonperpetrators increased in traditional bullying perpetration in the control and short intervention groups, nonperpetrators remained nonperpetrators in the long intervention group. For adolescents who were both cyber- and traditional bullies before the intervention, a decrease in traditional bullying was found in the short and long intervention groups. The long intervention thus prevented nonperpetrators from becoming perpetrators and reduced traditional bullying in students who already were perpetrators. Regarding *traditional victimization*, the analysis revealed that victimization increased in the control group while the long intervention prevented nonvictims from becoming victims and reduced traditional victimization in those adolescents who were victims before the intervention (Chaux et al., 2016).

The existing evaluation results and the results presented here, especially regarding the comparison between the two versions of "Media Heroes," implicate that effectiveness of the program increases with increasing duration of program implementation (cf. Wölfer et al., 2014). The "Media Heroes Project Day" seems suitable to maintain the status quo and to counteract development-related deteriorations while the "Media Heroes Curriculum" seems adequate to achieve long-term improvements. In case of resource shortage of the school, we recommend to at least implement the Project Day though the Curriculum is more ideal. In any case, "Media Heroes" presents an effective approach to address and counter cyberbullying among adolescents.

Acknowledgments

This project was funded by the DAPHNE III Program to combat violence against children, young persons, and women, funded by the European Commission (action no. JLS/2008/DAP3/AG/1211-30-CE-0311025/00-69; Cyberbullying in Adolescence: Investigation and Intervention in Six European Countries).

References

Ajzen, I. (1985). From intentions to actions. A theory of planned behavior. In J. Kuhl & J. Beckmann (Eds.), *Action control: From cognition to behavior* (pp. 11–39). Seattle, WA: Hogrefe & Huber.

Ajzen, I. (1991). The theory of planned behavior. *Organizational Behavior and Human Decision Processes*, *50*(2), 179–211. https://doi.org/10.1016/0749-5978(91)90020-t.

Ajzen, I., & Fishbein, M. (1980). *Understanding attitudes and predicting social behavior.* Englewood Cliffs, NJ: Prentice-Hall.

Bandura, A. (2002). Selective moral disengagement in the exercise of moral agency. *Journal of Moral Education*, *31*, 101–119.

Bussey, K., Fitzpatrick, S., & Raman, A. (2015). The role of moral disengagement and self-efficacy in cyberbullying. *Journal of School Violence*, *14*, 30–46. https://doi.org/10.1080/15388220.2014.954045.

Chaux, E., Scheithauer, H., Schultze-Krumbholz, A., & Zagorscak, P. (2014). Towards an effective and culturally appropriate prevention program against cyberbullying. Research project financed by Alexander von Humboldt Foundation. Berlin, Germany.

Chaux, E., Velásquez, A. M., Schultze-Krumbholz, A., & Scheithauer, H. (2016). Effects of the cyberbullying prevention program media heroes (Medienhelden) on traditional bullying. *Aggressive Behavior*, *42*, 157–165. https://doi.org/10.1002/ab.21637.

Childnet International (Producer). (2007). Let's fight it together. [Online Film] Retrieved from http://old.digizen.org/cyberbullying/fullFilm.aspx.

Festl, R., & Quandt, T. (2016). The role of online communication in long-term cyberbullying involvement among girls and boys. *Journal of Youth & Adolescence*, *45*, 1931–1945. https://doi.org/10.1007/s10964-016-0552-9.

Fishbein, M., & Ajzen, I. (1975). *Belief, attitude, intention and behavior: An introduction to theory and research.* Reading, MA: Addison-Wesley.

Gini, G., Pozzoli, T., & Hymel, S. (2014). Moral disengagement among children and youth: A meta-analytic review of links to aggressive behavior. *Aggressive Behavior*, *40*, 56–68. https://doi.org/10.1002/ab.21502.

Madden, T. J., Ellen, P. S., & Ajzen, I. (1992). A comparison of the theory of planned behavior and the theory of reasoned action. *Personality and Social Psychology Bulletin*, *18*, 3–9. https://doi.org/10.1177/0146167292181001.

Mrazek, P. J., & Haggerty, R. J. (1994). *Reducing risks for mental disorders: Frontiers for preventive intervention research.* Washington, D.C: The National Academic Press.

Obermann, M.-L. (2011). Moral disengagement among bystanders to school bullying. *Journal of School Violence*, *10*, 239–257. https://doi.org/10.1080/15388220.2011.578276.

Perren, S., Corcoran, L., Cowie, H., Dehue, F., Garcia, D. J., Mc Guckin, C., … Völlink, T. (2012a). Coping with cyberbullying: A systematic literature review. Final report of the COST IS 0801 Working Group 5. Retrieved from https://sites.google.com/site/costis0801/books-and-publications-1.

Perren, S., Corcoran, L., Cowie, H., Dehue, F., Garcia, D. J., Mc Guckin, C., et al. (2012b). Tackling cyberbullying: Review of empirical evidence regarding successful responses by students, parents, and schools. *International Journal of Conflict and Violence*, *6*, 283–292.

Quirk, R., & Campbell, M. (2015). On standby? A comparison of online and offline witnesses to bullying and their bystander behaviour. *Educational Psychology*, *35*, 430–448. https://doi.org/10.1080/01443410.2014.893556.

Salmivalli, C., Lagerspetz, K. M. J., Björkqvist, K., Österman, K., & Kaukiainen, A. (1996). Bullying as a group process: Participant roles and their relations to social status within the group. *Aggressive Behavior*, *22*, 1–15.

Schultze-Krumbholz, A., & Scheithauer, H. (2010). Cyberbullying unter Kindern und Jugendlichen—Ein Forschungsüberblick [Cyberbullying among children and adolescents—A research review]. *Psychosozial*, *122*, 79–91.

Schultze-Krumbholz, A., & Scheithauer, H. (2012). Das Medienhelden-Programm zur Prävention von Cybermobbing [The Media Heroes program for the prevention of cyberbullying]. In S. Drewes & K. Seifried (Eds.), *Krisen im Schulalltag—Prävention, Management und Nachsorge [Crises in everyday school life—Prevention, management and aftercare]* (pp. 210–219). Stuttgart: Kohlhammer.

Schultze-Krumbholz, A., Schultze, M., Zagorscak, P., Wölfer, R., & Scheithauer, H. (2016). Feeling cybervictims' pain—The effect of empathy training on cyberbullying. *Aggressive Behavior*, *42*, 147–156. https://doi.org/10.1002/ab.21613.

Schultze-Krumbholz, A., Wölfer, R., Zagorscak, P., & Scheithauer, H. (2012). Stakeholders' perception of the cyberbullying prevention program "Medienhelden". *Poster presented at the Conference "Bullying and cyberbullying: The interface between science and practice", Vienna, Austria*.

Schultze-Krumbholz, A., Zagorscak, P., Siebenbrock, A., & Scheithauer, H. (2012). *Medienhelden—Unterrichtsmanual zur Förderung von Medienkompetenz und Prävention von Cybermobbing [Media Heroes—Teaching manual for the promotion of media competence and the prevention of cyberbullying]*. München: Reinhardt Verlag.

Schultze-Krumbholz, A., Zagorscak, P., Wölfer, R., & Scheithauer, H. (2014a). Das Medienhelden-Programm zur Förderung von Medienkompetenz und Prävention von Cybermobbing: Konzept und Ergebnisse aus der Evaluation [Promotion of media competence and prevention of cyberbullying using the Medienhelden program: Results from an evaluation study]. *Praxis der Kinderpsychologie und Kinderpsychiatrie*, *63*, 379–394.

Schultze-Krumbholz, A., Zagorscak, P., Wölfer, R., & Scheithauer, H. (2014b). Prävention von Cybermobbing und Reduzierung aggressiven Verhaltens Jugendlicher durch das Programm Medienhelden: Ergebnisse einer Evaluationsstudie [Prevention of cyberbullying and reduction of aggressive behavior using the Medienhelden program: Results of an evaluation study]. *Diskurs Kindheits- und Jugendforschung*, *2014*(1), 61–79.

Shapka, J. D. (2011). Internet socializing snline: What are the risks? In *Paper presented at Curtin University of Technology, Perth, Australia*.

Stacey, E. (2009). Research into cyberbullying: Student perspectives on cybersafe learning environments. *Informatics in Education*, *8*, 115–130.

Topçu, Ç., Erdur-Baker, Ö., & Çapa-Aydin, Y. (2008). Examination of cyberbullying experiences among Turkish students from different school types. *CyberPsychology & Behavior*, *11*, 643–648. https://doi.org/10.1089/cpb.2007.0161.

Ttofi, M. M., & Farrington, D. P. (2011). Effectiveness of school-based programs to reduce bullying: A systematic and meta-analytic review. *Journal of Experimental Criminology*, *7*, 27–56. https://doi.org/10.1007/s11292-010-9109-1.

Van der Graaff, J., Branje, S., De Wied, M., Hawk, S., Van Lier, P., & Meeus, W. (2013). Perspective taking and empathic concern in adolescence: Gender differences in developmental changes. *Developmental Psychology*, *50*, 881–888. https://doi.org/10.1037/a0034325.

Wölfer, R., Schultze-Krumbholz, A., Zagorscak, P., Jäkel, A., Göbel, K., & Scheithauer, H. (2014). Prevention 2.0: Targeting cyberbullying @ school. *Prevention Science*, *15*, 879–887. https://doi.org/10.1007/s11121-013-0438-y.

Zagorscak, P., Schultze-Krumbholz, A., Siebenbrock, A., Wölfer, R., & Scheithauer, H. (2011). MEDIENHELDEN—Ein Programm zur Prävention von Cyberbullying im Schulkontext [Media Heroes—A program for the prevention of cyberbullying in the school context]. In: *Poster presented at the 13. Fachgruppentagung Pädagogische Psychologie der DGPs [Poster presented at the 13. Meeting of the DGPs Section Educational Psychology], September 14–16, Erfurt, Germany.*

Zagorscak, P., Schultze-Krumbholz, A., Wölfer, R., & Scheithauer, H. (in preparation). How does cyberbullying prevention work?—Efficacy of cyberbullying-prevention in relation to treatment intensity, changes in attitudes and changes in subjective norms—A cluster-randomized controlled trial.

Stronger than Bullying, a mobile application for victims of bullying: Development and initial steps toward validation

12

Isabelle Ouellet-Morin[*,†], *Marie-Pier Robitaille*[*,†]
[*]Research Centre of the Mental Health University Institute of Montréal, Montréal, QC, Canada, [†]Université de Montréal, Montréal, QC, Canada

Introduction

Name of program: Stronger than Bullying
Type of program: Mobile application
Suitable for ages: 12–16 years-old

It is now widely accepted among scientists, policymakers, and the general public that youth who are victims of bullying are more susceptible to experience a wide range of difficulties, including poor health and somatic complaints, low academic achievements as well as socioemotional problems (Arseneault, Bowes, & Shakoor, 2010; Craig et al., 2009; Sourander et al., 2016). The immediate suffering, along with the potential lingering impacts of bullying victimization, has exerted a powerful incentive to pass legislation sanctioning bullying behavior and asserting the responsibility of certain institutions, such as schools, to provide a safe environment for their students. Indeed, these policies appear to be associated with lower prevalence rates of bullying (Hatzenbuehler, Schwab-Reese, Ranapurwala, Hertz, & Ramirez, 2015). School- and community-wide interventions also hold the promise of making stable and positive changes in attitudes, social norms, and behavior toward bullying, which may benefit all youth. Most existing interventions have, however, not been empirically tested and only a minority has shown positive effects of, at best, a moderate size (Ttofi & Farrington, 2011). These interventions may not offer the extent of support needed by the 15% and 35% of youths who are involved in traditional bullying and cyberbullying, as victims or perpetrators (Modecki, Minchin, Harbaugh, Guerra, & Runions, 2014).

Targeted interventions designed to reach and help these youth have, to date, concentrated their efforts almost exclusively on the bullies, perhaps because of the long and rich history of research on childhood aggression (Olweus, 2013). While these interventions are necessary and may reduce bullying experienced by many victims, they may not be sufficient. Victims have, in some cases, experienced bullying for quite some time before actions have been taken to stop it and may be bullied by other peers. It thus also appears desirable to help victims acquire the skills to reduce these

Reducing Cyberbullying in Schools. https://doi.org/10.1016/B978-0-12-811423-0.00012-2

experiences and to foster resilience against subsequent difficulties. Surprisingly, relatively few interventions targeting victims of bullying have been empirically validated. This is certainly consistent with the perceptions of educators and parents who identify as problematic the lack of validated tools to help youth involved in bullying (Beran, 2006; Farrington & Ttofi, 2010).

Numeric platforms: A new opportunity to help bullying victims

The use of new technologies, including smartphones, is widespread in the general population—a trend that is even more prevalent among teens. About three-quarters of them own (or have access to) a smartphone (Lenhart et al., 2015). Specifically, while about half of middle school children own a smartphone, this proportion raises to 85% by the end of high school (Steeves, 2014). Not only do teens often own a smartphone, they also tend to prefer them to computers for a wide range of personal uses, including connecting with friends, playing games, and getting information about fashion, health, and entertainment (Connected Generation Report, 2010; Lenhart et al., 2015). While being present online may increase the risk of being bullied, these technologies also offer new opportunities to provide youth with more targeted health care services (Cuijpers, van Straten, & Andersson, 2008).

Accordingly, numeric platforms represent a new way to help bullying victims. Not only do they feel more confident talking or disclosing sensitive or embarrassing issues online or via an electronic device (Bradford & Rickwood, 2015; Jacobs, Vollink, Dehue, & Lechner, 2014; Webb, Burns, & Collin, 2008; Ybarra & Suman, 2006), these resources do not require them to disclose their experiences directly to someone, which many refuse to do out of fear of retaliation or embarrassment (Newman, Murray, & Lussier, 2001; Rigby, 2011; Webb et al., 2008). Mobile applications thus constitute a promising complementary platform to help youth (Havas, de Nooijer, Crutzen, & Feron, 2011), especially those who are not receiving help because of their reluctance to break their silence about their experiences.

This chapter outlines the development of Stronger than Bullying, a mobile application designed to help youth victims of bullying reduce their experiences and to foster their resilience in the face of mental health problems. We will first present an overview of Stronger than Bullying along with a brief description of its theoretical underpinnings, explain how Stronger than Bullying will be used, report the preliminary evidence of usefulness and outline future research and developments.

Overview of Stronger than Bullying

Stronger than Bullying has three specific objectives: (1) inform youth about bullying in an original, dynamic, and interactive manner; (2) help youth better understand their experiences and; (3) promote the experimentation of strategies to reduce bullying. Stronger than Bullying targets adolescents between 12- and 16-years-old because of the

Fig. 12.1 An overview of the main components of Stronger than Bullying.

remaining high prevalence of bullying victimization at this age, the relative complexity of the tasks proposed by the application, and the reluctance of older youths to divulge their experiences to an adult. Fig. 12.1 offers a visual presentation of the application.

Conceptual framework

In addition to refining the description of the impact of bullying on functioning, longitudinal studies comprising population-based cohorts of children have shed light on large individual differences in difficulties experienced by victims. One hypothesis to explain this heterogeneity lies in the way youth respond to bullying, both emotionally and behaviorally. Consistent with Lazarus and Folkman's (1984) Transactional model, youth who suffer the most from bullying may be those who are more inclined to use ineffective coping strategies (Lazarus & Folkman, 1984). Coping is generally defined as the individual's efforts to deal with the perceived threats and their immediate consequences (e.g., negative emotions; Lazarus, 2006). Little empirical work has been done so far to test the relevance of this conceptual model for bullying victimization [for an exception, see Hampel, Manhal, & Hayer, 2009]. Indirect evidence, however, shows that more often than not bullying victims select ineffective, emotion-focused strategies, such as distraction and denial, than nonvictims would (Cassidy, 2009; Hudson, Lambe, Committee, Pepler, & Craig, 2016). Additionally, victimized youth who chose poor coping strategies (e.g., aggression, self-blame) to deal with bullying also exhibit more externalizing problems (Dooley, Shaw, & Cross, 2012; Garnefski & Kraaij, 2014). Importantly, the Transactional model does not state that individuals' coping styles and skills are set in stone. Accordingly, one way to help youth reduce bullying victimization may be to facilitate the learning of better problem-solving techniques and to support the experimentation of more adaptive coping strategies when confronted with bullying (Garnefski & Kraaij, 2014; Jacobs, Dehue, Vollink, & Lechner, 2014).

Description of Stronger than Bullying

The structure and content of Stronger than Bullying were developed according to a coordinated sequence of four mechanisms of action considered to be at the core of problem-solving techniques. The first mechanism of action is to *learn empirically based and relevant information about bullying* to raise awareness about its occurrence and consequences. We included ten short videos featuring public figures popular with youth along with a virtual city map inviting users to identify places where bullying may occur, where it happened, and where to get help. Acquiring a better understanding of what bullying entails is thought to help users shift their causal attributions about victimization from being internal (due to themselves) to external [e.g., related to the situation; Juvonen & Graham, 2014]. They may then reconsider their perceived responsibility and become hopeful that it may eventually stop.

The application promotes a second mechanism of action involved in problem-solving techniques to come about—the idea that they can *take a more active role in reducing the bullying*. This is consistent with previous findings suggesting that future and prosocial orientations may help to buffer the negative impact of bullying (Griese & Buhs, 2014; Hamilton et al., 2015; Rudolph, Troop-Gordon, Monti, & Miernicki, 2014). For example, in the videos, youth personalities take a stand against bullying, show empathy regarding the victims' experiences, explain that other people like them were once victims of bullying and have gone on to have successful lives, and that a number of resources and tools exist to help them.

The third mechanism of action in problem-solving techniques embedded in this application is to help bullying victims to *clearly define the bullying problem* in order to adopt better strategies to respond to it. Some victims minimize their experiences (or think that they do not consist of bullying) while others overestimate them. Either way, these biases may affect their motivation to take steps to end bullying. To help victims define the problem more objectively, Stronger than Bullying collects information about bullying on a regular basis (every day, every other day, or once a week) using the items adapted from the Olweus bullying Questionnaire (Olweus, 1996) and compiles them in easy-to-understand graphs. These graphs illustrate which forms of bullying they experience the most, where it happens, and whether these experiences are increasing or decreasing over time. They can be shared with someone trustworthy, via email or in person, to facilitate breaking the silence about the victimization. Better understanding one's own experiences is hypothesized to help identify clear targets, a key step to display more effective strategies in response to bullying and to reduce victimization.

The fourth and final mechanism of action in problem-solving techniques targeted by Stronger than Bullying is to *brainstorm and evaluate the selected solutions*. By definition, victims of bullying come to think that it would be very hard for them to end it (Olweus, 2013), especially so if they have already tried a number of strategies that were not deemed useful or effective. Stronger than Bullying readily offers dozens of strategies along with a list of online and telephone resources to help them expand the pool of strategies to choose from. Each strategy includes a short description of what it entails and, if relevant, words of caution. The users are also invited to add their own strategies, which may stimulate further brainstorming, make them adapt to their situation, personal strengths, and limitations. Stronger than Bullying invites users to experiment with strategies and to evaluate them based on four dimensions of emotions (anger-serenity, sadness-happiness, insecure-confidence and anxiety-calmness) and the overall perception of usefulness. The goal is to promote experimentation of strategies in order to find which are most effective so they use them more often (e.g., talk to someone they trust) and that they gradually abandon those that do not work (e.g., crying alone, lashing out). Of note, the strategies included in Stronger than Bullying reflect prior work enquiring youth about the strategies they use (or would use) when confronted with bullying (Camodeca & Goossens, 2005; Hudson et al., 2016; Parris, Vayjas, Meyers, & Cutts, 2012; Slonje, Smith, & Frisén, 2013; Tenenbaum, Varjas, Meyers, & Parris, 2011; Weinstein et al., 2016) or are based on empirical work identifying factors shown to mitigate the impact of bullying on health and functioning [e.g., social support (Bowes, Maughan, Caspi, Moffitt, & Arseneault, 2010; Brendgen et al., 2014, 2013; Fridh, Lindstrom, & Rosvall, 2015)]. Less effective strategies have also been included (with words of caution) because they are often used by victims who could, through experimentation, recognize their relative ineffectiveness.

More generally, problem-solving techniques imply breaking down a problem into a small number of achievable steps in order to facilitate taking action to solve the larger problem without feeling overwhelmed or incapable to carry these tasks. Stronger than Bullying's layout mirrors this approach, dividing the content of the application into a number of menus and functions (see Fig. 12.1).

How the intervention is delivered?

Stronger than Bullying was developed to help youth reduce their experiences being bullied, even for victims who initially prefer not to disclose this information. This application can be downloaded, free of charge. Accordingly, the dissemination of this tool is expected to take place through features in the mainstream media, posters in schools, Facebook posts and marketing, word of mouth, etc. Alternatively, Stronger than Bullying could also be used by teachers or health care professionals (e.g., social workers, nurses or psychologists) to facilitate the disclosure of bullying experiences or as a complementary tool to help victims acquire or improve their problem-solving skills to reduce bullying victimization. At the time of this writing, the French-language version of Stronger than Bullying had been available for 2 months in the province of Québec, Canada. Despite the reception of many positive responses of youth, parents, educators and health care professionals about the perceived usefulness of this tool, it is still unknown whether Stronger than Bullying is as useful as a standalone tool as when it is used in the context of professionally-lead interventions. Similarly, future studies should also examine whether training professionals to use this tool in their interventions improves the effects of Stronger than Bullying on victimization.

Evidence for the program so far

Stronger than Bullying has been the object of one pilot study and two initial empirical investigations. The aims of the pilot study were to obtain a first indication of the perceptions of usefulness, attractiveness, and acceptability from youth, parents, and educators and to identify the weaknesses that required our attention while the application was still under development. The empirical investigations aimed to test, using a qualitative and quantitative design, whether the application was associated with a decrease in bullying victimization or changes in other areas of functioning relevant to these experiences, including the disclosure of victimization to someone they trust.

The pilot study

When a first version of Stronger than Bullying was completed, two groups of participants were invited to use the application during a 4-week period. The first comprised youth between the ages of 12 and 16 ($n=8$). The second group included parents and educators ($n=5$). Once the test period ended, we held two separate focus groups to gather the participants' general perceptions about Stronger than Bullying and to identify which features of the application they thought were the most helpful or needed improvement. Youth and adult participants unanimously stated that Stronger than Bullying may be useful to victims. They said it could also help to better inform youth in general (not just victims) about bullying. "*We talked about it (bullying) during three hours at school and I learned more about it with Stronger than Bullying in five minutes*"—14-year-old boy. Youth particularly appreciated the confidentiality (e.g., password), the number and diversity of proposed strategies, the virtual map, and the videos. The regular evaluation of bullying experiences was also reported to be a strength of the application "*It is like a personal diary*"—15-year-old girl. Of note, neither parents nor educators expressed concerns regarding the possibility that Stronger than Bullying could jeopardize (or be in conflict with) existing services. Like the younger participants, adults thought they could learn from it "*It is also a tool for the parents*"—a mother. Finally, a number of improvements were suggested by the participants, such as the visual presentation of the graphs.

The first investigation: A qualitative study

A qualitative study was preferred to first test Stronger than Bullying's usefulness considering how little we know about the tools and services perceived as useful by victims

(Levant & Hasan, 2008). Taking an inductive perspective, this methodology aimed to help understand how Stronger than Bullying may be of assistance to the victims by starting from their point of view.

Methods of Study 1

A total of 12 participants (nine girls and three boys) aged between 12- and 16-years-old were recruited through online advertisements and presentations offered in two youth centers located in the greater Montréal area, Canada. Participants were selected according to their score on the Multidimensional Peer-Victimization Scale [MPVS, 16 items; (Mynard & Joseph, 2000)], which was completed during an initial phone interview conducted by a trained research assistant. Parental oral consent was given over the phone before the interview. To be considered a victim, participants had to report a moderate-to-high level of bullying according to recommended thresholds [i.e., a total score between 16 and 21 or 22 and higher, respectively (Mynard & Joseph, 2000)]. When necessary, participants were provided with an iPhone. The research assistant outlined the study's instructions to participants (e.g., using Stronger than Bullying every day, trying and evaluating strategies). After the test period, the same research assistant asked participants to fill out the MPVS again and to participate in a semistructured interview. Four themes were explored during the interview: (1) the participant's opinions about Stronger than Bullying (e.g., visual presentation, user experience); (2) their experiences of bullying prior to Stronger than Bullying; (3) their experiences using the application and; (4) the perceived utility of Stronger than Bullying. Interviews lasted approximately 1 h and were recorded with verbatim transcription.

Analyses were conducted in two steps. First, a phenomenological examination of the verbatim interview was conducted, which helped to identify the participants' experiences in regards to the previously identified themes (Paillé & Mucchielli, 2003). Second, a thematic content analysis was performed to identify and group the themes addressed during the interviews. A coding chart was created with all codes attributed to every statement in the first few interviews. Codes were then hierarchically grouped and ranked (Paillé & Mucchielli, 2012). This chart was then used and adjusted, if needed, with the rest of the verbatim to bring out all the major themes (Danel, 2015). New participants were interviewed until saturation was obtained (i.e., new interviews did not bring new information to the understanding of the phenomenon; Pirès, 1997; Tesch, 1990). Inter-rater agreement was obtained between the research assistant and an experienced researcher, with NVivo10. The study protocol was approved by the Ethical Committee of the Montréal Mental Health University Institute.

Results of Study 1

Participants reported that they appreciated the confidentiality (e.g., password) and privacy (e.g., discrete logo) offered by Stronger than Bullying, which was reported to facilitate the disclosure of their experiences without feeling judged or pitied:

- "*It is more difficult to talk to someone (than using Stronger than Bullying) because they are going to remember only that afterward. I don't want that the person look at me and see pity. I want to talk about it but the pity that I see hurts me*"—13-year-old girl

- *"The adult, it's more a personal reaction. He/she is going to say « Oh, it's kind of hard what you're experiencing ». But we already know it's hard and then you see pity. I prefer this way (with Stronger than Bullying), you know, with the graphs to see for yourself it's serious and not that it's a person you see every day that is telling you, especially that you don't want everyone to know*"—13-year-old girl

They also reported that the immediate, 24 h, 7 days a week access along with the telephone and online references included in the application fulfilled their wish of autonomy (Danel, 2015).

Four changes were reported to have occurred while using Stronger than Bullying. First, all participants stated the application helped them to have more precise and realistic views of their experiences (e.g., nature, frequency, settings) "*The test (daily evaluations) makes you realize what you live, shows you how strong it is (the bullying). By telling you what you really live, it helps you to get the strategies to go better*"—13-year-old boy. Second, Stronger than Bullying was said to have helped them to disclose their experiences to someone they trusted. Indeed, while all participants initially refused to talk to someone, most (10 out of 12) broke the silence after the 4-week test period (Danel, 2015). Third, they described a renewed motivation to end bullying, which they attributed to the application.

- "*The strategies helped me to see good and bad things to do given your situation and as I tried some, I thought it was cool to have new things to do because before I was seeing only the negative whereas now I see that things could be done and that I can stop that*"—14-year-old girl
- "*Before Stronger than Bullying I was discouraged, I am still when I come back home, but with Stronger than Bullying, with the strategies, it helped me to have hope again. Before I had my own strategies but they were not the best ones, I'd say*"—14-year-old boy

Fourth, participants reported feeling more in control and empowered following the use of Stronger than Bullying.

- "*The fact of knowing that I have more strategies in my toolbox, I know more what to do, it definitively helped me to calm down and to see the reality*"—13-year-old boy
- "*Stronger than Bullying is really personal, it's your toolbox whereas if you talked to an adult, he/she is going to do something while with Stronger than Bullying, it has to be me that do really something with the help of Stronger than Bullying*"—14-year-old boy

To contextualize these preliminary qualitative findings, we also analyzed the MPVS scores reported before and after the use of Stronger than Bullying and observed a significant decrease of victimization using a repeated measures ANOVA [mean scores (SD): from 18.7 (4.1) to 12.2 (5.3); $F(1.00, 11.00) = 19{,}85$, $p = 0.001$]. Caution should, however, prevail in interpreting this finding considering the small size of the sample.

The second investigation: A quantitative study in schools

In this study, we examined the potential usefulness of Stronger than Bullying in reducing bullying victimization over time. To do so, we first tested, using a pretest- post-test control group design, whether the use of Stronger than Bullying was associated with a decrease in bullying experiences. Second, we explored whether the same patterns of findings could be detected in the data directly recorded by the application over the 4- to 6-week test period.

Methods of Study 2

Participants were recruited from two high schools, one public and one private, located in the province of Québec, Canada. Four waves of data collection were conducted. Each wave implied the completion of a selection questionnaire (including the MPVS; see Study 1) by the majority of students in four classrooms at the same grade level. Three groups of students were represented: (1) victims of moderate-to-high levels of bullying (MPVS scores of 16 and higher; $n=23$); (2) nonvictims (MPVS scores lower than 5; $n=12$) and; (3) occasional victims, who were also considered when not enough victims could be recruited (MPVS scores between 10 and 16; $n=5$). We thus had no a priori hypotheses regarding the magnitude of change in bullying experiences between the two victimized groups. Analyses were, however, conducted with and without the occasional victims to explore whether distinct patterns of findings could be detected. Parental consent was obtained for participants under 14 years of age while older students consented for themselves. A total of 40 students participated in this study, 23 boys and 17 girls. They used Stronger than Bullying for 4 to 6 weeks and filled the MPVS again after the test period. Another group of 170 same-aged youth who did not use Stronger than Bullying, but who were in the same classes, completed the MPVS simultaneously, at both time points. All participants were aged 12- to 16-years-old. The study protocol was approved by the Ethical Committee of the Montréal Mental Health University Institute.

Results of Study 2

Fig. 12.2 illustrates the experiences of bullying reported before and after using Stronger than Bullying for the victims (excluding and including the occasional victims), the nonvictims, and the controls. Repeated measures ANOVA showed that victims had greater levels of change in bullying victimization over time than nonvictims [$F(1, 34)=38.87, p<0.001$]. This pattern of finding remained when occasional victims were

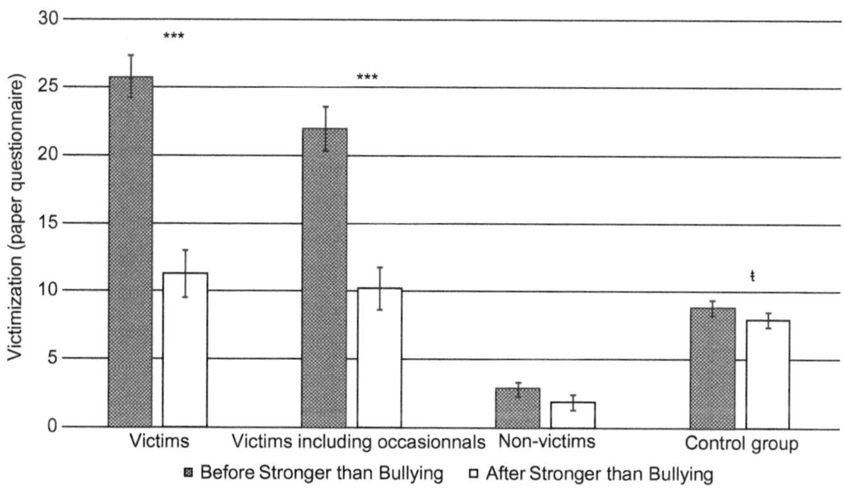

Fig. 12.2 Mean bullying experiences reported before and after using Stronger than Bullying. Notes: Repeated measures ANOVA. *SEM*, standard errors of mean. $^{***}p<.001$, $^{t}p=.07$.

considered along with the moderate-to-high victims [group x time: $F(1, 37)=30.71$, $p=0.001$]. Specifically, a significant decrease of bullying experiences was reported by moderate-to-high victims [$F(1, 21)=70.48$, $p<0.001$; $Eta^2=0.77$] as well as when all victims of bullying were considered [$F(1, 26)=70.29$, $p<0.001$; $Eta^2=0.73$]. No difference was detected, however, for nonvictims [$F(1, 11)=.03$, $p=0.86$; $Eta^2=0.00$]. These findings suggest that Stronger than Bullying may have played a role in the decline of bullying experiences over time. The effect size could tentatively be qualified of strong using Cohen's thresholds (Cohen, 1988). Fig. 12.2 also showed that the level of victimization remained relatively stable for the control group despite the fact that the repeated measures ANOVA pointed to a trend for lower levels of victimization over time [$F(1, 169)=3.36$, $p=0.07$; $Eta^2=0.02$]. The 16 time-fold larger decrease of victimization over the test period noted for the victims (or 11 time-fold when including the occasional victims) suggests, however, that the trend for reducing levels noted in the control group may not be clinically relevant nor comparable in magnitude to those noted for victims who used Stronger than Bullying.

Second, we explored whether the decreasing level of victimization noted using the paper questionnaire could also be detected using the data recorded repeatedly by the application during the same time period. We tested this possibility using a general linear mixed model with factorial effect of time and victimization. Victims and nonvictims differed in respect to their initial levels of bullying victimization [$F(1, 60.62)=6.20$, $p=.02$], which suggests that Stronger than Bullying can distinguish victims from nonvictims. We did not, however, detect a statistically significant difference in the decline of victimization over time between the victims and nonvictims [$F(5, 151.65)=0.51$, $p=.77$] nor a significant decrease for the victims [$F(5, 110.80)=1.77$, $p=.13$]. A visual inspection of Fig. 12.3 suggests nonetheless that bullying levels seemed to decrease over time in victims, especially so between weeks 4 and 5. To test this latter possibility, a pairwise comparison was conducted between these two time points. A trend for a significant decline of victimization between weeks four and five was noted [mean difference (standard error) = 1.72 (0.59), degree of freedom = 155.27, $p=0.06$]. While the statistical analyses conducted with this second set of data did not offer convincing

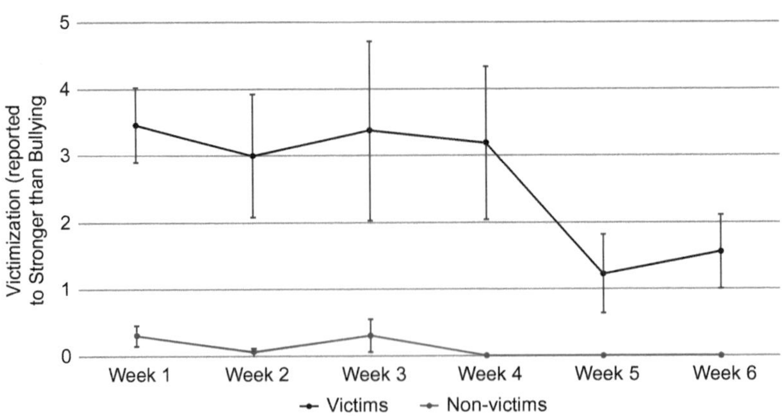

Fig. 12.3 Mean bullying experiences reported to Stronger than Bullying during the test period. Notes: *SEM*, standard errors of mean.

evidence of a decrease of bullying experiences over time, the magnitude of the estimated effect size could be tentatively qualified as moderate [Cohen's $d=0.5$; (Cohen, 1988)], which is somewhat consistent with the large effects noted when using the data collected with the paper questionnaires. Of note, the app was asking participants to specify whether bullying was taking place online and/or offline. The visual inspection of the data reported for specifically traditional and cyberbullying suggested a similar pattern of findings, although the low prevalence rates of cyberbullying during the 4 to 6 weeks testing period precluded separate analyses. Indeed, only 14 participants (35% of this selected sample) reported having been the victim of cyberbullying at least once during this period, and the vast majority (12 out of 14) reported cyberbullying at only one occasion.

Discussion and conclusion

The preliminary findings provided by the pilot study and the two initial investigations suggest that Stronger than Bullying may constitute a useful tool to help youth who are bullied to initiate actions to reduce these experiences. Three findings deserve attention. First, the qualitative and the quantitative studies offered preliminary evidence suggesting a decrease of victimization experiences during the test period. Specifically, using Stronger than Bullying was associated with more than a two-fold decrease of bullying experiences among moderate-to-high victims, an effect that remained of similar magnitude when occasional victims were also considered. These findings may indicate that, in addition to youth who are severely or frequently victimized, youth who are confronted with bullying on a more infrequent basis may also benefit from using the application. In the same way, the participants of the pilot study reported that Stronger than Bullying may help all youth, adults working with teens and parents learn more about bullying and become a source of reference when helping a friend, a student, or a child.

These preliminary findings depend, however, on the absence (or minimal influence) of measuring bias in the data collected using the paper questionnaires, notably social desirability and recall errors (Pellegrini & Bartini, 2000). To offer a complementary test of the possibility that using Stronger than Bullying is associated with a decrease of victimization over time, we examined in parallel the victimization information directly reported to the application. While these data are still self-reported, the nature of how they were collected may have tempered the impact of social desirability and recall errors because of the confidentiality offered by Stronger than Bullying and the completion of the evaluations on a regular basis (Bradford & Rickwood, 2015; Pellegrini & Bartini, 2000). In addition, the use of a pretest- post-test control group design revealed that the magnitude of the changes in victimization reported by the victims was several times higher than those noted for the nonvictims or the controls. Caution is nevertheless advised in interpreting these preliminary findings until the hypothesized effect of Stronger than Bullying in reducing bullying is properly tested with an experimental design including randomization of the participants, a larger sample size, multiple informants (e.g., teachers, parents), and follow-up data points examining the mid- and long-term gains associated with its use. Moreover, the findings provide no clear indication of the usefulness of Stronger than Bullying for cyberbullying because of the low incidence rate of online bullying reported in this sample. Future studies should thus attempt to replicate the present findings in larger samples (or by using oversampling techniques to ensure sufficient variance of cyberbullying victimization). Future studies should also attempt to evaluate how each four proposed mechanisms of action work together (or against each other) to decrease bullying and foster well-being. The preliminary findings cannot offer insights regarding these important questions at this point.

Furthermore, the preliminary findings suggest that Stronger than Bullying may need to be used for a certain amount of time before any meaningful change (statistically and clinically) in bullying could be detected. Based on the visual inspection of the data, we speculate at least 5 weeks may be required before a clear attenuation on victimization is noticeable. These findings, however, relied on just 17 participants who were allowed to use Stronger than Bullying for more than 4 weeks for logistical reasons. Future studies should thus examine more closely the question of dosage, which should also be extended to the time spent on the application, the number of completed evaluations and of experimented strategies.

Finally, the mixed methodology used in the two initial investigations allows us to go beyond the quantitative description of change in victimization and guide the formulation of specific hypotheses for future studies regarding the mechanisms that may underline the effect of Stronger than Bullying. In the qualitative study, the participants reported that Stronger than Bullying matched their wish of confidentiality and privacy, along with their initial preference of keeping these experiences secret. Most of them have nonetheless broken the silence with someone they trusted at the end of the 4-week test period. We speculate that this change may have been partly enabled by gently encouraging the users to reach out for help (in the videos and strategies, for example) and, more practically, by facilitating doing so with the graphs. The participants also identified two main functions of the application they stated helped them the most in taking actions to reduce bullying. Of note, these referred to the mechanisms of action involved in problem-solving techniques: seeing more objectively their own bullying experiences and realizing that they have a wide range of strategies to choose from and to experiment with. Altogether, they expressed that Stronger than Bullying made them believe that they could eventually end bullying and that they have the ability to do so. Importantly, future studies should, in addition to studying potential mediators, test more systematically possible moderators. For example, which strategies are associated with the greatest reduction in bullying experiences and for whom? Are some strategies more or less useful for boys in comparison to girls? Previous research suggests indeed that seeking social support may be more effective for girls while this strategy is less liked by peers for boys (Kochenderfer-Ladd & Skinner, 2002; Tenenbaum et al., 2011). All these fundamental questions deserve attention.

In conclusion, the preliminary investigation of the usefulness of Stronger than Bullying in reducing the experiences of bullying over time suggests that this tool is promising, although much remains to be done to test more rigorously its usefulness. As the development of English-language and Android versions are underway, we will consider the possibility of adapting Stronger than Bullying to other countries to increase the number of available and free of charge tools that may help youth who are bullied to reduce and overcome these experiences.

References

Arseneault, L., Bowes, L., & Shakoor, S. (2010). Bullying victimization in youths and mental health problems: 'Much ado about nothing'? *Psychological Medicine*, *40*, 717–729. https://doi.org/10.1017/S0033291709991383.

Beran, T. N. (2006). Preparing teachers to manage school bullying: The hidden curriculum. *The Journal of Educational Thought*, *40*, 119–128. http://www.jstor.org/stable/23767163.

Bowes, L., Maughan, B., Caspi, A., Moffitt, T. E., & Arseneault, L. (2010). Families promote emotional and behavioural resilience to bullying: Evidence of an environmental effect. *Journal of Child Psychology and Psychiatry*, *51*, 809–817. https://doi.org/10.1111/j.1469-7610.2010.02216.x.

Bradford, S., & Rickwood, D. (2015). Acceptability and utility of an electronic psychosocial assessment (myAssessment) to increase self-disclosure in youth mental healthcare: A quasi-experimental study. *BMC Psychiatry*, *15*, 305. https://doi.org/10.1186/s12888-015-0694-4.

Brendgen, M., Girard, A., Vitaro, F., Dionne, G., Tremblay, R. E., Perusse, D., & Boivin, M. (2014). Gene-environment processes linking peer victimization and physical health problems: A longitudinal twin study. *Journal of Pediatric Psychology*, *39*(1), 96–108. https://doi.org/10.1093/jpepsy/jst078.

Brendgen, M., Vitaro, F., Bukowski, W. M., Dionne, G., Tremblay, R. E., & Boivin, M. (2013). Can friends protect genetically vulnerable children from depression? *Developmental Psychopathology*, *25*, 277–289. https://doi.org/10.1017/S0954579412001058.

Camodeca, M., & Goossens, F. A. (2005). Children's opinions of effective strategies to cope with bullying: The importance of bullying role and school context. *Educational Research*, *47*, 93–105. https://doi.org/10.1080/0013188042000337587.

Cassidy, T. (2009). Bullying and victimization in school children: The role of social identity, problem-solving style, and family and school context. *Social Psychology of Education*, *12*, 63–76. https://doi.org/10.1007/s11218-008-9066-y.

Cohen, J. (1988). *Statistical power analysis for the behavioral sciences*. London: Routledge.

Connected Generation Report. (2010). The young people's help resource for under-25 s. Retrieved from London, UK.

Craig, W., Harel-Fisch, Y., Fogel-Grinvald, H., Dostaler, S., Hetland, J., Simons-Morton, B.…Pickett, W. (2009). A cross-national profile of bullying and victimization among adolescents in 40 countries. *International Journal of Public Health*, *54*(Suppl. 2), 216–224. https://doi.org/10.1007/s00038-009-5413-9.

Cuijpers, P., van Straten, A., & Andersson, G. (2008). Internet-administered cognitive behavior therapy for health problems: A systematic review. *Journal of Behavioural Medicine*, *31*, 169–177. https://doi.org/10.1007/s10865-007-9144-1.

Danel, A. (2015). Une application mobile pour les victimes d'intimidation par les pairs: examen des récits d'expérience et perceptions d'utilité.[A mobile application for bullying victims: an examination of narratives and perceptions of usefulness.] School of Criminology. Montréal, Canada, Université de Montréal.

Dooley, J. J., Shaw, T., & Cross, D. (2012). The association between the mental health and behavioural problems of students and their reactions to cyber-victimization. *European Journal of Developmental Psychology*, *9*, 275–289. https://doi.org/10.1080/17405629.2011.648425.

Farrington, D., & Ttofi, M. (2010). Systematic review for The Campbell Collaboration Crime and Justice Group.

Fridh, M., Lindstrom, M., & Rosvall, M. (2015). Subjective health complaints in adolescent victims of cyber harassment: Moderation through support from parents/friends—A Swedish population-based study. *BMC Public Health*, *15*, 949. https://doi.org/10.1186/s12889-015-2239-7.

Garnefski, N., & Kraaij, V. (2014). Bully victimization and emotional problems in adolescents: Moderation by specific cognitive coping strategies? *Journal of Adolescence*, *37*, 1153–1160. https://doi.org/10.1016/j.adolescence.2014.07.005.

Griese, E. R., & Buhs, E. S. (2014). Prosocial behavior as a protective factor for children's peer victimization. *Journal of Youth and Adolescence*, *43*, 1052–1065. https://doi.org/10.1007/s10964-013-0046-y.

Hamilton, J. L., Connolly, S. L., Liu, R. T., Stange, J. P., Abramson, L. Y., & Alloy, L. B. (2015). It gets better: Future orientation buffers the development of hopelessness and depressive symptoms following emotional victimization during early adolescence. *Journal of Abnormal Child Psychology*, *43*, 465–474. https://doi.org/10.1007/s10802-014-9913-6.

Hampel, P., Manhal, S., & Hayer, T. (2009). Direct and relational bullying among children and adolescents: Coping and psychological adjustment. *School Psychology International*, *30*, 474–490. https://doi.org/10.1177/0143034309107066.

Hatzenbuehler, M. L., Schwab-Reese, L., Ranapurwala, S. I., Hertz, M. F., & Ramirez, M. R. (2015). Associations between antibullying policies and bullying in 25 States. *JAMA Pediatrics*, *169*, e152411 https://doi.org/10.1001/jamapediatrics.2015.2411.

Havas, J., de Nooijer, J., Crutzen, R., & Feron, F. (2011). Adolescents' views about an internet plateform for adolescents with mental health problems. *Health Education*, *111*, 164–176. https://doi.org/10.1108/09654281111123466.

Hudson, C. C., Lambe, L., Committee, P.N.Y.A., Pepler, D., & Craig, W. M. (2016). Coping while connected: The association among cybervictimization, privacy settings, and reporting tools in youth. *Canadian Journal of School Psychology*, *31*(1), 3–16. https://doi.org/10.1177/0829573515619623.

Jacobs, N. C., Dehue, F., Vollink, T., & Lechner, L. (2014). Determinants of adolescents' ineffective and improved coping with cyberbullying: A Delphi study. *Journal of Adolescence*, *37*, 373–385. https://doi.org/10.1016/j.adolescence.2014.02.011.

Jacobs, N. C., Vollink, T., Dehue, F., & Lechner, L. (2014). Online Pestkoppenstoppen: Systematic and theory-based development of a web-based tailored intervention for adolescent cyberbully victims to combat and prevent cyberbullying. *BMC Public Health*, *14*, 396. https://doi.org/10.1186/1471-2458-14-396.

Juvonen, J., & Graham, S. (2014). Bullying in schools: The power of bullies and the plight of victims. *Annual Review of Psychology*, *65*, 159–185. https://doi.org/10.1146/annurev-psych-010213-115030.

Kochenderfer-Ladd, B., & Skinner, K. (2002). Children's coping strategies: Moderators of the effects of peer victimization? *Developmental Psychology*, *38*, 267–278.

Lazarus, R. S. (2006). Emotions and interpersonal relationships: Toward a person-centered conceptualization of emotions and coping. *Journal of Personality*, *74*(1), 9–46. https://doi.org/10.1111/j.1467-6494.2005.00368.x.

Lazarus, R. S., & Folkman, S. (1984). *Stress, appraisals, and coping*. New York: Springer.

Lenhart, A., Duggan, M., Perrin, A., Stepler, R., Rainie, L., & Parker, K. (2015). Teens, social media & Technology overview 2015. Smartphones facilitate shifts in communication landscape for teens. Retrieved from Washington, DC.

Levant, R. F., & Hasan, N. T. (2008). Evidence-based practice in psychology. *Professional Psychology: Research and Practice*, *39*, 658–662. https://doi.org/10.1037/0735-7028.39.6.658.

Modecki, K. L., Minchin, J., Harbaugh, A. G., Guerra, N. G., & Runions, K. C. (2014). Bullying prevalence across contexts: A meta-analysis measuring cyber and traditional bullying. *Journal of Adolescent Health*, *55*, 602–611.

Mynard, H., & Joseph, S. (2000). Development of the multidimensional peer-victimization scale. *Aggressive Behavior*, *26*(2), 169–178.

Newman, R. S., Murray, B., & Lussier, C. (2001). Confrontation with aggressive peers at school: Students' reluctance to seek help from the teacher. *Journal of Educational Psychology*, *93*, 398–410. https://doi.org/10.1037/0022-0663.93.2.398.

Olweus, D. (1996). *The revised Olweus Bully/victim questionnaire*. Norway: Bergen.

Olweus, D. (2013). School bullying: Development and some important challenges. *Annual Review of Clinical Psychology*, *9*, 751–780. https://doi.org/10.1146/annurev-clinpsy-050212-185516.

Paillé, P., & Mucchielli, A. (2003). *L'analyse qualitative en sciences humaines et sociales*. Paris: Armand Colin.

Paillé, P., & Mucchielli, A. (2012). *L'analyse qualitative en sciences humaines et sociales*. Paris: Armand Colin.

Parris, L., Vayjas, K., Meyers, J., & Cutts, H. (2012). High school students' perceptions of coping with cyberbullying. *Youth & Society*, *44*, 284–306. https://doi.org/10.1177/0044118X11398881.

Pellegrini, A. D., & Bartini, M. (2000). An empirical comparison of methods of sampling aggression and victimization in school settings. *Journal of Educational Psychology*, *92*, 360–366.

Pirès, A. P. (1997). Échantillonnage et recherche qualitative: essai théorique et méthodologique. In J. Poupart, J.-P. Deslauriers, L. Groulx, A. Laperrière, R. Mayer, & A. Pires (Eds.), *La recherche qualitative: enjeux épistémologiques* (pp. 113–169). Montréal: Gaëtan Morin.

Rigby, K. (2011). What can schools do about cases of bullying? *Pastoral Care in Education*, *29*, 273–285. https://doi.org/10.1080/02643944.2011.626068.

Rudolph, K. D., Troop-Gordon, W., Monti, J. D., & Miernicki, M. E. (2014). Moving against and away from the world: The adolescent legacy of peer victimization. *Developmental Psychopathology*, *26*, 721–734. https://doi.org/10.1017/S0954579414000340.

Slonje, R., Smith, P. K., & Frisén, A. (2013). The nature of cyberbullying and strategies for prevention. *Computers in Human Behavior*, *29*, 26–32. https://doi.org/10.1016/j.chb.2012.05.024.

Sourander, A., Gyllenberg, D., Brunstein Klomek, A., Sillanmaki, L., Ilola, A. M., & Kumpulainen, K. (2016). Association of bullying behavior at 8 years of age and use of specialized services for psychiatric disorders by 29 years of age. *JAMA Psychiatry*, *73*, 159–165. https://doi.org/10.1001/jamapsychiatry.2015.2419.

Steeves, V. (2014). Jeunes Canadiens dans un monde branché, Phase III: La vie en ligne. [Young Canadian in a connected world, Phase III: Life online.] Ottawa Habilos Médias.

Tenenbaum, L. S., Varjas, K., Meyers, J., & Parris, L. (2011). Coping strategies and perceived effectiveness in fourth through eighth grade victims of bullying. *School Psychology International*, *32*, 263–287. https://doi.org/10.1177/0143034311402309.

Tesch, R. (1990). *Qualitative research: Analysis types and software tools* (pp. 76–102). New York, NY: The Falmer Press.

Ttofi, M. M., & Farrington, D. P. (2011). Effectiveness of school-based programs to reduce bullying: A systematic and meta-analytic review. *Journal of Experimental Criminology*, *7*(1), 27–56. https://doi.org/10.1007/s11292-010-9109-1.

Webb, M., Burns, J., & Collin, P. (2008). Providing online support for young people with mental health difficulties: Challenges and opportunities explored. *Early Intervention Psychiatry*, *2*(2), 108–113. https://doi.org/10.1111/j.1751-7893.2008.00066.x.

Weinstein, E. C., Selman, R. L., Thomas, S., Kim, J.-E., White, A. E., & Dinakar, K. (2016). How to cope with digital stress: The recommendations adolescents offer their peers online. *Journal of Adolescent Research*, *31*, 415–441. https://doi.org/10.1177/0743558415587326.

Ybarra, M. L., & Suman, M. (2006). Help seeking behavior and the Internet: A national survey. *International Journal of Medical Information*, *75*(1), 29–41. https://doi.org/10.1016/j.ijmedinf.2005.07.029.

Stop Online Bullies: The advantages and disadvantages of a standalone intervention

13

Francine Dehue, Trijntje Völlink, Nicole Gunther, Niels Jacobs
Open University of the Netherlands, Heerlen, Netherlands

Name of program: Stop Online Bullies
Type of program: Individual program on website
Suitable for ages: Adolescents

Introduction

Cyberbullying intervention resources can be divided into school-based programs and individual standalone interventions. School-based interventions are programs containing for example, lessons, videos, presentations, discussions, and workshops, which are used in classrooms or whole schools. Standalone interventions are programs that can be used independently of schools and classrooms. Most standalone interventions are psychoeducational websites. There are many such sites containing tips, topics, and recommendations regarding cyberbullying. The problem is, however, that many of these standalone programs and materials, while well intentioned, lack research evidence. They are based on practical beliefs or common sense (Snakenborg, Van Acker, & Gable, 2011) and hence do not have a theoretical base, nor have the effectiveness of their materials been investigated (Völlink, Dehue, Mc Guckin, & Jacobs, 2016). There are some exceptions, however. In this chapter the development and content of the Dutch theory-based tailored intervention "Online Pestkoppenstoppen" or "Stop Online Bullies" will be described. The intervention is aimed at low academically achieving students of 12–15 years old who have experienced cybervictimization.

What is the content of the program and how is it delivered?

Content of the program

In their narrative review, Gunther, DeSmet, Jacobs, and De Bourdeaudhuij (2016) suggest a need to address victimization of traditional and cyberbullying simultaneously in intervention programs. Such combined intervention approaches may be most effective for three reasons: (1) the experience of combined traditional and cyberbullying victimization

Reducing Cyberbullying in Schools. https://doi.org/10.1016/B978-0-12-811423-0.00013-4

appears to be more strongly related to mental health problems than the experience of only traditional or only cyber victimization, (2) there is a large overlap between involvement in these two types of bullying behaviors, and (3) previous research indicates that targeting only one form of bullying causes an increase in another type of bullying (Campbell, Spears, Slee, Butler, & Kift, 2012; Dempsey, Sulkowski, Nichols, & Storch, 2009; Elledge et al., 2013; Erdur-Baker & Tanrikulu, 2010; Gradinger, Strohmeier, & Spiel, 2009; Juvonen & Gross, 2008; Raskauskas, 2010; Schneider, O'Donnell, Stueve, & Coulter, 2012; Steffgen, Vandebosch, Völlink, Deboutte, & Dehue, 2011). Therefore, Stop Online Bullies focuses on victims of traditional bullying as well as cyberbullying. The aim of the intervention is to decrease their victimization, to increase psychological well-being, and to decrease problem behavior, school problems, and truancy.

Both traditional- and cyberbullying-victimization peaks during the transition from middle to high school (Wade & Beran, 2011; Williams & Guerra, 2007). Moreover, low academically achieving adolescents tend to experience cyberbullying the most (Tokunaga, 2010; Walrave & Heirman, 2011). Therefore, Stop Online Bullies is developed for low academically achieving (cyber)bullying victims from 12 to 14 years old. It is a Dutch online computer-tailored intervention that is developed according to the Intervention Mapping protocol, which is a planned, systematic, and theory-based approach, an approach needed to increase the effectiveness of an intervention (Brug, Oenema, Kroeze, & Raat, 2005). Intervention mapping has proven to be very successful in the systematic development and planning of theory- and evidence-based health promotion interventions (Bartholomew, Parcel, Kok, & Gottlieb, 2006; Riper et al., 2007). The protocol emphasizes that intervention development should be based on a thorough understanding of the problem behavior and the determinants related to this behavior. The development of an intervention according to the Intervention Mapping protocol is an iterative process that consists of six steps (Bartholomew, Parcel, Kok, Gottlieb, & Fernández, 2011). The results of each step form the input of the next step. In the first step, a need assessment is conducted of the target group, their behavior, their situational conditions, and their mental health problems. The results of this step are the input of the second step. In this second step, anticipated changes as a result of the intervention are specified, by defining performance objectives and determinants, which are combined into change objectives. In the third step, these change objectives are combined with theory-based methods. These methods are translated into practical applications to effect changes in behavior of the target group and environmental agents, and in the fourth step all these theory-based practical applications are integrated in intervention components. The fifth and the sixth steps are on adoption and implementation of the intervention and on the process and effect evaluation. A thorough description of the results of the Intervention Mapping protocol for Stop Online Bullies is provided by Jacobs, Völlink, Dehue, and Lechner (2014a).

The input for the need assessment stems from a literature review. This need assessment forms the basis of the research on determinants of (cyber)bullying in the second step. The research in the second step consists of a three-round online Delphi study among 70 (inter)national experts on (cyber)bullying (most of them participants of the COST action IS0801), and a qualitative study among 66 adolescents. The Delphi study appeared to be effective in finding new and relevant determinants related to (cyber) bullying, such as self-efficacy related to adjusting one's behavior based on feedback, self-esteem, and communication style (Jacobs, Völlink, Dehue, & Lechner, 2014b). The first round yielded 171 determinants, predicting ineffective coping behavior (91) and improvement of coping behavior (80) regarding (cyber)bullying among adolescents. The result of the second and third rounds was a list of 62 relevant determinants of ineffective coping and 53 relevant determinants of improvement in coping (Jacobs et al., 2014b).

In the qualitative study, 66 low-academically achieving Dutch adolescents between 12 and 15 years old who attended secondary vocational education, participated in 10 focus group interviews, with the aim to gather in-depth information on performance objectives of (cyber)bullying. This study searched for answers on five research questions: (1) What kind of experiences do Dutch low-academically achieving cyberbullying victims have with cyberbullying victimization and perpetration, and what do they look like? (2) How do Dutch low-academically achieving cyberbullying victims perceive/consider experiences with cyberbullying and what is perceived as worse (traditional bullying, cyberbullying, different forms)? (3) Why do Dutch low-academically achieving cyberbullying victims think people (cyber)bully each other, who becomes/is a victim and who is a bully? (4) Which attitudes do Dutch low-academically achieving cyberbullying victims have toward (cyber)bullying? (5) How do Dutch low-academically achieving cyberbullying victims cope with (cyber)bullying, and how do they perceive these coping strategies? (Jacobs, Goossens, Dehue, Völlink, & Lechner, 2015). Most importantly, the study showed that not all the behaviors that are mentioned in the literature as cyberbullying are perceived as such by victims and that these perceptions often depends on the context (anonymity, characteristics of the bully, being in a fight or not). A complete overview of the results is described in Jacobs et al. (2015).

The theory-based methods and practical applications of step 3, used to change the objectives of step 2, are based on the principles of Rational Emotive (Behavioral) Therapy (RE(B)T) (Ellis, 2001). According to RE(B)T, evaluative thoughts influence the perception of events and the emotional, behavioral, and inferential reactions to these events (Ellis, 1995, 2001; MacInnes, 2004). Several theoretical and evidence-based methods are selected for the intervention. For example, consciousness raising is used to increase awareness of the relation between thoughts, feelings and behavior (Ringrose & Nijenhuis, 1986), modeling and guided practice are used to increase self-efficacy (Bandura, 1997), arguments and persuasive communication are used to increase knowledge and to influence attitudes (Bartholomew et al., 2011), and coping plans are used to link concrete, suitable, and effective responses to future risk situations (Sniehotta, Scholz, & Schwarzer, 2005).

In the fourth step, intervention components are developed, using all the theory-based methods and practical applications of step three. This resulted in an intervention consisting of three web-based topics in sessions delivered over 3 months. Topic 1 is called "Think strong, feel better." In this topic, the focus is on the 5G-schema (Ringrose & Nijenhuis, 1986), which gives insight in the relation between an event (Gebeurtenis), the thoughts (Gedachten) evoked by the event, the emotions (Gevoelens) evoked by the thoughts, the behavior (Gedrag) evoked by the emotions, and the resulting consequences (Gevolg). The schema is explained in a video by a famous Dutch actor, and demonstrated by comics and digital guides. Adolescents learn to work with this schema by performing several tasks, in order to recognize and replace irrational thoughts into rational thoughts, and to examine emotions in response to events. They also form action plans to use the 5G-schema in the future. Topic 2 is called "Stop the bully now," and is mainly concentrated on effective and ineffective coping behavior. The adolescents receive information on the dynamics of (cyber)bullying, are provided with video models demonstrating examples of ineffective and effective coping strategies and become aware of ineffective strategies, and learn effective strategies. In this topic, coping plans are formulated including assertive reactions. Topic 3 is called "You are doing great, can you do better?" In this topic, the plans made in Topics 1 and 2 are evaluated on usability and are adjusted, if necessary. The skills learned in topics 1 and 2 are summarized into three steps (Think, Act, and Closure), which form the skill conflict resolution. Moreover, based on this skill conflict resolution and tailored on progress, adolescents receive written and spoken feedback on their irrational thoughts and coping. Tailored additional lessons are provided in working with the 5G-schema, in recognizing and replacing irrational thoughts, and rehearsing social skills and coping behavior. Finally, in topic 3 adolescents learn to use the Internet and the mobile phone in a safe and secure manner. Each topic is preceded by several questionnaires that take about half an hour to complete. The questionnaires measure, for example, personality, irrational thoughts, coping, self-efficacy, psychological well-being, behavioral problems and experiences with traditional bullying, and are used to tailor the topics and to measure the effects of each topic. The topics were developed in close cooperation with the members of the target group and were adapted after the pre- and pilot tests with the target group.

Several tools are used throughout the intervention such as general and tailored information, digital guides (4), video clips (41), pictures (27), comics (11), and animations (4). The amount of text was kept as short as possible and was also delivered as spoken text by the digital guides, two of them in the age of the target group, and two of them several years older. These guides provide information, ask questions, demonstrate and explain desired skills, provide opportunities to practice these skills, and provide feedback. The gender and contexts of the four guides are matched to the gender of adolescents. Furthermore, in the video clips, models demonstrate and explain effective and ineffective problem-solving behavior, recognize and replace irrational thoughts. These videos were professionally recorded at a schoolyard, in a classroom, in the school's canteen, and in a studio, which was decorated as a boy's and girl's bedroom, using a professional adult actor and several young actors.

A personal page provides access to the questionnaires, topics, and additional lessons, and contains a summary of all important information, the video clips, pictures and comics used in each topic, as well as the elaboration of all tasks and exercises and feedback.

Program delivery

"Stop Online Bullies" is a fully automated online standalone intervention, which should be completed individually. Adolescents can complete the intervention independently; involvement of teachers or other adults is not necessary. No training is needed. Each topic takes approximately 45 min to complete; the three topics should be completed within 3 months. Based on research findings that an explicit selection approach underestimates the problem (Vandebosch & van Cleemput, 2009; Walrave &

Heirman, 2011), an implicit approach selects the victims of cyberbullying. Individuals indicate the frequency of experiences with 17 different cyberbullying behaviors and are included in the intervention when they experience at least one behavior once a month.

Evidence for effectiveness

To test the effectiveness of "Stop Online Bullies," a randomized controlled trial was conducted, in which the outcomes of the experimental condition at baseline, and 1, 2, 6, and 12 months later were compared with the outcomes of a control group, which received general information, and the outcomes of a control group, which received no information. All secondary vocational education schools in the Netherlands were approached via about 600 contact persons. They were told that their participation could help reduce cyberbullying and associated problems, and information on cyberbullying and a description and screenshots of the intervention were provided. The researchers visited the schools that indicated willingness to participate and gave a short introductory presentation to all students. Since the first recruitment round did not generate enough participants, a second recruitment round was conducted, in which teachers introduced the intervention and the study to their students by means of videos developed by the research team. Students received a written information letter and informed consent, which had to be signed by both the participant and his or her parent(s). In this first round, students were included as a victim when they experienced at least three of 17 forms of cyberbullying acts at least once a month, or at least one form two or three times a month during the past 6 months (Vandebosch & van Cleemput, 2009). In the second round, it was decided to broaden these inclusion criteria by also including students who experienced one or two cyberbullying acts once a month, because a single action (e.g., uploading an embarrassing video or picture) can result in repeated humiliation (Dooley, Pyzalski, & Cross, 2009). About 56% of the students (>2000) of participating schools clicked the "I participate" button on the website of the intervention. Instead of the expected 25%, only 18% of the students (360) matched the criteria of being a victim of cyberbullying. Half of these students, 183, completed the informed consent, and 170 started the first measurement, a number that declined to 59 by the second measurement. Unfortunately, throughout the intervention the dropout continued to remain very high, which meant that an effectiveness study was not possible. To understand the processes responsible for the unsuccessfulness of the intervention (e.g., high dropout) and to provide guidelines for future interventions, a process evaluation was conducted (Baranowski & Stables, 2000; Hulscher, Laurant, & Grol, 2003).

In general, adolescents were rather positive about the website. The three topics received overall appreciation scores ranging from 7.3 to 7.7 on a scale from 1 (not appreciated at all) to 10 (very much appreciated). The appreciation related to interestingness, comprehensibility, believability, amount of information, the novelty of information, the helpfulness of information in stopping cyberbullying and personal relevance was relatively high. On a five-point scale (1 = I totally disagree, 5 = I totally agree), scores ranged from 2.8 to 4.3. The first topic, focused on thoughts, was rated as most comprehensible. The second topic was rated as being the most helpful in stopping (cyber)bullying, probably because this session aimed to change actual behavior. The information in the third topic was rated as the most novel. The majority watched the movies, pictures, and comics completely and did the exercises of the three sessions. The personal page however was not used frequently: some adolescents indicated they did not look at this page and half of them looked only once or twice.

In addition to questionnaires, qualitative data were gathered by email and phone calls. It appeared that the questionnaires preceding the topics were perceived as too long, tedious and difficult, which explains part of the dropout. Moreover, some of the adolescents mentioned that they simply forgot to return to the website, despite automatically and manually sent emails and text messages.

Benefits and drawbacks of Stop Online Bullies

Monitoring and regulating the usage on the Internet by adults can be difficult, since there can be a generational divide in Internet usage. Children and young people may feel that parents are often less than experts in the new communication technologies (Subrahmanyam & Greenfield, 2008; Wong, 2010). Moreover, children and young people value their privacy and therefore often exclude their parents from their Internet activities (Subrahmanyam & Greenfield, 2008). So, parents are frequently unaware of the activities of their children on the Internet, and even worse, they are frequently unaware of their child being involved in cyberbullying (Dehue, Bolman, & Vollink, 2008; Hoff & Mitchell, 2009; Perren et al., 2012). Victims of cyberbullying are reluctant to report to their parents that they are involved in cyberbullying because of the fear of losing computer privileges and hence being isolated from peers (Bath, 2008; Kraft & Wang, 2009; Mishna, Saini, & Solomon, 2009). Literature shows that children and young people prefer to get anonymous help (Webb, Burns, & Collin, 2008) and report a need for help through the Internet (Havas, de Nooijer, Crutzen, & Feron, 2011). Therefore, the best method to deliver cyberbullying interventions seems to be over the Internet. The most important benefit of Stop Online Bullies therefore is related to the fact that it is a web-based standalone intervention that can be completed without the help of adults.

Web-based interventions such as Stop Online Bullies have several advantages. For example, they can reach a lot of people in a relatively inexpensive way and can be used whenever and wherever the individual prefers. But most importantly they can be tailored to the individual, which appears to be a successful health promotion technique (Krebs, Prochaska, & Rossi, 2010; Noar, Benac, & Harris, 2007). To be effective, first of all, interventions should fit the personality of the student. Several personality traits have been linked to coping strategies. For example, prior research has shown that children and young people who are resilient, tend toward a problem-solving approach of coping, such as deleting unwelcome messages, blocking contacts in the context of cyberbullying, seeking social support from peers and adults, or confronting the bully online (D'Haenens, Vandoninck, & Donoso, 2013; Hunter, Boyle, & Warden, 2004; Machmutow, Perren, Sticca, & Alsaker, 2012; Matsunaga, 2011; Perren et al., 2012).

Those who are not resilient, tend to use an emotion-solving approach of coping, such as ignoring the bully or bullying the bully, using aggression, reacting submissively, avoiding the situation or acting helpless (Acirak, 2009; Dehue et al., 2008; Perren et al., 2012; Riebel, Jäger, & Fischer, 2009). Furthermore, research in biology and epidemiology shows that optimism is also linked to coping. Optimism can be defined as the general tendency to have positive rather than negative outcome expectancies. Ursin and Eriksen (2010) showed that individuals who generally have positive outcome expectancies use active coping strategies, whereas individuals who generally have negative outcome expectancies perceive the situation as uncontrollable and their possible actions as useless and hence use passive coping strategies. Indeed, research has shown that compared to general information, interventions that fit the personality of the user are perceived as more personal and relevant, are more often read, saved, remembered, and discussed (Brug, Oenema, & Campbell, 2003), and result in more improvement in behavior (Krebs et al., 2010). However, not only personality characteristics influence the use of coping strategies. Contextual features like the kind of relationship between victims and perpetrators (Vandebosch & van Cleemput, 2009) and the kind of emotion evoked by the cyberbullying experience also influence coping. Threats may evoke anxiety, humiliating pictures may evoke shame and name calling, or gossiping may evoke anger. So, the effectiveness of a coping strategy may depend on the specific experience. The importance of tailored topics is reflected in the results of the process evaluation of Stop Online Bullies. The second topic of the intervention, dedicated to effective and ineffective coping behavior, was tailored to the individual's experiences with coping strategies and was perceived as most relevant and interestingly, being the most helpful in stopping cyberbullying. Thus, the most important advantage of Stop Online Bullies is the fact that the intervention provides tailored advice.

Paradoxically, the fact that Stop Online Bullies is a web-based standalone intervention that can be completed without the help of adults also shows the most important drawback: the lack of guidance. The target group seems to need guidance in regulation and motivation activities (De Boer, Reinards, & Reubel, 1993; Den Boer, Mittendorff, & Sjenitzer, 2004). Indeed, Jacobs, Völlink, Dehue, and Lechner (2014c) concluded that their target group lacked the motivation and discipline to complete the intervention on an individual basis, and that more guidance and structure in using the intervention is needed. The lack of guidance by adults, such as explaining to children and young people the usefulness and the benefits of the intervention, and reminding them to return to the intervention, can partly explain the large dropout.

Another factor that may have influenced this dropout was the design of the intervention, which had some drawbacks. Previous research shows that program length and the number of sessions decrease the use of interventions (Bouwer et al., 2009; Glasgow, 2007). As well, interest in returning to interventions seems to decrease over time and revisits are uncommon in interventions (Gustafson et al., 2001; Schulz et al., 2014). Intervention website visits should not be longer than 17 min (Verheijden, Jans, & Hildebrandt, 2008), whereas Stop the Bully contains three topics of 45 min each, to be completed at fixed times with a time interval of at least 1 month. Furthermore, the number and negative content of the measurements, which are necessary to tailor and to measure the effectiveness of the intervention, may have influenced the dropout rate (Bunker, Howell, & Weaver, 2007; Jacobs et al., 2014c). In addition, the login procedure was too complicated and the procedure at the start of Stop Online Bullies was different from the procedure at the follow up sessions.

Although all materials were positively evaluated, some other drawbacks were related to the presentation of the content of the intervention. Low academically achieving students, and thus our target group, do not like to read and need teaching methods that use a concrete manner of working (De Boer et al., 1993; Den Boer et al., 2004). The first topic "Think strong, feel better" does not use a concrete manner of working since it mostly focuses on thoughts and feelings and concerns the understanding of the relation between the 5Gs, and hence may be too abstract.

Conclusion

As described, Stop Online Bullies provides online tailored information for victims of both traditional and cyberbullying to decrease their victimization, but also provides topics to increase psychological well-being, and to decrease problem behavior, school problems, and truancy.

The intervention was based on the assumption that victims of bullying behavior prefer to get anonymous help delivered via the Internet, without the intervention of adults. Although all three topics were evaluated as rather positive, personally relevant, and helpful, an online approach to combat cyberbullying appeared to be less effective than expected. The experience with the delivering of the intervention and the process evaluation, however, provided many important insights and several recommendations for future interventions.

First of all, the several studies and the process evaluation of Stop Online Bullies clearly suggest that it is of utmost importance that information and topics in future cyberbullying online standalone interventions are tailored for the individual.

Second, the many advantages of online standalone interventions like Stop Online Bullies seem not to fit the ability of victims to independently use the intervention. Low-academically achieving adolescents seem to need more guidance and external motivation to continue and finish such an intensive online intervention. Therefore, for future intervention, it is important to deliver anonymous help via the Internet, but at the same time researchers should face the challenge to incorporate some assistance and structure provided by adults. An online blended approach meets these criteria, by providing an online standalone intervention in combination with face-to-face classroom methods provided by teachers, for example feedback on the exercises done in the standalone intervention.

Third, victims probably need freedom to obtain help when needed, without interruptions and several sessions. Multisession interventions have been found to have a low reach (Glasgow, 2007), and interest in returning to intervention websites appears to decrease over time (Gustafson et al., 2001). Revisits are uncommon in interventions (Schulz et al., 2014), as was experienced in testing Stop Online Bullies. Despite the emails and text messages, participants did not return. The three topics of Stop Online Bullies could only be completed at fixed times, with a month interval, although the

Internet provides 24-h access. So the challenge for future online interventions is to target different areas without the requirement of multiple sessions.

This leads to the fourth recommendation: standalone interventions should be kept as short as possible, especially for low-academically achieving adolescents. This implies that the questionnaires needed for tailoring and research purposes should be short. The number and length as well as the negative content of measurements could be one reason that the young people dropped out (Bunker et al., 2007). However, reducing the number of questions can influence the validity of the measurement. Hence, for future researchers, it is a challenge to develop interventions with a balance between the number of questions and the validity of the measurements.

The fifth recommendation concerns the login procedure. Online interventions should have an easy login procedure (Bouwer et al., 2009; Schneider, van Osch, Schulz, Kremers, & de Vries, 2012).

Finally, the acceptability of the materials appeared to depend on how helpful it was. This also emphasizes the importance of tailoring the interventions. Moreover, the acceptability of the material also depended on the novelty of the information. This implies that for future interventions it is important to keep the information up to date, especially when it concerns information on using specific social media in a safe way, since the popularity of these specific media rapidly changes over time. Therefore, it is probably easier to incorporate links to sites on the Internet that provide these safety tips. Finally, future interventions should pay less attention to abstract concepts, and instead use more concrete information, as low academically achieving adolescents do not like to read and need concrete teaching methods (De Boer et al., 1993; Den Boer et al., 2004). Although all materials of Stop Online Bullies were evaluated as positive by the young people, and almost all indicated that they read the texts, watched the movies, pictures, and comics, and did the exercises of the three sessions, earlier research found that the use of and exposure to the content of online interventions is often less than optimal (Campbell et al., 2002; Cunningham, Gulliver, Farrer, Bennett, & Carron-Arthur, 2014; Leslie, Marshall, Owen, & Bauman, 2005; Mañanes & Vallejo, 2014). Games have been found to improve attractiveness of the sites and consequently longer visits (Vandelanotte & Mummery, 2011). Future interventions should therefore pay less attention to abstract concepts, and instead use more novel and concrete information. Standalone online tailored interventions should be restricted to effective coping strategies, social skills, insights in social norms, behavior, and manners, and differences between online and offline contacts. Abstracts concepts like the five G-scheme, the effects and restructure of irrational thoughts, and the negative effects of harassments on self-esteem are probably more suitable when more guidance is possible, as in a face-to-face classroom part of a blended approach, linked to safety programs in schools. In a study among 309 primary and secondary Flanders schools, it was found that 92% of the teachers consider it their duty to inform young people about cyberbullying. However, 87% reported to receive insufficient professional support and 85% reported to receive insufficient guidelines to prevent and combat cyberbullying (Vandebosch, Poels, & Deboutte, 2014). Materials of Stop Online Bullies that are too abstract for an online standalone approach could be redeveloped in a blended approach for teachers in school.

References

Acirak, O. T. (2009). Psychiatric symptomatology as predictor of cyberbullying among university students. *Eurasian Journal of Educational Research, 34*, 167–184.

Bandura, A. (1997). *Self-efficacy: The exercise of control.* New York, NY: W.H. Freeman.

Baranowski, T., & Stables, G. (2000). Process evaluation of the 5-a-day projects. *Health Education & Behavior, 27*, 157–166. https://doi.org/10.1177/109019810002700202.

Bartholomew, L. K., Parcel, G. S., Kok, G., & Gottlieb, N. H. (2006). *Planning health promotion programs: An intervention mapping approach.* San Francisco, CA: Jossey-Bass.

Bartholomew, L. K., Parcel, G. S., Kok, G., Gottlieb, N. H., & Fernández, M. E. (2011). *Planning health promotion programs: An intervention mapping approach.* San Francisco, CA: Jossey-Bass.

Bath, C. S. (2008). Cyber bullying: Overview and strategies for school counsellors, guidance officers, and all school personnel. *Australian Journal of Guidance & Counselling, 18*, 53–66.

Bouwer, W., Oenema, A., Crutzen, R., de Nooijer, J., de Vries, N. K., & Brug, J. (2009). What makes people decide to visit and use an internet-delivered behavior-change intervention?: A qualitative study among adults. *Health Education, 109*, 460–473. https://doi.org/10.1108/09654280911001114.

Brug, J., Oenema, A., & Campbell, M. (2003). Past, present, and future of computer-tailored nutrition education. *The American Journal of Clinical Nutrition, 77*(4), 1028S–1034S. Retrieved from http://ajcn.nutrition.org/content/77/4/1028S.abstract.

Brug, J., Oenema, A., Kroeze, W., & Raat, H. (2005). The internet and nutrition education: Challenges and opportunities. *European Journal of Clinical Nutrition, 59*, S130–S139. https://doi.org/10.1038/sj.ejcn.1602186.

Bunker, K. D., Howell, C. C., & Weaver, M. (2007). Children for research in schools. *Western Journal of Nursing Research, 29*, 501–514.

Campbell, M. A., Spears, B., Slee, P., Butler, D., & Kift, S. (2012). Victims' perception of traditional and cyberbullying, and the psychological correlates of their victimization. *Emotional and Behavioral Difficulties, 17*(3–4), 389–401. https://doi.org/10.1080/13632752.2012.704316.

Campbell, M. K., Tessaro, I., DeVellis, B., Benedict, S., Kelsey, K., Belton, L., et al. (2002). Effects of a tailored health promotion program for female blue-collar workers: Health works for women. *Preventive Medicine, 34*(313–323), 34. https://doi.org/10.1006/pmed.2001.0988.

Cunningham, J. A., Gulliver, A., Farrer, L., Bennett, K., & Carron-Arthur, B. (2014). Internet interventions for mental health and addictions: Current findings and future directions. *Current Psychiatry Reports, 16*. https://doi.org/10.1007/s11920-014-0521-5.

D'Haenens, L., Vandoninck, S., & Donoso, V. (2013). *How to cope and build online resilience?* London, UK: EU Kids Online Network.

De Boer, B., Reinards, R., & Reubel, F. (1993). *Zelfstandig leren in beroepsopleidingen: meer kansen op de Europese arbeidsmarkt* [Independent learning in vocational schools: More chances at the labour market]. Groningen: Wolters-Noordhoff.

Dehue, F., Bolman, C., & Vollink, T. (2008). Cyberbullying: youths' experiences and parental perception. *CyberPsychology & Behavior, 11*, 217–223.

Dempsey, A. G., Sulkowski, M. L., Nichols, R., & Storch, E. A. (2009). Differences between peer victimization in cyber and physical settings and associated psychosocial adjustment in early adolescence. *Psychology in Schools, 46*, 962–972. https://doi.org/10.1002/pits.20437.

Den Boer, P., Mittendorff, K., & Sjenitzer, T. (2004). *Beter kiezen. Onderzoek naar keuzeporocessen van jongeren in het vmbo en mbo* [Choose better. Research on choise processes of youngsters on the vmbo and mbo]. Delft: Deltapunt. Retrieved from http://www.mittendorffonderwijsadvies.nl/wp-content/uploads/2011/10/Link-10.pdf, August 17, 2016.

Dooley, J. J., Pyzalski, J., & Cross, D. (2009). Cyberbullying versus face-to-face bullying. *Zeitschrift Fur Psycholoie*, [Journal of Psychology], *217*, 182–188. https://doi.org/10.1027/0044-3409.217.4.182.

Elledge, L. C., Williford, A., Boulton, A. J., DePaolis, K. J., Little, T. D., & Salmivalli, C. (2013). Individual and contextual predictors of cyberbullying: The influence of children's provictim attitudes and teachers' ability to intervene. *Journal of Youth and Adolescence*, *42*, 698–710. https://doi.org/10.1007/s10964-013-9920-x.

Ellis, A. (1995). Changing rational-emotive therapy (RET) to rational, emotive behavior therapy (REBT). *Journal of Rational-Emotive & Cognitive-Behavior Therapy*, *13*(2), 85–89.

Ellis, A. (2001). *Overcoming destructive beliefs, feelings and behaviors: New directions for rational emotive therapy*. New York, NY: Prometheus Books.

Erdur-Baker, O., & Tanrikulu, I. (2010). Psychological consequences of cyber bullying experiences among Turkish secondary school children. *Procedia—Social and Behavioural Science*, *2*(2), 2771–2776. https://doi.org/10.1016/j.sbspro.2010.03.431.

Glasgow, R. E. (2007). eHealth evaluation and dissemination research. *American Journal of Preventive Medicine*, *32*, 119–126. https://doi.org/10.1016/j.amepre.2007.01.023.

Gradinger, P., Strohmeier, P., & Spiel, C. (2009). Traditional bullying and cyberbullying. Identification of risk groups for adjustment problems. *Zeitschrift für Psychologie*, [Journal of Psychology]*217*(4), 205–213. https://doi.org/10.1027/044-3409.217.4.205.

Gunther, N., DeSmet, A., Jacobs, N. C. L., & De Bourdeaudhuij, I. (2016). Comparing associated harm with traditional bullying cyberbullying: A narrative overview of mental, physical and behavioral negative outcomes. In T. Völlink, F. Dehue, & C. Mc Guckin (Eds.), *Cyberbullying: From theory to interventions. Current issues in social psychology*. New York, NY: Taylor & Francis.

Gustafson, D. H., Hawkins, R., Pingree, S., McTavish, F., Arora, N. K., & Salner, A. (2001). Effect of computer support on younger women with breast cancer. *Journal of General Internal Medicine*, *16*, 435–445. https://doi.org/10.1046/j.1525-1497.2001.016007435.x.

Havas, J., de Nooijer, J., Crutzen, R., & Feron, F. (2011). Adolescents' views about an internet platform for adolescents with mental health problems. *Health Education*, *111*, 164–176. https://doi.org/10.1108/09654281111123466.

Hoff, D. L., & Mitchell, S. N. (2009). Cyberbullying: Causes, effects, and remedies. *Journal of Educational Administration*, *47*, 652–665. https://doi.org/10.1108/09578230910981107.

Hulscher, M., Laurant, M., & Grol, R. (2003). Process evaluation on quality improvement interventions. *Quality & Safety in Health Care*, *12*, 40–46. https://doi.org/10.1136/qhc.12.1.40.

Hunter, S. C., Boyle, J. M. E., & Warden, D. (2004). Help seeking amongst child and adolescent victims of peer-aggression and bullying: The influence of school-stage, gender, victimization, appraisal, and emotion. *British Journal of Educational Psychology*, *74*(3), 375–390. https://doi.org/10.1348/0007099041552378.

Jacobs, N. C. L., Völlink, T., Dehue, F., & Lechner, L. (2014a). Online Pestkoppenstoppen: Systematic and theory-based development of a web-based tailored intervention for adolescent cyberbully victims to combat and prevent cyberbullying. *BMC Public Health*, *14*, 396. https://doi.org/10.1186/1471-2458-14-396.

Jacobs, N. C. L., Völlink, T., Dehue, F., & Lechner, L. (2014b). Determinants of adolescents' ineffective and improved coping with cyberbullying: A Delphi study. *Journal of Adolescence*, *37*, 373–385. https://doi.org/10.1016/j.adolescence.2014.02.011.

Jacobs, N. C. L., Völlink, T., Dehue, F., & Lechner, L. (2014c). Procesevaluatie van Online Pestkoppenstoppen. Intern Open Universiteit Rapport. [Process evaluation of Online Pestkoppenstoppen. Internal Open University Report, Heerlen:Open University]. Heerlen:Open University.

Jacobs, N. C. L., Goossens, L., Dehue, F., Völlink, T., & Lechner, L. (2015). Dutch cyberbullying victims' experiences, perceptions, attitudes and motivations related to (coping with) cyberbullying: Focus group interviews. *Societies*, *5*, 43–64. https://doi.org/10.3390/soc5010043.

Juvonen, J., & Gross, E. F. (2008). Extending the school grounds? Bullying experiences in cyberspace. *The Journal of School Health*, *78*(9), 496–505. https://doi.org/10.1111/j.1746-1561.200800335.x.

Kraft, E. M., & Wang, J. (2009). Effectiveness of cyber bullying prevention strategies: A study on students' perspectives. *International Journal of Cyber Criminology*, *3*, 513–535.

Krebs, P., Prochaska, J. O., & Rossi, J. S. (2010). A meta-analysis of computer-tailored interventions for health behavior change. *Preventive Medicine*, *51*, 214–221. https://doi.org/10.1016/j.ypmed.2010.06.004.

Leslie, E., Marshall, A. L., Owen, N., & Bauman, A. (2005). Engagement and retention of participants in a physical activity website. *Preventive Medicine*, *40*, 54–59. https://doi.org/10.1016/j.ypmed.2004.05.002.

Machmutow, K., Perren, S., Sticca, F., & Alsaker, F. D. (2012). Peer victimisation and depressive symptoms: Can specific coping strategies buffer the negative impact of cybervictimisation? *Emotional and Behavioural Difficulties*, *17*(3–4), 403–420. https://doi.org/10.1080/13632752.2012.704310.

MacInnes, D. (2004). The theories underpinning rational emotive behaviour therapy: Where's the supportive evidence? *International Journal of Nursing Studies*, *41*, 685–695.

Mañanes, G., & Vallejo, M. A. (2014). Usage and effectiveness of a fully automated, open-access, Spanish web-based smoking cessation program: Randomized controlled trial. *Journal of Medical Internet Research*, *16*, https://doi.org/10.2196/jmir.3091.

Matsunaga, M. (2011). Underlying circuits of social support for bullied victims: An appraisal-based perspective on supportive communication and postbullying adjustment. *Human Communication Research*, *37*(2), 174–206. https://doi.org/10.1111/j.1468-2958.2010.01398.x.

Mishna, F., Saini, M., & Solomon, S. (2009). Ongoing and online: Children and youth's perceptions of cyber bullying. *Children and Youth Services Review*, *31*, 1222–1228.

Noar, S. M., Benac, C. N., & Harris, M. S. (2007). Does tailoring matter? Meta-analytic review of tailored print health behavior change intervention. *Psychological Bulletin*, *133*(4), 673–693. https://doi.org/10.1037/0033-2909.133.4.673.

Perren, S., Corcoran, L., Cowie, H., Dehue, F., Garcia, D., & Völlink, T. (2012). Tackling cyberbullying: Review of empirical evidence regarding successful responses by students, parents, and schools. *International Journal of Conflict and Violence*, *6*(2), 283–292.

Raskauskas, J. (2010). Text-bullying: Associations with traditional bullying and depression among New Zealand adolescents. *Journal of School Violence*, *9*(1), 74–97. https://doi.org/10.1080/15388220903185605.

Riebel, J., Jäger, R. S., & Fischer, U. C. (2009). Cyberbullying in Germany—An exploration of prevalence, overlapping with real life bullying and coping strategies. *Psychology Science Quarterly*, *51*(3), 298–314.

Ringrose, H. J., & Nijenhuis, E. H. (1986). *Bang zijn voor andere kinderen* [Being afraid for other children]. Groningen: Wolters-Noordhoff.

Riper, H., Smit, F., van der, Zanden, R., Conijn, B., Kramer, J., & Mutsaers, K. (2007). *E-mental health—high tech, high touch, high trust.* Utercht: Trimbos-Instituut.

Schneider, S. K., O'Donnell, L., Stueve, A., & Coulter, R. W. S. (2012a). Cyberbullying, school bullying, and psychological distress: A regional census of high school students. *American Journal of Public Health*, *102*, 171–177. https://doi.org/10.2105/AJPH.2011.300308.

Schneider, F., van Osch, L.A.D.M., Schulz, D. N., Kremers, S. P. J., & de Vries, H. (2012b). The influence of user characteristics and a periodic email prompt on exposure to an internet-delivered computer-tailored lifestyle program. *Journal of Medical Internet Research, 14*, 28–41. https://doi.org/10.2196/jmir.1939.

Schulz, D. N., Kremers, S. P. J., Vandelanotte, C., Van Adrichem, M. J. G., Schneider, F., Candel, M.J.J.M., et al. (2014). Effects of a web-based tailored multiple-lifestyle intervention for adults: A two-year randomized controlled trial comparing sequential and simultaneous delivery modes. *Journal of Medical Internet Research*, 16. https://doi.org/10.2196/jmir.3094.

Snakenborg, J., Van Acker, R., & Gable, R. A. (2011). Cyberbullying: Prevention and intervention to protect our children and youth. *Preventing School Failure, 55*, 88–95. https://doi.org/10.1080/1045988x.2011.539454.

Sniehotta, F. F., Scholz, U., & Schwarzer, R. (2005). Bridging the intention-behaviour gap: Planning, self-efficacy, and action control in the adoption and maintenance of physical exercise. *Psychology & Health, 20*(2), 143–160.

Steffgen, G., Vandebosch, H., Völlink, T., Deboutte, G., & Dehue, F. (2011). Cyberbullying in the Benelux-Countries: First findings and ways to address the problem. In Mora.

Subrahmanyam, K., & Greenfield, P. (2008). Online communication and adolescent relationships. *The Future of Children, 18*(1), 119–146.

Tokunaga, R. S. (2010). Following you home from school: A critical review and synthesis of research on cyberbullying victimization. *Computers in Human Behavior, 26*, 277–287. https://doi.org/10.1016/j.chb.2009.11.014.

Ursin, H., & Eriksen, H. R. (2010). Cognitive activation theory of stress (CATS). *Neuroscience and Biobehavioral Reviews, 34*(6), 877–881.

Vandebosch, H., & van Cleemput, K. (2009). Cyberbullying among youngsters: Profiles for bullies and victims. *New Media Society, 11*(8), 1349–1371.

Vandebosch, H., Poels, K., & Deboutte, G. (2014). Schools and cyberbullying: Problem perception, current actions and future needs. *International Journal of Cyber Society and Education, 7*, 29–48.

Vandelanotte, C., & Mummery, W. K. (2011). Qualitative and quantitative research into the development and feasibility of a video-tailored physical activity intervention. *International Journal of Behavioral Nutrition and Physical Activity, 8*(1), 70.

Verheijden, M. W., Jans, M. P., & Hildebrandt, V. H. (2008). Web-based tailored lifestyle programs: Exploration of the target group's interest and implications for practice. *Health Promotion Practice, 9*(1), 81–92. https://doi.org/10.1177/1524839906289515.

Völlink, T., Dehue, F., Mc Guckin, C., & Jacobs, N. (2016). An introduction in cyberbullying research. In T. Völlink, F. Dehue, & C. Mc Guckin (Eds.), *Cyberbullying: From theory to interventions. Current issues in social psychology*. New York, NY: Taylor & Francis.

Wade, A., & Beran, T. (2011). Cyberbullying: The new era of bullying. *Canadian Journal of School Psychology, 26*(1), 44–61. https://doi.org/10.1177/0829573510396318.

Walrave, M., & Heirman, W. (2011). Cyberbullying: Predicting victimisation and perpetration. *Children & Society, 25*, 59–72. https://doi.org/10.1111/j.1099-0860.2009.00260.x.

Webb, M., Burns, J., & Collin, P. (2008). Providing online support for young people with mental health difficulties: Challenges and opportunities explored. *Early Intervention in Psychiatry, 2*(2), 108–113. https://doi.org/10.1111/j.1751-7893.2008.00066.x.

Williams, K. R., & Guerra, N. G. (2007). Prevalence and predictors of Internet bullying. *The Journal of Adolescent Health, 41*, S14–S21. Retrieved from http://linkinghub.elsevier.com/retrieve/pii/S1054139X0700362X?showall=true.

Wong, Y. C. (2010). Cyber-parenting: Internet benefits, risks and parenting issues. *Journal of Technology in Human Services, 28*, 252–273.

Further reading

Campbell, M. A. (2005). Cyber bullying: an old problem in a new guise? *Australian Journal of Guidance and Counselling*, *15*, 68–76. https://doi.org/10.1375/ajgc.15.1.68.

Merchan, J., & Jäger, Th. (Eds.) Cyberbullying: A cross-national comparison. Verlag. Empirische Pädagogik, Landau, Germany, 2011.

Cyberbullying prevention within a socio-ecological framework: The ViSC social competence program

14

Petra Gradinger, Dagmar Strohmeier
University of Applied Sciences Upper Austria, Linz, Austria

Name of program: ViSC social competence program
Type of program: Manualized educational program for teachers and students
Suitable for ages: Lower secondary and middle school (11–15 years old)

In line with a socioecological understanding of bullying, international comparison studies suggest that cyberbullying is frequent in countries where traditional bullying rates are also high (Livingstone, Haddon, Görzig, & Ólafsson, 2011). Furthermore, cyberbullying actually co-occurs with traditional bullying (Kowalski, Giumetti, Schroeder, & Lattanner, 2014) indicating that cyberbullying might be part of a systemic school problem. Thus, it is conceivable to assume that programs or strategies tackling traditional bullying are also effective in preventing cyberbullying (Cross, Li, Smith, & Monks, 2012). Recently, guidelines how to best prevent cyberbullying have been published (e.g., Välimäki et al., 2012), and several programs about how to specifically tackle cyberbullying have been developed (e.g., Menesini, Nocentini, & Palladino, 2012; Ortega-Ruiz, Del Rey, & Casas, 2012; Pieschl & Porsch, 2013; Schultze-Krumbholz, Zagorscak, Woelfer, & Scheithauer, 2014). However, as long as longitudinal and experimental research on risk and protective factors regarding cyberbullying and cybervictimization is sparse and specific etiological models for cyberbullying and cybervictimization are lacking, it is rather difficult to develop specific anticyberbullying programs based on empirical grounds.

Therefore, this chapter examines the merits of the ViSC social competence program—a socioecological program to prevent traditional bullying—to change cyberbullying and cybervictimization, and summarizes the insights we gained during the crossnational implementation of this systemic whole school program in Austria, Cyprus, Romania, and Turkey.

Prevention of cyberbullying

Many terms have been used for cyberbullying (e.g., cyberaggression, cyberharassment) but most often, the term cyberbullying is used for bullying through electronic means. Based on Smith et al. (2008), cyberbullying can be defined as “An aggressive, intentional act carried out by a group or individual, using electronic forms of contact, repeatedly and over time against a victim who cannot easily defend him or herself” (p. 376).

Reducing Cyberbullying in Schools. https://doi.org/10.1016/B978-0-12-811423-0.00014-6

Table 14.1 ViSC course for ViSC coaches

Semester	Month	Target group	Activity
First semester	September	ViSC coaches	Two-day workshop at university
	September	Teachers	First pedagogical conference in the school
	September–October	Teachers	In-school training
	October–February	Teachers	Coaching of the school team
	February	Teachers	Second pedagogical conference in the school
Second Semester	February	ViSC coaches	Two-day workshop at the university
	February–March	Teachers	In-school training
	March–June	Teachers	Class and school team coaching
	June	ViSC coaches	One-day workshop at the university
	June	Teachers	Third pedagogical conference in school

Note: Activities during one school year starting at begin of September and ending at begin of July.

Content	School level	Class level	Individual level
State-of-the-art knowledge about bullying research Knowledge about standards of evidence Overview of the ViSC program Detailed instructions on how to implement the program at the school level General information about the program to all teachers Definition and recognition of the problem Tackling acute cases How best to implement preventive measures at the school level How to engage as many people as possible in the school How to involve parents Parents' meeting Reflection about the implementation process at school level and how best to continue the activities	School poster, parents' meetings, teacher trainings, and supervision		Recognizing and handling acute bullying cases
Reflection on the implementation processes in the schools and the professional role of the ViSC coaches Detailed instructions on how to implement the program at the class level Continuation of the implementation at the school level Preventive measures at the class level: Content and implementation of the class project How to continue activities at the school level How best to implement the units of the class project Reflection on the implementation processes in the schools and the professional role of the ViSC coaches Reflection on implementation of the program and how best to continue the activities in the next school year without the help of the ViSC coach	Teacher trainings and supervision	Class project	Recognizing and handling acute cases

Based on the socioecological model of bullying (Swearer & Espelage, 2004), risk and protective factors for cyberbullying perpetration and victimization are located on several systemic levels. On the individual level, cybervictimization, traditional bullying and traditional victimization, age, and internet usage have been identified as cross-sectional risk factors for cyberbullying perpetration (Kowalski et al., 2014), while gender effects are mixed (Barlett & Coyne, 2014). On the class level, good class climate has been shown to be a protective factor for both traditional and cyberbullying perpetration based on cross-sectional data (Eisner & Malti, 2012; Kowalski et al., 2014). In line with the socioecological framework, programs with longer duration and components for students, teachers, and parents have been shown to be more effective in reducing traditional bullying than programs with shorter duration and fewer components (Fox, Farrington, & Ttofi, 2012; Ttofi & Farrington, 2011). Thus, based on theoretical and empirical grounds, it is conceivable that a systemic whole school prevention program is not only able to reduce traditional but also cyberforms of bullying perpetration and victimization.

The ViSC social competence program

The ViSC Social Competence Program was developed, implemented, and evaluated as one component of the Austrian national strategy "*Together against violence*" in Austrian secondary schools between 2008 and 2013 (Spiel & Strohmeier, 2011, 2012). The program conceptualizes the prevention of perpetration behavior and victimization as a whole school task with the initial implementation of the program lasting one school year. Thus, the program not only aims to change the behavior of the students (on an individual and class level), but also aims to foster knowledge and competences among teachers to be able to initiate several change processes at the school level. During program implementation, several routines at the school level (e.g., the handling of acute bullying cases) are changed. The program is implemented via several in-school-teacher trainings and a class project for students (Strohmeier, Hoffmann, Schiller, Stefanek, & Spiel, 2012).

Program structure and target groups

The main goal of the ViSC program is to reduce aggressive behavior and bullying and foster social and intercultural competencies in secondary schools. In Austria, secondary schools serve grades 5–8, with students aged 11–15 years. The ViSC program intends to promote the vision "*Together against violence*" as a commonly shared principle in schools and approaches the school as a whole using a systemic perspective. During the first semester, the program covers preventive measures and interventions at the school, and teachers are the primary target group for change (see Table 14.1). Preventive measures at the class level are introduced to the teachers during the second semester. During this semester, the target groups are both teachers and students, as teachers train their students during the ViSC class project.

Implementation model

To foster knowledge transfer between research and practice and to empower sustainable preventive attitudes and behaviors in teachers, a cascaded train-the-trainer model has been developed and applied; researchers train multipliers (called ViSC coaches), multipliers train teachers, and teachers train their students (see Fig. 14.1). Researchers are the program developers in Austria, or certified researchers located in the partner countries. ViSC coaches are professionals working in the school or in a support system surrounding the school, e.g., school psychologists, specialized teachers, counselors, and school social workers. This approach ensures training professionals who are potentially able to support teachers even after the initial program implementation. It is well known that support systems are especially relevant to initiate sustainable change, as otherwise programs are initially implemented but then quickly abandoned (Fixsen, Schultes, & Blase, 2016). Teachers are the most important change agents and the goal is to foster their knowledge about bullying and to change their attitudes and behaviors toward the students. When delivering the structured program modules and the student-centered interactions, the teachers reflect on their own teaching style.

The main goal during the program implementation is to create a school development process during which as many teachers as possible are committed to work together against violence. The ViSC program aims to foster shared responsibility among teachers, which in turn implies that as many teachers in the school as possible have worked out a common understanding of the problem, agreed on procedures for tackling acute cases, and jointly implement preventive measures at the school and class levels. The theory behind this approach is that bullying is promoted in an environment where the problem is not taken seriously or is overlooked and that bullying can be stopped in an environment where there is a consensus that such behavior will not be tolerated.

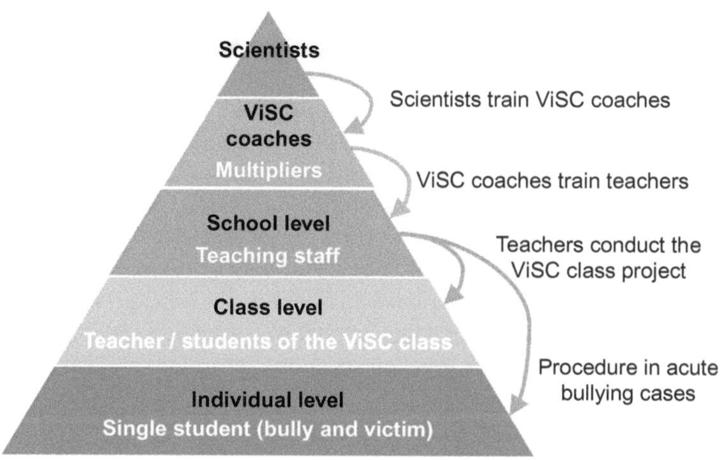

Fig. 14.1 Implementation model of the ViSC program. Note: Cascaded train-the-trainer model.

The ViSC coach has a central role during this process. This person is an expert who provides state-of-the-art knowledge and introduces specific procedures for how best to tackle the problem and implement concrete preventive measures at the school and class levels. This person is also a coach who must be able to integrate the existing expertise of the teachers in order to commit and empower as many of them as possible. The ability of the ViSC coach to foster ownership of the program by the school staff is considered central to initiate a sustainable school development process. Besides the implementation of this philosophy of the program, the ViSC coach also offers many practical tools during the in-school training for the teachers.

ViSC teacher trainings

Two in-school teacher training opportunities are offered during program implementation (see Table 14.1). During the first training session that is offered at the beginning of the first semester, teachers are trained on how to recognize bullying, how to tackle acute bullying cases, and how to implement preventive measures at the school level. The second training session is offered at the beginning of the second semester and the goal is to introduce the philosophy and materials of the ViSC class project to enable them to implement it in their classes. In accordance with the philosophy of the program, the training contains many interactive elements to foster the development of a commonly shared perspective among as many teachers as possible. In total, the in-school training consists of four modules.

Module 1: Definition and recognition of the problem

To provide an overview of the lay definitions of violence, aggression, and bullying versus social and intercultural competencies, the ViSC coach prompts a brainstorming discussion among the teachers. The goal is to collect ideas without judging them as right or wrong. During this discussion, it becomes clear whether there are contradictory opinions among the teachers and whether and to what extent teachers have already worked on these topics. Next, the coach introduces the scientific perspective by discussing the broad definition of violence from the World Health Organization and the much narrower definition of bullying. The scientific definitions of social competence are also discussed. By acknowledging the previous knowledge of the teachers, the ViSC coach leads them to the insight that it is very helpful for prevention and intervention to have a common understanding of the problem and that bullying is a serious issue that needs to be tackled. Next, the teachers work in small groups and analyze hypothetical bullying cases. The goal is to discuss how to detect bullying and how to differentiate it from reactive aggression, rejection, shyness, or voluntary solitude. These discussions usually reveal that it is not always easy to detect bullying and that it is very helpful that teachers work together to get the information needed.

Module 2: Tackling acute bullying cases

It is very important for both intervention and prevention that the teachers follow a common procedure in addressing acute bullying cases. Based on the work of Roland

and Vaaland (2006) and in line with their suggestions, a manualized best practice procedure is introduced to the teachers. To tackle a bullying case, the teachers need to talk with the victimized student first. Second, they need to talk with the bullying students by clearly stating that this behavior is wrong and needs to be stopped immediately. These conversations need to be firm but respectful. If a group of students has bullied another student, the conversations need to be conducted in such a way as to weaken the social bonds of the bullying students. Third, it is necessary to inform the parents. The teachers are provided with a detailed manual including examples of exact words in how to conduct these conversations. Extending the work of Roland and Vaaland (2006), the manual also covers example conversations with students who both bully others and are victimized by others, and their parents.

Module 3: Preventive measures at school level

Even before participating in the ViSC program, many schools would have already implemented some preventive measures. The ViSC coach aims to integrate these existing measures in a common school wide approach to prevent violence. For instance, some schools have already implemented peer education approaches that are suitable complementary methods to the ViSC program. Some teachers are experts in peer mediation techniques; these are not suitable for tackling bullying cases, but they can be integrated in a school wide approach to solve conflicts between parties of equal strength. The task of the ViSC coach is to clarify which method is suitable for which goals. The coach aims to commit teachers to tackle acute bullying cases according to the guidelines presented in the manual and works on an agreement that clarifies who in the school will be responsible for conducting these conversations. The teachers who are willing to coordinate the activities at the school level are nominated as members of the school team. These teachers also prepare information sheets about the ViSC program for students and parents. Finally, the ViSC coach works on an agreement on how best to implement a ViSC class project during the second semester. The team needs to clarify which classes will participate in the class project, which teachers will implement it, and how the teaching units needed for the class project can best be integrated in the academic curriculum of these classes.

Module 4: ViSC class project

The class project consists of 13 units divided into 2 main parts (see Table 14.2). During units 1–8, the students are trained in various social skills while during units 9–13, they work together to achieve a positive, common goal. Thus, the class project is not an antibullying program in a narrow sense. Instead, the program trains a broad spectrum of competencies considered important for the development of social and intercultural competencies. The idea behind this approach is that different students need to learn different competencies. In many classes, a rather large group of students neither feels responsible for what happens around them nor intervenes in critical situations. Therefore, all students are trained to feel responsible when something negative is going on in their class and to react in a way that is likely to improve the situation. Furthermore, in many lower secondary school classes, there is a group of

Table 14.2 ViSC class project: phases, units and contents

Phase	Unit	Content
Impulse	Unit 1	What is the class project, and why are we participating? Why are rules important in our lives, and what rules do we want in our class?
	Unit 2	How can we recognize critical social situations, and what can we do to help improve the situation?
	Unit 3	How can we recognize the emotions of others, and what can we do to help them feel better?
	Unit 4	How can we recognize our own emotions, and what can we do to cope with them to feel better?
	Unit 5–6	What can we do if we are treated in a mean and unfair way by others? What is the best thing to do in such situations, and why?
	Unit 7–8	What can we do if we don't understand the behavior of our classmates who come from another country? What is the best thing to do in such situations, and why?
Reflection	Unit 9	What have we learned during the project so far, and what do we want to learn in the remaining units? Which common activity do we want to carry out during our project day? How can we plan and organize the common activity in a way that every classmate is able to make a valuable contribution?
Action	Unit 10–13	Carrying out the common activity by creating a process that leads to the experience of a common success.

preadolescents who are not able to manage their negative emotions in a nonaggressive way. Therefore, all students are trained to recognize their own emotions and the emotions of others and to cope with these emotions in a positive, nonaggressive way. Third, it is necessary to empower students who might be victimized easily because they might invite attacks with their unassertive behavior. Thus, all students are trained how best to react when others are picking on them. Taken together, the program empowers victims and bystanders, and helps bullies and bully-victims to cope with anger and frustration in a social competent way. The class project does not include units to directly change the behavior of bullying students; instead the class project aims to create an environment in which it is less likely that bullying will occur. To train these competencies, concrete materials are provided in the class manual. Each unit is designed for a 2-hour lesson and consists of worksheets for individual students, sheets for small group work, summary sheets, and a detailed implementation plan. The task of the teacher is to lead the class and work with the materials provided in the manual. The units are designed to foster exchange and discussions among the students. The teacher is encouraged to use interactive games, role plays, and other interactive pedagogical methods. During unit 9, the focus of the class project changes. To transfer the social competencies into real life, the class is assigned to find a common, positive, and realistic activity that can be carried out *together* during a project day. The role of the teacher is to create a group process that enables cooperative learning and the experience of common success. Thus, the teacher helps the students find a cooperative structure and supervises them as they plan and carry out the activity. A huge variety of activities has been carried out during ViSC project days. Some classes produced photos, short films, songs, or newspapers. Others conducted interviews with students in other classes, people on the street, and local politicians and asked them about their contribution to prevent violence. Still others organized parents' meetings during which they wrote a performance to demonstrate what they had learned during the class project. To summarize, the theoretical idea is that aggressive behavior is less likely to occur in an encouraging, structured, and friendly environment where students are able to feel part of a group and are able to create common successes.

Program evaluation

The ViSC program was developed in several phases. During the years 1999–2005, the program consisted of the class project only and was implemented by external experts and not by teachers (Atria & Spiel, 2007). Evaluation results showed encouraging short-term effects but failed to produce any long-term changes (Atria & Spiel, 2007; Gollwitzer, 2005; Gollwitzer, Banse, Eisenbach, & Naumann, 2007; Gollwitzer, Eisenbach, Atria, Strohmeier, & Banse, 2006). During 2008 and 2013, the program was substantially improved and rolled out in about 100 secondary schools in Austria. In this phase, the program was evaluated with the highest possible research standards to gain evaluation results with high statistical conclusion validity (Gradinger, Yanagida, Strohmeier, & Spiel, 2014, 2016; Yanagida, Strohmeier, & Spiel, 2016). Since 2012, the program was also rolled out internationally and is currently used in schools located in Cyprus, Romania, and Turkey (Dogan et al., 2017; Solomontos-Kountouri, Gradinger, Yanagida, & Strohmeier, 2016; Trip et al., 2015).

Program evaluation regarding cyberbullying and cybervictimization

To investigate whether a general whole school prevention program is also able to change cyberbullying and cybervictimization, (a) the effectiveness and (b) the sustainability of the ViSC program regarding cyberbullying and cybervictimization, controlling for several covariates, was conducted in Austria within a cluster randomized control study (Gradinger et al., 2016). It was hypothesized that cyberbullying and cybervictimization has a greater change over time in the intervention group than in the control group, when controlling for baseline levels of class climate and ethnic diversity at the class level, as well as of traditional and cyberbullying/victimization, age, gender, and internet usage on the individual level (Model 1). Secondly, class climate and ethnic diversity as class-level moderators of program effectiveness and sustainability were examined (Model 2) as well as individual level variables, such as gender, age, internet usage, traditional bullying/victimization (Model 3).

Effectiveness

Results of Model 1 investigating program effectiveness showed an increase in cyberbullying and cybervictimization in the control group between pretest and posttest (cyberbullying: $b=0.529$, $p<.05$; cybervictimization: $b=.287$, $p<.05$). For the intervention group, there was a decrease in cyberbullying ($b=-0.749$, $p<.05$) and a lower increase for cybervictimization ($b=-0.274$, $p<.05$). The results demonstrate effectiveness of the intervention for cyberbullying and cybervictimization when controlling for several covariates at individual and class level (see Fig. 14.2).

In Model 2, neither class climate nor ethnic diversity moderated the intervention effects for cyberbullying or cybervictimization. In Model 3, only traditional victimization was a moderator of program effectiveness ($b=0.129$, $p<.05$) indicating the higher traditional victimization at pretest the smaller the decrease in cyberbullying in the intervention group (i.e., smaller intervention effects).

Sustainability

Results showed an increase in cyberbullying in the control group between posttest and follow-up test ($b=0.281$, $p<.05$). Cybervictimization stabilized in the control group between posttest and follow-up test ($b=-0.044$, $p=.690$). After posttest, there was an *intervention* effect for cyberbullying ($b=-0.590$, $p<.05$) and cybervictimization

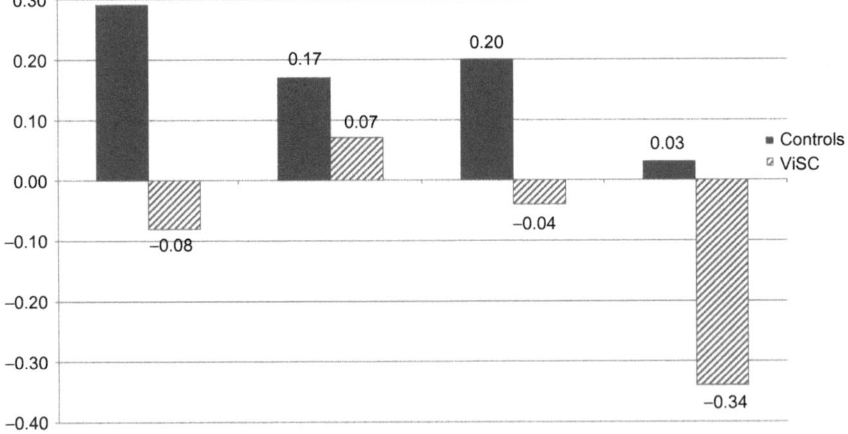

Fig. 14.2 Program effectiveness and sustainability regarding cyberbullying and cybervictimization in Austria. Note: Difference scores (Δ) between waves separately by group (ViSC vs controls).

($b = -0.327$, $p < .05$) indicating a decrease in cyberbullying and cybervictimization in the intervention group.

In sum, the evaluation results indicated a sustainable intervention effect for cyberbullying and cybervictimization when controlling for several covariates at individual and class level (see Fig. 14.2). Importantly, neither class climate nor ethnic diversity moderated the intervention effects for cyberbullying or cybervictimization (see Model 2) and no individual level covariates were moderators of program effectiveness (see Model 3).

Lessons learned, drawbacks, and implications

The ViSC program has several strengths. To begin with, the ViSC program is well grounded on the socioecological framework of bullying and uses state-of-the art methods and initiates change processes to prevent bullying on several systemic levels (Fox et al., 2012; Swearer & Espelage, 2004). In Austria, the program was implemented within a national strategy, and it was possible to investigate program effectiveness on the class and the individual level within a large sample of schools within a large cluster randomized control study (Gradinger et al., 2014, 2016; Yanagida et al., 2016). Thus, evaluation results from Austria are solid and also provide insights regarding the mechanisms of change on class level and regarding teacher's behavior (Schultes, Stefanek, van de Schoot, Strohmeier, & Spiel, 2014). Furthermore, the ViSC program was transported to three other countries without major adaptations (Dogan et al., 2017; Solomontos-Kountouri et al., 2016; Trip et al., 2015). To summarize, the program is both highly structured including a large number of materials and also adaptive to create ownership and a sustainable change process on school level.

Regardless of the benefits of ViSC program, there are several drawbacks. To begin with, program implementation is a very complex task because the *whole* school needs to engage in a developmental process. Because sustainable changes need time, it is not always possible that teachers see changes among their students quickly (see Trip et al., 2015). Consequently, several schools start disengaging with bullying prevention after the initial first year of implementation. In Cyprus and Turkey, we also found sensitizing effects, and only on the long run preventive effects were detected (see Dogan et al., 2017; Solomontos-Kountouri et al., 2016). However, our studies clearly demonstrate that schools where teachers show high program responsiveness profited most (see Schultes et al., 2014).

To summarize, the ViSC program is effective and shows sustainable effects regarding cyberbullying, cybervictimization, aggressive behavior and victimization, and can easily be adapted to new countries. Although the program is not specifically designed to prevent cyberbullying and cybervictimization, it obviously also tackles the underlying mechanisms of cyberforms of bullying indicating that cyberbullying is indeed part of a systemic school problem. However, it is important that well-designed, theoretically sound programs like ViSC are implemented sustainable and with high fidelity in practice. Finally yet importantly, we would strongly recommend to also include specific units to prevent cyberbullying in any general antibullying program, because we are convinced that a combined strategy will yield the most effective results in the long run.

Acknowledgments

The implementation and evaluation of the ViSC program in Austria was funded by the Austrian Federal Ministry for Education, Arts and Cultural Affairs between 2008 and 2011. The writing of the present study was funded by the Platform for Intercultural Competences, University of Applied Sciences Upper Austria in 2016 and 2017. We are very grateful to the whole ViSC project team consisting of Christiane Spiel, Takuya Yanagida, Eva-Maria Schiller, Elisabeth Stefanek, Christoph Burger, Bianca Pollhammer, Katharina Derndarsky, Marie Therese Schultes, and Christine Hoffmann for their invaluable work during the intervention studies conducted in Austria. We also want to thank the ViSC coaches and teachers who implemented the program in their schools and classes. We thank all schools and students who participated in the studies in Austria, Cyprus, Romania, and Turkey.

References

Atria, M., & Spiel, C. (2007). The Viennese Social Competence (ViSC) training for students: Program and evaluation. In J. E. Zins, M. J. Elias, & C. A. Maher (Eds.), *Bullying, victimization and peer harassment: A handbook of prevention and intervention* (pp. 179–198). New York, NY: The Haworth Press.

Barlett, C., & Coyne, S. M. (2014). A meta-analysis of sex differences in cyber-bullying behavior: The moderating role of age. *Aggressive Behavior*, *40*, 474–488. https://doi.org/10.1002/ab.21555.

Cross, D., Li, Q., Smith, P., & Monks, C. (2012). Understanding and preventing cyberbullying: Where have we been and where should where should we be going? In Q. Li, D. Cross, & P. Smith (Eds.), *Cyberbullying in the global playground: Research from international perspectives* (pp. 287–305). Chichester: Wiley-Blackwell.

Dogan, A., Keser, E, Şen, Z., Yanagida, T., Gradinger, P., & Strohmeier, D. (2017). Evidence based bullying prevention in Turkey: Implementation of the ViSC Social Competence Program.

Eisner, M., & Malti, T. (2012). The future of research on evidence-based developmental violence prevention in Europe—Introduction to the focus section. *International Journal of Conflict and Violence*, *6*, 166–175. https://doi.org/10.4119/UNIBI/ijcv.319.

Fixsen, D. L., Schultes, M.-T., & Blase, K. A. (2016). Bildung-psychology and implementation Science. *European Journal of Developmental Psychology*, *13*, 666–680. https://doi.org/10.1080/17405629.2016.1204292.

Fox, B. H., Farrington, D. P., & Ttofi, M. M. (2012). Successful bullying prevention programs: Influence of research design, implementation features, and program components. *International Journal of Conflict and Violence*, *6*, 27–56. http://ijcv.org/index.php/ijcv/article/viewFile/245/pdf_65.

Gollwitzer, M. (2005). Könnten Anti-Aggressions-Trainings in der Schule wirksamer sein, wenn sie weniger standardisiert wären? [Could antiaggression training programs be more effective if they were less standardized?]. In A. Ittel & M. von Salisch (Eds.), *Lästern, Lügen, Leiden lassen: Aggressives Verhalten von Kindern und Jugendlichen* [Lying, backbiting, bullying. Aggressive behavior in children and adolescents] (pp. 276–291). Stuttgart: Kohlhammer.

Gollwitzer, M., Banse, R., Eisenbach, K., & Naumann, E. (2007). Effectiveness of the Vienna social competence training on implicit and explicit aggression. Evidence from an aggressiveness IAT. *European Journal of Psychological Assessment*, *23*, 150–156. https://doi.org/10.1027/1015-5759.23.3.150.

Gollwitzer, M., Eisenbach, K., Atria, M., Strohmeier, D., & Banse, R. (2006). Evaluation of aggression-reducing effects of the "Viennese Social Competence Training". *Swiss Journal of Psychology*, *65*, 125–135. https://doi.org/10.1024/1421-0185.65.2.125.

Gradinger, P., Yanagida, T., Strohmeier, D., & Spiel, C. (2014). Prevention of cyberbullying and cyber victimization: Evaluation of the ViSC Social Competence Program. *Journal of School Violence*, *14*, 87–110. https://doi.org/10.1080/15388220.2014.963231.

Gradinger, P., Yanagida, T., Strohmeier, D., & Spiel, C. (2016). Effectiveness and sustainability of the ViSC Social Competence Program to prevent cyberbullying and cyber-victimization: Class and individual level moderators. *Aggressive Behavior*, *42*, 181–193. https://doi.org/10.1002/ab.21631.

Kowalski, R. M., Giumetti, G. W., Schroeder, A. N., & Lattanner, M. R. (2014). Bullying in the digital age: A critical review and meta-analysis of cyberbullying research among youth. *Psychological Bulletin*, *140*, 1073–1137. https://doi.org/10.1037/a0035618.

Livingstone, S., Haddon, L., Görzig, A., & Ólafsson, K. (2011). *Risks and safety on the internet: The perspective of European children. Full Findings*. London: EU Kids Online/LSE.

Menesini, E., Nocentini, A., & Palladino, B. (2012). Empowering students against bullying and cyberbullying: Evaluation of an Italian peer-led model. *International Journal of Conflict and Violence*, *6*, 314–321. https://doi.org/10.4119/UNIBI/ijcv.253.

Ortega-Ruiz, R., Del Rey, R., & Casas, J. (2012). Knowing, building and living together on internet and social networks: The ConRed cyberbullying prevention program. *International Journal of Conflict and Violence*, *6*, 303–313. https://doi.org/10.4119/UNIBI/ijcv.250.

Pieschl, S., & Porsch, T. (2013). Das Praeventionsprogramm Surf-Fair gegen Cybermobbing—Eine Einfuehrung [The prevention program Surf-Fair against cyberbullying—An introduction]. *Psychologie in Oesterreich*, *1*, 14–21.

Roland, E., & Vaaland, G. (2006). *ZERO teacher's guide to the zero anti-bullying programme*. Stavanger: Centre for Behavioural Research, University of Stavanger.

Schultes, M.-T., Stefanek, E., van de Schoot, R., Strohmeier, D., & Spiel, C. (2014). Measuring implementation of a school-based violence prevention program Fidelity and teachers' responsiveness as predictors of proximal outcomes. *Zeitschrift für Psychologie*, *222*, 49–57. https://doi.org/10.1027/2151-2604/a000165.

Schultze-Krumbholz, A., Zagorscak, P., Woelfer, R., & Scheithauer, H. (2014). Praevention von Cybermobbing und Reduzierung aggressiven Verhaltens Jugendlicher durch das Programm Medienhelden. Ergebnisse einer Evaluationsstudie [Prevention of cyberbullying and reduction of adolescent's aggressive behavior using the Medienhelden program. Results from an evaluation study]. *Diskurs Kindheits- und Jugendforschung*, *9*, 61–79.

Smith, P., Mahdavi, J., Carvalho, M., Fisher, S., Russell, S., & Tippett, N. (2008). Cyberbullying: Its nature and impact on secondary school pupils. *The Journal of Child Psychology and Psychiatry*, *49*, 376–385. https://doi.org/10.1111/j.1469-7610.2007.01846.x.

Solomontos-Kountouri, O., Gradinger, P., Yanagida, Y., & Strohmeier, D. (2016). The implementation and evaluation of the ViSC program in Cyprus: Challenges of cross-national dissemination and evaluation results. *European Journal of Developmental Psychology*, *13*, 737–755. https://doi.org/10.1080/17405629.2015.1136618.

Spiel, C., & Strohmeier, D. (2011). National strategy for violence prevention in the Austrian public school system: Development and implementation. *International Journal of Behavioral Development*, *35*, 412–418. https://doi.org/10.1177/0165025411407458.

Spiel, C., & Strohmeier, D. (2012). Evidence-based practice and policy: When researchers, policy makers, and practitioners learn how to work together. *European Journal of Developmental Psychology*, *9*, 150–162. https://doi.org/10.1080/17405629.2011.616776.

Strohmeier, D., Hoffmann, C., Schiller, E.-M., Stefanek, E., & Spiel, C. (2012). ViSC Social Competence Program. *New Directions for Youth Development*, *133*, 71–84. https://doi.org/10.1002/yd.20008.

Swearer, S. M., & Espelage, D. L. (2004). Introduction: A social-ecological framework of bullying among youth. In D. L. Espelage & S. M. Swearer (Eds.), *Bullying in American schools: A social-ecological perspective on prevention and intervention* (pp. 1–12). Mahwah, NJ: Lawrence Erlbaum.

Trip, S., Bora, C., Sipos-Gug, S., Tocai, I., Gradinger, P., Yanagida, T., et al. (2015). Bullying prevention in schools by targeting cognitions, emotions and behavior: Evaluating the effectiveness of the REBE-ViSC Program. *Journal of Counseling Psychology*, *62*, 732–740. https://doi.org/10.1037/cou0000084.

Ttofi, M. M., & Farrington, D. P. (2011). Effectiveness of school-based programs to reduce bullying: A systematic and meta-analytic review. *Journal of Experimental Criminology*, *7*, 27–56. https://doi.org/10.1007/s11292-010-9109-1.

Välimäki, M., Almeida, A., Cross, D., O'Moore, M., Berne, S., Deboutte, G., et al. (2012). *Guidelines for preventing cyber-bullying in the school environment*. https://sites.google.com/site/costis0801/guideline (1.10.2016).

Yanagida, T., Strohmeier, D., & Spiel, C. (2016). Dynamic change of aggressive behavior and victimization among adolescents: Effectiveness of the ViSC Program. *Journal of Clinical Child & Adolescent Psychology*, *1–15*, 2016. https://doi.org/10.1080/15374416.2016.1233498.

The ConRed program: Educating in cybercoexistence and cyberbullying prevention by improving coexistence projects in schools

15

Jose A. Casas, Rosario Del Rey†, Rosario Ortega-Ruiz*,‡*

*University of Cordoba, Cordoba, Spain, †University of Sevilla, Sevilla, Spain, ‡University of Greenwich, London, United Kingdom

Name of program: The ConRed program
Type of program: Practical school lessons
Suitable for ages: Secondary school students

Introduction

The last decade has witnessed a dramatic transformation in the social life of human beings due to the dissemination of digital devices that allow rapid communication in real time with other people. This has not only affected communication in general, but has also accelerated the development of interpersonal relationships, thus enhancing the sociability of individuals. Smartphones, tablets, laptops, and mobile digital devices with Internet connection have enabled such changes as they offer multiple options for communicating with others both nearby and hundreds or thousands of kilometers away. Social network profiles, instant mobile messaging applications, and videoconferencing have now become so common and widespread that it is rare to find people who do not have or use any of these services or devices in geographical areas where this form of communication is available.

Unquestionably, the Internet and Internet-enabled devices form an essential part of many spheres of people's lives today. Indeed, the majority of the activities that we engage in on a daily basis, from searching for information and shopping to communicating with others, as well as other important aspects of our lives such as work, leisure, or interpersonal relationships, now require technology to be carried out properly. As a result, we live in a society that is developing between two large dimensions: the physical or real and the technological or virtual.

This rapid and profound transformation that has affected most social spheres is even more pronounced in the younger generations. These so-called digital natives are boys and girls who have been born and are being educated and socialized in this new real and virtual society (Prensky, 2005). In the lives of young people today, virtual

Reducing Cyberbullying in Schools. https://doi.org/10.1016/B978-0-12-811423-0.00015-8

environments play a paramount role in establishing and maintaining relationships with peers due to their fascination with all that is new or the additional technological advantages that these environments provide them. Beyond their passion for technological innovation, the massive use of digital spaces by young people may also be related to the independence such communication media afford youth and the lack of adult supervision of the social activities they engage in through them, as well as the perhaps false belief in the lower technological competence of adults compared to adolescents and youth (Revilla Muñoz, Alpiste Penalba, Fernández Sánchez, & Santos, 2017).

Cyberbullying is the clearest example of the additional risks of using digital devices and the one that has received most attention in the scientific literature (Zych, Ortega-Ruiz, & Del Rey, 2015). Cyberbullying is defined as an intentional and repeated act of aggression by means of digital media and devices based on an imbalance of power among those involved (Tokunaga, 2010). Due to the prevalence of cyberbullying and the serious consequences that such behavior can have on young people, among them suicide, this is one of the risks that has become a major topic of public concern.

What is the program and how is it delivered

The ConRed program has been designed to promote and raise awareness among the educational community of the importance of using the Internet and social networks in a safe, positive, and beneficial manner, and to incorporate this view into schools' coexistence plans. The implementation of this program also involves a research-based analysis and diagnosis to identify the needs of the schools regarding the use of technology, which serves as the starting point for the program.

ConRed aims to address three key goals: (1) educate about the ethical and legal aspects of inappropriate activities conducted in virtual environments; (2) educate about the risks and benefits of one's own and others' activities related to the use of social networks and digital communication devices; and (3) organize activities and provide practical examples of how certain behaviors do not lead to peer acceptance and do not reflect the norms of the group. ConRed also provides the educational community training in the skills and knowledge needed to use the Internet and social networks in a safe and responsible manner. Although ConRed has a set framework, the program can be tailored to the needs of those involved (students, teachers, and families) through three independent but interconnected lines of action. Each line addresses the major objectives of the program, but can be modified to take into account the perspective, needs, and prior competence of each of the groups or recipients to whom it is targeted. The following recommendations or guidelines for students are examples of these actions:

- Take a few minutes to configure safety settings in your social networks so you can avoid potential problems.
- Protect your information and privacy. Remember that your contacts include different types of friends.
- Read what you accept on a social network. Try to control your clicks.
- Make it clear how you want others to use your information or images.
- Don't do things to others that you wouldn't like them to do to you. Respect the privacy of others.

- If you have questions or need help, don't remain silent. Talk to an adult.
- Don't waste time: use the Internet, but don't get hooked.

In short, the practical lessons of ConRed cover the following aspects: (a) the Internet and social networks; (b) the benefits of using these digital media and instrumental competence; and (c) information about the risks and advice on use. These areas of intervention have three general objectives: (a) to highlight the importance of knowledge about technology, the Internet, and social networks in order to use them responsibly; (b) instruct users in the basic concepts and functions of digital tools to promote safe and responsible use; and (c) develop a strategies-based plan of action for schools in situations of risk. The performance of educational agents, teachers, parents, and school counselors is also implemented in eight sessions. The first one explores basic ideas and knowledge about relationships in social networks that serve as both initial assessment and contact with the focus of the program. Sessions two and three deal with aspects related to the conceptualization and definition of Social Networks. Relevant and current data on frequency and forms of networking are shown. They teach how to investigate privacy and identity in Social Networks, showing its importance and the negative consequences that may lead to not having security or privacy in the acts performed in them. Subsequently develop a dynamic practice of strategies and forms of action on risky events. An example of dynamics is a simulation of a report of an inappropriate fact that the school may have suffered (a photo of itself that has been used abusively, maliciously, etc.). The fourth session extends the work on specific risks of victimization in the Networks, providing competence for the reflection and the operability of the fight against this type of aggression. The fifth session addresses the positive use of Social Networks and information and communication technologies (ICT), showing their own benefits, mainly academic and social and leisure, aimed especially at the prosocial use of the activity. Positive use is included for the benefit of others, that is, solidarity, the encouragement of friendship, etc. The sixth session focuses particularly on cyberbullying as one of the most important risk and victimization phenomena in the years of compulsory schooling. In it, we insist on the continuity that cyberbullying has of the phenomenon best known by school children or traditional bullying, since there has been a great overlap between this and traditional bullying. Then there is an activity, Webquest, to synthesize and advance the knowledge and key ideas that have been developed in the program. It is a question of the students learning to face real or simulated cases of aggression in Social Networks, and cyberbullying using a tool created by them, where a device or guide containing a reservoir for solving specific cases has been recorded. Finally, the eighth session is devoted to evaluating the program and conducting an assembly on the keys to making safe and healthy use of social networks.

Theoretical basis of the program

The incorporation of virtual environments and applications in young people's peer relationships has become a reality. Instant messaging via text, images, or video are particularly effective ways to remain connected with peers where the place, time, or action does not matter for communication to occur. The content of messages is usually very brief: an image, one hundred and forty alphanumeric characters or a video of no more than 5 min in length is sufficient. Evidence has shown that this is time enough to create a constant sense of presence among peers that exchange messages and adopt very similar behaviors and styles in their respective profiles, which in turn strengthens their sense of belonging to the peer group.

These tools provide multiple benefits, such as the elimination of physical barriers to communication, increased social support, or the possibility of housing an inexhaustible source of information. Unfortunately, however, virtual environments also reproduce negative aspects of the socialization of human beings and entail significant risks. In this line, the scientific community has focused on describing and identifying the main risks that occur or acquire a larger scope through the use of online technologies (Staksrud, Ólafsson, & Livingstone, 2013).

Given that the massive use of such media affects the social relations of youth and adolescents, it is time to recognize that both the benefits and risks of the widespread use of digital communication devices should be incorporated into the educational system as key elements of learning and development. Schools need to educate digital citizens in both purely technological competences as well as in moral values to prevent cyberbullying. But this is a major challenge. Schools receive young people who have grown up on par with technological advances, the digital natives. Moreover, those who are responsible for educating these digital natives do not always have the necessary technological skills and knowledge to do so with sufficient authority. However, this may not be the only problem. The educational models that schools use to promote values and prevent social problems such as bullying often overlook the digital social lives of youth. In this regard, we have proposed that the whole policy model, which has proven to be successful in preventing bullying (Ortega-Ruiz & Zych, 2016), also address virtual social networks in a global project of coexistence that takes into account not only direct interpersonal relationships, but also those that are produced by means of digital devices, what we call cybercoexistence.

Conocer, Construir y Conviviren la Red or the ConRed program (Ortega-Ruiz, Del Rey, & Casas, 2012) has been designed in line with the evidence-based practice approach, developed in a systematic way, and evaluated rigorously. To date, the program has been implemented in a total of six schools (Del Rey, Casas, & Ortega, 2016). Grounded in the theory of normative social behavior (Rimal, Lapinski, Cook, & Real, 2005), which posits that human behavior is heavily influenced by perceived social norms and social consensus, ConRed designed a coexistence plan to prevent cyberbullying in the participating schools; an intervention that we refer to as cybercoexistence. The theory of normative social behavior holds that conventional norms are largely constructed by imitating others, especially when there is no clear set of agreed-upon rules. This is an aspect that is very present in virtual environments, since there are no established norms or rules of conduct viewed as being positive or negative; it is simply assumed that the usage of such media will conform to a more or less shared set of norms, without questioning the risks or consequences such conduct may have for their own or others' lives.

From coexistence to cybercoexistence

For more than two decades in Spain, the coexistence model has underlined the importance of the quality of interpersonal relationships and the expression of emotions, feelings, and values in the school setting, especially through global programs (whole policy) to enhance the emotional and relational climate of schools and prevent bullying and other problems. Plans for peace and coexistence education are designed in a similar way to school curricula: teachers encourage communication and negotiation as skills to resolve conflict and improve the social life of students. In recent years, schools have been working to foster a better social climate based on empathy, reciprocity, and moral values as a means to achieving a more peaceful coexistence. Democratic classroom management, cooperative group work, the discussion and negotiation of rules and norms, together with emotional education and increasing the self-esteem of victims and the empathy of bullies have been lines of work to promote social adjustment and a positive sense of identity and solidarity among peers, as well as a global way of preventing bullying (Ortega & Del Rey, 2004).

Most education authorities in Spain (there are seventeen autonomous communities in Spain, each of which has jurisdiction over educational policy) have legislated on how to promote coexistence as part of their educational goals. The so-called Plan de Convivencia (Coexistence Plan) is understood as a core element of the autonomous communities' overall educational project, that is, it is a whole policy whose norms and standards teachers are required to reflect and implement in all aspects of the school curriculum. Coexistence plans are set out in a document, which specifies the organization and functioning of the schools and establishes the lines of action to be taken and the objectives to achieve.

Nevertheless, these coexistence plans have yet to address the challenges involved in relationships developed through the use of digital devices, thus overlooking or not yet effectively taking account of the potentialities and risks of cyberconduct. For example, the sending of an embarrassing picture of a student in a messaging application or a social network is not included in school regulations. Research has shown that many cases of cyberbullying take place as a continuation of traditional bullying and vice versa (Patchin & Hinduja, 2012). The use of digital devices has not only changed the way we relate to others, but also our norms, beliefs, attitudes, and other processes, thus redefining and transforming school life in a certain sense, while maintaining or revealing social problems that already existed in direct social networks; what we call cybercoexistence (Ortega-Ruiz, Casas, & Rey, 2014). This is a new challenge for schools, students, and especially teachers, who must redefine the current coexistence intervention models to include cybercoexistence in at least the following ways:

- *Teacher intervention.* Teachers must rethink how they give instruction, their teaching styles, or how they guide learning, as well as the rules and norms they establish regarding social relations, their discipline policy, or how they punish improper behavior. Teachers should also incorporate the so-called digital tutoring into their teaching practice (which requires the recognition of teaching on social networks), understand that students are participants in these environments, and use them in a supervised manner for the benefit of all. Teachers must understand and be aware that although they may not be expert users of social networks or mobile devices, they have sufficient experience to assist students in the safe and responsible use of digital technology and the capacity to help them in solving problems that may arise when using these digital tools.

- *Family-school partnerships* are an essential element of educational coexistence. How schools manage relationships with families has been widely recognized in the scientific literature as an important factor in achieving a positive school climate. In recent years, recommendations and guidelines have been developed to ensure that families and schools work together to set the direction of a child's school career (Harper, 2016). For this reason, it is important that digital parental supervision forms part of this dimension of education. Families need to inquire into the activities that their children engage in on the Internet and exercise parental control over its use in order to assist them and provide support in the event of problems. Moreover, schools should provide families advice and training in digital parental supervision as they are key to achieving cybercoexistence.
- *Attention to the interpersonal relations between students.* This traditional element of coexistence in schools refers to the quality of the interactions and communication between students; their codes of conduct, conventions, and implicit rules; subtle systems of power; phobias and obsessions; and how they intervene in conflicts or provide support and help regarding what is done and how it is done in the school and the classroom. Improving such peer relations has been one of the most important focuses of the work on educational coexistence in recent years. Cybercoexistence must continue in a similar line but incorporate new aspects such as the social media relations of students. These include the online social activity of students, social networking, and the use of instant messaging applications. Common online activities, such as updating profiles, visiting friends' profiles, increasing the number of contacts, and other actions to maintain and strengthen relationships with friends, etc. are aspects that all educational institutions must take into account to determine how students develop and engage in relations with their peers. In doing so, schools can effectively promote the values of respect, solidarity, and cooperation. Schools must therefore continue to work toward fostering respect for others not only in the physical but also the virtual reality of the school environment.
- *Address specific problems of social exclusion, bullying and cyberbullying, or other social risks*. Efforts to prevent or minimize these problems in schools have a practical as well as a scientific tradition. For example, multiple interventions, plans, and programs to combat bullying have been developed with differing degrees of success (Ttofi & Farrington, 2010), and have shed much insight on this serious problem. Different strategies have also been designed in this regard, among them peer mediation, peer support, or specific programs to reduce the risk of bullying. However, in light of the risks described, particularly cyberbullying, cybercoexistence requires specific actions to support the responsible use of the Internet, social networks, and instant-messaging applications. These include requesting permission to use the personal information of others, knowing how to report an online aggression, and responding to attacks calmly, among others; all of which must form part of the daily work of schools. Similarly, in order to promote safe Internet usage, it is necessary that the entire educational community be familiar with and know how to use the available resources to keep computers and social networks safe and secure, as well as be aware of the importance of protecting personal or private information appropriately. The abusive use or technological dependence on these media is another issue that must be addressed. Feelings of distress or becoming upset when access to the Internet is limited or denied or the need to be constantly connected have been shown to have a negative effect on the school climate (Casas, Del Rey, & Ortega-Ruiz, 2013). Therefore, promoting the healthy use of the Internet and social networks is an additional aspect to consider in order to ensure a safe and healthy coexistence in both physical and virtual environments.

Educating for cybercoexistence should not be understood as a break with traditional coexistence plans. Indeed, the approach involves the analysis and diagnosis of phenomena related to both direct (offline) and digital social interactions (online) that affect the lives of students and the social reality of schools, as well as intervention. An analysis of the school setting should therefore include the type of platforms or applications most widely used by the educational community, the social networks present in the school and their particular characteristics, as well as the use or abuse of these virtual environments by families, teachers, and students alike. In this regard, it is necessary to develop an effective troubleshooting strategy for detecting the problems that arise in virtual communication. Current systems to detect such problems and conflicts among students do not take into account the negative feelings students experience when they are intentionally excluded from an online group although this is one of the main forms of cyberbullying. Evidence-based practice (EBP) is important to understand the direct and virtual environments in which students interact. Almost two decades ago (Davies, 1999) pointed to the importance of utilizing the existing scientific evidence to improve educational practice. Cybercoexistence programs for the prevention of bullying and cyberbullying must be grounded in evidence-based practice if they hope to be successful in the schools in which they are implemented.

Evidence for effectiveness

During the experimental phase, the ConRed program was evaluated in eight working sessions with students, two with families, and two with teachers. During the sessions, the participants discussed the opportunities and benefits of social networks and the importance of privacy and identity, particularly the negative effects of the lack of protection. The issue of prosocial behavior and solidarity was also addressed, with special emphasis given to the risks of social networking sites and the consequences of their inappropriate use. Finally, strategies for dealing with problems in these media and tips for their proper use were discussed.

An evaluation of the ConRed cyberbullying intervention program yielded positive results regarding its main objectives. A quasiexperimental design with a control group and pre-post data collection provided interesting results (Del Rey et al., 2016).

Some of the most remarkable results are the significant decrease in the perceived control of information and personal data on the Internet and social networks. That is, participants perceived that they have no real control over personal information that they post on their social networking profiles. This was interpreted as a heightened awareness of the risks involved in disclosing personal information and the need to increase the safety and security of content circulating on the Internet. Problems associated with dependence or addiction also decreased, although to a different extent between boys and girls. While the need to connect and interact with others in social networks significantly decreased among boys, girls maintained higher levels of use, indicating that ConRed did not have a significant impact on this group. Cyberbullying also decreased in terms of both aggression and victimization, thus indicating that the ConRed program achieved one of its main objectives.

Due to the good results of ConRed, the program is now being taken into account by the public administration to develop strategies aimed at improving online relationships and preventing problems such as cyberbullying. Indeed, it is crucial that these strategies be implemented on a large scale, and not be subject simply to the good intentions and available resources of individual schools. In this regard, ConRed makes an interesting contribution to the debate on whether intervention against cyberbullying and traditional bullying should be global (whole policy) or specific and differentiated. Given that both types of bullying share common traits in terms of interpersonal relations, we believe that the measures taken to combat one type can also be used to combat the other provided that the analysis of the social ecosystem of cyberconduct is included as part of the wider social environment (cybercoexistence).

To conclude, it is important to highlight some weaknesses of the ConRed program. ConRed has been implemented by researchers who are outsiders to the school ecosystem. As a result, when the program is implemented by teachers, there may be certain aspects that require further testing and evaluation due to their different expertise. Another weakness stems from the fact that in evaluating the program, the experimental group was larger than the control group, which should be taken into account when replicating and evaluating the effects of ConRed.

References

Casas, J. A., Del Rey, R., & Ortega-Ruiz, R. (2013). Bullying and cyberbullying: Convergent and divergent predictor variables. *Computers in Human Behavior*, *29*, 580–587. https://doi.org/10.1016/j.chb.2012.11.015.

Davies, P. (1999). What is evidence-based education? *British Journal of Educational Studies*, *47*, 108–121. https://doi.org/10.1111/1467-8527.00106.

Del Rey, R., Casas, J. A., & Ortega, R. (2016). Impact of the ConRed program on different cyberbullying roles. *Aggressive Behavior*, *42*, 123–135. https://doi.org/10.1002/ab.21608.

Harper, L. J. (2016). Supporting young children's transitions to school: Recommendations for families. *Early Childhood Education Journal*, *44*, 653–659. https://doi.org/10.1007/s10643-015-0752-z.

Ortega, R., & Del Rey, R. (2004). *Construir la Convivencia.* [English translation] Barcelona: Edebé.

Ortega-Ruiz, R., Casas, J. A., & Rey, R. Del. (2014). Towards the construct of cyberconvivencia. *Infancia yAprendizaje*, *37*, 602–628. https://doi.org/10.1080/02103702.2014.957537.

Ortega-Ruiz, R., Del Rey, R., & Casas, J. A. (2012). Knowing, building and living together on internet and social networks: The ConRed cyberbullying prevention program. *International Journal of Conflict and Violence*, *6*, 303–313.

Ortega-Ruiz, R., & Zych, I. (2016). La ciberconducta y la psicología educativa: Retos y riesgos. *Psicología Educativa*, *22*, 1–4. https://doi.org/10.1016/j.pse.2016.04.001.

Patchin, J. W., & Hinduja, S. (2012). *Cyberbullying prevention and response: Expert perspectives*. New York, NY: Routledge.

Prensky, M. (2005). Listen to the natives. *Educational Leadership*, *63*, 8–13.

Revilla Muñoz, O., Alpiste Penalba, F., Fernández Sánchez, J., & Santos, O. C. (2017). Reducing techno-anxiety in high school teachers by improving their ICT problem-solving skills. *Behaviour & Information Technology*, *36*(3), 255–268. https://doi.org/10.1080/0144929X.2016.1221462.

Rimal, R. N., Lapinski, M. K., Cook, R. J., & Real, K. (2005). Moving toward a theory of normative influences: How perceived benefits and similarity moderate the impact of descriptive norms on behaviors. *Journal of Health Communication, 10*, 433–450.

Staksrud, E., Ólafsson, K., & Livingstone, S. (2013). Does the use of social networking sites increase children's risk of harm? *Computers in Human Behavior, 29*, 40–50.

Tokunaga, R. S. (2010). Following you home from school: A critical review and synthesis of research on cyberbullying victimization. *Computers in Human Behavior, 26*, 277–287. https://doi.org/10.1016/j.chb.2009.11.014.

Ttofi, M. M., & Farrington, D. P. (2010). Effectiveness of school-based programs to reduce bullying: A systematic and meta-analytic review. *Journal of Experimental Criminology, 7*, 27–56. https://doi.org/10.1007/s11292-010-9109-1.

Zych, I., Ortega-Ruiz, R., & Del Rey, R. (2015). Scientific research on bullying and cyberbullying: Where have we been and where are we going. *Aggression and Violent Behavior, 24*, 188–198. https://doi.org/10.1016/j.avb.2015.05.015.

Smartphone Summit: Children's initiative to prevent cyberbullying and related problems

16

*Kazuo Takeuchi**, Kaito Abe*†, Motoko Miyake*‡, Yuichi Toda*§
*University of Hyogo, Hyogo, Japan, †Teens Online Japan, Japan, ‡Okayama University, Okayama, Japan, §Osaka University of Education, Osaka, Japan

Name of program: Smartphone Summit
Type of program: Student voice
Suitable for ages: Late elementary/middle school/high school/university

In this chapter, we present a child-centered practice, the Smartphone Summit, to prevent cyberbullying and other problems related to smartphone usage in Japan. The Smartphone Summit is a child-centered and cross-age program that may be a model for efforts in other countries. In this chapter, we describe the development of the program, include early findings from a preliminary method for evaluating such programs, and consider future perspectives on child-centered practices for preventing cyberbullying and related problems.

A short history of the Smartphone Summit

The reason for the Smartphone Summit started in 2005. It was the children's initiative after a widely publicized revenge incident of face-to-face bullying resulted in the killing of a teacher in an elementary school where the 17-year-old perpetrator graduated from (Takeuchi, 2011). That incident amplified problems of other graduates from the elementary school, and so junior high-school teachers decided to listen to these students to learn how to improve the school. The teachers asked the students what they wanted to do. The students proposed eliminating bullying. As bullying was a city-wide issue, they suggested working with other junior high-school students in the city. This conversation led to the formation of the Neyagawa Junior High School Summit in 2007. As this summit ideas spread to other regions, and began to involve other parties such as high-school students, parents, teachers, police officers, the name "Junior High School Summit" was no longer applicable. Yet, "school summit" or "children's summit" would have been ambiguous. Since the main issue was determined by the participating children, the program was called the "Smartphone Summit."

Interschool activities in Neyagawa city

In 2007, student council members met to discuss what they could do for their peers working as the Neyagawa Junior High School Summit. They created and distributed

Reducing Cyberbullying in Schools. https://doi.org/10.1016/B978-0-12-811423-0.00016-X

advocacy guidelines, including “tackling bullying.” Focusing on bullying issues, the students created a handwritten questionnaire on bullying and produced antibullying dramas. The DVD recordings of their dramas were distributed at all 12 Junior High School and 24 elementary schools in the city. This process was later used when students recognized that cyberbullying was a problem they wanted to tackle.

In Japan, 93.6% of high-school students and 45.8% of junior high-school students are now using smartphones (Cabinet Office, Government of Japan, 2016). After another Neyagawa Junior High School Summit in 2009, the first author received numerous phone calls and emails from various organizations across Japan. The first author was told that they learned about the Summit through TV programs and newspaper articles. This way, news of the project was not disseminated through scientific papers or governmental initiatives, but through media coverage and online social networks.

Kansai Smartphone Summit

When asked what problem they wanted to address, children across the Kansai region suggested problems surrounding smartphones, including cyberbullying and “later bed times” (Lemola, Perkinson-Gloor, Brand, Dewald-Kaufmann, & Grob, 2015, p. 406), “meeting online contacts offline” (Livingstone, Haddon, Görzig, & Ólafsson, 2011, p. 5), “solicitation” (Smith, Thompson, & Davidson, 2014, p. 360), and purchasing “in-game contents” on online games (Hamari et al., 2017, p. 538). This was when the name was changed to the “Smartphone Summit.” Various organizations have sponsored the summits in every prefecture in the Kansai area, to meet the growing need for child-led rule-making on smartphone usage.

In 2010 in the Hyogo prefecture, city-level junior high-school summits emerged to share their experience and messages with the general public. Since 2014, the Kyoto Smartphone Summit has been sponsored by the Kyoto Prefectural Police. The Shiga Smartphone Summit has been funded by the Shiga Parent-Teacher Association. Osaka and Hyogo Smartphone Summits have been supported by the Departments of Youth Safety and Development in their respective prefectures. Wakayama and Nara prefectural Summits have been supported by their respective Boards of Education. Since 2015, integrating all these prefectural-level summits, the Kansai Smartphone Summit, sponsored by several prefectural Parent-Teacher Associations, has invited representative children from all six prefecture-level summits to share and spread the children's activities and messages.

Smartphone Summit in Okayama

The Smartphone Summit has also been implemented in the Okayama Prefecture. The Okayama Prefecture is located outside but near Kansai area, with a population of around 1.92 million. The Governor has focused on education policy, aiming to reduce problems in schools and improve students' academic achievement.

The Smartphone Summit in Okayama was organized by a newspaper company in conjunction with the Board of Education of both Okayama Prefecture and Okayama City. The newspaper company, the Sanyo Shimbun, is headquartered in Okayama city, with most subscribers in Okayama Prefecture. It had been looking for ideas how the media could contribute to protecting children from the harmful effects of the Internet and smartphones—in the wake of coverage of many problems concerning children.

The company came up with the idea of fostering children's ability to deal properly with the Internet and smartphones, and asked the first author to implement the Smartphone Summit there. The first author invited an external researcher who had not been involved in the former summits to assist in evaluating the practice. As the practice itself is different from most prevention programs, we next explain the frameworks of the Summit and describe our method of evaluating the practice in a manner that is consistent with the frameworks.

The Smartphone Summit framework

The Smartphone Summit has a different framework from most prevention programs. Three characteristics of that framework are the cascade for dissemination, interschool activity, and intergenerational collaboration. The third aspect includes adults outside schools. Media, police, and corporations play important roles in the summit. Although the practice is similar to the World Café practice (a structured conversational process intended to foster personal relationships and collaborative learning, Tan & Brown, 2005), it developed as a child-centered effort to solve perceived problems of cyberbullying in their schools.

Cascade model for dissemination

Prevention programs are designed to change participants' behavior. This usually means that researchers develop a program and choose the participants, based on their school or class year to evaluate it. The Smartphone Summit practice differs from typical prevention programs in two ways. The Smartphone Summit seeks to not only change participants' behavior but also to empower them to change the climate and behavior of their peers. Moreover, participants are the students who actively express their interest to their teacher recruiters, which allows the program to boost their motivation to help peers. The implementation model of the ViSC program consists of a cascaded train-the-trainer model in which the program developers (researchers) train ViSC coaches (e.g., school psychologists, teacher trainers) who, in turn, train teachers, and then these teachers train their students (Strohmeier, Hoffmann, Schiller, Stefanek & Spiel, 2012). The Smartphone Summit however implemented a cascade of children's ideas to other children. In this model, children are not only recipients of the program but also active change agents. For this to be effective, it is important to select students who are popular not only among well-behaved students but also among less-compliant students. Identifying and promoting such students relies on the teachers' knowledge of their students' characteristics.

Interschool activity model

Most prevention programs are administered in individual schools that function independently. Even in multiple-schools' trials such as Sheffield project (Smith & Sharp, 1994), cooperation among the participant schools was rare. Recently, the KiVa program in Finland has biannual KiVa conference days where teachers from different schools exchange their experience and ideas for improving the program in each school (Salmivalli, Kärnä, & Poskiparta, 2010). Following this direction, as for the Smartphone Summit, all the schools in a city, or at least several schools, are invited to participate in the program. This kind of participation is actually an interschool activity. It is interesting to note that not all the schools in Neyagawa city attended the Summit from the beginning. The children met several times with some schools joining later.

In 2016, Smartphone Summits began to spread outside the Kansai region. At one Summit, a junior high-school student proposed "I want to talk with children in urban areas, to learn if they are using smartphones any differently." Highlighting their curiosity to meet children of other regions, remarks like this led us to consider creating a space for interregional interactions.

To make this accessible to everyone interested, our approach in the future will be to use free video conferencing to connect multiple Summits. This will enable both children and adult supervisors to cut down costs while cultivating further collaboration between children in different parts of Japan. The children may even begin to tackle various types of inequalities between rural and urban areas, as students from different schools have addressed regional-scale challenges.

The framework of interschool activities has merits and challenges. According to the tradition of Japanese bullying, *ijime* research, *ijime* is considered to be "a disease of a class" (Morita & Kiyonaga, 1994, p. 181). This implies that if a certain class was affected by *ijime*, it would be difficult to change the situation from inside the class. Some kind of intervention from outside the class is necessary. For prevention, mutual influence between classes or even between schools would be effective for generating ideas and learning effective ways to work together. This is the underlying philosophy of this practice, which is particularly important in the case of cyberbullying, which is not confined to one school or class and easily crosses school boundaries.

Intergenerational collaboration

The Smartphone Summit includes participants of various ages. High-school students and junior high-school students, aged 12–18, work with each other, while university students facilitate their group discussions. These university students are supervised by a university faculty advisor.

The idea of such intergenerational collaboration comes from peer support practice; but in this instance, there are not only students and teachers but also other professionals who support children to come together and talk freely.

An interesting aspect of this approach is that some teachers and adults are now asking the children for advice and thanking them for getting hints about how to think about the problems. In many areas of life, adults are assumed to be more knowledgeable because they have acquired expertise throughout their lives. However, for smartphone usage, children are often much more experienced and skilled than adults who spent their younger days with a home telephone or old-style mobile phones. For smartphone knowledge and skills, the developmental order among adults and children generally does not reflect that adults know more than children. That is why adults are learning from children.

But adults can do more in their areas of expertise. The media report the children's activities and bring the idea to other schools and teachers. Children and parents are happy seeing their ideas on the news and local people are proud of the children. Some municipal assemblymen praised the activity to their local educational committee, saying, "We will raise the budget for the board of education." Thanks to the free-of-charge programming lessons and coding guidance from a smartphone game company, children attendees at Osaka Smartphone Summit developed an Android app called "mom-app," where a mother figure admonishes the user for excessive use of smartphones (The Asahi Shimbun Company, 2016).

Reflecting on the frameworks, we may define the Smartphone Summit as an interschool World Café meeting by intergenerational participants to disseminate safer usage of the Internet and Smartphone and reduce cyberbullying.

The logistics of the Smartphone Summit

Overview

Any Smartphone Summit consists of a series of three meetings: (1) Introduction/idea meeting, (2) analysis/activity meeting, and (3) sharing/dissemination meeting. Here is one example of the meetings.

At the introduction/idea meeting, thirty or more junior- and high-school students from a variety of schools meet for the first time. The meeting lasts for 4 hours in the afternoon: 1 hour of icebreaker activities and the coordinator's presentation and 3 hours of group work. After the icebreaker activities, the coordinator talks briefly about the impact of technological advancement on our society. Then each student thinks about pros and cons of smartphone usage and writes them down on sticky notes. After that, they work in groups to categorize their notes. When all the groups, including one adult group, finishes presenting, every attendee votes to select the best presentation in the room. Once the winner is announced and all the groups' contributions are appraised, the students move on to discuss what they want to do to reduce cyberbullying and related problems for their peers. In the past, several students have volunteered to develop a questionnaire to investigate how their peers are using smartphones. Adults, including teachers, have distributed the students' handwritten questionnaire. Another time, a game company employee worked on data entry and the coordinator of the event prepared the survey results to be shown on slides.

One month later, they meet again for the analysis/activity meeting. The agenda consists of icebreakers, 2 hours of group work, 1 hour of lunch, and 1 hour of script writing and video writing. At one such meeting, survey results were available to the students. The students looked at graphs and discussed the analysis. Then, similar to the introduction/idea meeting, the groups took part in presentation tournaments. During that meeting, some students produced 30-second videos, with the university students' support who distributed them to all schools in the region. Before closing, each school came up with ideas for their own grassroots activities, such as writing theme songs and making posters, to work on for the next 6 months.

A variety of the following grassroots activities

After the analysis/activity meeting, students initiate various grassroots activities to convey what they learnt through the Summit. The reach of their messages can range from their immediate peers (Peer Impact) to younger children and parents (Intergenerational Impact).

Peer Impact initiatives have included organizing a poster competition at their own schools and making theme songs about safer and kinder smartphone use to be played between class periods. Intergenerational Impact projects have been that one high-school invited junior high-school students for a collaborative summit, under the university students' supervision. The junior high-school students created the Smartphone Guidelines to reduce cyberbullying and related problems, with the discussion facilitated by the high-school students. Another high school wanted to convey their messages to elementary-school children. Under the university students' guidance, the students visited local elementary schools and taught classes on how to use smartphones safely. The students noticed that the elementary-school children were not choosing to play except online. The university students allowed them to experience the playfulness of playing offline reminding the children of simple group plays and the enjoyment they had together at the end of each lesson. Furthermore, these high-school students educated parents of the young children. During their smartphone classes at a local elementary school, many children reported not using parental control service on their devices. Subscription to parental control, though optional, blocks the child's access to harmful websites. The high-school students knew this. Feeling energized by the meeting, they visited local cellphone stores to collect filtering service brochures for the parents of the younger pupils.

The Smartphone Summit day

Half a year later, students from several analysis/activity meetings gather at the sharing/dissemination meeting. This meeting serves as an opportunity for students to share their findings and grassroots activities. After presenting on their survey findings and grassroots activities, the student volunteers and adult representatives participate in a panel discussion. They share their opinions on the survey results. The students' honest voices sometimes astonish adults, but the coordinator helps adults understand the students' perspectives. At the end of one meeting, a student testified, “Although it is the one of the most important things for us, we don't talk about it at school. I really want to have a discussion like this regularly at school.” This meeting was featured in several newspaper articles and TV news programs.

Evaluation of the Smartphone Summit

Comments from adult participants

As well as providing a platform for children to engage in discussions on the Internet and smartphone problems, the Smartphone Summit aims to facilitate interactive learning among adults and children. The following individuals from various organizations found the Summits effective in addressing the causes they work toward. A former head of a Parent-Teacher Association said, "Numerous parents learned from the voices of children at the Summits that smartphone problems can affect any child." A Board of Education member stated, "Students' autonomous thinking about rules would help teachers be aware of and cope with the potential problems before they become too difficult to tackle." A representative from a game company testified, "We believe it is crucial for users to gain knowledge on the Internet, like at the Summits." A police officer said, "Continuing the Summits is effective in developing children's morality and ability to tackle the Internet problems."

Preliminary evidence from Neyagawa city

The 2007 Neyagawa Junior High School Summit, a prototype of the Smartphone Summit model, offered preliminary but hard evidence of the effects of the summit. In order to assess the effect of the activities, the number of bullying cases in Neyagawa city reported in 2009 was compared with that of 2006. According to the statistics compiled by the Neyagawa City Board of Education, it was found that the number of bullying cases reported decreased from 58 to 30 (Takeuchi, 2010). Furthermore, the number of school absentees halved (Takeuchi, Aoyama, Kanayama, & Toda, 2012). There are no control groups to compare these results with, however, there are no such trends in the available nation-wide statistics from the Japanese Government.

Effects of practice

Statistical evidence might be a necessary but not sufficient condition for validating the impact of an educational program. Voices and actions of teachers, parents, and municipalities following the Summit illustrate the effect on them. Many parents, after reading the newspaper article about the Neyagawa Junior High School Summit, reported having discussed cellphone and cyberbullying problems with their children.

Furthermore, after the first author presented the idea of the summit at the Japan Peer Support Conference, many municipalities replicated the process. Although these pieces of qualitative evidence do not sufficiently prove that children changed because of the summit, the community in Japan viewed this model as a powerful, much-needed solution to the contemporary challenges of cyberbullying and other problems of smartphone use.

Because the summits are designed to inspire participants to initiate change in their schools, we developed a questionnaire to assess participants' beliefs about the impact of the summit on themselves and their classmates (Miyake, Takeuchi, & Toda, in preparation). The items described seven behaviors (see Fig. 16.2) in which they and their classmates might engage in the immediate future and longer term. Response options ranged from 1 (not at all) to 4 (extremely plausible).

Fig. 16.1 shows the overview of the structure of the questionnaire.

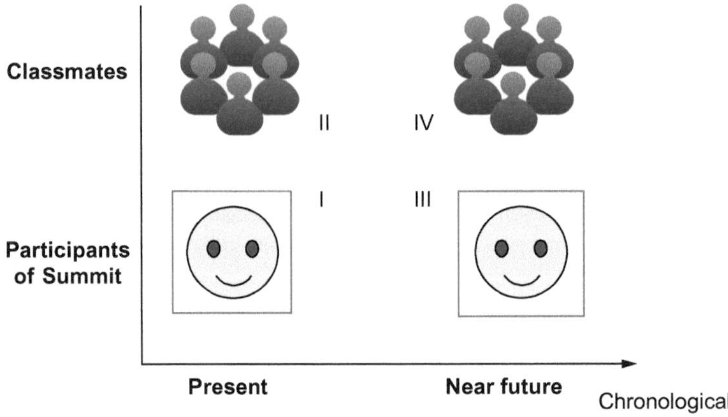

Fig. 16.1 Two types of person(s) and present/anticipated future behavior.

First, we examined whether the 26 male and female participants (almost all attendees) anticipated using the Internet and smartphones more appropriately in the future and whether their classmates would do so. Their responses showed that the participants expected their own and their classmates' anticipated future smartphone usage to be more appropriate than their present usage. Participants rated their classmates' future usage significantly better than their present usage concerning all items except for "respecting privacy" in the paired *t*-tests ($p < .05$). This indicates that the participants expect positive impacts of their grassroots activities on their classmates' anticipated smartphone usage. The tendency of expecting improved anticipated future usage than present usage was similar concerning their own usage. By joining in the Summit, the participants may have obtained efficacy to make an impact on their peers as well as a sense of confidence to improve their own future smartphone usage.

Second, in order to examine the patterns of participants' "impact expectation" toward their peers, we conducted a cluster analysis (Ward method) based on the total scores of their classmates' usage (present and anticipated future). The result revealed three groups of impact expectation toward their classmates (see Fig. 16.2.).The largest cluster ($n = 13$) was relatively moderate in their evaluation of their classmates for both present and anticipated future behavior. The second cluster ($n = 8$) showed relatively lower evaluation of classmates. The third cluster ($n = 5$) showed relatively higher evaluation. Fig. 16.2 also shows the ratings for participants' own present and anticipated future behavior by cluster. There was no significant difference among three clusters in the total scores of both present and anticipated future behavior of the respondents, in contrast to the significant differences among three clusters in the impact expectations for classmates.

However, some children are likely to have faced difficulties when they tried to share the activities with their classmates. Such participants might know the reasons for the difficulty of changing their classmates' behavior. For future verification of the effect of the Summit, it will be necessary to document how activities are expanded on

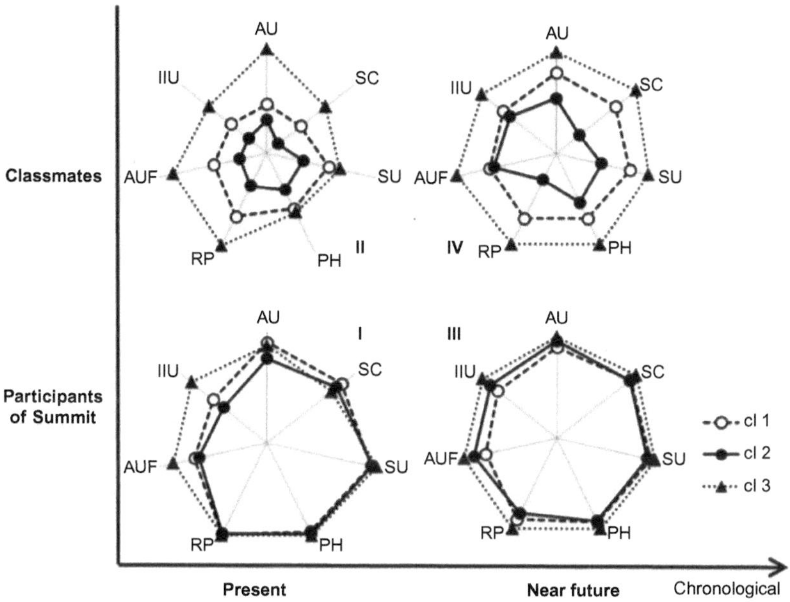

Fig. 16.2 Estimated impact patterns of three clusters by person(s) by time points (present behavior/anticipated future behavior). Note: *AU*, thinking about appropriate usage; *SC*, self-control to prevent overuse; *SU*, safe Internet usage; *PH*, prevention of hurting others; *RP*, respecting privacy; *AUF*, talking about appropriate usage with familiar people; *IIU*, intervening familiar people's inappropriate usage.

in participants' own classrooms and how participants can be supported in implementing their ideas with possibly reluctant classmates.

Future directions

The Smartphone Summit has been well received in Japan. The three components of the practice (cascade model of dissemination, interschool activities, and crossgenerational collaboration) could be implemented in other countries. The notion of engaging students in solving problems is also recognized as a teaching method of reflective and critical thinking skills (Hermanowicz, 1961). The problem of cyberbullying is one that exists in all countries in which it has been studied, and using this child-centered, cross-age practice is one of appropriate ways to address the problem. Since 2016, this summit practice has been proposed as an archetype for US-Japan youth program to reduce cyberbullying. The underlying philosophy is that children, not adults, define the central theme of the program. As Takeuchi (2011, p. 348) concluded, we "must believe in the children. Only they know the way." It is of our firm belief that listening to children will be the first step to design an effective prevention practice on cyberbullying, despite cultural and linguistic differences.

References

Cabinet Office, Government of Japan. (2016). *Heisei 27nendo seishonen no intanetto riyou kankyou jittai chousa* [2015 report of research on the Internet usage of youth]. Retrieved from http://www8.cao.go.jp/youth/youth-harm/chousa/h27/net-jittai/pdf/2-1-1-1.pdf.

Hamari, J., Alha, K., Järvelä, S., Kivikangas, J. M., Koivisto, J., & Paavilainen, J. (2017). Why do players buy in-game content? An empirical study on concrete purchase motivations. *Computers in Human Behavior, 68*, 538–546. https://doi.org/10.1016/j.chb.2016.11.045.

Hermanowicz, H. (1961). Problem solving as teaching method. *Educational Leadership, 18*, 299–306.

Lemola, S., Perkinson-Gloor, N., Brand, S., Dewald-Kaufmann, J., & Grob, A. (2015). Adolescents' electronic media use at night, sleep disturbance, and depressive symptoms in the smartphone age. *Journal of Youth and Adolescence, 44*, 405–418. https://doi.org/10.1007/s10964-014-0176-x.

Livingstone, S., Haddon, L., Görzig, A., & Ólafsson, K. (2011). *EU kids online II final report.* Retrieved from http://eprints.lse.ac.uk/39351/1/EU_kids_online_final_report_%5BLSERO%5D.pdf. November 9.

Miyake, M., Takeuchi, K., & Toda, Y. (in preparation). Perspectives of JHS students who has participated in Smartphone Summit for appropriate usage of the Internet and smartphones. Manuscript in preparation.

Morita, Y., & Kiyonaga, K. (1994). *Ijime: Kyoshitsu no yamai.* Tokyo: Kaneko Shobo.

Salmivalli, C., Kärnä, A., & Poskiparta, E. (2010). Development, evaluation, and diffusion of a national anti-bullying program, KiVa. In B. Doll, W. Pfohl, & J. Yoon (Eds.), *Handbook of youth prevention science* (pp. 238–252). New York, NY: Routledge.

Smith, P. K., & Sharp, S. (1994). *School bullying: Insights and perspectives.* London: Routledge.

Smith, P. K., Thompson, F., & Davidson, J. (2014). Cyber safety for adolescent girls: Bullying, harassment, sexting, pornography, and solicitation. *Current Opinion in Obstetrics and Gynecology, 26*, 360–365. https://doi.org/10.1097/GCO.0000000000000106.

Strohmeier, D., Hoffmann, C., Schiller, E. M., Stefanek, E., & Spiel, C. (2012). ViSC Social Competence Program. *New Directions for Youth Development, 133*, 71–84. https://doi.org/10.1002/yd.20008.

Takeuchi, K. (2010). A practical study of peer support program by school council of all junior high schools in a city: Focus on a play which aims to eradicate cyber bullying; By Osaka pref. Neyagawa City Junior High School Students Summit [in Japanese]. *Japanese Annals of Peer Support, 7*, 19–27. Retrieved from http://www.peer-s.jp/bulletin_paper.html#ttl07.

Takeuchi, K. (2011). Children's own initiative to change their school: A glimmer of hope after a tragic incident. In R. H. Shute, P. T. Slee, R. Murray-Harvey, & K. L. Dix (Eds.), *Mental health and wellbeing: Educational perspectives* (pp. 347–350). Adelaide, SA: Shannon Research Press.

Takeuchi, K., Aoyama, I., Kanayama, K., & Toda, Y. (2012). *City-wide anti-cyberbullying activities initiated by students: City-wide evaluation according to school surveillance.* In: *Poster presented at the meeting of the International Conference on Cyberbullying COST IS0801, Sorbonne, Paris.*

Tan, S., & Brown, J. (2005). The world café in Singapore: Creating a learning culture through dialogue. *Journal of Applied Behavioral Science, 41*, 83–90. https://doi.org/10.1177/0021886304272851.

The Asahi Shimbun Company. (2016). *"Eekagennishiya" Okan apuri, chojikan sumahoni keihou* ["Don't go too far" mom-app alarms long-hour use of smartphones]. The Asahi Shimbun Company.Retrieved from http://www.asahi.com/articles/photo/AS20161218001654.html, December 19.

Further reading

Takeuchi, K., & Abe, K. (2015). "Smartphone Summit" by children for sharing rules and strategies to tackle Internet-related delinquency. *Japanese Journal of Morality Development, 9*, 76–83. Retrieved from http://jssepmd.jp/kikannsi.htm.

An intervention using the Information-Motivation-Behavioral Skills Model: Tackling cyberaggression and cyberbullying in South African adolescents

17

Maša Popovac, Philip Fine
University of Buckingham, Buckingham, United Kingdom

Name of program: Information-Motivation-Behavioral Skills
Type of program: School lessons
Suitable for ages: Adolescents

Introduction

Children and adolescents are growing up in the digital age and Information and Communication Technologies (ICTs) have become an integral part of daily life. In addition to a range of available technologies, there are also numerous online activities for social interaction, entertainment, and information seeking. Adolescents' use of ICTs is particularly high and on the rise globally, especially in more affluent Western societies (Denissen, Neumann, & van Zalk, 2010; Eurostat, 2015). However, there has been a rapid surge in the uptake of ICT use in developing countries through mobile phones, a key entry point for internet adoption in this context (Calandro, Stork, & Gillwald, 2012). In South Africa, internet access among adolescents is particularly high, with 81% owning a mobile phone, 46% having internet access on their mobile phone, and 54% owning a computer, laptop, or tablet (Burton & Leoschut, 2012).

Although South Africa-based research is limited, a national study on school violence, which included questions on cyberbullying, found that 21% of adolescents had been victimized online (Burton & Leoschut, 2012). Further research shows that 28% of 13–15-year-olds were victims and 16% were perpetrators of cyberbullying (Pillay, 2012). A third of 13–18-year-olds reported receiving threats from others on their mobile phone (Odora & Matoti, 2015). These prevalence rates are similar to those indicated by a meta-analysis of international research (Tokunaga, 2010).

Negative online experiences, especially cyberbullying, have been linked to many psychological, emotional, and behavioral problems (Dempsey, Sulkowski, Nichols, & Storch, 2009; Hinduja & Patchin, 2007; Kim & Leventhal, 2008; Litwiller & Brausch, 2013; Van Geel, Vedder, & Tanilon, 2014) and negative school outcomes (Bauman, 2007; Patchin & Hinduja, 2006), leading to cyberbullying being described as a serious

Reducing Cyberbullying in Schools. https://doi.org/10.1016/B978-0-12-811423-0.00017-1

societal level health concern (Tokunaga, 2010). However, current online safety strategies in South Africa are fragmented due to a lack of formal guidelines to address cyberbullying incidents, leaving schools to their own initiative in this regard (De Lange & Von Solms, 2011), and this is not just the case in South Africa (Perren et al., 2012; Snakenborg, Van Acker, & Gable, 2011).

This chapter describes an intervention that focuses on addressing cyberaggression, including cyberbullying (and also other online risks not described in this chapter). Cyberaggression, a broader term encompassing a range of different experiences including cyberbullying, harassment, and stalking that occur online, is defined as "intentional harm delivered by the use of electronic means to a person or a group of people irrespective of their age who perceive(s) such acts as offensive, derogatory, harmful or unwanted" (Grigg, 2010, p. 152). Experiences of cyberbullying are forms of cyberaggression, but only cyberbullying shows intentionality, imbalance of power, and repetition (see Corcoran, Guckin, & Prentice, 2015; Menesini et al., 2012; Slonje & Smith, 2008). These distinctions in definitions are important for accurately measuring the behaviors in research contexts, but have little bearing for those experiencing these behaviors or those aiming to address them (Patchin & Hinduja, 2015). Thus, this intervention considers both cyberaggression and cyberbullying.

The intervention applied the Information-Motivation-Behavioral Skills (IMB) model (Fisher & Fisher, 1992) and was piloted on female adolescents in South Africa. The intervention involves addressing deficits in (1) information, (2) motivation, and (3) behavioral skills to increase individuals' online risk perception, which is a prerequisite for eliciting positive behavioral change and increasing online safety. The intervention is delivered in groups and was implemented to test the utility of the IMB model in this context. Although targeting individuals, it forms part of a broader strategy incorporating a multilevel approach to online safety including teacher training and parental involvement. The following sections outline the (i) theoretical rationale for the intervention, (ii) description of the program, including school-level aspects needed to conduct the intervention effectively, (iii) preliminary evidence for the effectiveness of the IMB model in online safety efforts and, finally (iv) implications and evaluation of the intervention, including a link to further resources.

Theoretical rationale for the program

The Information-Motivation-Behavioral Skills model is an empirically validated and comprehensive health behavior change framework (Fisher & Fisher, 1992). Originally used as a framework to understand a range of health-related risk behaviors (e.g., Kalichman et al., 2002; Kelly, Melnyk, & Belyea, 2012; Osborn & Egede, 2010; Peltzer, Preez, Ramlagan, & Anderson, 2010) where it has proven useful in enacting positive behavior change (Chang, Choi, Kim, & Song, 2014; Gavgani, Poursharifi, & Aliasgarzadeh, 2010; Kiene et al., 2013; Mayberry & Osborn, 2014), the model is increasingly being applied more broadly to promoting prosocial behaviors (e.g., Chang, 2011; Glasford, 2008; Seacat & Northrup, 2010). Thus, it was of interest to determine whether this behavior change framework is applicable in the context of online safety.

The framework is made up of two cognitive factors (Information and Motivation) and one behavioral factor (Behavioral Skills) as shown in Fig. 17.1, argued to be fundamental to behavior change (Fisher & Fisher, 1992). The IMB model posits that information about risks alone is not sufficient to alter people's risky behavior, but individuals also require motivation to act on the risk information they receive and the necessary behavioral skills to enact positive behavior change (Fisher, Fisher, Bryan, & Misovich, 2002).

Motivation to alter risk behaviors and engage in positive behaviors can be personal (having positive attitudes toward not being involved in the behavior) and social (considering social norms and peer acceptance toward the behavior). Others' reactions and views influence an individual's own behavior (Amico, Toro-Alfonso, & Fisher, 2005; Fisher et al., 2002). For example, adolescents whose peers display positive attitudes and greater acceptance toward cyberbullying were found to be more likely to cyberbully others (Heirman & Walrave, 2012). Thus, both the social context of risky behaviors and personal attitudes are important motivators for change.

The third component, behavioral skills, determines whether those who are well informed and well motivated are capable of behavior change. This relates to practical skills needed to increase online safety (e.g., adjusting privacy settings and other risk-reducing behaviors) as well as an individual's self-confidence about their capabilities (e.g., managing online risks, knowledge of reporting mechanisms), sometimes termed self-efficacy. Behavioral skills thus determine how likely individuals are to initiate or effectively sustain risk-reducing behaviors.

Given that all three of these components are necessary to foster behavior change, the intervention focused on informing, motivating, and enhancing behavioral skills. The aim was to increase adolescents' online risk perception, a prerequisite for behavior change (Gerrard, Gibbons, Benthin, & Hessling, 1996), as those with higher risk perception are less likely to engage in risk behaviors. Risk perception is influenced by individuals' knowledge, personal experience, peer and societal norms, and cost-benefit appraisals of their actions (Boholm, 1998; Kasperson et al., 1988; Slovic & Peters, 2006). When an activity is viewed positively, the risks are deemed lower

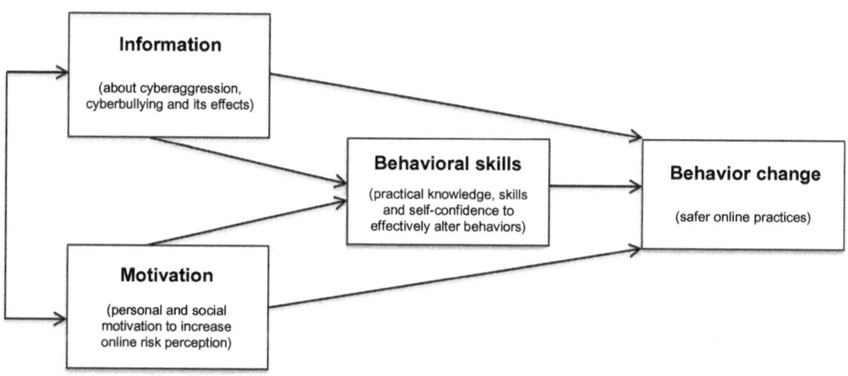

Fig. 17.1 The IMB model.

compared to the benefits; when viewed negatively, risks are deemed higher and benefits lower (Alhakami & Slovic, 1994; Finucane, Alhakami, Slovic, & Johnson, 2000). Thus, even though there may be consequences to the risk behaviors, individuals may still engage in them if the perceived benefits seem to outweigh the risk. Individuals also tend to perceive lower risk for themselves compared to others despite potentially engaging in the same risk behavior (Popovac, Mwaba, & Roman, 2011; Sjoberg, 2000): this is true for cyberbullying (Chapin, 2014).

Adolescents in particular tend to have higher feelings of invulnerability to risks, engage in more risk taking and experimentation, associated with their cognitive development during this period (Steinberg, 2008, 2010), and make more risky decisions than either children or adults, indicating that adolescence is a particularly vulnerable time for risk taking (Paulsen, Platt, Huettel, & Brannon, 2011). Adolescents perceive higher benefits than costs for a behavior when they engage in it themselves and tend to normalize the behavior by thinking that more people engage in it than actually do (Benthin, Slovic, & Severson, 1993). Researchers argue that adolescents, although not actively pursuing risks, do not appreciate them (Cohn, Macfarlane, Yanez, & Imai, 1995; Johnson, McCaul, & Klein, 2002; Wolburg, 2001), which makes it harder to warn them about risky behaviors (Greene et al., 2000). Thus, a multifaceted approach is needed (Johnson et al., 2002)—hence the application of the IMB model.

In the IMB model, risk perception plays a crucial role in behavior change by increasing individuals' personal and social motivation. Low risk perception sustains risk behaviors due to lowered perception of personal vulnerability to harm. In terms of perpetration, lower risk perception and understanding of the effects of their behaviors make adolescents more likely to continue with the behavior. The intervention, therefore, focuses on increasing online risk perception by providing both information and motivation about cyberaggression and cyberbullying from the perspectives of victims, perpetrators, and witnesses. It also addresses the necessary practical skills for eliciting positive behavior change in relation to these different roles given that the same individuals can often be victims in one context and perpetrators in another (Bauman, Toomey, & Walker, 2013; Mishna, Khoury-Kassabri, Gadalla, & Daciuk, 2012; Modecki, Minchin, Harbaugh, Guerra, & Runions, 2014). The ultimate goal of the intervention is to increase online safety.

The program

The program utilizing the IMB framework is designed for adolescents. It is facilitated in a group setting, with the goal of increasing online risk perception, ultimately resulting in behavior change.

Interventions adopting the IMB model are usually tailored to individuals' current information, motivation, and behavioral skills (Kalichman et al., 2002; Osborn & Egede, 2010). This makes the intervention particularly effective since it targets specific risk behaviors and perceptions (DiClemente, Crosby, & Kegler, 2009; Fisher & Fisher, 1992; Suls & Wallston, 2008), which are seen to be personally relevant, making it more likely that participants will internalize and reflect on the risks and adjust their risk perception. This tailoring is an important aspect to the program. Thus, an initial baseline questionnaire should be administered to the group of adolescents being targeted by the intervention in order to screen their online behaviors, perceptions, and experiences.

This questionnaire should ask adolescents about their online risk perception and various online risk behaviors. It can focus on their experience and involvement in both cyberaggression and cyberbullying as victims, perpetrators, and witnesses, but there is scope for flexibility in terms of what is included. In our pilot study, victimization and perpetration of eight cyberaggression behaviors were explored, including name calling, spreading rumors, and impersonation, according to the categories of behaviors outlined by Patchin and Hinduja (2006) and Willard (2007). Cyberbullying was assessed subjectively, by asking adolescents whether they had ever been cyberbullied, as our previous focus group data from schools in South Africa indicated that adolescents had a good understanding of what constituted cyberbullying actions. Items relating to the emotional effects of these experiences were also included to gauge the severity of these online experiences. The different sections of the baseline questionnaire and example items are shown in Table 17.1.

The baseline questionnaire can be administered in a class session, and due to the highly personal and potentially sensitive information provided by students, it should be anonymous, perhaps utilizing an online survey service such as Survey Monkey (https://www.surveymonkey.com). Moreover, Survey Monkey can automatically generate simple results relating to prevalence rates that are needed to plan the intervention, without needing any complicated and time-consuming analyses by those undertaking the intervention. This can reduce the time between the baseline questionnaire and the intervention, enabling practitioners to focus their efforts on preparing the tailored activities. Although variation of online behaviors and experiences within the same class is to be expected, the focus in the intervention should be on the students' most commonly reported behaviors and experiences. To protect students' confidentiality and anonymity, it is best to use closed-ended questions and not ask for details about specific incidents. Practitioners should omit any details regarding specific incidents from the intervention, and be sensitive to ensuring confidentiality of what students may have reported in the baseline questionnaire.

The information in the baseline questionnaire leads to the development of a focused, targeted intervention, as the practitioner now has an understanding of the key issues. This information is used to inform the content of the program, with participants (i) receiving relevant information about cyberaggression and cyberbullying, (ii) being motivated to make a change in their behaviors, and (iii) enhancing their practical skills and self-confidence to elicit behavior change.

For the information component of the model, participants receive feedback about the prevalence rates of cyberaggression and cyberbullying in their grade and discuss the possible consequences of victimization and perpetration. The different types of behaviors that are experienced (e.g., online threats, name-calling, etc.) are also discussed in more detail. Multimedia learning is recommended (Mayer, 2005), through the use of short video clips, newspaper articles, images, and current research to guide discussions. Participants are also informed about the prevalence rates of witnessing cyberaggression and cyberbullying and reflect on their role as bystanders. During these

Table 17.1 Baseline Questionnaire sections and example items

Section	Description	Example items
Online Risk Perception	Fifteen items with response options ranging from Strongly Agree to Strongly Disagree	– I worry about things that can go wrong when I am on the internet – I cannot control the things that happen to me on the internet – I am afraid of being harassed or threatened on the internet
Cybervictimization	Eight items with response options ranging from Never to 6 or more times	– I have been cyberbullied – I have been called a hurtful name or received a hurtful or rude comment, email, text or message – I have had rumors or gossip spread about me on the internet – I have had someone take or put up a picture of me online to embarrass me
Cyberperpetration	Eight items with response options ranging from Never to 6 or more times	– I have taken a private message someone sent me and forwarded it on to others or posted it online for all to see – I have posted comments or questions to hurt or embarrass someone on the internet – I have sent threatening emails, texts, messages or made such calls to someone
Witnessing of cyberbullying	Two items with response options ranging from Never to Very Often	– How often do you witness someone else being cyberbullied online? – How often has someone you know, like a friend or sibling, been cyberbullied?
Emotional Experiences	Three items with response options ranging from Never to 6 or more times	– I have been scared or worried about something someone did or said to me on the internet – I have been hurt or made to feel sad about something someone did or said to me on the internet – I have not wanted to go to school on some days because of something someone did or said to me on the internet

discussions, the practitioner's role is to present the key issues and facilitate group discussion in a multimedia environment. The practitioner could also introduce alternative perspectives in order to challenge views and correct any myths and misconceptions that might be held (e.g., victim blaming attitudes).

Understanding the short- and long-term effects of cyberaggression and cyberbullying and discussing these from multiple viewpoints (as victims, perpetrators, and witnesses) can motivate behavior change and create negative social norms relating to these behaviors. It can also increase empathy, encourage help seeking, and engage bystanders. Thus, reflecting on and discussing the issues they face is important in enhancing both personal and social motivation among adolescents. Two activities were particularly effective in this regard. Firstly, students are asked to draw cards containing various cyberaggression or cyberbullying scenarios from the perspective of victims, perpetrators, or witnesses, which were developed for the intervention (see Box 17.1 for examples). For each scenario, students discuss in pairs (i) how they would feel, and (ii) what they could do, if this happened to them. A class discussion follows. This activity encourages students to think about both consequences and strategies to address the issues. Secondly, students are asked to advise one another about an incident of cyberaggression or cyberbullying they were currently (or previously) experiencing, each of which was written anonymously on a piece of paper at the start of the workshop. Advising someone else about a real-life scenario potentially gives participants the opportunity to problem solve about issues that they might themselves encounter online in the future. It also allows participants to give one another relevant advice, promoting peer support and positive social norms in the class.

Although similar, these exercises are quite distinct. The first is more general and allows students to reflect on emotions and effects of behaviors and allows them to begin thinking about possible solutions. This leads to the second exercise, which is

Box 17.1 Scenario Activity Examples

Task: Students randomly select a card containing a scenario relating to cyberaggression or cyberbullying and (i) reflect on how they would feel if this happened to them and (ii) what they could do if this happened to them. Scenarios were written either from the perspective of a victim, perpetrator, or witness.

Scenario Examples:

- You found out that someone had created a fake social media profile in your name and was using it to post things as if they were coming from you.
- You had an argument with a member of your class during school and in anger posted something about the incident on social media but did not mention them by name. However, people from your school worked out who the post was about and started liking your post and commenting hurtful things about the person on your profile.
- You notice that a page had been created about a member of your class and that it was being used to post altered images of the person in various settings that are not flattering and would likely cause a great deal of embarrassment to them if they found out.

more personal as it relates to a peer's real experience. Both activities address personal and social motivation as well as behavioral skills through practical knowledge and by enhancing self-confidence in online contexts. It also encourages participation of all students in the intervention. If time allows, students can work in groups and think of strategies that could be useful to address the scenarios they have been given in both exercises more broadly, such as in their class and in their school. Coming up with problem-solving strategies related to cyberaggression and cyberbullying is very useful as the students' ideas could feed into broader school strategies.

In addition to these exercises aimed at enhancing self-confidence related to online safety issues, practitioners should also discuss practical skills (e.g., privacy settings, blocking websites) and the available resources and support both within and outside the school (e.g., reporting mechanisms at school). The main aspects of the intervention program are summarized in Table 17.2. Further resources relating to the intervention (i.e., sample questionnaire, teacher guide, and activity plans) can be found at https://www.buckingham.ac.uk/cyberbullying.

This intervention, tailored to adolescents' own behaviors and experiences, along with a focus on addressing all three components of the IMB model, encourages adolescents to take ownership of their online safety, to be mindful of their online behaviors and their potential impact on others, and to take action as bystanders through increased self-confidence and understanding of the support available to them. The steps in the program thus include (i) administering an initial questionnaire to screen adolescents' perceptions and experiences, (ii) developing a focused intervention using the information provided

Table 17.2 The IMB model components in the intervention

Information	• Discussion of positive and negative aspects of the internet • Presentation of participants' self-reported risk behaviors highlighting the key issues • Information on why some behaviors are risky through examining examples in the media, current research etc.
Motivation	• Reflection on potential consequences and effects of cyberaggression and cyberbullying on victims, perpetrators, and witnesses • Thinking about what one could do when facing a situation of cyberaggression or cyberbullying • Reflection on what to do when witnessing cyberbullying and why engaging bystanders is important • Ideas around internet etiquette ("netiquette") • Building social motivation and addressing peer norms through peer support
Behavioral Skills	• Taking ownership of online safety: Discussion about practical skills and online privacy • Problem solving about negative online incidents (reflecting on solutions and strategies) • Information about resources available to support help seeking and reporting of cyberaggression and cyberbullying within the school and external sources

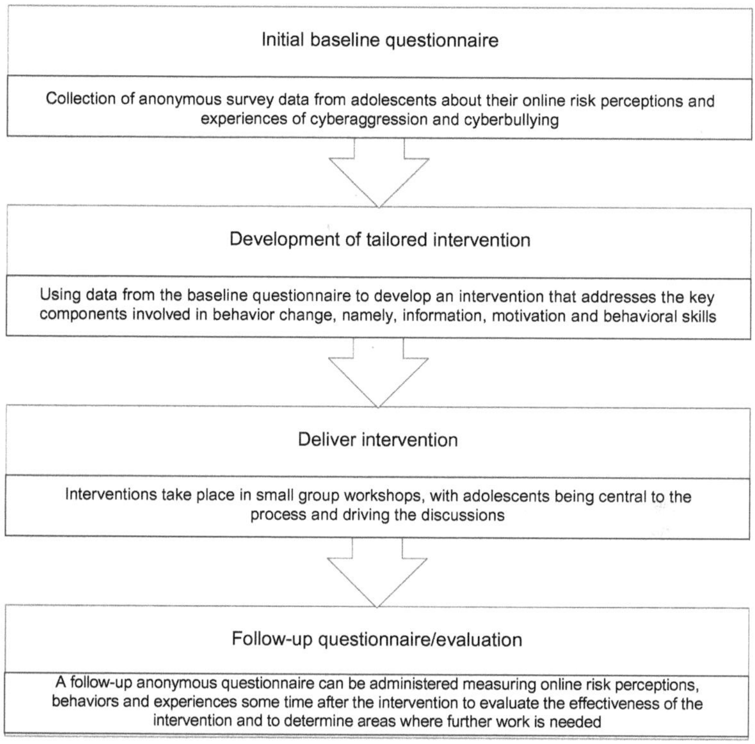

Fig. 17.2 Steps in the intervention.

by participants and addressing all three components of the IMB model, and (iii) facilitating the workshop by promoting discussion and problem solving (see Fig. 17.2). Practitioners can re-administer the baseline questionnaire (or parts thereof) periodically to assess further areas to work on, especially given the pace with which technology evolves, as well as to evaluate the effectiveness of the intervention. A tailored intervention provides practitioners with the flexibility to customize the program to the current issues being experienced by participants, ensuring that the workshop is appropriate, relevant, and comprehensively addresses the issues through the IMB framework.

Evidence for the intervention's effectiveness

Participants

The study was conducted at an all-female high school in Cape Town, South Africa, due to reports of differences in online activities and risk experiences between males and females (e.g., Mitchell, Finkelhor, Jones, & Wolak, 2012; Ybarra, Alexander, & Mitchell, 2005). Extensive data about online risk behaviors and perceptions were collected for 91 grade 8 and 9 students at the end of the 2013 school year. The intervention took place 7 months later, and was conducted with the original participants,

Table 17.3 Participants: grade, proportion, and mean age (years)

Grade	% Of total	Mean age
8	35.6% (n=63)	13.6
9	32.8% (n=58)	14.5
10	31.6% (n=56)	15.5

Note: The intervention was delivered to 177 adolescents but 3 participants were excluded in the later analyses due to missing data.

now in grades 9 and 10. The intervention was tailored for these participants. The new grade 8 students of 2014 were also included in the intervention, enabling them to benefit from it. However, since they did not complete the baseline questionnaire, their intervention was not tailored, allowing an exploratory comparison of the effectiveness of a tailored versus non-tailored intervention.

A total of 177 females between the ages of 13–16 years (M=14.5) participated in the intervention, representing early and middle adolescence (see Table 17.3). Each participating grade (8, 9 and 10) consisted of three classes. The first author facilitated one 50-min workshop with each of the 9 classes. The intervention received the necessary ethical approval. Consent and assent for participation in the initial questionnaire and the intervention workshop was obtained from the parents and adolescents, respectively. No parent withheld consent and none of the adolescents chose not to participate in the intervention.

The baseline questionnaire: Behaviors and perceptions to target in the intervention

The initial questionnaire showed that 71% of females had experienced cyberaggression, of whom 35% indicated that they had ever been cyberbullied. Most participants knew the identity of the perpetrator (87%) and were most likely to tell a friend about the experience (44%). Half also admitted that they had perpetrated cyberaggression (51%). Most (72%) had witnessed cyberbullying, with 16% witnessing it often. The majority also knew someone who had been cyberbullied (64%). Unsurprisingly, given these findings, 68% of participants believed that cyberbullying was currently a very serious issue. Further examples of cyberaggression experiences reported at baseline are shown in Table 17.4. Reliability analyses of the scale showed a Cronbach's alpha of .82.

The severity of these online experiences is reflected in the emotional distress reported by some adolescents (see Table 17.5). Examples of online risk perception items are also shown in Table 17.5, showing the participants' concerns and their perceptions of how controllable the risks are, which were addressed in the intervention through enhancing behavioral skills.

Assessing the intervention's effectiveness

The intervention was evaluated using the online risk perception scale from the baseline questionnaire. This 15-item scale was developed from existing risk perception literature

Table 17.4 Examples of cybervictimization and cyberperpetration ($n = 91$)

Cybervictimization	
Been called a rude or hurtful name in an online space	55.0%
Had my picture posted online to embarrass me	38.0%
Had rumors or gossip spread about me online	32.0%
Cyberperpetration	
Called someone a rude or hurtful name	29.8%
Put up a picture of someone online to embarrass them	25.0%
Spread rumors or gossip about someone online	8.3%

Table 17.5 Emotional experiences, concerns, and controllability of online risks ($n = 91$)

Emotional experiences	
Been hurt or made to feel sad about something that happened online	44.6%
Felt scared or worried about something that happened online	32.9%
Did not want to go to school on some days due to an online experience	22.0%
Concern and fear	
I worry about things that can go wrong when I am on the internet	52.4%
I am afraid of being harassed or threatened online	34.5%
Controllability	
I would not know what to do if I was faced with a dangerous situation on the internet	50.0%
I do not have control over what happens to me on the internet	24.1%

(e.g., Benthin et al., 1993; Boholm, 1998; Turow & Nir, 2000). Validity testing of the scale showed that the items reflected four categories of risk perception, including: (i) costs vs. benefits of the internet (e.g., "The benefits of the internet are far bigger than any dangers"); (ii) knowledge of risks (e.g., "People on the internet are usually honest about who they are"); (iii) fear and controllability of risks (e.g., "I cannot control the things that happen to me on the internet"); and (iv) desire for regulation (e.g., "It is important that adults keep a watch over teenagers' internet behaviors"). Participants indicated their agreement or disagreement on a 5-point Likert scale, with a midpoint neutral option. The scale demonstrated adequate reliability (Cronbach's alpha = .78).

The risk perception scale was administered either before or after the intervention. One randomly selected class per grade completed the questionnaire before the intervention (control group), the other two classes completing it after the intervention (intervention group). It was not feasible in the time available for participants to complete the instrument both before and after the intervention, and participants might have recalled their responses, potentially confounding the results. Moreover, this would have reduced the time available for the intervention. Thus, independent groups with 50 participants in the control and 124 in the intervention were used to evaluate the effectiveness of the IMB Skills model as an intervention for cyberaggression and cyberbullying.

An overall online risk perception score was calculated for each participant. Negatively worded items were reverse scored and response options were assigned scores of −2, −1, 0, +1, and +2, resulting in overall scores ranging from −30 to +30. A higher score reflected higher risk perception (i.e., greater appreciation of risk) and a lower score reflected lower risk perception.

Two verification analyses were conducted prior to the main analysis. Firstly, online risk perception of the new grade 8 students were compared with those of the previous year (i.e., 2014 students vs. 2013 students) using independent samples t-tests. Since the new students did not complete the baseline questionnaire, it was important to ensure that they did not significantly differ from the previous grade 8's. The results confirmed that there was no significant difference in online risk perception between the two groups (2013 grade 8's: M = 1.42; 2014 grade 8's: M = 1.88).

Secondly, the differences in risk perception between the (i) baseline questionnaire, (ii) control and (iii) intervention groups were compared (one-way ANOVA). There was a significant difference between the groups, $F(2, 255)=5.10$, $p=.007$, $\eta^2=.04$. This was due to the intervention group having significantly higher risk perception scores (M = 3.52, SD = 5.69, SE = 0.51) compared to both other groups, providing initial evidence that the intervention increased online risk perception. No significant difference was found between the baseline questionnaire (M = 1.40, SD = 6.86, SE = 0.76) and the control group (M = 0.60, SD = 6.44, SE = 0.91). As both occurred prior to the intervention, this ruled out a significant maturation effect over the 7-month period between data collection and the intervention.

The control and intervention groups were then compared for each grade. Main effects were found for both group (control and intervention) and grade (8, 9, and 10). The intervention group had significantly higher risk perception than the control, as established in the verification analysis above, $F(1, 174)=11.65$, $p=.001$, $\eta^2=.07$. Risk perception was also significantly lower with each subsequent grade for both groups combined, i.e., risk perception in grade 8 was highest (M = 3.90, SE = 1.29), followed by grade 9 (M = 1.87, SE = −0.84) and grade 10 (M = −0.25, SE = 0.92), $F(2, 174)=5.96$, $p=.003$, $\eta^2=.07$. With the difference between grades 8 and 10 being significant ($p=.017$), this suggests that risk perception decreased with age. A significant negative correlation between grade and risk perception further demonstrates this ($r=-0.21$, $p=.007$). This pattern has also been established in previous research: although risk taking and risky decision making generally decrease with age (Gardner & Steinberg, 2005), mid-adolescence has been identified as a period of heightened vulnerability in risky behavior (Steinberg, 2008, 2010). The current study likewise indicates that middle adolescence may also be a particularly vulnerable period for cyberaggression and cyberbullying. Although the interaction was nonsignificant, there was a larger proportional difference in risk perception scores between the control and intervention groups in the higher grades (see Fig. 17.3), possibly because they received the tailored intervention. This suggests that the intervention may be especially effective during middle adolescence when it is tailored to participants' risk behaviors and experiences. During the intervention itself, many participants were surprised by the prevalence rates of cyberaggression and cyberbullying in their grade. A tailored

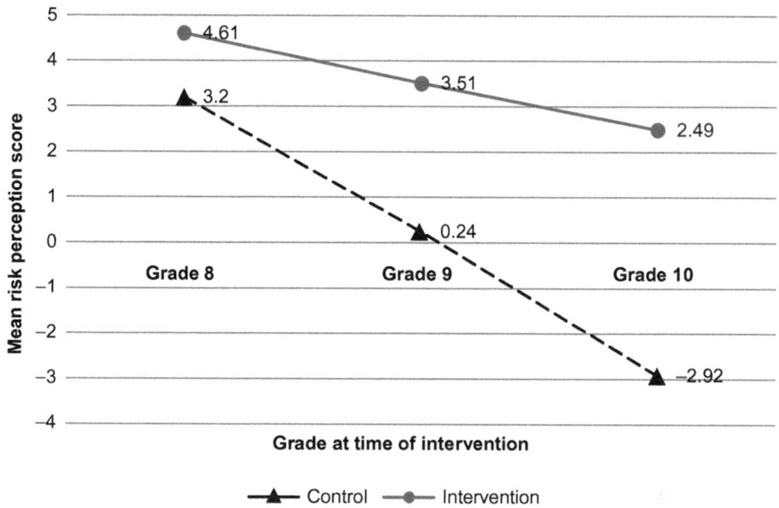

Fig. 17.3 Mean risk perception scores for the control and intervention groups for each grade ($n=174$).

intervention likely makes it more difficult to dismiss the personal relevance of the issues, which is important in enhancing risk perception. Knowing that others are encountering similar experiences may also be powerful in influencing risk perception.

Despite the small effect sizes of these findings, preliminary analysis suggests that the intervention had some positive effect on risk perception. The individual items in the risk perception scale show this (see Table 17.6). For example, fewer adolescents in the intervention group thought that the benefits of the internet outweigh any risks. This is a positive shift as the intervention is aimed at enhancing understanding and appreciation of risks in order to make informed behavioral choices when using technology.

These results provide preliminary evidence for the IMB model as an effective framework for online safety efforts, which should form part of broader strategies (see later). It also highlights the importance of tailored interventions and targeting those at middle adolescence in particular. Further interventions with additional pre- and post-test groups are underway to clarify these links.

Table 17.6 Differences in risk perception between the control and intervention groups

	Control	Intervention
The internet is very safe	76%	32%
The benefits of the internet are far bigger than any dangers	56%	29%
Adults make too much of a fuss when it comes to risks of the internet	42%	24%
The internet should not have an age restriction and everyone should be able to access anything they like	33%	17%

Implications and evaluation of the intervention

Cyberaggression and cyberbullying warrant serious attention within policy and intervention efforts, especially due to their psychological and behavioral effects and their influence on the offline world such as the school environment (Casas, Del Rey, & Ortega-Ruiz, 2013). This exploratory study was the first to apply the IMB model in the context of online behaviors. Preliminary results from an intervention conducted among 177 female adolescents in South Africa indicate that Information, Motivation, and Behavioral Skills are relevant factors in developing comprehensive interventions relating to online safety at the individual level, in conjunction with broader level efforts. The findings highlighted several important points, discussed below.

Firstly, an intervention using the IMB model did increase adolescents' online risk perception, indicating the utility of the model for addressing cyberaggression and cyberbullying, and providing further support for the model's use in nonhealth-related behavioral contexts. Secondly, while interventions targeting all age groups are important, the results highlight the need to target those in middle adolescence as they emerged as a particularly vulnerable group in terms of risk perception and behavior.

Thirdly, the effectiveness of the current intervention may be that it was tailored to adolescents' reported online risk behaviors, perceptions, and experiences. Tailored interventions enhance participants' evaluation of the information presented as being personally relevant, thereby promoting more accurate cost-benefit appraisals. The lower proportional increase in risk perception among the grade 8 students (for whom the intervention was not tailored and was presented as a general intervention) supports this, although there may be more scope for an increase in risk perception in older adolescents due to their lower baseline risk perception. One of the key challenges in current interventions is that many teachers feel ill-equipped to talk about online safety with their students at an appropriate level (e.g., De Lange & Von Solms, 2012; Eden, Heiman, & Olenik-Shemesh, 2013). Tailoring an intervention to a group not only highlights relevant issues to be addressed in an age-appropriate way, but makes the adolescents themselves key players in the intervention. This also takes some pressure off practitioners, whose role in facilitating the program is to ensure that the three core components of the IMB model are addressed.

Finally, the intervention can be used as a long-term strategy to introduce and then continue to support issues of online safety within the school. Schools can conduct a follow-up survey of adolescent online risk perceptions and behaviors in order to determine areas that require further attention. These evaluations can also serve to inform whole-school policies and procedures, and pinpoint areas for teacher training.

While the IMB model provides a framework for interventions aimed at individuals, it is important that this is only one part of broader efforts. Upon the completion of the interventions, the first author held a feedback session with teachers to discuss the (i) behaviors targeted in the intervention, (ii) theoretical framework used, (iii) activities and discussions relating to the IMB model, and (iv) technology more broadly and the issues adolescents face. This ensured that teachers were aware of what had been conducted, and they were given ideas for how to continue to engage in this area further.

Follow-up work related to this intervention aims to include formal teacher training and longer-term engagement with schools. Although this intervention is relatively easy to implement by practitioners who are already working in this area, training of school staff will be essential in future work. More specifically, this training will include (i) a tutorial on administering the baseline questionnaire, (ii) an overview of the theoretical framework, (iii) guides and resources relating to the intervention and its activities, and (iv) ongoing support and information relating to technology and cyberaggression and cyberbullying to enhance self-efficacy of teachers and practitioners to conduct the interventions. Once this is in place, schools can continue with these efforts through conducting top-up sessions and extending the intervention to other grades. Efforts can then also be put into place to engage parents. Thus, it is envisaged that this intervention will also incorporate the two most immediate environments in adolescents' lives, namely, the home and school contexts. Formal training and ongoing engagement also means that the intervention can become more detailed and be conducted as a series of workshops, which is likely to hold further benefits.

Although more research is in progress, the pilot study reflects a number of benefits of the intervention (see Box 17.2).

Overall, the findings are promising given the random allocation of classes in the same school to the control and intervention groups, which reduces the impact of contextual factors on any differences found between groups. However, there are also a number of

Box 17.2 Benefits of this Intervention for Educators and Practitioners

- *Relatively simple implementation*
  The steps in the intervention involve (i) administering a survey to determine the risk perceptions and behaviors to be targeted in the intervention (sample items are shown in Table 17.1), (ii) designing the intervention with this information in mind, and (iii) facilitating the intervention as a workshop. Although further work is being done in terms of teacher training, those already working in the area will be able to implement the intervention. Further guides and resources for conducting the intervention are also available on our website https://www.buckingham.ac.uk/cyberbullying.
- *Adolescents are central to the intervention*
  The practitioner's role is to encourage reflection, discussion and to carry out the practical exercises in the workshop, which relate to the three core aspects of the Information-Motivation-Behavioral Skills Model. Practitioners add important points and ideas where required, but adolescents take on a key role in the intervention as coeducators.
- *Potential for ongoing work*
  The intervention can be an excellent way of introducing the issues of cyberaggression, cyberbullying, and other online risks into the school by creating a dialog between adolescents and adults. After the intervention there is potential for ongoing work, keeping the issue of cyberaggression and cyberbullying, and online safety more generally, at the forefront. For example, further surveys can be administered to determine future areas of focus as technology evolves, and further informal discussions over time can also serve to reinforce important points and issues raised.

limitations, which should be acknowledged and which future work in this area can address. Firstly, in order to further explore the generalizability of the IMB model, the intervention is being extended to other groups, including males, those in late adolescence and other schools in South Africa and elsewhere. Secondly, other relevant factors that may have impacted on changes between the control and intervention groups should be explored, such as potential social desirability bias in the intervention group. Longer-term assessment of the intervention's effectiveness will thus be important, and should also include measures of behavior change directly (in addition to changes in risk perception). Finally, as mentioned, the importance of the whole-school approach to online safety is recognized and longer-term engagement with schools and appropriate staff training will be essential.

Conclusion

This chapter highlights the utility of the IMB model in addressing cyberaggression and cyberbullying through not only informing adolescents about risk behaviors but also providing motivation and behavioral skills to elicit behavior change. The initial evidence lends support to the model as a relevant framework within larger-scale online safety efforts. The study also suggests that tailoring interventions to participants' own online risk behaviors and perceptions rather than engaging them more generally may be important. The findings also reflect the importance of early prevention efforts prior to and during early adolescence as well as interventions during middle adolescence, which appears to be a critical period in relation to online safety. Further research in this area is underway, and it is important to extend the intervention to other groups to evaluate its efficacy more broadly. The chapter presented key steps that can be implemented by practitioners, utilizing an effective framework for engaging adolescents and facilitating interventions in this area.

References

Alhakami, A. S., & Slovic, P. (1994). A psychological study of the inverse relationship between perceived risk and perceived benefit. *Risk Analysis*, *14*(6), 1085–1096.

Amico, K. R., Toro-Alfonso, J., & Fisher, J. D. (2005). An empirical test of the information, motivation and behavioral skills model of antiretroviral therapy adherence. *AIDS Care*, *17*(6), 661–673.

Bauman, S. (2007). *Cyberbullying: A virtual menace*. In: *Paper presented at the National Coalition Against Bullying National Conference, November 2–4, Melbourne, Australia*. Retrieved from http://www.ncab.org.au/Assets/Files/Bauman%20S%20Cyberbullying.pdf.

Bauman, S., Toomey, R. B., & Walker, J. L. (2013). Associations among bullying, cyberbullying, and suicide in high school students. *Journal of Adolescence*, *36*(2), 341–350.

Benthin, A., Slovic, P., & Severson, H. (1993). A psychometric study of adolescent risk perception. *Journal of Adolescence*, *16*(2), 153–168. https://doi.org/10.1006/jado.1993.1014.

Boholm, A. (1998). Comparative studies of risk perception: A review of twenty years of research. *Journal of Risk Research*, *1*(2), 135–163. https://doi.org/10.1080/136698798377231.

Burton, P. & Leoschut, L. (2012). School Violence in South Africa. Results of the 2012 National School Violence Study. Centre for Justice and Crime Prevention, CJCP. Monograph Series No. 12.

Calandro, E., Stork, C. & Gillwald, A. (2012). Internet going mobile: Internet access and usage in 11 African countries. Research ICT Africa Policy Brief. No. 2.

Casas, J. A., Del Rey, R., & Ortega-Ruiz, R. (2013). Bullying and cyberbullying: Convergent and divergent predictor variables. *Computers in Human Behavior*, *29*(3), 580–587.

Chang, C.-C. (2011). A study of E-waste recycling behavior-adopting from IMB model. Retrieved from http://thesis.lib.ncu.edu.tw/ETD-db/ETD-search/view_etd?URN=984203043.

Chang, S. J., Choi, S., Kim, S.-A., & Song, M. (2014). Intervention strategies based on information-motivation-behavioral skills model for behavior change: A systematic review. *Asian Nursing Research*, *8*(3), 172–181.

Chapin, J. (2014). Adolescents and cyber bullying: The precaution adoption process model. *Education and Information Technologies*, 1–10.

Cohn, L. D., Macfarlane, S., Yanez, C., & Imai, W. K. (1995). Risk-perception: Differences between adolescents and adults. *Health Psychology: Official Journal of the Division of Health Psychology, American Psychological Association*, *14*(3), 217–222.

Corcoran, L., Guckin, C. M., & Prentice, G. (2015). Cyberbullying or cyber aggression? A review of existing definitions of cyber-based peer-to-peer aggression. *Societies*, *5*(2), 245–255.

De Lange, M., & Von Solms, R. (2011). *The importance of raising e-Safety awareness amongst children in South Africa*. In *Proceedings of the 13th Annual Conference on World Wide Web Applications, September 13–16, Johannesburg, South Africa*. Retrieved from: http://www.zaw3.co.za/index.php/ZAWWW/2011/paper/viewFile/423/131.

De Lange, M., & Von Solms, R. (2012). *An e-Safety educational framework in South Africa*. In *Proceedings of the Southern Africa Telecommunications Networks and Applications Conference (SATNAC)*.

Dempsey, A. G., Sulkowski, M. L., Nichols, R., & Storch, E. A. (2009). Differences between peer victimization in cyber and physical settings and associated psychosocial adjustment in early adolescence. *Psychology in the Schools*, *46*(10), 962–972.

Denissen, J. J. A., Neumann, L., & van Zalk, M. (2010). How the internet is changing the implementation of traditional research methods, people's daily lives, and the way in which developmental scientists conduct research. *International Journal of Behavioral Development*, *34*(6), 564–575.

DiClemente, R. J., Crosby, R. A., & Kegler, M. (2009). *Emerging theories in health promotion practice and research*. John Wiley & Sons.

Eden, S., Heiman, T., & Olenik-Shemesh, D. (2013). Teachers' perceptions, beliefs and concerns about cyberbullying. *British Journal of Educational Technology*, *44*(6), 1036–1052.

Eurostat (2015). Being Young in Europe Today—Digital World. Available Online: http://ec.europa.eu/eurostat/statisticsexplained/index.php/Being_young_in_Europe_today_-_digital_world#Main_statistical_findings.

Finucane, M. L., Alhakami, A., Slovic, P., & Johnson, S. M. (2000). The affect heuristic in judgments of risks and benefits. *Journal of Behavioral Decision Making*, *13*(1), 1–17. https://doi.org/10.1002/(SICI)1099-0771(200001/03)13:1<1::AID-BDM333>3.0.CO;2-S.

Fisher, J. D., & Fisher, W. A. (1992). Changing AIDS-risk behavior. *Psychological Bulletin*, *111*(3), 455.

Fisher, J. D., Fisher, W. A., Bryan, A. D., & Misovich, S. J. (2002). Information-motivation-behavioral skills model-based HIV risk behavior change intervention for inner-city high school youth. *Health Psychology*, *21*(2), 177.

Gardner, M., & Steinberg, L. (2005). Peer influence on risk taking, risk preference, and risky decision making in adolescence and adulthood: An experimental study. *Developmental Psychology*, *41*(4), 625–635. https://doi.org/10.1037/0012-1649.41.4.625.

Gavgani, R. M., Poursharifi, H., & Aliasgarzadeh, A. (2010). Effectiveness of Information-Motivation-Behavioral Skill (IMB) model in improving self-care behaviors & Hba1c Measure in Adults with Type 2 Diabetes in Iran-Tabriz. *Procedia—Social and Behavioral Sciences*, *5*, 1868–1873.

Gerrard, M., Gibbons, F. X., Benthin, A. C., & Hessling, R. M. (1996). A longitudinal study on the reciprocal nature of risk behaviors and cognitions in adolescents: What you do shapes what you think, and vice versa. *Health Psychology*, *15*(5), 344–354.

Glasford, D. E. (2008). Predicting voting behavior of young adults: The importance of information, motivation, and behavioral skills. *Journal of Applied Social Psychology*, *38*(11), 2648–2672.

Greene, K., Krcmar, M., Walters, L. H., Rubin, D. L., Jerold, & Hale, L. (2000). Targeting adolescent risk-taking behaviors: The contributions of egocentrism and sensation-seeking. *Journal of Adolescence*, *23*(4), 439–461. https://doi.org/10.1006/jado.2000.0330.

Grigg, D. W. (2010). Cyber-aggression: Definition and concept of cyberbullying. *Journal of Psychologists and Counsellors in Schools*, *20*(2), 143–156.

Heirman, W., & Walrave, M. (2012). Predicting adolescent perpetration in cyberbullying: An application of the theory of planned behavior. *Psicothema*, *24*(4), 614–620.

Hinduja, S., & Patchin, J. W. (2007). Offline consequences of online victimization: School violence and delinquency. *Journal of School Violence*, *6*(3), 89–112.

Johnson, R. J., McCaul, K. D., & Klein, W. M. P. (2002). Risk involvement and risk perception among adolescents and young adults. *Journal of Behavioral Medicine*, *25*(1), 67–82.

Kalichman, S., Stein, J. A., Malow, R., Averhart, C., Dévieux, J., Jennings, T., ... Feaster, D. J. (2002). Predicting protected sexual behavior using the information-motivation-behavior skills model among adolescent substance abusers in court-ordered treatment. *Psychology, Health & Medicine*, *7*(3), 327–338. https://doi.org/10.1080/13548500220139368.

Kasperson, R. E., Renn, O., Slovic, P., Brown, H. S., Emel, J., Goble, R., ... Ratick, S. (1988). The social amplification of risk: A conceptual framework. *Risk Analysis*, *8*(2), 177–187. https://doi.org/10.1111/j.1539-6924.1988.tb01168.x.

Kelly, S., Melnyk, B. M., & Belyea, M. (2012). Predicting physical activity and fruit and vegetable intake in adolescents: A test of the information, motivation, behavioral skills model. *Research in Nursing & Health*, *35*(2), 146–163. https://doi.org/10.1002/nur.21462.

Kiene, S. M., Fisher, W. A., Shuper, P. A., Cornman, D. H., Christie, S., MacDonald, S., ... Fisher, J. D. (2013). Understanding HIV transmission risk behavior among HIV-infected South Africans receiving antiretroviral therapy: An information-motivation-behavioral skills model analysis. *Health Psychology*, *32*(8), 860–868.

Kim, Y. S., & Leventhal, B. (2008). Bullying and suicide. A review. *International Journal of Adolescent Medicine and Health*, *20*(2), 133–154.

Litwiller, B. J., & Brausch, A. M. (2013). Cyber bullying and physical bullying in adolescent suicide: The role of violent behavior and substance use. *Journal of Youth and Adolescence*, *42*(5), 675–684.

Mayberry, L. S., & Osborn, C. Y. (2014). Empirical validation of the information-motivation-behavioral skills model of diabetes medication adherence: A framework for intervention. *Diabetes Care*, *37*(5), 1246–1253.

Mayer, R. E. (Ed.), (2005). *The Cambridge handbook of multimedia learning*. USA: Cambridge University Press.

Menesini, E., Nocentini, A., Palladino, B. E., Frisén, A., Berne, S., Ortega-Ruiz, R., ... Smith, P. K. (2012). Cyberbullying definition among adolescents: A comparison across six European countries. *Cyberpsychology, Behavior and Social Networking*, *15*(9), 455–463.

Mishna, F., Khoury-Kassabri, M., Gadalla, T., & Daciuk, J. (2012). Risk factors for involvement in cyber bullying: Victims, bullies and bully–victims. *Children and Youth Services Review, 34*(1), 63–70.

Mitchell, K. J., Finkelhor, D., Jones, L. M., & Wolak, J. (2012). Prevalence and characteristics of youth sexting: A national study. *Pediatrics, 129*(1), 13–20.

Modecki, K. L., Minchin, J., Harbaugh, A. G., Guerra, N. G., & Runions, K. C. (2014). Bullying prevalence across contexts: A meta-analysis measuring cyber and traditional bullying. *Journal of Adolescent Health, 55*(5), 602–611.

Odora, R. J., & Matoti, S. N. (2015). The nature and prevalence of cyber bullying behaviors among South African high school learners. *International Journal of Educational Sciences, 10*(3), 399–409.

Osborn, C. Y., & Egede, L. E. (2010). Validation of an information-motivation-behavioral skills model of diabetes self-care (IMB-DSC). *Patient Education and Counseling, 79*(1), 49–54. https://doi.org/10.1016/j.pec.2009.07.016.

Patchin, J. W., & Hinduja, S. (2006). Bullies move beyond the schoolyard a preliminary look at cyberbullying. *Youth Violence and Juvenile Justice, 4*(2), 148–169.

Patchin, J.W. & Hinduja, S. (2015). Measuring cyberbullying: Implications for research. Aggression and Violent Behavior. Retrieved from http://www.sciencedirect.com/science/article/pii/S1359178915000750.

Paulsen, D. J., Platt, M. L., Huettel, S. A., & Brannon, E. M. (2011). Decision-making under risk in children, adolescents, and young adults. *Frontiers in Psychology, 2*. https://doi.org/10.3389/fpsyg.2011.00072.

Peltzer, K., Preez, N. F., Ramlagan, S., & Anderson, J. (2010). Antiretroviral treatment adherence among HIV patients in KwaZulu-Natal, South Africa. *BMC Public Health, 10*(1), 111. https://doi.org/10.1186/1471-2458-10-111.

Perren, S., Corcoran, L., Cowie, H., Dehue, F., Garcia, D., Mc Guckin, C., ... Völlink, T. (2012). Tackling cyberbullying: Review of empirical evidence regarding successful responses by students, parents, and schools. *International Journal of Conflict and Violence, 6*(2), 283.

Pillay, C. L. (2012). Behavioral and psychosocial factors associated with cyberbullying. University of Zululand. Unpublished Masters Thesis. Retrieved from http://196.21.83.35/handle/10530/1225.

Popovac, M., Mwaba, K., & Roman, N. V. (2011). Smoking behavior, risk perception and attitudes toward anti-smoking legislation among a sample of South African students: Physical activity and health. *African Journal for Physical Health Education, Recreation and Dance, 17*(3), 473–480.

Seacat, J. D., & Northrup, D. (2010). An information–motivation–behavioral skills assessment of curbside recycling behavior. *Journal of Environmental Psychology, 30*(4), 393–401.

Sjoberg. (2000). Factors in risk perception. *Risk Analysis: An Official Publication of the Society for Risk Analysis, 20*(1), 1–11.

Slonje, R., & Smith, P. K. (2008). Cyberbullying: Another main type of bullying? *Scandinavian Journal of Psychology, 49*(2), 147–154.

Slovic, P., & Peters, E. (2006). Risk perception and affect. *Current Directions in Psychological Science, 15*(6), 322–325. https://doi.org/10.1111/j.1467-8721.2006.00461.x.

Snakenborg, J., Van Acker, R., & Gable, R. A. (2011). Cyberbullying: Prevention and intervention to protect our children and youth. *Preventing School Failure: Alternative Education for Children and Youth, 55*(2), 88–95.

Steinberg, L. (2008). A social neuroscience perspective on adolescent risk-taking. *Developmental Review, 28*(1), 78–106. https://doi.org/10.1016/j.dr.2007.08.002.

Steinberg, L. (2010). A dual systems model of adolescent risk-taking. *Developmental Psychobiology*, *52*(3), 216–224. https://doi.org/10.1002/dev.20445.

Suls, J., & Wallston, K. A. (2008). *Social psychological foundations of health and illness*. John Wiley & Sons.

Tokunaga, R. S. (2010). Following you home from school: A critical review and synthesis of research on cyberbullying victimization. *Computers in Human Behavior*, *26*(3), 277–287. https://doi.org/10.1016/j.chb.2009.11.014.

Turow, J., & Nir, L. (2000). The internet and the family: The view from parents, the view from kids. The Annenberg Public Policy Center of the University of Pennsylvania. Retrieved from http://www.annenbergpublicpolicycenter.org/downloads/information_and_society/20000516_internet_and_family/20000516_internet_and_family_report.pdf.

Van Geel, M., Vedder, P., & Tanilon, J. (2014). Relationship between peer victimization, cyberbullying, and suicide in children and adolescents: A meta-analysis. *JAMA Pediatrics*, *168*(5), 435–442.

Willard, N. E. (2007). *Cyberbullying and cyberthreats: Responding to the challenge of online social aggression, threats, and distress*. Research Press.

Wolburg, J. (2001). The "risky business" of binge drinking among college students: Using risk models for PSAs and anti-drinking campaigns. *Journal of Advertising*, *30*(4), 24–39.

Ybarra, M. L., Alexander, C., & Mitchell, K. J. (2005). Depressive symptomatology, youth Internet use, and online interactions: A national survey. *Journal of Adolescent Health*, *36*(1), 9–18.

A short intervention on cyberbullying for students in middle school and their parents

18

Leslie Ramos Salazar, Anthony J. Roberto†, Jen Eden‡, Matthew Savage§, Douglas Deiss¶*

*West Texas A&M University, Canyon, TX, United States, †Arizona State University, Tempe, AZ, United States, ‡Marist College, Poughkeepsie, NY, United States, §San Diego State University, San Diego, CA, United States, ¶Glendale Community College, Glendale, CA, United States

Name of program: Cyberbullying talk
Type of program: Forty-five minute talk
Suitable for ages: Middle school students and parents

Introduction

The tech savviness of U.S. adolescents contributes to their vulnerability to experiencing bullying in online social environments. To date, cyberbullying has become a widespread societal problem given adolescents' high use of communication technology with Internet access. The U.S. Department of Education and National Center for Education Statistics (2016) reports that students in middle school are more likely to experience bullying and cyberbullying than those in high school or college. A recent meta-analytical review of 58 studies on middle-school student cyberbullying victimization reported that perpetration of cyberbullying ranges from 1% to 41%, cyberbullying victimization ranges from 3% to 72%, and both cyberbullying perpetration and victimization ranges from 2.3% to 16.7% (Selkie, Fales, & Moreno, 2016). Interestingly, Juvonen and Gross's (2008) study found the highest level for the prevalence of cyberbullying (e.g., receiving threats or mean online messages) to be 75%. Another middle-school study found that 11% had been victims of cyberbullying, 4% reported cyberbullying others, and 7% reported experiencing both in the past 2 months (Kowalski & Limber, 2007). These alarming prevalence rates in middle-school students along with several news stories regarding adolescent suicides instigated primarily by cyberbullying attacks have triggered numerous cyberbullying intervention investigations across the fields of communication, psychology, social work, education, and criminal justice.

This chapter describes a school-based intervention that has been used for middle-school students and their parents to prevent cyberbullying. Two school-based intervention studies on the intervention using constructs from the Extended Parallel Process Model (EPPM) are presented. Recommendations to middle-school students,

Reducing Cyberbullying in Schools. https://doi.org/10.1016/B978-0-12-811423-0.00018-3

parents, educators, and administrators, and future directions for intervention researchers of cyberbullying prevention complete the chapter.

Theoretical basis for the program

To scientifically assess the student and parent school-based cyberbullying interventions, the researchers used The Extended Parallel Process Model (EPPM) (Witte, 1992) to evaluate the effectiveness of the fear appeals used in the presentation materials of the student and parent interventions. The EPPM is a message-based model that explains that susceptibility, severity, response efficacy, and self-efficacy play a significant role in individuals' intentions and behaviors. Both perceived threat (susceptibility and severity) and perceived efficacy (response-efficacy and self-efficacy) explain individuals' differing reactions to threatening messages (Roberto & Witte, 2010). *Susceptibility* refers to feeling vulnerable to experiencing cyberbullying victimization. *Severity* refers to the intensity of the threat of experiencing cyberbullying victimization. *Response-efficacy* refers to the ability to control cyberbullying behavior. *Self-efficacy* refers to the perceived competency one feels to engage in constructive behaviors to prevent or reduce the cyberbullying behavior.

The EPPM suggests that adolescents may react differently to the exposure of the fear appeals used in cyberbullying messages. When a cyberbullying message is perceived to be unthreatening to the adolescents, then adolescents will feel that they are not susceptible to cyberbullying and may ignore the message, and thus, do nothing about the cyberbullying behavior. If adolescents' cyberbullying experiences are perceived to be highly self-threatening and if they perceive their efficacy to be high, then EPPM suggests that adolescents will engage in danger control, which means that students will follow through with the recommendations offered by the cyberbullying intervention (Witte, 1992). On the other hand, if adolescents perceive cyberbullying experiences to be highly self-threatening, but have low efficacy, then adolescents may engage in fear control (or abstain from complying with the presenter's recommendations by ignoring them) (Witte, 1992). Thus, the researchers evaluated the responses to the intervention using constructs from the EPPM, first with the middle-school students and second with the middle-school parents.

What is the program and how is it delivered?

Student component

In 2011, the Arizona Attorney General, Terry Goddard, introduced an intervention entitled the "Social Networking Safety Promotion and Cyberbullying Prevention" to spread awareness about cyberbullying and social networking site safety issues. For the purposes of the two intervention studies reported in this chapter, cyberbullying was defined as "the deliberate and repeated misuse of communication technology by an individual or group to threaten or harm others" (Roberto & Eden, 2010, p. 201). The interventions adopted the following definition for social network: "a socialization framework that links individuals through some common purpose, interest, or characteristic" (Hinduja & Patchin, 2009, p. 77). Social networking sites (SNS) such as Facebook,

Myspace, Bebo, Friendster, and Xanga enable adolescents to share messages, pictures, and videos with their social networking friends. This program is an example of a school-based intervention used to prevent cyberbullying in middle-school students in Phoenix, Arizona. The intervention consisted of a presenter who spoke for 45 minutes to the students about safety precautions in social networking sites such as Facebook, the use of communication technologies such as cell phones and e–mail, and specific recommendations to prevent cyberbullying behaviors. Social networking message examples were provided within the presentation to illustrate adolescents' vulnerability to the risks involved in social networking sites. For example, the presenter "friended" several middle-school students prior to the presentation via the school's Facebook page and he illustrated how easy it was to obtain students' personal information from their Facebook profile such as their full names, addresses, and phone numbers, and how complete strangers can locate where they lived via Google Maps (Roberto, Eden, Savage, Ramos-Salazar, & Deiss, 2014). To induce adolescents' perceived threat in cyberbullying, the presentation included cyberbullying messages such as several cyberbullying cases such as Megan Mier's suicide story, other newsworthy stories of perpetrators who got caught and arrested for cyberbullying other adolescents, and Arizona's cyberbullying prevention laws (Roberto et al., 2014). The objectives of the intervention consisted of (a) changing students' attitudes, intentions, and behaviors, (b) stimulating the relevancy and seriousness of the threats, and (c) reducing the perceived threats though constructive preventative behaviors (Roberto et al., 2014).

Parent component

The intervention was later adapted to the parents of middle-school students. First, the intervention educated parents about the risk factors of cyberbullying to enhance the self-efficacy or competency of the parents so that they can identify and prevent cyberbullying before it occurs to their own children. Because some parents might not be technologically savvy in regards to new forms of social media such as Pinterest, Foursquare, Instagram, and Yik Yak, parents might not be able to identify the risks associated with their usage without obtaining any training. To educate the parents about cyberbullying, several examples of cyberbullied adolescents and news stories about cyberbullying were provided in the presentation. These examples also served to trigger parents' perceived risks regarding their children's probability of getting cyberbullied through social networking sites. Second, the parental intervention primarily focused on addressing cyberbullying behaviors rather than the safety issues regarding social networking site use. Third, the intervention highlighted three recommendations against cyberbullying, which included a) save the evidence, b) do not retaliate, and c) tell a trusted adult or an authority figure.

Evidence for the intervention to date

Student component

Roberto et al. (2014) evaluated a 45-minute speaker intervention that was adopted by a public middle school in Phoenix, AZ. The presenter shared recommendations regarding social networking safety promotion and cyberbullying issues to sixth, seventh, and eight grade middle-school students. Two-thirds of the presentation focused on social networking safety promotion and one-third on cyberbullying prevention. The field study examined the short-term effects of this intervention on these middle-school students by randomly assigning students to either the control group or the experimental group using a post-test-only control-group design with random assignment at the classroom level. The study examined the intervention's use of social networking safety promotion, cyberbullying prevention, and cyberbullying perpetration and victimization. The study also examined the effectiveness of the intervention's social safety networking promotion by comparing both groups. The social networking safety promotion consisted of the five recommended behaviors:

(1) Keep your social networking site profile private.
(2) Do not friend people who you do not know.
(3) Do not post photos that you do not want others to download without your permission.
(4) Do not meet face to face with someone you only met online.
(5) Tell a trusted adult when someone suspicious attacks you.

For the social networking safety (SNS) promotion, the intervention had positive effects in one or more grades (e.g., 6th graders, 7th graders) on two specific intentions (e.g., not posting photos, not meeting face to face). The main effect for the intervention across grades included severity, response efficacy, attitudes, and general intentions to practice the safe SNS behaviors. The intervention also affected the following two specific behavioral intentions: to not friend strangers and to keep their SNS profile private (Roberto et al., 2014).

This study also revealed that severity, self-efficacy, and response efficacy predicted behavioral intentions, and severity and self-efficacy predicted attitude for social networking safety (Roberto et al., 2014). Main effects for grade level were found for the three specific intentions to do the recommendations for social networking safety, which included making sure information is unavailable via SSNs, keeping SSNs private, and not friending strangers (Roberto et al., 2014).

In addition, the study examined the effects of the intervention's cyberbullying preventative strategies. The aims of the intervention were to change students' attitudes, intentions, and behaviors about cyberbullying (Roberto et al., 2014). Another aim was to convince students that cyberbullying is relevant to them and that it is a serious threat. Students were subsequently provided with effective strategies to reduce their threats and to be able to confront cyberbullying issues. When examining the effectiveness of the intervention on cyberbullying prevention, the intervention had positive effects in one or more grades (e.g., 7th grade) for severity and susceptibility. Similarly, across grades, the intervention had positive main effects on two specific intentions (not retaliate and tell a trusted adult).

Further, findings revealed that severity was also a predictor of behavioral intentions and attitudes about cyberbullying. When examining both groups, the intervention impacted two key intentions of the experimental group: to avoid retaliating and the intentions to tell a trusted adult (Roberto et al., 2014). There was also an interaction effect with grade level with two variables: perceived severity and perceived susceptibility. For example, the effects of the cyberbullying prevention had an impact on the severity especially on the sixth and eighth grade students. The interaction effects by condition and grade were evident in the susceptibility reports by grade. Also, the intervention had an impact on attitudes of the seventh graders, but there were clear differences in attitude across the grades. In terms of behavioral intentions, there were differences across the grades as well. The intervention also made an impact on two of the recommended preventative behaviors against cyberbullying, which included (a) saving the evidence and (b) telling a trusted adult across all the grade levels. These findings suggest that the middle-school student cyberbullying prevention intervention did have short-term effects in this population's attitudes and behavioral intentions. This intervention may be replicated in other middle-school systems to determine whether obtaining a credible speaker to speak to middle-school students helps administrators and educators prevent cyberbullying perpetration at their schools.

Finally, the authors also discuss the use of technology by middle-school students. The study found differences in the reported access to technology by grade. The majority of the sixth (78.6%), seventh (90.8%), and eighth (94.5%) graders reported having access to a personal e-mail account. Interestingly, the eighth graders (80.7%) reported having a higher access to a personal cell phone in comparison to the sixth (63.0%) and seventh (69.9%) graders. Most of the middle-school students (98.4%–100%) reported having access to a computer and all of them indicated having access to the Internet across the grade levels. Most seventh (71.2%) and eighth (86.2%) graders reporting having access to social networking sites (e.g., Facebook) in comparison to the sixth graders (53.5%). These prevalence reports suggest that most middle-school students have access to a variety of technological tools and U.S. middle schools may benefit from the implementation of social networking safety (SNS) promotion and cyberbullying interventions.

Parent component

Few school-based intervention studies exist to educate parents about their children's risks of cyberbullying perpetration and victimization. In a public middle school in Phoenix, AZ, an intervention was conducted and a group of researchers examined the intervention's effectiveness of parents' perceptions about cyberbullying using a separate sample pretest-post-test quasiexperimental design with random assignment approach (Deiss, Savage, Eden, Ramos-Salazar, & Roberto, 2012). The intervention educated parents primarily about cyberbullying and it was designed to alert parents how to protect their children against cyberbullying perpetration. Parents who were interested in protecting their child against cyberbullying attended an evening presentation. The intervention consisted of a presenter who informed parents about three recommendations to talk about with their children, which included:

(1) Saving all the evidence
(2) Avoid retaliating
(3) Telling a trusted adult or authority figure

First, because cyberbullying incidents occur primarily through communication technology, children can save evidence such as e-mails, Facebook messages, Tweets, texts, and instant message scripts. Saving the evidence empowers the students and their parents to report cyberbullying incidents. Second, parents were told to tell their children to avoid retaliating back to the bullies by replying negatively back to the received messages. Studies have found that individuals who reported cyberbullying victimization reported retaliating against the offender to attain vengeance for the cyberbullying offense (Crosslin & Golman, 2014; Runions, 2013). Another study found that student retaliation was not perceived to be an effective strategy to cope with cyberbullying (Price & Dalgleish, 2010). Third, parents were told to let their children know to tell a trusted adult or authoritative figure when encountering cyberbullying incidences. A study by Crosslin and Golman (2014) found that children who tell a peer tend to engage in behaviors that escalates the cyberbullying behavior. However, children who share their cyberbullying victimization experiences with a trusted adult such as a parent or a teacher who is informed about cyberbullying perpetration are more likely to gain the social support needed to be able to confront and manage the cyberbullying behavior (Machmutow, Perren, Sticca, & Alsaker, 2012; Aricak et al., 2008). For the most part, the presenters' three recommendations are confirmed by scholarly evidence to be effective ways of coping with cyberbullying.

Deiss et al. (2012) examined parents' behavioral intentions of talking to their children about the three recommended behaviors following the intervention. The study used a separate-sample pretest-post-test design with random assignment to conditions. For this design, parents in the control group completed the survey with the outcome variables prior to viewing the presentation, and parents in the experimental group completed the survey with the outcome measures after viewing the presentation. The goal of this study was to determine whether the presentation impacted parents' perceptions about their children's susceptibility to cyberbullying behaviors and whether they would talk to their children about the three recommendations.

The study found that parents in the experimental group reported perceiving higher susceptibility of their child to experience cyberbullying and they also reported positive behavioral intentions to communicate with their children about the three recommendations suggested in the presentation. This study's findings suggest that parental cyberbullying prevention interventions in middle schools can impact parents' short-term attitudes and intentions. This intervention model can be utilized to educate parents about their children's risks about cyberbullying and how to talk to their children to reduce cyberbullying in middle schools.

Recommendations & future directions

There are several applicable recommendations for middle-school students and parents, school officials, and for intervention researchers that can be derived from the review of these evidence-based cyberbullying prevention studies. First of all, parent-child interactions about cyberbullying are crucial to enable parents to develop their children's trust and social support. Parents are encouraged to talk to their children about cyberbullying issues to protect their children from being victimized. Second, students and parents may benefit from knowing about the two evidence-based recommendations that deal with cyberbullying, which include to not retaliate and to tell a trusted adult.

Middle-school students who understand the importance of not retaliating, despite the temptation to do so, may prevent the cyberbullying issue from escalating, or from getting worse. Also, students who understand the value of telling an adult or a trusted authority about the cyberbullying issue may be more likely to cope and reduce the cyberbullying behavior. Unfortunately, a few middle-school students prefer dealing with problems by themselves instead of telling adults about their cyberbullying problems (Aricak et al., 2008; Froeschle, Mayorga, Castillo, & Hargrave, 2008). Third, school officials may benefit from enabling cyberbullying speakers to talk to middle-school students and parents about cyberbullying perpetration and social networking safety strategies to prevent cyberbullying issues at their middle schools. Fourth, future cyberbullying and cybersafety interventions may benefit from communication scholarship that includes the use of models such as the Extended Parallel Process Model (EPPM) to design their interventions to examine the interaction patterns of students and their parents and the effects of the intervention on their attitudes, intentions, and behaviors. Future cyberbullying prevention interventions may also examine the longitudinal effects of bringing the same cyberbullying speaker over time, or a series of speakers to talk to middle-school students and their parents about cyberbullying prevention approaches.

Concluding thoughts

A description of a research-based intervention that has been used to prevent cyberbullying in middle-school students and parents was presented. As far as we know, this is the only evidence-based intervention that has been adapted to both middle-school students and parents, which authorizes the use of knowledgeable external presenters on the topic of cyberbullying and social networking site safety. Two research-based intervention studies about the cyberbullying prevention using the EPPM were also described. The use of the EPPM as a theoretical underpinning strengthened both studies. The EPPM was helpful to determine the effectiveness of the cyberbullying prevention intervention among both middle-school students and parents, which suggests that communication models and theories may benefit cyberbullying intervention scholarship. Recommendations to middle-school educators and administrators, middle-school parents, and future directions for intervention researchers of cyberbullying were presented. Cyberbullying continues to be a societal problem that impacts U.S. adolescents, and there is still a need to develop and evaluate cyberbullying prevention interventions using a communication approach.

References

Aricak, T., Siyahhan, S., Uzunhasanoglu, A., Saribeyoglu, S., Ciplak, S., Yilmaz, N., et al. (2008). Cyberbullying among Turkish adolescents. *CyberPsychology & Behavior*, *11*(3), 253–261. https://doi.org/10.1089/cpb.2007.0016.

Crosslin, K., & Golman, M. (2014). "Maybe you don't want to face it"—College students' perspectives on cyberbullying. *Computers in Human Behavior*, *41*, 14–20. https://doi.org/10.1016/j.chb.2014.09.007.

Deiss, D. M., Savage, M. W., Eden, J., Ramos-Salazar, L., & Roberto, A. J. (2012). Outcome evaluation results of school-based cybersafety promotion and cyberbullying prevention intervention for middle school parents. In *Paper presented to the Interpersonal Communication Interest Group of the Western States Communication Association, Albuquerque, NM*.

Froeschle, J. G., Mayorga, M., Castillo, Y., & Hargrave, T. (2008). Strategies to prevent and heal the mental anguish caused by cyberbullying. *Middle School Journal*, *39*, 30–35.

Hinduja, S., & Patchin, J. W. (2009). *Bullying beyond the schoolyard: Preventing and responding to cyberbullying*. Thousand Oaks, CA: Corwin Press.

Juvonen, J., & Gross, E. F. (2008). Bullying experiences in cyberspace. *The Journal of School Health*, *78*, 496–505.

Kowalski, R. M., & Limber, S. P. (2007). Electronic bullying among middle school students. *Journal of Adolescent Health*, *41*, S22–S30.

Machmutow, K., Perren, S., Sticca, F., & Alsaker, F. D. (2012). Peer victimization and depressive symptoms: Can specific coping strategies buffer the negative impact on cybervictimization? *Emotional and Behavioural Difficulties*, *17*(3–4), 403–420.

Price, M., & Dalgleish, J. (2010). Cyberbullying: Experiences, impacts and coping strategies as described by Australian young people. *Youth Studies Australia*, *29*(2), 51–59.

Roberto, A. J., & Eden, J. (2010). Cyberbullying: Aggressive communication in the digital age. In T. A. Avtgis & A. S. Rancer (Eds.), *Arguments, aggression, and conflict: New directions in theory and research* (pp. 198–216). New York, NY: Routledge.

Roberto, A. J., Eden, J., Savage, M. W., Ramos-Salazar, L., & Deiss, D. M. (2014). Outcome evaluation results of school-based cybersafety promotion and cyberbullying prevention intervention for middle school students. *Health Communication*, *29*, 1029–1042. https://doi.org/10.1080/10410236.2013.831684.

Roberto, A. J., & Witte, K. (2010). Fear appeals. In S. Priest (Ed.), *Encyclopedia of science and technology communication* (pp. 295–298). Thousand Oaks, CA: Sage.

Runions, K. C. (2013). Toward a conceptual model of motive and self-control in cyber- aggression: Rage, revenge, reward, and recreation. *Journal of Youth & Adolescence*, *42*, 751–771. https://doi.org/10.1007/s10964-013-9936-2.

Selkie, E. M., Fales, J. L., & Moreno, M. A. (2016). Cyberbullying prevalence among US middle and high school-aged adolescents: A systematic review and quality assessment. *Journal of Adolescent Health*, *58*, 125–133. https://doi.org/10.1016/j.jadohealth.2015.09.026.

U.S. Department of Education, National Center for Education Statistics. (2016). Indicators of school crime and safety: 2015. NCES. Retrieved from https://nces.ed.gov/fastfacts/display.asp?id=719.

Witte, K. (1992). Putting the fear back into fear appeals: The extended parallel process model (EPPM). *Communication Monographs*, *59*, 329–349. https://doi.org/10.1080/03637759209376276.

Further reading

Bauman, S., & Belllmore, A. (2015). New directions in cyberbullying research. *Journal of School Violence*, *14*, 1–10. https://doi.org/10.1080/15388220.2014.968281.

Chibnall, S., Wallace, M., Leicht, C., & Lunghofer, L. (2006). i-Safe evaluation: Final report (research report no. 213715). Retrieved from National Criminal Justice Reference Service website: https://www.ncjrs.gov/pdffiles1/nij/grants/213715.pdf.

Craig, W. M., Pepler, D. J., & Shelley, D. (2004). *Summary of interventions to address bullying problems at school*. Queen's Park: Ontario Ministry of Education.

Davidson, J., Martellozzo, E., & Lorenz, M. (2009). Evaluation of CEOP ThinkUKnow Internet safety programme and exploration of young people's Internet safety knowledge (CATS report July 2009). Retrieved from Kingston University London, Centre for Abuse and Trauma Studies website: http://www.cats-rp.org.uk/pdf%20files/Internet%20safety%20report%204-2010.pdf.

Della Cioppa, V., O'Neil, A., & Craig, W. (2015). Learning from traditional bullying interventions: A review of research on cyberbullying and best practice. *Aggression and Violent Behavior*, *23*, 61–68.

Felix, E. D., Sharkey, J. D., Green, J. G., Furlong, M. J., & Tanigawa, D. (2011). Getting precise and pragmatic about the assessment of bullying: The development of the California Bullying Victimization Scale. *Aggressive Behavior*, *37*, 234–247. https://doi.org/10.1002/ab.20389.

Greenawalt, J. A. (2010). Review of cyber crime fighters: Tales from the trenches. *Activities, Adaptation, & Aging*, *34*, 165–166. https://doi.org/10.1080/01924781003793144.

Kite, S. L., Gable, R., & Filippelli, L. (2010). Assessing middle school students' knowledge of conduct and consequences and their behaviors regarding the use of social networking sites. *The Clearing House*, *83*, 158–163.

Kowalksi, R. M., & Limber, S. P. (2013). Psychological, physical, and academic correlates of cyberbullying and traditional bullying. *Journal of Adolescent Health*, *53*, S13–S20. https://doi.org/10.1016/j.jadohealth.2012.09.018.

Kowalski, R. M., Giumetti, G. W., Schroeder, A. N., & Lattanner, M. R. (2014). Bullying in the digital age: A critical review and meta-analysis of cyberbullying research among youth. *Psychological Bulletin*, *140*, 1073–1137.

Lenhart, A. (2015). Teens, social media & technology overview 2015. Retrieved from http://www.pewinternet.org/2015/04/09/teens-social-media-technology-2015/.

Li, Q. (2006). Cyberbullying in schools: A research of gender differences. *School Psychology International*, *27*, 157–170. https://doi.org/10.1177/0143034306064547.

Olweus, D. (1993). *Bullying at school: What we know and what we can do*. Cambridge, MA: Blackwell.

Olweus, D. (1994). Bullying at school: Basic facts and effects of a school based intervention program. *Journal of Child Psychology & Psychiatry & Allied Disciplines*, *35*, 1171–1190.

Olweus, D. (2003). A profile of bullying at school. *Educational Leadership*, *60*, 12–17.

Ortega-Ruiz, R., Del Rey, R., & Casas, J. A. (2012). Knowing, building and living together on Internet and social networks: The ConRed cyberbullying prevention program. *International Journal of Conflict and Violence*, *6*, 303–313.

Patchin, J., & Hinduja, S. (2006). Bullies move beyond the schoolyard: A preliminary look at cyberbullying. *Youth Violence and Juvenile Justice*, *4*, 148–169. https://doi.org/10.1177/1541204006286288.

Salmivalli, C. (2010). Bullying and the peer group: A review. *Aggression and Violent Behavior*, *15*, 112–120. https://doi.org/10.1016/j.avb.2009.08.007.

Schenk, A. M., Fremouw, W. J., & Keelan, C. M. (2013). Characteristics of college cyberbullies. *Computers in Human Behavior*, *29*, 2320–2327. https://doi.org/10.1016/j.chb.2013.05.013.

Smith, P. K., Mahdavi, J., Carvalho, M., Fisher, S., Russell, S., & Tippett, N. (2008). Cyberbullying: Its nature and impact in secondary school pupils. *Journal of Child Psychology and Psychiatry*, *49*, 376–385. https://doi.org/10.1111/j.1469-7610.2007.01846.x.

Studer, J. R., & Mynatt, B. S. (2015). Bullying prevention in middle schools: A collaborative approach. *Middle School Journal*, *1*, 25–32.

Tynes, B. M. (2007). Internet safety gone wild? Sacrificing the educational and psychosocial benefits of online social environments. *Journal of Adolescent Research*, *22*, 575–584. https://doi.org/10.1177/0743558407303979.

Varjas, K., Henrich, C. C., & Meyers, J. (2009). Urban middle school students' perceptions of bullying, cyberbullying, and school safety. *Journal of School Violence*, *8*, 159–176. https://doi.org/10.1080/15388220802074165.

Willard, N. E. (2007). *Cyberbullying and cyberthreats: Responding to the challenge of online social aggression, threats, and distress*. Champaign, IL: Research Press.

Williford, A., Elledge, L. C., Boulton, A. J., DePaolis, K. J., Little, T. D., & Salmivalli, C. (2013). Effects of the KiVa antibullying program on cyberbullying and cybervictimization frequency among Finnish youth. *Journal of Clinical Child & Adolescent Psychology*, *42*, 820–833. https://doi.org/10.1080/15374416.2013.787623.

Part Three

Reflections

Commentary: Ways of preventing cyberbullying and evidence-based practice

19

Peter K. Smith
Goldsmiths, University of London, London, England

The 20th century has seen an explosion of use of the internet. This has transformed the lives of children and adults. Much of this has been beneficial, enriching our lives and widening our opportunities. But the dark side of the internet—cyberbullying and harassment, trolling, grooming—has grown alongside this. These negative aspects can disproportionately affect children and young people. Preadolescent children lack some wider knowledge of the world that may give adults some protection, and adolescents may have more knowledge but are also more likely to engage in risk-taking behaviors as they seek to explore the virtual as well as the real world, and to impress others as they seek peer status.

Much concern has focused around the concept of cyberbullying. Issues around definition are discussed in Chapter 1 of this book, and clearly there are both more narrow and more broad definitions that may affect the kinds of prevalence rates reported. But however defined, research on cyberbullying has increased exponentially over the last decade (Smith & Berkkun, 2017; Zych, Ortega-Ruiz, & del Rey, 2015). In a sample of studies abstracted in Web of Science, Zych et al. found the earliest articles on cyberbullying in 2003, with just 4 articles before 2006. Of 72 articles sampled (as the most cited) between 2006 and 2013, most were on the nature and dynamics of cyberbullying, and related variables; none were scored in the prevention and intervention category.

Smith and Berkkun (2017) also used articles abstracted in Web of Science, but scored all articles on cyberbullying (from the Abstracts), using keywords cyber* and bully*; cyber* and victim*; electronic bullying; internet bullying; and online harassment; they also extended the search up through 2015. From 2000 to 2015 they found 538 abstracts, averaging 33.6 per year. From 2000 to 2006, there was a small trickle of articles (range: 0–5 per year); from 2007 to 2011, a substantial but still modest number of articles (range: 14–38 per year); but from 2012 on, a very large number of articles (range: 85–131 per year). The year 2015 saw 131 articles, meaning about 2.5 new articles every week.

Of all these articles, the great majority ($n = 454$) provided original empirical data. Of these, 39, or some 9%, had a focus on resources for dealing with cyberbullying, or on interventions to reduce or prevent it. Although not documented quantitatively, this appears to be increasing further, with for example chapters in the volume edited by Völlink, Dehue and McGuckin (2016), and a special issue of *Aggressive Behavior* 42(2), 2016, devoted to such interventions; and of course this present volume.

Reducing Cyberbullying in Schools. https://doi.org/10.1016/B978-0-12-811423-0.00019-5

Resources and interventions to reduce traditional or offline bullying go back to the 1980s, with a great deal of work done in the 1990s and 2000s (Olweus, 2013; Smith, Pepler, & Rigby, 2004; Ttofi & Farrington, 2011). The efforts to counter cyberbullying are naturally much more recent but now growing fast. Can we expect this to have an impact?

Are rates of bullying and cyberbullying getting better or worse?

The Health Behaviour in School-aged Children (HBSC) surveys have provided data on incidence rates of being bullied and bullying others, at four-year intervals since the 1990s. Molcho et al. (2009) presented trends over time, between 1993/1994 and 2005/2006. Decreases were observed in the majority of the 27 countries for which there were data over all the time points. The most striking finding was for chronic bullying of others; the country average fell from 19.3% in 1993/1994, to 16.1% in 1997/1998, 11.1% in 2001/2002, and 10.6% in 2005/2006; on a larger set of countries, this figure fell further from 10.7% in 2005/2006 to 10.1% in 2009/2010. It does appear to have risen slightly in 2013/14, this being the first survey to include questions on cvberbullying.

Apart from the HBSC surveys, Rigby and Smith (2011) reviewed findings from independent studies in England, Wales, Finland, and Australia. These too generally supported evidence for a decline. Another example comes from Waasdorp, Pas, Zablotsky and Bradshaw (2017), who reported ten-year trends from 109 schools in Maryland, USA. Between 2005 and 2014, many bullying indicators showed a fairly steady decline over this period. For example, reports of being victimized showed a drop from 28.5% in 2005 to 13.4% in 2014. Reports of having witnessed bullying showed a monotonic decline every year from 66.4% in 2005 to 42.7% in 2014.

Given that we know that antibullying interventions generally have some, albeit partial, success (Ttofi & Farrington, 2011), it is plausible that increased awareness and implementation of antibullying interventions has helped produce this decline. However as of yet, the evidence mainly concerns traditional bullying. There is much less evidence for a decline in cyberbullying, and some evidence of an increase.

Obviously cyberbullying increased as the relevant technology has become more and more accessible in the early years of this century. Jones, Mitchell and Finkelhor (2012) reported data from Youth Internet Safety Surveys in the USA conducted in 1999–2000, 2005 and 2010. The data closest to cyberbullying are that on internet harassment; the surveys showed an increase in this from 6% to 9% and then 11%, this being more marked for girls. A composite measure of amount of internet use increased from .24 to .41 and then .49 over the three time points.

Olweus (2012) reported data from a very large US sample from 2007 to 2010; no systematic time trends were found, although if anything the trend is slightly upward. The Maryland study by Waasdorp et al. (2017) included data specifically on cyberbullying. Whereas most bullying measures showed a nearly or perfectly monotonic yearly decline over the period 2005–14, the data on being victimized by cyberbullying appear to show a more curvilinear trend, with an increase in the first half of the period (up to 2010) before a decrease in the second half.

Olweus (2012) also analyzed data from 41 Norwegian schools for 2006–10, and again found little systematic trend, although if anything the direction is slightly downward. In Europe more widely, the EU Kids online study (Livingstone et al., 2011) carried out surveys in 2010 of children aged 9–16 years, in 25 European countries; a follow-up in seven countries from 2010 to 2013/14 has suggested some rise in cyberbullying, especially for girls, from around 7% to 12% (Hasebrink, 2014).

In summary, there is good evidence that in many countries rates of involvement in traditional bullying have declined over the last 10 or 20 years. There is much less evidence about cyberbullying involvement; but it clearly increased in the early years of this century, and has proliferated into different forms as the proportion of students having access to mobile phones and the internet increased. This penetration may now be approaching saturation in many communities; there is mixed evidence about whether rates of cyberbullying are continuing to rise, are rather stable, or may even be declining in some studies.

A fundamental aim of cyberbullying research should be to help design effective ways of reducing cyberbullying and the harm it causes. The apparent partial success in tackling traditional bullying, and the mixed picture regarding cyberbullying, points to the need to develop (or continue developing) resources and intervention strategies further for cyberbullying, as has been done for traditional bullying. This book brings together an important and diverse set of such attempts.

Interventions can vary along various dimensions. One dimension is technological versus relationship oriented. A second is general (bullying) versus specific (cyberbullying). A third is where interventions focus on an ecological dimension from individual to small group to institution to society.

Technological versus relationship oriented interventions

As posed very clearly in Chapter 3, technological interventions aim to make bullying or cyberbullying more difficult to do, or the costs more obvious. They do not directly tackle the relationship issues thought to underlie bullying, in a way that many other interventions (for example all those described for traditional bullying in Chapter 2) do. Chapter 3 gives an excellent overview of such interventions for cyberbullying, while also pointing out the paucity of evaluation of such measures. However, there is no reason to suppose that they could not be implemented together with relationship-based measures. Also, as Chapter 6 makes clear, technological approaches such as online social marketing can tackle relationship issues such as empathic attitudes. Another example is the text-messaging program BullyDown for bullying generally (Ybarra, Prescott, & Espelage, 2016).

Legal measures are not technological, but can also be seen as not concerned with relationships *per se*, but as signaling the wrongness of cyberbullying and making some form of negative outcome for perpetrators more likely. Chapter 4 sets out some important issues regarding legal approaches, especially in Australia, the UK and the

USA. Again, we know little of how effective legal approaches really are, but there are a couple of studies from the USA. Hatzenbuehler et al. (2015) compared 25 states, and (after partialing out some confounding factors) found that having some legislative component to antibullying laws was associated with reduced rates of being both bullied and cyberbullied. This was a cross-sectional study, but Ramirez et al. (2016) using a more longitudinal design, examined rates of being bullied in the US state of Iowa in 2005 (just before an antibullying law was introduced), 2008, and 2010. They found an increase in rates of being bullied in 2008, possibly due to increased reporting, but then a decrease by 2010. However, being cyberbullied (one of four aspects of being bullied, and the least frequent) did not decrease by 2010. While both these studies have drawbacks, they are a beginning to evaluating the impact of legal measures.

Specialized versus generalized interventions

Should resources and interventions be targeted very specifically for cyberbullying, or can we rely on those devised for bullying generally, or even specifically for offline bullying (see Chapter 2), to generalize? The chapters in this book present a range of actions along this dimension. Purely technical actions, as exemplified in Chapter 3, can be for bullying or cyberbullying; and similarly many countries have laws about bullying or harassment generally, but there is also discussion of laws specifically on cyberbullying, as demonstrated in Chapter 4. Again there are many curricular resources for bullying, but specific curricula for cyberbullying, for example e-safety teaching, can be utilized, for example Chapter 11. This can include specific coping strategies for dealing with cyberbullying. All these resources may be rather specific to cyberbullying, or part of a more general curricula approach, such as social and emotional learning and general anti-bullying prevention work.

MARC (Chapter 8) has material on bullying generally, but also (especially for older students) more specialized curricula material on cyberbullying. NoTrap! (Chapter 10) has both general bullying and specific cyberbullying elements. Cyber-Friendly Schools (Chapter 7) has many components specifically on cyberbullying, but also material on bullying generally.

ConRed (Chapter 15) focuses mainly on cyberbullying, including e-safety and relationship education (*convivencia*). MediaHeroes (Chapter 11) mainly focuses on cyberbullying, as does the IMB model (Chapter 17) and EPPM model (Chapter 18) interventions, with curricula material on cyberbullying.

Stop Online Bullies (Chapter 13) specifically argues for the advantages of targeting both traditional and cyberbullying. In fact, we know that there is considerable overlap between pupil involvement in traditional and cyberbullying (Modecki et al., 2014; and Chapter 1). This means we can expect interventions primarily focused on traditional bullying to have some positive effects in reducing cyberbullying as well. Just such carryover effects have been reported for the KiVa program in Finland (Williford et al., 2013; and Chapter 7), and for the ViSC Social Competence Program in Austria (Gradinger et al., 2016; and Chapter 14). For example, both general empathy training and modifying beliefs supportive of aggression could be helpful in reducing all kinds of bullying including cyberbullying (Ang, 2015). However, resources and interventions tailored more specifically for cyberbullying are very likely to be important too. It is worth noting that the KiVa program does include some specific cyberbullying elements in its curricula work (Chapter 9). Interestingly, MediaHeroes (Chapter 11) is much more specifically on cyberbullying, but has carryover effects for traditional bullying.

An ecological perspective

Another dimension to consider comes from the ecological perspective (Cross et al., 2015; Hong & Espelage, 2012). Moving outward from the center of Bronfenbrenner's model, we can consider the individual, his/her immediate social groups (parents, siblings, teachers, peers), the school, the community, and the wider society. Cross et al. (2015) extend this model by introducing online influences between peer and community level. A whole-school approach (e.g., Chapter 7, Chapter 8) can embrace much of this. Several aspects are covered for example in NoTrap! (Chapter 10; whole school, peers, and individuals) and in Media Heroes (Chapter 11; individual, class and parents).

Interventions at the level of individual factors would include attempts to enhance social skills and empathy, and reduce moral disengagement, as is aimed for in many curriculum interventions; and also to improve coping strategies for victims, as for example in NoTrap! (Chapter 10) and + *Fort* (Chapter 12).

Considering the immediate social group, family (parents and siblings) are clearly important. Parent-child and sibling relationships affect the likelihood of being involved in bully or victim roles (Lereya et al., 2013; Wolke et al., 2015); and parents also have an important role in working with schools, supporting antibullying initiatives, and liaising with schools if they have concerns about a child's behavior (Axford et al., 2015). Given that much cyberbullying is initiated outside school, they also have a particular, but difficult, role in discussing e-safety and cyberbullying issues with their children, giving guidance on acceptable internet practice, and being involved without being overly restrictive (Sasson & Mesch, 2014). Chapter 5 lays out important issues around parental roles regarding cyberbullying.

Chapter 7 provides an example of a parent component as part of a whole-school approach. Interestingly it suggests that the often-touted digital divide may be beginning to lessen, in some respects at least, as incoming generations of parents are more internet aware. Nevertheless, the authors point to important misconceptions that parents may have about the risks their child may be taking and how best to deal with them. In this respect, more parental guidance continues to have an important role. Intergenerational collaboration is an important aspect in the Smartphone Summit approach in Japan (Chapter 16) (with adults sometimes learning from children). There are parent components in Media Heroes (Chapter 11) and the EPPM model intervention (Chapter 18).

An under-researched area appears to be the role of siblings in cyberbullying. We know something of the importance of siblings in bullying generally (Wolke et al., 2015), but not in cyberbullying specifically. Do siblings share experiences on the internet? Do they cyberbully each other? Or do they support each other if one is experiencing cyberbullying? And what variables (such as age gap, gender) affect these?

Within the school teachers have an influential role, especially at primary ages. So far as general bullying is concerned, we know that teacher aspects such as openness in communication, and perceived importance of bullying, are important predictors of success in the Olweus Bullying Prevention Program (Olweus, 2004); and in KiVa, the general pupil perception of homeroom teacher's attitude to bullying was a significant predictor of levels of victimization (Saarento et al., 2013). The MARC (Chapter 8), KiVa (Chapter 9), and ViSC (Chapter 14) programs emphasize teacher training components.

Perhaps even more important than family and teachers by secondary school age is the peer group. We know the importance of class norms (descriptive and injunctive) about bullying (Saarento et al., 2013); the protective effect of a friend who is able to protect a victim (Fox & Boulton, 2006), and that bystander intervention can be increased (Polanin, Espelage, & Pigott, 2012) and can be effective especially if defenders have high status in the peer group (Caravita et al., 2009). This knowledge is built on in KiVa (Chapter 9), and bystanders' responsibility is also emphasized in NoTrap! (Chapter 10). Peers can also act as mentors and this is an aspect of MARC (Chapter 8).

Many interventions at the individual and peer group level may have positive effects at the school level, as assessed for example by school climate measures. For example, peer support schemes may often have limited effects on victim rates (Flygare, Gill & Johansson, 2013; Ttofi & Farrington, 2011) but do appear to improve school climate (Cowie & Smith, 2010). Between school studies have found links of school climate to bullying rates (e.g., Elgar et al., 2009). There is also an obvious need to ensure that cyberbullying is explicitly included in school antibullying policies (Smith et al., 2012).

Although interventions are mainly school based and focus on individual, family, peer group, and whole-school aspects, wider aspects in the ecological model are important. Considering online level influences (Cross et al., 2015), social media companies and internet service providers are under pressure to do more to enhance internet safety and reporting of abuse (Chapter 3; and Coyne & Gountsidou, 2013).

The media generally often show violence, and some studies have established links between violent media exposure, and involvement in bullying or cyberbullying. For example, Calvete, Orue, Estévez, Villardón, and Padilla (2010) in Spain, Fanti, Demetriou and Hawa (2012) in Cyprus, and den Hamer, Konijn and Keijer (2014) in the Netherlands all found links from violent media exposure (on television, internet, movies, video games), to both cyberbullying and cybervictimization. den Hamer et al. (2014) supported a "Cyclic Process" model that adolescent victims of (mainly traditional) bullying feel anger and frustration, they may then tend to use violent media more, as a way of coping with or finding outlets for their anger feelings, and that this exposure in itself may lead to cyberbullying behaviors, for example through desensitization, imitation, or modeling of action scripts. The model is "cyclic" because the cyberbullying might then increase the chances of being a victim again.

How cyberbullying is portrayed in the media (such as newspapers) may also be important. Vandebosch et al. (2013) analyzed 1599 newspaper articles from 8 countries, over the period 2004–11, which covered cyberbullying. While raising awareness of the topic is vitally important, these authors also pointed out the dangers of creating a "moral panic," and the difficulties in achieving balanced reporting on the issue.

At the community level, there is evidence that levels of neighborhood violence may change normative beliefs about aggression, as shown in a US study by Schwartz and Proctor (2000). Children who had witnessed community violence were more likely to be aggressive to classmates; and those who had been victims of community violence were more likely to be victims at school as well. A study in Colombia by Chaux, Molano and Podlesky (2009) also related violence at the municipality level, as well as poverty and inequality, to bullying involvement. These studies did not explicitly study cyberbullying, but given the high overlap between online and offline bullying, may well be relevant.

At the society level, issues regarding legal provisions have already been discussed (Chapter 4). However, we also know that factors such as country wealth and distribution of wealth may be important (at least for traditional bullying). Research comparing countries (using for example HBSC data) has found that income inequality, as a measure of power differentials between those who have access to resources and those who do not, is a strong predictor of country differences in bullying involvement (Chaux et al., 2009; Due et al., 2009; Elgar et al., 2009). Elgar et al. (2009) argued that "it is possible that redistributing wealth and creating more egalitarian societies would do more for reducing bullying than school-level policies or individual-level intervention" (p. 358). However, such political change may be even more difficult to achieve than changes at lower levels in the ecological model.

Sample characteristics

Should interventions be tailored to individual characteristics, or to sample characteristics such as age, gender, disability, or culture? The most effective might be tailoring to the individual circumstances of the young person, but this is obviously difficult for school or class based interventions. However, it was done in the Stop Online Bullies' (Chapter 13) project, which was adult-free, with a computer program adjusted to the pupil's level of knowledge and skills. This was also for low academically achieving pupils, but unfortunately perhaps because of this, the program lacked sustainability through repeat visits. Some element of tailoring was also present in ConRed (Chapter 15), and at the workshop level, in the IMB model intervention (Chapter 17).

Age is an important factor in bullying intervention research, with most programs showing less effectiveness in secondary compared to primary school ages (Yeager et al., 2015). For example, KiVa has been found to be more effective with younger pupils (Chapter 9). Nevertheless, and appropriately given a somewhat shifted age curve for cyber compared to face-to-face bullying (Kowalski et al., 2014), many of the interventions in this volume target secondary school students; NoTrap! (Chapter 10), Media Heroes (Chapter 11), *+Fort* (Chapter 12), Stop Online Bullies (Chapter 13), ViSC (Chapter 14), and the IMB model intervention (Chapter 17). Interestingly, the IMB model intervention found more effect on risk perception at higher grades. In contrast to age, there has been less discussion of gender as an issue. Tailoring by gender would anyway be difficult in mixed-sex schools (it would be less difficult in, for example, India, where many classes are sex segregated; Schäfer et al., 2018). By and large, different rates of effectiveness were not expected by gender. This was explicitly found in NoTrap! (Chapter 10), and was also the case in the Cyberprogram 2.0 intervention reported by Garaigordobil and Martinez-Valderrey (2016).

Interventions may also work differently, in different cultures. We know there are considerable differences in bullying rates between different countries, even if these are difficult to measure reliably (Smith, Robinson, & Marchi, 2016). Following the EU Kids online model (Livingstone & Helsper, 2013), these might be explained by factors such as cultural values, education system, technological infrastructure, regulatory framework, and socioeconomic stratification. Besides differences in prevalence, there may be differences in what is considered to be bullying, the types of bullying that occur, attitudes to bullying and seeking help (e.g., Smith, Kwak, & Toda, 2016), and even issues affecting assessments such as social desirability and reference group effects (Guillaume & Funder, 2016).

The interventions described in this book are mostly from western countries, although the Smartphone Summit was in Japan (Chapter 16) and the IMB model intervention in South Africa (Chapter 17). Interventions are also developed within one cultural setting. Translating an intervention from one country to another can be problematic; for example, the OBPP has been very successful in Norway but less so in the USA (Smith, 2014). Nevertheless, some interventions have been tried elsewhere with some success, for example KiVa in Italy (Nocentini & Menesini, 2016) and several other countries, ViSC (Chapter 14) in three other countries (though with more mixed success than in Austria), and MediaHeroes (Chapter 11) is being tested elsewhere. The kinds of issues (such as cultural values) that affect differences in prevalence and attitudes may have implications for certain components of interventions. For example, it is interesting that getting pupils to take part in a sequence of voluntary activities was achieved successfully in a collectivist country such as Japan (Smartphone Summit. Chapter 16) but much less so in a more individualist society, Belgium (Stop Online Bullies, Chapter 13).

Some issues in intervention research

A couple of distinctive issues come from reading the chapters in this collection. One is the idea of "pupil voice" or pupil participation in the intervention. The other is the role of theory in designing interventions.

Pupil voice: "Don't do it about us, without us" is a slogan heard in relation to involving pupils in meaningful ways in designing and implementing interventions. There are various ways of doing this, and a number are exemplified in this collection. In Chapter 6 we see young people involved in design of online social marketing. In Cyber-Friendly Schools (Chapter 7), student cyberleaders develop activities. In NoTrap! (Chapter 10), peer educators play an important role. Children decide the topic initiative in Smartphone Summit (Chapter 16); and pupils advise one another in the EPPM model intervention (Chapter 17). Another example of pupil participation is in the Cross-Age teaching Zone (CATZ) model, in which 11-year-old students acted as e-safety tutors for 9 year olds (Boulton et al., 2016).

Role of theory: some interventions have relatively unarticulated theoretical backgrounds. As noted, a background philosophy is often to intervene at various levels on the ecological model, and to increase awareness and empathy, change attitudes, and change behavior. One theoretical background to bullying intervention was proposed by Hawley and Williford (2015). They used Ajzen's Theory of Planned Behavior to advocate changes in *perceptions* (for example of what bullying is), *attitudes* (about bullying behavior and toward victims; reporting bullying and intervening), *subjective norms* (how do others think or expect I should behave?), and *efficacy beliefs* (feeling confident that actions such as reporting or defending will be successful and not result in negative consequences) in order to achieve desired changes in actual *behaviors*. In addition, they took ideas from organizational science to argue the necessity of targeting these with pupils, teachers, and other staff in the school or relevant to the school, in order to change school culture and school climate.

This is an ambitious blueprint, but some of the interventions in this book go some way toward this, using the same or similar theoretical models. The Ajzen Theory of Reasoned Action/Planned Behavior is invoked in MediaHeroes (Chapter 11). A theory of normative social behavior is used in ConRed (Chapter 15). An Information-Motivation-Behavioral (IMB) Skills' model is adopted in Chapter 17, and an Extended Parallel Process model (EPPM) in Chapter 18. These all target some aspects of attitudes, norms, intentions, self-efficacy, and behavior. From a somewhat different perspective, REBT is used in Stop Online Bullies (Chapter 13).

Implementation and evaluation

There are a range of issues to be considered in the actual implementation of interventions, and their evaluation (see for example Ryan & Smith, 2009). Here I consider aspects under four main headings: Feasibility (can you do it?); Fidelity (is it done?); Follow-up or sustainability (will it continue to be done?); and Efficacy (does it work?).

Feasibility: the ecological model, and the theoretical rationale proposed by Hawley and Williford (2015), suggest that a successful intervention will be multifaceted in terms of various target groups and outcome objectives. This could involve a major investment of time and resources. Even if feasible in an experimental study, can this be subsequently generalized to other schools without intensive input from researchers? Perhaps the best example of this so far is the KiVa program, which has been taken up by most schools in Finland. This has however been enabled by substantial financial support from the Finnish Ministry of Education and Culture (Chapter 9).

Some examples are much more modest, and consequently less costly to implement, but generally have more limited targets or outcome objectives. For example, the IMB model intervention (Chapter 17) has one 50-min workshop, with a main outcome of changing pupil risk perception. Similarly, the EPPM model intervention (Chapter 18) has one 45-min session. Stop Online Bullies (Chapter 13) has low cost as a standalone procedure (not needing adult guidance), but this in itself may have contributed to a large dropout rate over sessions (especially for low academically achieving young people). *+Fort* (Chapter 12) uses a mobile app (focused on coping strategies), which can be downloaded for free.

Another way to increase feasibility is to employ some kind of "train the trainer" or cascade model of introducing the intervention. MARC (Chapter 8) and MediaHeroes (Chapter 11) used train the trainer in this way, and ViSC (Chapter 14) used a cascade model for teacher training.

Smartphone Summit (Chapter 16) used a cascade model for dissemination by children.

Fidelity: How well are program interventions followed? For bullying generally, this issue was highlighted by Flygare, Gill and Johansson (2013). They found that in Sweden, bully intervention programs were implemented such that components were mixed from more than one program. Rather than evaluating programs they switched to evaluating components. This is an endemic problem. In Cyber-Friendly Schools (Chapter 7), only about one-third of the intervention was implemented by classroom teachers, In Kiva, schools varied greatly in implementation; in primary schools, teachers delivered on average 8.7 out of 10 lessons in the initial RCT trial, but this fell to 7.8 during the first year of the national rollout, and to 7.2 in the second year (Salmivalli & Poskiparta, 2012).

Fidelity does appear to be important. In Kiva, it correlated with victim and bully reductions (Salmivalli & Poskiparta, 2012). In the OBPP, it was an important predictor of success (Olweus, 2004). The ViSC project (Chapter 14) found more effects on teachers who implemented the program with greater fidelity.

Follow-up, Sustainability: Do programs continue effectively once the researchers have left?

Schober et al. (2016) emphasized the importance of implementation research to connect with intervention research and to work with policy makers and practitioners from the start; ViSC being an example of this. Indeed ViSC (Chapter 14) reported continuing positive effects of the intervention at follow-up.

Efficacy: How well do interventions actually work? In order to ascertain this, the Randomized Control Trial (RCT) has been seen as the gold standard, in terms of ruling out most alternative explanations for findings. Many reports in this book have used RCT at some level: Cyber-Friendly Schools (Chapter 7), KiVa (Chapter 9) in their initial study, and ViSC (Chapter 14) used RCTs by random assignment of schools; MediaHeroes (Chapter 11) and the IMB model intervention (Chapter 17) used RCT by random assignment of classes; and Stop Online Bullies (Chapter 13) planned RCT by random assignment at the individual level but was unable to complete this due to heavy dropout. RCTs are indeed likely to be the most convincing, but they are not without problems, including how natural (and ethical) it is to require schools to follow an experimental or control procedure that they might not have followed if given free choice.

Sometimes RCTs are not feasible for such practical reasons. It is then possible to use an experimental/control pre/post-test design, which is still very effective at ruling out alternative explanations of effects if initial differences between experimental and control groups are taken account of. Such nonrandomized designs were employed by NoTrap! (Chapter 10), +*Fort* (Chapter 12), and ConRed (Chapter 15). The IMB model intervention (Chapter 17) also compared experimental and control classes.

Even if there are no control schools, evaluation of an intervention can be made using an Extended Selection Cohorts' design (comparing same-age children who have not or have experienced the intervention, in successive years). This controls for age effects, but not history effects (Smith, 2014). This has been used in OBPP evaluations, and for the KiVa nationwide rollout of the program (when control schools were not so feasible). In addition, given imperfect fidelity of implementation, the correlation of fidelity with outcome, or the dosage-response relationship, can also inform on the effects of intervention.

Finally, "softer" evaluation procedures can be employed and still give useful information, albeit not so convincing as those given earlier. These can include more qualitative assessments, for example of how the implementation was perceived by stakeholders. The Smartphone Summit (Chapter 16) is an example of this. However, qualitative methods can be combined powerfully with quantitative methods to give more insight into process (Ryan & Smith, 2009). MARC (Chapter 8) mixed qualitative and quantitative methods in a quasiexperimental design, and +*Fort* (Chapter 12) and Stop Online Bullies (Chapter 13) used both qualitative and quantitative evaluations.

Clearly the most desired for outcomes are changes in behaviors, but changes in knowledge and attitudes, empathy and feelings of efficacy, may be way stations toward this (Hawley & Williford, 2015). Positive effects on attitudes as well as behavior were reported in KiVa (Chapter 9), on awareness, empathy and behavior in NoTrap! (Chapter 10), and on empathy, and cyberbulling perpetration (but not cybervictimization) in Media Heroes (Chapter 11). MARC (Chapter 8) reports more on knowledge and attitudes than on behaviors.

A related issue is who are the informants for the outcomes. Ryan and Smith (2009) advocated a multi-informant assessment; for example, self, peers, and teachers. Cyber-Friendly Schools (Chapter 7) provides an example of multiple informants (students, including cyberleaders, and school staff).

Generally, outcomes reported are positive, or else nonsignificant. However, the possibility of iatrogenic effects (negative effects resulting from the intervention) have to be faced. Some interventions could be counterproductive. An example is some kinds of peer support (Cowie & Smith, 2010; Flygare et al., 2013) which may be stigmatizing either of those who seek support (e.g., buddy bus stops) or of peer supporters themselves (e.g., uniforms that can be made fun of). Other examples might be certain kinds of social skills' training, which might simply enhance the skills put to negative ends by bullies; or encouraging victims to tell about bullying without effective follow-up.

Cost effectiveness: Even if an intervention is demonstrated to have effectiveness in terms of desired outcomes, whether it will be more widely adopted is likely to depend on how cost effective it is. This links to issues of feasibility discussed earlier, but also takes account of quantifying the benefits of the intervention. If bullying is reduced, then fewer pupils are likely to have mental health problems, and more are likely to live productive lives. Persson and Svensson (2013), and Beckman and Svensson (2015), considered the costs of two Swedish antibullying programs, Friends, and the OBPP; and weighed them against actual costs of court settlements brought by individuals against schools or education authorities for being bullied in school; and to a survey of what taxpayers were prepared to pay to reduce school bullying. On these measures, the programs were deemed to be cost effective.

Summary

Antibullying interventions have a history of some 30 years, but those targeted at or to include cyberbullying have a history of only a few years. This volume illustrates a range of attempts to tackle it. The diversity of approaches is, at this stage, to be welcomed. The interventions described have varying levels of ambition, and varying levels of success. Interventions that are wider in scope are likely to be more successful, but may also be more costly. Among a range of issues brought forward for consideration in this chapter, the cost effectiveness of interventions deserves more scrutiny if we hope to have a wide take-up as well as a useful impact. Also, the issue of pupil voice, or pupil participation in designing interventions, may be particularly relevant for cyberbullying. Our challenge is to further develop and refine a range of approaches and resources so that young people can be safer in cyberspace.

References

Ang, R. P. (2015). Adolescent cyberbullying: A review of characteristics, prevention and intervention strategies. *Aggression and Violent Behavior*, *25*, 35–42.

Axford, N., Farrington, D. P., Clarkson, S., Bjornstad, G. J., Wrigley, Z., & Hutchings, J. (2015). Involving parents in school-based programmes to prevent and reduce bullying: what effect does it have? *Journal of Children's Services*, *10*, 242–251. https://doi.org/10.1108/jcs-05-2015-0019.

Beckman, L., & Svensson, M. (2015). The cost-effectiveness of the Olweus Bullying Prevention Program: Results from a modeling study. *Journal of Adolescence*, *45*, 127–139. https://doi.org/10.1016/j.adolescence.2015.07.020.

Boulton, M. J., Boulton, L., Camerone, E., Down, J., Hughes, J., Kirkbride, C., … Sanders, J. (2016). Enhancing primary school children's knowledge of online safety and risks with the CATZ cooperative cross-age teaching intervention: Results from a pilot study. *Cyberpsychology, Behavior, and Social Networking*, *19*, 609–614. https://doi.org/10.1089/cyber.2016.0046.

Calvete, E., Orue, I., Estévez, A., Villardón, L., & Padilla, P. (2010). Cyberbullying in adolescents: Modalities and aggressors' profile. *Computers in Human Behavior*, *26*, 1128–1135. https://doi.org/10.1016/j.chb.2010.03.017.

Caravita, S., DiBlasio, P., & Salmivalli, C. (2009). Unique and interactive effects of empathy and social status on involvement in bullying. *Social Development*, *18*, 140–163. https://doi.org/10.1111/j.1467-9507.2008.00465.x.

Chaux, E., Molano, A., & Podlesky, P. (2009). Socio-economic, socio-political and socio-emotional variables explaining school bullying: A country-wide multilevel analysis. *Aggressive Behavior*, *35*, 520–529. https://doi.org/10.1002/ab.20320.

Cowie, H., & Smith, P. K. (2010). Peer support as a means of improving school safety and reducing bullying and violence. In B. Doll, W. Pfohl, & J. Yoon (Eds.), *Handbook of youth prevention science* (pp. 177–193). New York: Routledge.

Coyne, I., & Gountsidou, V. (2013). The role of the industry in reducing cyberbullying. In P. K. Smith & G. Steffgen (Eds.), *Cyberbullying through the new media: Findings from an international network* (pp. 83–98). Hove: Psychology Press.

Cross, D., Barnes, A., Papageorgiou, A., Hadwen, K., Hearn, L., & Lester, L. (2015). A socio-ecological framework for understanding and reducing cyberbullying behaviours. *Aggression and Violent Behavior, 23,* 109–117. https://doi.org/10.1016/j.avb.2015.05.016.

den Hamer, A., Konijn, E. A., & Keijer, M. G. (2014). Cyberbullying behavior and adolescents' use of medias with antisocial content: A cyclic process model. *Cyberpsychology, Behavior, and Social Networking, 17,* 74–81. https://doi.org/10.1089/cyber.2012.0307.

Due, P., Merlo, J., & Harel-Fisch, Y. (2009). Socioeconomic inequality in exposure to bullying during adolescence: a comparative, cross-sectional, multilevel study in 35 countries. *American Journal of Public Health, 99,* 907–914. https://doi.org/10.2105/ajph.2008.139303.

Elgar, F. J., Craig, W., Boyce, W., Morgan, A., & Vella-Zarb, R. (2009). Income inequality and school bullying: Multilevel study of adolescents in 37 countries. *Journal of Adolescent Health, 45,* 351–359. https://doi.org/10.1016/j.jadohealth.2009.04.004.

Fanti, K. A., Demetriou, A. G., & Hawa, V. V. (2012). A longitudinal study of cyberbullying: Examining risk and protective factors. *European Journal of Developmental Psychology, 9,* 168–181. https://doi.org/10.1080/17405629.2011.643169.

Flygare, E., Gill, P. E., & Johansson, B. (2013). Lessons from a concurrent evaluation of eight antibullying programs used in Sweden. *American Journal of Evaluation, 34,* 170–189. https://doi.org/10.1177/1098214012471886.

Fox, C. L., & Boulton, M. J. (2006). Friendship as a moderator of the relationship between social skills problems and peer victimisation. *Aggressive Behavior, 32,* 110–121. https://doi.org/10.1002/ab.20114.

Garaigordobil, M., & Martinez-Valderrey, V. (2016). Impact of Cyberprogram 2.0 on different types of school violence and aggressiveness. *Frontiers in Psychology, 7.* https://doi.org/10.3389/fpsyg.2016.00428. article 428.

Gradinger, P., Yanagida, T., Strohmeier, D., & Spiel, C. (2016). Effectiveness and sustainability of the ViSC social competence program to prevent cyberbullying and cyber-victimization: Class and individual level moderators. *Aggressive Behavior, 42*(2), 181–193. https://doi.org/10.1002/ab.21631.

Guillaume, E., & Funder, D. (2016). Theoretical and methodological issues in making cross-national and cross-cultural comparisons. In P. K. Smith, K. Kwak, & Y. Toda (Eds.), *School bullying in different cultures: Eastern and western perspectives* (pp. 211–228). Cambridge: Cambridge University Press.

Hasebrink, U. (2014). *Children's changing online experiences in a longitudinal perspective.* www.eukidsonline.net.

Hatzenbuehler, M. L., Schwab-Reese, L., Ranapurwala, S. I., Hertz, M. F., & Ramirez, M. R. (2015). Associations between antibullying policies and bullying in 25 states. *JAMA Pediatrics, 169*(10), e152411https://doi.org/10.1001/jamapediatrics.2015.2411.

Hawley, P. H., & Williford, A. (2015). Articulating the theory of bullying intervention programs: Views from social psychology, social work, and organizational science. *Journal of Applied Developmental Psychology, 37,* 3–15. https://doi.org/10.1016/j.appdev.2014.11.006.

Hong, J. S., & Espelage, D. L. (2012). A review of research on bullying and victimization in school: An ecological system analysis. *Aggression and Violent Behavior, 176,* 311–322. https://doi.org/10.1016/j.avb.2012.03.003.

Jones, L. M., Mitchell, K. J., & Finkelhor, D. (2012). Trends in youth internet victimization: Findings from three youth internet safety surveys 2000–2010. *Journal of Adolescent Health, 50,* 179–186. https://doi.org/10.1016/j.jadohealth.2011.09.015.

Kowalski, R. M., Giumetti, G. W., Schroeder, A. N., & Lattanner, M. R. (2014). Bullying in the digital age: A critical review and meta-analysis of cyberbullying research among youth. *Psychological Bulletin, 140,* 1073–1137. https://doi.org/10.1037/a0035618.

Lereya, S. T., Samara, M., & Wolke, D. (2013). Parenting behavior and the risk of becoming a victim and a bully/victim: A meta-analysis study. *Child Abuse & Neglect, 37,* 1091–1108. https://doi.org/10.1016/j.chiabu.2013.03.001.

Livingstone, S., Haddon, L., Görzig, A., & Ólafsson, K. (2011). *Risks and safety on the internet: The perspective of European children. Full findings*. LSE, London: EU Kids Online.

Livingstone, S., & Helsper, E. J. (2013). Children, internet and risk in comparative perspective. *Journal of Children and Media, 7*(1), 1–8. https://doi.org/10.1080/17482798.2012.739751.

Modecki, K. L., Minchin, J., Harbaugh, A. G., Guerra, N. G., & Runions, K. C. (2014). Bullying prevalence across contexts: A meta-analysis measuring cyber and traditional bullying. *Journal of Adolescent Health, 55,* 602–611. https://doi.org/10.1016/j.jadohealth.2014.06.007.

Molcho, M., Craig, W., Due, P., Pickett, W., Harel-Fisch, Y., Overpeck, M., the HBSC Bullying Writing Group. (2009). Cross-national time trends in bullying behaviour 1994–2006: Findings from Europe and North America. *International Journal of Public Health, 54,* S1–S10. http://springerlink.com/content/j15430j1x087r023/fulltext.pdfol.

Nocentini, A., & Menesini, E. (2016). KiVa anti-bullying program in Italy: Evidence of effectiveness in a randomized control trial. *Prevention Science*, https://doi.org/10.1007/s11121-016-0690-z.

Olweus, D. (2004). The Olweus bullying prevention programme: Design and implementation issues and a new national initiative in Norway. In P. K. Smith, D. Pepler, & K. Rigby (Eds.), *Bullying in schools: How successful can interventions be?* (pp. 13–36). Cambridge University Press: Cambridge.

Olweus, D. (2012). Cyberbullying: An overrated phenomenon? *European Journal of Developmental Psychology, 9,* 520–538. https://doi.org/10.1080/17405629.2012.682358.

Olweus, D. (2013). School bullying: Development and some important challenges. *Annual Review of Clinical Psychology, 9,* 751–780. https://doi.org/10.1146/annurev-clinpsy-050212-185516.

Persson, M., & Svensson, M. (2013). The willingness to pay to reduce school bullying. *Economics of Education Review, 35,* 1–11. https://doi.org/10.1016/j.econedurev.2013.02.004.

Polanin, J. R., Espelage, D. L., & Pigott, T. D. (2012). A meta-analysis of school-based bullying prevention programs' effects on bystander intervention behavior. *Educational Psychology, 41*(1), 47–65.

Ramirez, M., Ten Eyck, P., Peek-Asa, C., Onwuachi-Willig, A., & Cavanaugh, J. E. (2016). Evaluation of Iowa's anti-bullying law. *Injury Epidemiology, 3,* 15. https://doi.org/10.1186/s40621-016-0080-9.

Rigby, K., & Smith, P. K. (2011). Is school bullying really on the rise? *Social Psychology of Education, 14,* 441–455. https://doi.org/10.1007/s11218-011-9158-y.

Ryan, W., & Smith, J. D. (2009). Antibullying programs in schools: how effective are evaluation practices? *Prevention Science, 10,* 248–259. https://doi.org/10.1007/s11121-009-0128-y.

Saarento, S., Kärnä, A., Hodges, E. V. E., & Salmivalli, C. (2013). Student-, classroom-, and school-level risk factors for victimization. *Journal of School Psychology, 51,* 421–434. https://doi.org/10.1016/j.jsp.2013.02.002.

Salmivalli, C., & Poskiparta, E. (2012). KiVa antibullying program: Overview of evaluation studies based on a randomized controlled trial and national rollout in Finland. *International Journal of Conflict and Violence*, *6*, 294–302.

Sasson, H., & Mesch, G. (2014). Parental mediation, peer norms and risky online behavior. *Computers in Human Behavior*, *33*, 32–38. https://doi.org/10.1016/j.chb.2013.12.025.

Schäfer, M., Stoiber, M., Bramböck, T., Letsch, H., Starch, K., & Sundaram, S. (2018). Participants' roles in bullying: What data from Indian classes can tell us about the phenomenon. In P. K. Smith, S. Sundaram, B. Spears, C. Blaya, M. Schäfer, & D. Sandhu (Eds.), *Bullying, cyberbullying and pupil well-being in schools: Comparing European, Australian and Indian perspectives*. Cambridge: Cambridge University Press.

Schober, B., Brandt, L., Kollmayer, M., & Spiel, C. (2016). Overcoming the ivory tower: Transfer and societal responsibility as crucial aspects of the Bildung-Psychology approach. *European Journal of Developmental Psychology*, *13*, 636–651. https://doi.org/10.1080/17405629.2016.1231061.

Schwartz, D., & Proctor, L. J. (2000). Community violence exposure and children's social adjustment in the peer group: The mediating roles of emotion regulation and social cognition. *Journal of Consulting and Clinical Psychology*, *68*, 670–683. https://doi.org/10.1037/0022-006x.68.4.670.

Smith, P. K. (2014). *Understanding school bullying*. London: Sage Publications.

Smith, P. K., & Berkkun, F. (2017). How research on cyberbullying has developed. In C. Mc Guckin & I. Corcoran (Eds.), *Bullying and cyberbullying: Prevalence, psychological impacts and intervention strategies* (pp. 11–27). Hauppauge, NY: Nova Science.

Smith, P. K., Kupferberg, A., Mora-Merchan, J. A., Samara, M., Bosley, S., & Osborn, R. (2012). A content analysis of school anti-bullying policies: A follow-up after six years. *Educational Psychology in Practice*, *28*, 61–84. https://doi.org/10.1080/02667363.2011.639344.

Smith, P. K., Kwak, K., & Toda, Y. (2016). Reflections on bullying in eastern and western perspectives. In P. K. Smith, K. Kwak, & Y. Toda (Eds.), *School bullying in different cultures: Eastern and western perspectives* (pp. 399–419). Cambridge: Cambridge University Press.

Smith, P. K., Pepler, D., & Rigby, K. (Eds.), (2004). *Bullying in schools: How successful can interventions be?* Cambridge: Cambridge University Press.

Smith, P. K., Robinson, S., & Marchi, B. (2016). Cross-national data on victims of bullying: What is really being measured? *International Journal of Development Science*, *10*, 9–19. https://doi.org/10.3233/dev-150174.

Ttofi, M. M., & Farrington, D. P. (2011). Effectiveness of school-based programs to reduce bullying: A systematic and meta-analytic review. *Journal of Experimental Criminology*, *7*, 27–56. https://doi.org/10.1007/s11292-010-9109-1.

Vandebosch, H., Simulioniene, R., Marczak, M., Vermeulen, A., & Bonetti, L. (2013). The role of the media. In P. K. Smith & G. Steffgen (Eds.), *Cyberbullying through the new media: Findings from an international network* (pp. 99–118). Hove: Psychology Press.

Völlink, T., Dehue, F., & McGuckin, C. (2016). *Cyberbullying: From theory to intervention*. London: Routledge.

Waasdorp, T. E., Pas, E. T., Zablotsky, B., & Bradshaw, C. P. (2017). Ten-year trends in bullying and related attitudes among 4th- to 12th-graders. *Pediatrics*, *139*, e20162615.

Williford, A., Elledge, L. C., Boulton, A. J., DePaolis, K. J., Little, T. D., & Salmivalli, C. (2013). Effects of the KiVa antibullying program on cyberbullying and cybervictimization frequency among Finnish youth. *Journal of Clinical Child and Adolescent Psychology*, *42*, 820–833. https://doi.org/10.1080/15374416.2013.787623.

Wolke, D., Tippett, N., & Dantchev, S. (2015). Bullying in the family: Sibling bullying. *The Lancet Psychiatry*, *2*, 917–929. https://doi.org/10.1016/s2215-0366(15)00262-x.

Ybarra, M. L., Prescott, T. L., & Espelage, D. L. (2016). Stepwise development of a text messaging-based bullying prevention program for middle school students (BullyDown). *JMIR mHealth*, *4*(2), e60. https://doi.org/10.2196/mhealth.4936.

Yeager, D. S., Fong, C. J., Lee, H. Y., & Espelage, D. L. (2015). Declines in efficacy of anti-bullying programs among older adolescents: Theory and a three-level meta-analysis. *Journal of Applied Developmental Psychology*, *37*, 36–51. https://doi.org/10.1016/j.appdev.2014.11.005.

Zych, I., Ortega-Ruiz, R., & del Rey, R. (2015). Scientific research on bullying and cyberbullying: Where have we been and where are we going. *Aggression and Violent Behavior*, *23*, 1–21. https://doi.org/10.1016/j.avb.2015.05.015.

Summary

20

*Sheri Bauman**, *Marilyn Campbell*†
*University of Arizona, Tucson, AZ, United States, †Queensland University of Technology (QUT), Brisbane, QLD, Australia

There is no disagreement that cyberbullying is a serious global problem, and that strategies to combat the problem are sorely needed. Without evidence-based interventions readily available, practitioners are left to their own devices to create programs, sometimes in collaboration with researchers. In this book, we have provided the most current information available on efforts to reduce cyberbullying in schools. The reader will notice that the strength of the evidence of effectiveness varies among the programs, but all at least show preliminary findings that hold promise. Readers will need to weigh the results of these evaluations with care, and note whether the context for the interventions will make it possible to adapt the program for their own setting. For example, in some countries, students remain together as a class throughout the day, while in others, secondary students change classes (and classmates) multiple times each day. This means that programs based on a cohort will be difficult to apply where classes are not as cohesive.

To facilitate understanding of the program-specific chapters, we included several introductory chapters that provided important background information. In this final chapter, we summarize what we have learned from the contributors.

In Chapter 1, we reviewed basic information, including definitions of both bullying and cyberbullying, and discussed the available data on prevalence of the problem. We pointed out that there are still disagreements about definitions and measures, and that reported prevalence rates vary widely across studies as a result. We talked about ways in which cyberbullying differs from traditional bullying, and pointed out the significant overlap in the two forms of bullying. It is important to note that studies have found a large proportion of cyberbullying-involved youth are both cyberbullies and cybervictims, whereas with traditional bullying, the bully-victim group is usually quite small. Although there are still many unknowns on the topic, we do know that in some cases, the consequences of being cyberbullied have been severe, and efforts to curtail it are imperative.

In Chapter 2, Rigby and Griffiths discussed how schools approach traditional bullying, and propose that many of the same strategies can be relevant for cyberbullying. Schools may employ proactive approaches, designed to prevent cyberbullying before it happens, or reactive responses to situation that have occurred. Within those broad categories of responses, several different approaches are described so that readers are able to consider, which might be best for their context, and how those approaches have fared in evaluations. Olweus (1993) whole-school approach is reviewed; despite its popularity and longevity, the effectiveness of the program is not clearly established. More recent emphasis on programs targeting bystander empowerment (e.g., the KiVa

Reducing Cyberbullying in Schools. https://doi.org/10.1016/B978-0-12-811423-0.00020-1

antibullying program from Finland), the growth of interest in social-emotional learning programs, and the application of circle time to address bullying make this review very relevant for readers. The chapter also discusses reactive strategies such as punishing the perpetrator(s), intervening to strengthen the victim, applying mediation programs to bullying and cyberbullying. These authors also cover important nonpunitive strategies (e.g., restorative practices, the support group method, the Method of Shared Concern, and more recently, Motivational Interviewing), as they can be applied to cyberbullying in the school context. These approaches are all suitable for the school setting, but all require a commitment from all stakeholders to be effective. What is clear in this chapter is that many of the approaches that have been successful with traditional bullying are also applicable to cases of cyberbullying, but that evidence for how well these approaches fare with cyberbullying is lacking.

Chapter 3 looks at what is known about technological solutions. After all, if cyberbullying is uniquely tied to the digital world, perhaps digital approaches are most consistent with the method. This chapter looks at what various sectors can provide to assist in reining in this problem by focusing on ISPs, e-mail service providers (e.g., Yahoo and Gmail), messaging apps, and software designed to allow users (and parents of users) to exert control over what happens online. The rapidity with which new platforms and types of social media emerges makes it impossible to be up to date on every development, but understanding the role each of these technological solutions can play will help practitioners and their clients make more informed decisions.

The legal aspect of cyberbullying, or how the law might assist in reducing cyberbullying, is reviewed in Chapter 4. Professor Butler focuses on three English-speaking countries with similar legal foundations, Australia, the U.K., and the U.S. He particularly analyzes what legal basis might be for school interventions, and provides a cogent analysis of what legal limits and recourses are available when cyberbullying can be tied to educational settings. The news is that laws are not likely to be the intervention of choice for either prevention or intervention. In addition, laws vary widely by country, and within countries among smaller administrative units (e.g., states or provinces), so it is always necessary to familiarize oneself with local statutes. Ultimately, when someone suffers harm from cyberbullying, it is likely for the foreseeable future that existing laws (against slander, or stalking, or threats to life, etc.) will be invoked rather that new legislation designed specifically to combat cyberbullying.

The final chapter (5) of the background section of the book focuses on the role of parents in combating cyberbullying. These authors contend that since parents are typically the source of technological access for their children (purchasing devices), they bear ultimate responsibility for their child's digital behaviors. They do so by direct monitoring of the child's online world (e.g., using parental monitoring software), engaging in conversations with their children about online behavior, and their modeling of appropriate internet behavior. Parental actions are classified as either restrictive mediation or educative mediation, with the authors clearly favoring the latter. A study of 908 Irish parents on their own Internet experiences found that a large majority of their sample felt confident in their ability to manage their children's online activities, and three-quarters of the parents reported they felt sufficiently involved and able to protect their child from digital harm. However, only a third of parents thought their children knew how to protect themselves in cyberspace. Despite the parental confidence, these authors pointed out that youth use very different social media platforms from their parents, and as a consequence were likely to underestimate the dangers of the currently popular sites. The authors express the need for available parent training so they are better prepared to support their children's online safety.

The interventions covered in Part II of this volume can be grouped by the way the interventions were developed and how they are delivered. First, there are two strategies that use digital technology to deliver the programs. These approaches utilize the same technology that is such an essential part of the lives of this digital generation, and may appeal to youth who are accustomed to accomplishing many of their life tasks online. Another group of strategies were developed to tackle traditional bullying, but were found to have an impact on cyberbullying behaviors as well, showing that although the medium is different, perhaps the underlying motivations are similar enough that well-designed interventions are useful for all kinds of peer victimization. Several other chapters describe programs that were originally developed to address traditional bullying but which have been adapted in some way to explicitly include cyberbullying. Others describe short-term interventions, whose evaluative approaches generally utilized feedback about the content from those who received the interventions. A number of the projects are built upon a model designed and implemented by youth themselves, with one of these designed to extend into the larger community and one working within the school system. So the readers have a variety of approaches to consider, keeping their own context in mind.

Online social marketing is the domain of advertisers, and as anyone who uses social media and the internet knows, it can be very effective. We do some shopping for a new purse online, and lo and behold there are ads for purses everywhere we look online. And they seem to know what kind of purses are of interest. That is not surprising, since marketing researchers are experts in selling things to consumers. In Chapter 6, Spears and her colleagues consider harnessing those strategies to "sell" attitudes and beliefs that underlie behaviors related to cyberbullying, much as is done in the field of public health. Knowing that the target audience for such marketing messages (youth and adolescents) are far more aware of their needs related to cyberbullying, the team of researchers included young people in the design of the media campaigns. Four different but related media campaigns were created, piloted, and studied. Although the statistical results were not exceptional, the contribution of this study is that we must include youth in the design of programs designed for youth, and that in the case of cyberbullying, the perspectives of youth are particularly salient. Further, this initial foray into the land of social media marketing was ground breaking and opens the door to digital solutions to the uniquely digital problem of cyberbullying, especially since cyberbullying is not restricted to schools or schoolmates. The chapter left us thinking about teams of educators, researchers, marketing specialists, and public health experts putting their heads together, informed by youth, continuing this line of work.

Since Olweus' (1993) ground-breaking work, the field has embraced whole-school approaches to bullying prevention, and this notion has been utilized in cyberbullying prevention as well. An example is the Cyber-Friendly Schools' project (Cross and her colleagues, Chapter 7), which incorporates a whole-school approach and youth as collaborators in a multilevel multicomponent platform, with a wealth of online resources. Although many programs could be described as "whole-school" approaches, the design of this project was unique in that a school team of adults and a leadership team of youth (10th grade students) collaborated to plan and deliver a curriculum to students in 8th and 9th grades. The teachers deliver the curriculum, and the students implement whole-school activities that they develop using program resources. The program includes a wealth of resources for the teams to draw upon, and the curriculum for each grade is sequential. The school teams, both teachers and students, receive training via workshops. Parents are included via online resources and a parent workshop presented by the staff and student cyberleaders. The evaluation of this project was extensive, involving large samples and multiple methods (surveys, interviews, etc.). The findings were positive in terms of reductions in perpetration and victimization by cyberbullying in grade 9 from grade 8 levels. In reviewing the results, the biggest barrier to success in the program was the difficulty finding time for delivery of the curriculum. This is a common struggle; schools are pressured to ensure that their academic curriculum is challenging and meets high expectations, leaving little time for other activities, regardless of the merit of those activities. It seems that it will require a major shift in educational policy for schools to embrace the notion that education involves more than just academic knowledge. We must prepare graduates to enter the world with skills they need to survive and thrive, and managing the online world respectfully is one of those skills.

In Chapter 8, we learned about the Massachusetts Aggression Reduction Center's commitment to a whole-school approach in a US state that mandates antibullying training for educators and students. A unique aspect of the cyberbullying prevention program described here (McCoy & Englander) is the use of university students, considered high-status peer models, to educate K-12 students. The center provides training for teachers, and also conducts Train the Trainer faculty programs to equip participating faculty with more information and skills. Parent workshops are also offered. The training for students, which is conducted by the university students, is offered in a variety of formats, from assemblies to small groups. A unique aspect of this program is the development of activities designed specifically for advisory periods, which are 20–30 min daily blocks of time when students meet in smaller groups with a faculty advisor. This time is allocated for activities outside the curriculum, such as advising, career planning, social-emotional learning, and others. In most schools, the faculty advisor is responsible for planning for that time, and many are not comfortable planning outside their academic areas, and the time can easily revert to being a study hall. This program offers a curriculum specifically designed for those periods. Evaluations focused on participant satisfaction with the program, and their self-assessment of increased knowledge or skills derived, although there are data from a pre-post questionnaire about bullying and cyberbullying knowledge, taken by teachers, that showed a significant increase. A student survey showed increase in willingness to talk to adults at schools if they were targeted by bullying following an assembly. There were also positive ratings by students who had participated in the Advisory Period programming and those who had completed the CyberSkills Curriculum.

The KiVa Antibullying program (Chapter 9), developed in Finland and translated for use in several other countries, is a well-known whole-school approach with curriculum and online games that support the classroom activities. It is based on Salmivalli's work on participant roles in bullying situations; the program focuses on empowering bystanders to take an active role in stopping bullying. KiVa includes lessons for all students and a process for intervention when serious cases of bullying occur. The actual lessons are not prescribed; the teacher material includes a variety of activities from which the teacher selects those most suited to her class. The approach has been rigorously evaluated, and found to reduce bullying and victimization in KiVa schools. Although cyberbullying is given attention in topics covered in the program, it is not the focus because the developers do not view cyberbullying as a separate phenomenon. However, the evaluation research found a significant reduction in cyberbullying and cybervictimization in KiVa schools compared to control schools. Age was a factor in the effects with middle-school youth: significant differences were found for younger students, almost significant for students at the mean age for the sample, and nonsignificant for older students. Follow-up data (no control schools) showed continued reductions in cybervictimization over time. This program is worthy of consideration by schools who have the commitment to invest the time for lessons and other activities, as evaluations using rigorous methods, have demonstrated the positive effects of KiVa on cyberbullying.

Like the KiVa program, the *NoTrap!* program (Menesini and her colleagues, Chapter 10) is directed toward both bullying and cyberbullying and has been subjected to rigorous evaluation procedures. Readers should attend closely to the section of the chapter that describes the series of studies undertaken to assess the effectiveness of the program, as they could be a model for others seeking to evaluate a program. *NoTrap!* is based on an ecological approach that considers the various levels of influence that extend beyond the school. This program targets secondary students in grades 7–10, and is designed to encourage bystanders to take action to stop bullying or cyberbullying. It has demonstrated reductions in victimization and increases in defending behavior. The program, delivered over about four months, engages students and peer educators, and has an online component. The effort to increase bystander action involves increasing empathy toward victims and teaching effective coping strategies. It is important for readers to keep in mind that the structure of Italian schools is such that students remain with their classmates throughout the day and over multiple years. Training is provided to teachers and students; those who become peer educators receive eight hours of training to learn listening skills, emotional competence and empathy, and problem solving and coping strategies for both bullying and cyberbullying. They also have a role in responding to requests for help from adolescents on the program website. The peer educators also lead two workshops for their classmates. In addition to reductions in all forms of bullying, which were sustained six months after the intervention concluded, the researchers found that for cybervictimization, participants had a significant reduction in internalizing symptoms.

Chapter 11 describes a program specifically designed to prevent cyberbullying. *Media Heroes* was developed in Germany for German schools, and is currently undergoing a trial of a Spanish version. It targets students in grades 7–10, along with their teachers and parents, and aims to impart online self-protection skills. The model is a Train the Trainer model, providing information and skills to school personnel who then are provided with resources to deliver the program in their usual context. The program focuses on developing skills in empathy and perspective taking, as research links the absence of these skills to increases in bullying and cyberbullying behaviors. Two versions of the program are available: a 10-week program that includes 90 minutes per week of lessons and activities, and a one-day workshop with four sections of 90 min each. Although the developers of the program prefer the longer format, they acknowledge the difficulties that have been encountered finding time for weekly lessons, and want to ensure that at least some prevention activities occur in each school. The program targets individuals, classes, and parents, so as to provide different perspectives and include important environmental contexts. The parent component is a workshop for parents planned and delivered by students, reinforcing the skills they have learned. This program does not provide a component to deal with serious cyberbullying when it occurs. The program evaluation utilized a pre- post- follow-up design with a waitlist control group that did not receive the intervention. The data showed that almost half the students liked the program either a lot, or very much and that the teachers were very satisfied. The perceptions of students and teachers were that cyberbullying decreased as a result of the program. Results also showed positive effects on empathy, perspective taking, cyberbullying perpetration and victimization, and self-esteem and health. The positive effects were maintained at the six-month postintervention time point. The authors also note that the 10-week program had, as expected, greater effects than the single-day workshop.

In Chapter 12, a technological project—an app for mobile phones—was developed and tested. It has an overall goal of teaching more effective strategies to respond to bullying. The password-protected app first provides accurate information about bullying, and uses short videos of celebrities popular with youth. The figures in the videos take an active role in combating bullying, modeling better coping strategies than many youth are known to use. The app collects data about bullying experiences on a regular basis (daily to weekly) and presents the information in graphic form. The app offers a large number of strategies and resources that are believed more effective than the typical responses made by victimized youth. The app encourages youth to experiment with, and evaluate new strategies in a quest to find the most effective ones for each user. It could be used as an adjunct to other interventions, or as a standalone app. It has only recently been released, and is currently only available in French. Qualitative data were very positive about the program, and a very small quantitative study reduced victimization in participants. Another quantitative study found that victims showed greater reductions in victimization than controls. Because the analyses were conducted with small groups, the evidence, although positive, is hardly definitive. However, we agree with the authors that this strategy has promise and look forward to reading about further studies with larger samples. We also acknowledge that although cyberbullying was not specifically addressed in the app, the skills and resources would likely be helpful, as was found with other programs. We hope the authors will add a cyberbullying component, and find resources to make the program available in other languages.

One might argue that school-based interventions do not reach all youth, and perhaps are likely to exclude many vulnerable groups. In Chapter 13, Dehue and her colleagues describe a Dutch standalone intervention designed for low-academically achieving students who are 12–15 years old and who have been cybervictimized. Because many youth are victimized in traditional ways in addition to cyberforms, the intervention targets both kinds of peer victimization. The program is online, and was developed using an Intervention Mapping Protocol to ensure a rigorous model is followed. After conducting an exhaustive literature review, the research team conducted focus groups with representatives of the target audience. This was followed by applying the principles of Rational Emotive Behavior Therapy (REBT) to the intervention design, which included three topics, accessed via the Internet, that were delivered monthly for three months. The amount of text was minimal and more appealing delivery used video clips, images, comics, animations, and digital guides. Each student had a personal page that included exercises and information summaries. Approximately 18% of students in recruited programs were considered to cybervictims. The study experienced high rates of attrition, so that the planned effectiveness study could not be conducted. The participants who did complete measures rated the website quite positively, found the first topic to be the most understandable, the second most useful for stopping cyberbullying, and the third topic was rated as the most unique. The personal page was not utilized much. The authors conclude that the target population may have had difficulty using the website independently, and perhaps a feature connecting the youth to assistance would be a good addition. They also concluded that such standalone intervention should be short, and measures used to assess the program also be as short as possible while retaining good psychometric properties.

The social ecological framework was along the theoretical basis for the development of the ViSC program in Austria (Chapter 14). Like Kiva, this program was developed to address traditional bullying, and the researchers examined the effects on cyberbullying as well. It is a whole-school program that includes teacher training and a class project completed by students in grades 5–8. The key person in each school is the ViSC coach, who is trained by the researchers and who then conducts teacher training at the school level. Two trainings are conducted, one at the beginning of first semester and the other at the beginning of the second semester. The program includes four sequential modules: in the first, teachers learn to define and recognize bullying. Scientific evidence is presented to ensure the teachers' information is factual and accurate. The second module involves training in how to address serious cases of bullying when they occur. A manualized best practice is conveyed to the teachers, and in module three, the teachers discuss what preventive measures already exist in the school. It is in this module that the specific procedures and logistics for program implementation are determined. The last module is the class project, in which students first receive social skills' training, and then work together as a group to achieve a class-determined goal. The collaborative effort is believed to create a more positive class climate in which bullying and other forms of aggression are less likely. The program has been evaluated using the most rigorous methods of analysis, and has also been disseminated to three other countries (Cyprus, Romania, and Turkey). The findings show strong support for the effectiveness of the intervention on cyberbullying and cybervictimization, with results showing a decrease in cyberbullying and victimization in the months following the end of the intervention.

Convivencia is a national model that promotes positive interpersonal relationships in Spanish schools (Ortega-Ruiz and her colleagues, Chapter 15). The goal is to create more positive and accepting social climates in which aggression is rare. With the advent of cyberbullying, the concept was expanded to include cyberbullying, and is known is *cyberconvivencia.* The program uses training and workshops for teachers, students, and parents in its effort to reduce interpersonal problems associated with the digital world. The program uses short lessons to teach about the Internet and social networks, the benefits of digital media, and information about risks. There are eight sessions that promote knowledge of digital technology and the various media, the safe ways to use digital tools, and to generate an action plan for the school. The content of each session is described in the chapter. Schools are obligated to expand their *convivencia* programs to address cyberbullying and other digital behaviors. The authors cite their previously published work regarding effectiveness, noting that participants gained awareness of the lack of control over information that is on the Internet. Importantly, both cyberbullying and cybervictimization decreased after the intervention. Note that the program to date has been delivered by the researchers; the next step is to evaluate the program when delivered by teachers in the schools.

Chapter 16 turns to a child-directed program used with youth in Japan (Takeuchi and his colleagues). It began in one school, and has expanded to include young people in a wider geographical area. The model is based on a cross age structure, with children disseminating their ideas to other children. Students involved represented a cross-section of the school in terms of age, popularity, status, etc. and all had a desire to participate. The Smartphone Summits, as they are called, involve youth from multiple schools, and the crossfertilization of ideas is a valuable benefit of the model. In addition, the plan is cross age, with university faculty supervising university students, who facilitate group discussion among the high-school and junior high-school students. Many of the projects created in the summits involve educating elementary children about safe ways to use smartphones. Adults assist in generating media coverage of events, and by inviting local officials to the summits in which the children describe their projects. Logistically, each summit involves a series of meetings: an introductory session to generate ideas. One group decided to survey students in their school, and adults helped them distribute their questionnaire. At the next meeting, the students actually work on their project plans and give a presentation to the entire group. The final activity occurs six months later, when the projects have been implemented. Each group shares what they have accomplished. After one summit, a group, supervised by university students, created a minitextbook for elementary children, and presented lessons in elementary classrooms. The chapter mentions a variety of products that came out of the summits. Evaluation of a sample of participants using a researcher-developed questionnaire revealed positive beliefs on the part of participants on their own and their classmates improved behavior with smartphones. The Smartphone Summit has grown in Japan and received favorable publicity in local press, generating even more interest. The model could be applied in other countries and settings to take advantage of youth's desire to have a voice and an impact on their lives and those of their peers.

The Information-Motivation-Behavioral Skills' (IMB) model was the approach to intervention development taken by Popovac and Fine (Chapter 17) whose workshops were piloted with adolescent girls in South Africa. The approach, best known in health behavior programs, aims to impart increased information, motivation, and behavioral skills to reduce problem behaviors and promote positive change. An essential target in this program is risk perception; adolescents are often described as believing in their own invulnerability, which decreases their responses to what others might perceive as dangerous. To make the program relevant to a given group of youth, an anonymous baseline questionnaire is administered to gather data on their digital behaviors and beliefs. The authors recommend free programs such as Survey Monkey to quickly obtain basic analyses that can be used to tailor the content of the single 50-minute workshop. In addition to the information about the prevalence of cyberbullying and other digital behaviors in the school, the workshop should be interactive and engage the participants in discussions of potential consequences of involvement in cyberbullying. The authors recommend using a variety of media to engage the students, including video, articles from recent news, etc. After the presentation of information, students work with scenarios of situations developed by the researchers, and discuss how they would feel if they were the target, and how they would respond. These are first shared in pairs, and then presented for discussion by the whole group. To evaluate the program, the researchers used a risk-perception scale administered before the intervention for the control group and after the intervention for intervention groups. Analysis revealed that the intervention group had significantly higher risk perception than the control, and risk perception decreased with the increase in grade. Since increased risk perception was a goal of the program, authors considered this to be evidence of effectiveness.

The final chapter describing interventions, Chapter 18, describes a single-session intervention that is based on the Extended Parallel Process Model (EPPM), which conveys messages directed toward factors believed to have an impact on an individual's behavior: susceptibility (to victimization), perceived severity of the threat, response efficacy to control cyberbullying behaviors, and general self-efficacy for employing constructive behaviors to reduce cyberbullying. The program uses "fear appeals" to increase the sense of susceptibility of the youth. The intervention was a 45-minute presentation to middle-school students that utilized information gathered about students via their school Facebook profiles, demonstrating that it is easy for someone to obtain personal information. The presentation included high-profile examples of tragic outcomes of cyberbullying. Then the presentation offered constructive behaviors that would prevent cyberbullying if students would use them. The intervention was also modified and presented to parents. The authors present the findings of a study of effectiveness, citing earlier papers, but the reader is not given the statistical information in this chapter, so must rely on the authors' reports. This intervention is unique in that it is very brief, relies on generating fear, which is then allayed if the speaker's recommendations are followed.

Peter Smith's commentary brings all the major points of the book into sharp focus, pointing out how the interventions are considered along three dimensions of technical vs. relationship; general bullying or a specific focus on cyberbullying and which levels of the ecological model are targeted. He also mentions how age, gender, culture, and disability are considered. There is a discussion of student voice and what role theory does and should play in reducing cyberbullying. Finally, Peter discusses issues about how the programs are implemented and evaluated considering factors such as feasibility, fidelity, follow-up, and efficacy.

Well, congratulations to you the reader for getting through the whole book (or just reading this chapter or even if you only turned to this last page! ☺). This feat actually shows that as a practitioner you want to make a difference for young people and reduce the harm of cyberbullying. And that motivation is crucial in changing young people's perceptions and attitudes about cyberbullying which hopefully will lead to a change in behavior. You as a teacher or adult working with young people can make a difference in influencing their attitudes and behaviors. Although many of the programs in this book are aimed at secondary school students many studies have shown that elementary and middle-school students' attitudes and behaviors are more easily influenced by adults than older students. So start early. Most of these programs also show evidence of reduction of both traditional and cyberbullying whether the program targeted one of the other or both, giving credence to the notion that the underlying mechanisms and motivations for all forms of bullying are similar. As with any learning also once is not enough. If it takes us as parents about ten years to instill an automatic "please" and "thank you" in our children, we must continually be teaching them about civility and kindness, not to resort to or join in any form of bullying and to stand up for anyone who is victimized.

Reference

Olweus, D. (1993). *Bullying at school: What we know and what we can do*. Blackwell: Cambridge.

Index

Note: Page numbers followed by *b* indicates boxes, *f* indicate figures, *t* indicate tables and *np* indicates footnotes.

R

S

FSC
www.fsc.org
MIX
Papier | Fördert gute Waldnutzung
FSC® C083411

Kolibri 360 GmbH
Ferdinand-Jühlke-Straße 7
99095 Erfurt, Deutschland
produktsicherheit@kolibri360.de